# THE MISMEASURE
# OF DESIRE

# IDEOLOGIES OF DESIRE

**David M. Halperin**
**Series Editor**

*The Female Thermometer*
Eighteenth-Century Culture and the Invention of the Uncanny
TERRY CASTLE

*Gide's Bent*
Sexuality, Politics, Writing
MICHAEL LUCEY

*The Erotic Imagination*
French Histories of Perversity
VERNON A. ROSARIO II

*Roman Homosexuality*
Ideologies of Masculinity in Classical Antiquity
CRAIG A. WILLIAMS

*Great Mirrors Shattered*
Homosexuality, Orientalism, and Japan
JOHN WHITTIER TREAT

*The Mismeasure of Desire*
The Science, Theory, and Ethics of Sexual Orientation
EDWARD STEIN

# THE MISMEASURE OF DESIRE

*The Science, Theory, and Ethics of Sexual Orientation*

**Edward Stein**

OXFORD
UNIVERSITY PRESS

# OXFORD
UNIVERSITY PRESS

Oxford   New York
Athens   Auckland   Bangkok   Bogotá   Buenos Aires   Calcutta
Cape Town   Chennai   Dar es Salaam   Delhi   Florence   Hong Kong   Istanbul
Karachi   Kuala Lumpur   Madrid   Melbourne   Mexico City   Mumbai
Nairobi   Paris   São Paulo   Shanghai   Singapore   Taipei   Tokyo   Toronto   Warsaw

and associated companies in
Berlin   Ibadan

Copyright © 1999 by Edward Stein

First published by Oxford University Press, Inc.
198 Madison Avenue, New York, New York 10016

First issued as an Oxford University Press paperback, 2001

Oxford University Press is a registered trademark of Oxford University Press

Library of Congress Cataloging-in-Publication Data

Stein, Edward, 1965–
The mismeasure of desire: the science, theory, and ethics of sexual orientation
/ Edward Stein.
p.   cm. — (Ideologies of desire)
Includes bibliographical references and index.
ISBN 0-19-509995-8
ISBN 0-19-514244-6 (Pbk.)
1. Homosexuality—Research.   2. Homosexuality—Philosophy.
3. Homosexuality—Moral and ethical aspects.   4. Sexual orientation—
Research.   5. Sexual orientation—Philosophy.   6. Sexual
orientation—Moral and ethical aspects.   I. Title.   II. Series.
HQ76.25.S69   1999   306.76'6—dc2198-55079   98–55079

10 9 8 7 6 5 4 3 2 1

Printed in the United States of America
on acid-free paper

For Laskar A. Wechsler, my grandfather,
for nurturing my intellectual curiosity

# CONTENTS

# PREFACE

**M**any people find sex pleasurable. Many people also find talking and thinking about sex to be fun and interesting. At the same time, many people find it difficult to talk about sex, and for some, sex is the source of anxiety and discomfort. In the last decade, a substantial portion of the thinking and talking concerning sex has focused on sexual desires, in particular, the various sexual desires that people have and the source of these varied desires. Sexual desire, it seems, comes in different forms. Some people are primarily attracted to men and others are primarily attracted to women. Where do these different sexual orientations come from? Are they based on biological differences, environmental differences, individual choices, or some combination of these and perhaps other factors? And what is the relevance of these differences in sexual orientation? In this book, I consider these questions in a detailed fashion. In particular, I critically examine scientific research on sexual orientation. This scientific research has received a great deal of attention in the last several years from many people with a wide variety of political and intellectual perspectives. Although science has the potential to emerge as the central perspective for thinking about sexual orientation, I will argue that, despite interesting and provocative current scientific research on sexual orientation, there are various grounds for questioning its assumptions, its methods, and its relevance.

As the subtitle of this book suggests, in addition to looking at scientific perspectives on sexual orientation, I also consider various theoretical and ethical questions about sexual orientation and sexual desires generally. I consider what sexual orientations are, how they develop, and their ethical and legal status. In the process of uncovering the undefended assumptions in our thinking about sexual desire, I drawn on and reflect on scientific research, social scientific research, lesbian and gay studies, lesbian and gay politics, feminist theory, and philosophy. Despite its broad range, this book is written for a wide audience. Interested readers of any sort should find this book interesting, engaging, and provocative.

I started writing about sexual desire and sexual orientations while work-ing toward my doctorate in philosophy at the Massachusetts Institute of Tech-nology. My work was shaped by my training in contemporary Anglo-American philosophy, especially philosophy of mind, philosophy of science, and episte-mology. I was also influenced by the political climate for lesbians and gay men, and the emerging academic field of lesbian and gay studies. When I joined the faculty in the philosophy department at New York University, I developed a course called "The Philosophy of Sex" and collaborated on the development of a course called "Introduction to Lesbian and Gay Studies." I continued to write and teach about sexual orientation while I was a faculty member of the philoso-phy departments at Mount Holyoke College and Yale University. At Yale, the Fund for Lesbian and Gay Studies helped, in various ways, to support my teach-ing and research. When I became a student at the Yale Law School, concern with issues relating to sexual orientation continued to animate my thinking.

Along the way, I talked to many of my classmates, colleagues, students, and friends about sexual desire and sexual orientation. Their comments, ques-tions, and support sustained my interest in the issues that are central to this book. In particular, I want to thank Ernie Alleva, Carol Alpert, Eric Altman, Michael Bailey, Ned Block, Paul Bloom, Lee Bowie, Michael Bronski, Judy Butler, Jules Coleman, Angela Curran, Ronnie DaSousa, David Eppel, Joe Gordon, Larry Gross, Judith Halberstam, Janet Halley, David Halperin, David Hull, Tracy Isaacs, Diane Jeske, Paul Kahn, Jacinta Kerin, Suzanne Kessler, Harold Koh, Tom Kohut, David Lam, Peter Lipton, Robert Marshall, Brett McDonnell, Meredith Michaels, Tim Murphy, Richard Pillard, David Richards, Bill Rubenstein, Paul Rubin, Bill Ruddick, Udo Schüklenk, David Shengold, Lincoln Shlensky, Reva Siegel, William Snyder, Roy Sorensen, Steve Stich, Chris Straayer, Yuko Uchikawa, Virginia Vander Jagt, Blakey Ver-meule, Tom Wartenberg, Jami Weinstein, Rob Wilson, Karen Wynn, and Kenji Yoshino. I also want to thank my parents, Neil and Ellen, my sister Karen, and my extended family for their support and interest.

Other people deserve to be singled out for their help. Sydelle Kramer, my agent, provided important advice, especially at the beginning and end of this project. Cheshire Calhoun, Hilary Kornblith, and Wendy McKenna all read a complete draft of this book and gave me extensive comments that guided me as I substantially revised the book. Gene Buckley, Teresa Chandler, and Theresa Yuan read the entire penultimate draft of the book; each of them provided im-portant assistance at a crucial phase of the project. At several junctures, Gary Marcus provided crucial suggestions.

Over the past few years, I have had the good fortune to collaborate on various writing projects related to the topic of this book. In particular, my collaborations with Bill Byne, Bill Eskridge, and Morris Kaplan have shaped my thinking about sexual orientation in a myriad of ways. Each has taught me a great deal and provided substantial intellectual support for this project. Although the three of them will surely disagree with some of my arguments in this book, each should recognize his influence on my ideas.

Finally, my deepest thanks to Steve Lin. He has provided me with tremendous emotional support and day-to-day assistance throughout this entire project. If that weren't enough, he read the entire manuscript with great precision and provided numerous comments, large and small. In countless ways, he made this book possible.

Two chapters of this book have appeared in print in a modified form. Some parts of chapter 10 are adapted from my article "The Relevance of Scientific Research Concerning Sexual Orientation to Lesbian and Gay Rights," which appeared in the *Journal of Homosexuality* 27 (1994). These portions appear with the permission of Haworth Books. A version of chapter 11 appeared in *Bioethics* 12 (1998) under the title "Choosing the Sexual Orientation of Children." It appears here with the permission of Blackwell Publishers.

# THE MISMEASURE
# OF DESIRE

# INTRODUCTION

## Questions

The setting of Plato's classic dialogue, *The Symposium,* is a drinking party. Socrates, Aristophanes, and several others are celebrating the success of their friend Agathon (who was, like Aristophanes, a playwright) at the annual Athens theater festival. The celebration involved drinking and taking turns giving speeches to each other about love. As part of his speech, Aristophanes told a story about how humans came to be in their current form. According to Aristophanes' myth, the human race was once made up of three sexes, "that is to say, besides the two sexes, male and female, . . . there was a third which partook of the nature of both, which we [call] . . . 'hermaphrodite' . . . a being which was half male and half female" (Plato 1935b, 189d–e). The human race, in addition to having an additional sex, looked rather different. Each human was "globular in shape, with . . . four arms and legs, and two faces, both on the same cylindrical neck, and one head, with one face on one side and one on the other, and four ears, and two lots of privates" (189e–190). Because these humans were too powerful and threatened the power of the gods, Zeus split each human in half down the middle, leaving "each half with a desperate yearning for the other" (191). Once they had been divided, the three original types of humans gave rise to different types of people, defined by the kind of other-half he or she desired.

> The man who is a slice of the hermaphrodite sex . . . will naturally be attracted by women . . . and the women who run after men are of similar descent . . . . But the woman who is a slice of the original female is attracted by women rather than by men . . . while men who are slices of the male are followers of the male. (191d–e)

3

A natural (though, as I will show, a contentious) interpretation of this myth says Aristophanes was talking about heterosexuals, lesbians, and gay men and that he was claiming sexual orientation is an important, defining, and inborn feature of a person.

Like Socrates and his companions, most humans spend a great deal of time talking about, thinking about, trying to have, and (if we are lucky) having sex. Most of us have a desire for sex, what is sometimes called a sexual appetite or a sex drive. We vary widely, however, with respect to the particular forms our sexual appetite takes, what might be called our sexual desires, our sexual interests, or our sexual tastes. Some people, for example, like to have sex outdoors; some people want to have sex with multiple partners; some people like to engage in certain specific kinds of sexual acts, for example, nonreciprocal oral sex; some people like to have sex with particular kinds of people, for example, people with blond hair or people with long legs. The list of possible variations in sexual tastes is almost endless. In this sense, the variation among people with respect to sexual desires is like the desire for food—almost everyone has the general desires for sex and food, but in each individual the desires are manifested in very different ways.

A person's sexual orientation is one part of a person's overall sexual desires. Just as whether a person likes to have sex indoors or outdoors is part of a person's sexual desires, whether a person is (primarily) attracted to and likes to have sex with men or women is also part of a person's sexual desires. This part of a person's sexual desires is his or her sexual orientation. Today, in North America and in many other parts of the world, discussions about sex and sexual desire frequently concern sexual orientation. In particular, there has been a remarkable increase in discussions concerning homosexuality. Not more than a hundred years ago, engaging in sexual acts with a person of the same sex was a "love that dare not speak its name." Today, whether to celebrate or deride it, homosexuality is frequently discussed in public forums, in films, on television, in court rooms, and in almost every other context. The love that dare not speak its name is now unwilling to keep quiet. Among the issues that are frequently discussed are: Should lesbians and gay men be discriminated against in employment, housing, or military service? Should people of the same sex be allowed to marry? Is homosexuality inborn? Is homosexuality a choice? These days, questions about sexual orientation abound in our society. In all sorts of contexts, we want to know who a person has had sex with, whether a person is *really* heterosexual or homosexual, and what causes people to have one sexual orientation rather than another. Although the questions clearly took different forms, Socrates, Aristophanes, and their friends were clearly interested in matters sexual as well. We may claim to know a great deal more about human sexual desire than Aristophanes did, but do we?

This book is about sexual orientation: what it is, how it develops, and what its significance is. Much has been written about sexual orientation and sexual desire more generally, but this book examines the basic underlying questions about these issues in a way that few have tried to do. I will carefully examine what we mean by the term sexual orientation. I will also examine how this term gets deployed in the sciences, the social sciences, the humanities, the law, and everyday thinking. I will also examine various ethical and political issues connected to sexual orientation. In general, I shall attempt to convince you that much of what most people think about sexual orientations is probably wrong, or at least misguided. Many people think that a person's sexual orientation is inborn in the sense that a person's eye color is inborn. Most of the popular scientific theories concerning the origins of human sexual orientation—as well as our commonsense theories about them—accept this claim or one similar to it. Further, many people of various political stripes think that this claim and the scientific theories that relate to it are relevant to ethical and legal questions relating to sexual orientations. I am skeptical of each of these commonly held views, and in subsequent chapters, I will provide reasons for this skepticism. I will argue that much of what is widely believed about human sexual orientations is not that much more likely to be true than Aristophanes' story about the origin of humans and our varied sexual tastes. Aristophanes' theory and contemporary theories of the nature and origin of sexual orientation, in effect, *mismeasure* desire.

This book has three parts: the metaphysical part, the scientific part, and the ethical part. *Metaphysics* is the branch of philosophy that concerns the underlying nature of the world. Aristotle wrote books on almost every philosophical subject of his time (for example, *Ethics, Politics, Physics, Poetics*). The book he wrote after *Physics* was called *Metaphysics* (literally "after physics"), and it concerned features of the world that he considered more abstract and farther from human perception than the things dealt with in *Physics* (which included most of what today we would call science). Although the line between metaphysics and science is somewhat blurry, philosophers typically understand metaphysics as the study of the kind of things that there are and the forms that their existence takes, whereas science is concerned with the details of the entities that exist and the laws that operate on them. In the parts of the book that concern metaphysics and science, I explore a range of questions about the nature of sexual orientation including:

- What is it to have a sexual orientation?
- How many sexual orientations are there?
- How does a person develop a sexual orientation?
- Does a person in any sense *choose* his or her sexual orientation?
- Does it make sense to talk about a person in a dramatically different culture as having a sexual orientation?
- Does it make sense to talk of other primates as having a sexual orientation? Nonprimates?
- Is sexual orientation amenable to scientific study? If so, in what way?
- Is it useful for our understanding of human nature to divide people into categories in virtue of their sexual desires?

These issues are intrinsically interesting and important. Understanding human sexual desire is, I will argue, an important part of understanding human nature.

Socrates aside, philosophers as a group—and, until recently, most researchers (though certainly not all)—have had remarkably little to say about human sexual desires, leaving this matter to the poets, novelists, and other of their ilk. Although artists have had—and continue to have—much of interest to say about sex and sexual desire, there is no need for the rest of us to ignore sex and sexual desire in our intellectual pursuits. Insofar as we are interested in human nature, we should be interested in human sexual nature. In fact, given our special interest in having sex, and in knowing who has had sex and with whom, it seems that our interest in sex and sexual desire should be a crucial part of our attempt to understand ourselves. There is no obvious reason why science, social science, and philosophy should be silent about sex and sexual desire.

There is, however, another set of reasons to be interested in sexual desires. Metaphysical and scientific matters connect, albeit in complex and contested ways, to ethical, political, and legal matters. An understanding of human nature is (in some way) relevant to what we ought to do (ethics), how society ought to be structured (politics), and what our laws should be (legal). If after the drinking party Socrates and one of his comrades (they were all men) engaged in particular sorts of sexual acts (but not others), they would have been subject to severe social sanctions. If, for example, a young man at the party not yet old enough to be a citizen of Athens inserted his penis into the anus of a willing Socrates, Socrates would have been viewed as behaving shamefully. In England in the late nineteenth century, for example, men who engaged in such behavior faced severe legal penalties.

Many people today think that scientific evidence about how people develop sexual orientations is relevant to ethical and legal matters concerning sex

and sexuality. For example, some scientists, lawyers, and lesbian and gay advocates have argued that if a person's sexual orientation is innate or immutable,
then it follows that people should not be discriminated against in virtue of their
sexual orientation. Whether or not this argument is a strong one will be taken
up in the third part of this book, but, even setting this argument aside, there
seems at least a plausible connection between the metaphysics of sex and sexual desire and the ethics of sex and sexual desire (by which I mean to include
ethical, legal, and political matters relating to sex and sexual desire). Given this
possible connection, it is appropriate that the third part of this book deals with
ethical issues that stem from the metaphysical and scientific issues of the first
two parts of this book. Among the issues I examine are:

- Is scientific research on sexual orientation relevant to ethical questions?
- Are there ethical considerations that bear on whether such research
  should be done and the form it should take?
- What are lesbian and gay rights?
- Are there ethical considerations that bear on what a person's sexual be-
  havior (or sexual desires) should (or shouldn't) be?
- Should parents try to affect the sexual orientation of their children?

Although these issues connect to quite general issues about "sexual
morality" and "sexual ethics," I do not attempt a detailed or systematic discussion of these issues in general or of lesbian and gay rights in particular. Instead,
I focus on some (but not all) of the more pressing ethical, political, and legal
questions that are connected (or at least plausibly connected) to the metaphysical questions surrounding sexual desires and sexual orientations in particular.


## Interdisciplinary Background

The subject matter of this book is multifaceted and multidisciplinary. I draw
considerably on lesbian and gay studies, the scientific study of sex and sexuality, feminism, and the lesbian and gay political movement. The method of this
project comes from the discipline of philosophy. This might be somewhat surprising since philosophers have had less to say about sex and sexual desire than
might have been expected (Baker and Elliston 1984). Although I draw on both
lesbian and gay studies and the scientific study of sex and sexual orientation,
I raise questions about what is probably the central theoretical principle of
each of these emerging interdisciplinary fields. With respect to lesbian and gay

studies, I raise doubts about constructionism, the thesis that sexual orientations are mere social constructs. With respect to the scientific study of sex, I raise doubts about essentialism, the thesis that, in contrast to constructionism, sexual orientations are more than mere social constructs. Additionally, the ethical portion of my book is informed both by feminism and by what is sometimes called *queer politics*. In what follows, I say something about these interdisciplinary influences on my project. In the next section, I discuss philosophy, which provides my primary methodology.

### The Scientific Study of Sex

In the last several years, scientific research on sexual orientation has garnered a great deal of attention in various realms. Some scientists and some nonscientist commentators have gone so far as to suggest that a *new scientific paradigm* for the study of human sex and sexuality is emerging. Scientific research on sex and sexual orientation is a primary catalyst for my project, and its claims will be prominently discussed throughout.

If we want to understand the phenomenon of sex and the human desires involved with it, contemporary science seems the right place to turn. Science has great explanatory power, and in this century, it has made dramatic strides towards understanding human nature. It seems certain that, in the long term, science will make important contributions to our understanding of sex, sexual orientation, and sexual desire. For this reason, a detailed discussion of scientific research on sexual orientation is central to my project. Throughout this book, I will be drawing on research in the sciences and the social sciences, in particular as it relates to sexual orientation. This is not, however, because I necessarily believe that the theories science currently has to offer are true. Looking back over the history of science, one can see that scientists, like practitioners of other fields of inquiry, make mistakes and unquestioningly accept premises that are later rejected. It is quite possible that much of the research on sexual orientation that is grabbing headlines in the 1990s will prove to have been nothing more than a wrong turn in the development of the advanced scientific understanding of human sexual desire that, for all we know, might develop in the latter part of the twenty-first century. For this reason, I do not assume the validity of the most recent scientific studies but, rather, engage and critique them. At times, I will do so from within, but I will also examine the putative emerging paradigm from without, for example, by looking at its theoretical assumptions and its ethical implications.

## *Lesbian and Gay Politics*

In 1969, a group of gay men and drag queens were arrested as part of what was, for that time and place, a not-atypical raid on a gay bar, this one at the Stonewall, a bar in the Greenwich Village section of New York City. The group resisted, and over the next couple of days, a series of riots broke out pitting members of the gay community against New York City police officers (D'Emilio 1983; Duberman 1993). Although this event has developed something like biblical significance for lesbians, gay men, and transgendered people in the United States and many other parts of the world, it was hardly the first act of resistance by lesbians and gay men nor necessarily the most significant. In the middle of the nineteenth century, Karl Heinrich Ulrichs, a German jurist and writer, single-handedly and quixotically urged the repeal of all laws that criminalized same-sex sexual activity (Kennedy 1988); some have claimed that this was the first time a self-proclaimed homosexual publicly spoke out for lesbian and gay rights (Dynes 1990, 1339; LeVay 1996, 11–16). Even in the United States, there was significant lesbian and gay political activity before Stonewall—just after World War II, the Mattachine Society and the Daughters of Billitis began organizing gay men and lesbians for mutual support and to struggle for legal and political goals (D'Emilio 1983). A more vocal lesbian and gay political movement coalesced around the time of Stonewall partly due to the influence of the women's movement and the civil rights movement (Blasius and Phelan 1997; Newton 1997; Radicalesbians 1973). At a time in which feminists examined the sexism inherent in society and demanded equal rights and African Americans proclaimed "Black is beautiful" and fought for racial justice, it does not seem surprising, in retrospect, that lesbians and gay men responded to deeply entrenched homophobia and discrimination on the basis of sexual orientation by organizing their own political movement. Nevertheless, Stonewall has become perhaps the most important symbol of the emergence of the contemporary lesbian and gay movement.

A decade or so after Stonewall, lesbians, gay men, and their allies had a higher profile and had obtained some of their political goals. In the process, gay liberation, with its goal of changing the sexual character of society and "bringing out the homosexual in everyone" (Wittman 1997, 388), had been replaced by a more mainstream assimilationist strategy that emphasized the commonalities between heterosexuals and homosexuals. For assimilationists, the goal was to be treated fairly and to be left alone. The dramatic impact of AIDS on gay men starting in the 1980s was both a huge setback and a remarkable catalyst for lesbian and gay social and political action around the world, especially in America and Western Europe. ACT-UP, a loosely knit collection of local political action groups that primarily used confrontational tactics to address the wide array of social and political issues associated with the AIDS crisis, marked something of a return to the gay liberationist politics of the 1970s, but with greater success in getting national and international attention (Blasius and Phelan 1997, 561–708). In the late 1980s, Queer Nation brought the confrontational style and grassroots organizational structure of ACT-UP to the full range of lesbian and gay political issues ("Queers Read This" 1997). Queer politics rejected assimilationism as well as the labels "lesbian" and "gay." The lesbians, gay men, bisexuals, transgendered people, and others who embraced the label "queer" did not want to assimilate, and they proudly announced their difference from heterosexuals by their slogan "We're here; we're queer; get used to it."

Through its multiple origins and varied forms, lesbian and gay activism has made possible the development of an open, self-affirming, politically active, culturally involved, and intellectually engaged lesbian and gay community. Without this community, a book like this one would simply not be possible.

### Lesbian and Gay Studies

Just as the civil rights movement to some extent spawned the interdisciplinary field of African American studies and the women's movement spawned women's studies, the interdisciplinary field of inquiry known as *lesbian and gay studies* began to emerge in the shadows of the gay liberation movement (Escoffier 1990). Gay men, lesbians, and their allies began to openly and self-consciously study themselves and how they were represented in history and culture. This has led them to inquire how sex and sexual orientations have been and are constructed and conceptualized. The resulting field of lesbian and gay studies examines same-sex desires, preferences, orientations, erotics, lifestyles, sentiments, and conceptions—how they differ (and remain the same) when the variables of time, place, culture, gender, class, race, and so forth, are changed; how they are constructed and interpreted; and how they interact with other human phenomena such as law, scientific inquiry, medicine, government, art, popular culture, family, and education (see, for example, the essays in Abelove et al. [1993]). Research in lesbian and gay studies has focused attention on the importance of historical and cultural factors in situating these issues. Lesbian and gay studies raises critical questions that challenge the controlling gaze long directed at homosexuals by disciplines and professions primarily focused on and populated by heterosexuals. Lesbian and gay studies both informs my project and provides some of its subject matter.

*Queer theory* emerged from lesbian and gay studies, but it also has roots in the more radical strands of the lesbian and gay community and its activism in the 1980s. The relationship between queer theory and lesbian and gay studies can be understood in various ways. On one reading, queer theory is simply the theoretical wing of lesbian and gay studies, roughly like the relationship between historiography and history or literary theory and the study of literature. On another reading, queer theory is both more radical and more all-encompassing than lesbian and gay studies (Warner 1993). According to this view, whereas lesbian and gay studies attempts to use existing disciplinary lenses (for example, history, political science, literature) to look at homosexuals and sexual orientation in a more positive light than they had been previously, queer theory attempts to "queer" these disciplines, that is, to change them by weeding out the deep heterosexist biases within them. "Queer commentary shows that much of what passes for general culture is riddled with heteronormativity [the view that heterosexuality is and should be the norm]" (Berlant and Warner 1995, 349). What makes queer theory *queer* is not that it concerns homosexuality or that its practitioners are lesbians and gay men, but that it questions assumptions that are steeped, often subtly, in heterosexist biases. Based on this interpretation, whereas lesbian and gay studies, applied to history, might chronicle the lives of ostensibly lesbian and gay historical figures like Michelangelo, Shakespeare, and Socrates (Garde 1964; Rowse 1977), a queer theory approach to history might eschew our contemporary categories of sexual orientation and look instead at sexual deviance in history. I offer this example of what might be considered the main difference between lesbian and gay studies and queer theory, although I believe this view of the difference between them suggests a negative assessment of lesbian and gay studies. In truth, a substantial portion of lesbian and gay studies scholarship adopts a queer-theoretical approach albeit under a different rubric (Altman 1971; Bronski 1984; Newton 1972; Weeks 1977).

The present project draws on lesbian and gay studies in various ways. My subject is sexual orientation and sexual desire, how we conceptualize, study, and experience them. Lesbian and gay studies provides a foothold on this topic. By focusing on same-sex desires, I approach sexual desire and orientation from the margins. Because I question the adequacy of our categories of sexual orientation as they are used in science, theory, and ethics, this project can be appropriately called queer.

## Philosophy

What is philosophy? If you asked a physicist or a historian what it is that practitioners in her field study, she would probably be able to give a rather straightforward answer. No doubt, there might be a difference of opinion among some historians or physicists as to the nature of their subject matter and their method. The same question posed to a philosopher, however, is rather more complex. This is because the question, What is philosophy? is itself a philosophical question, while the question, What is physics? is not in the same way a question for physics; in fact, the question What is physics? is probably a philosophical question. With that disclaimer in mind, I shall try to say something about what philosophy is. Philosophy is the critical examination of fundamental concepts, concepts that ground human thought, both of the everyday and the academic sort. Perhaps the best way to understand what "the critical examination of fundamental concepts" means is through examples; throughout the book, there will be many examples of this sort of critical reflection. For now, I pick two, both of which are outside the main purview of this book; I do this in order not to confuse the nature of my specific topic with the nature of philosophy in general.

Consider the concept of a person. Certainly, this concept is a basic and fundamental one. Consider, for example, how the concept "person" functions in law—*people* have certain rights, certain responsibilities, certain legal relationships with others—and how it functions in our everyday talk—as in, "There were fifty *people* in the movie theater yesterday." In both contexts, the concept "person" is a central one. But what constitutes a person? What are the necessary and sufficient conditions for being a person? Or similarly, what constitutes being the *same* person over time? What are the necessary and sufficient conditions for being the *same* person? We think, for example, that I am the same person who began writing this book a couple of years ago and that I am the same person who several decades ago was quite small, had no teeth and very little hair, and spent most of the day crying, suckling, and looking around a crib. Why do we think that the person writing this book somewhere in front of a computer is the very same person as that baby called "Eddie"? After all, that baby and this adult have very little in common physically and intellectually.

Or consider this possibility. What if my brain were removed and destroyed and Bill Clinton's brain were put into my skull and attached to my spinal cord? Would the resulting person be me or Bill Clinton, or would I be dead and replaced (in some sense of the term) by some new and distinct person with a body like mine and a brain like Bill Clinton's? Or what if scientists developed a human photocopier that could make an exact physiological and psychological copy of a person? Would the output of a human photocopier (that is, a physiological and psychological copy of the person being copied) be a person? And more interestingly, especially to my mother, if I were put in such a device, would the resulting person be *me?* If so, does this make it the case that the photocopying process alters my status as a person? After the photocopying process, would there now be *two* people competing for the label "Edward Stein"? Or would we just say that after the photocopying process I would be twice as large as I am now?

These questions may seem lifted from an episode of *Star Trek,* but they have deep importance—they push us to articulate the nature of personhood. If you think such questions are unimportant or uninteresting, think not only about how frequently we use the concept person, but think also about the debates surrounding abortion and the question of when a developing fertilized egg becomes a person. Such questions fall into the broad area of philosophy known as metaphysics. As I mentioned before, metaphysics is the part of philosophy concerned with the kinds of things that there are and the forms that their existence take. The question, What kind of thing is a person? thus fits into metaphysics. Chapters 1 through 4 concern metaphysical questions relating to sexual desire and sexual orientation.

Another example of a philosophical question, a question that involves critical examination of a fundamental concept, concerns knowledge. We all think we *know* lots of things: how many people there are in a particular room at a particular moment, the name of the president of the United States, the result of multiplying 17 by 19, and that it is morally unacceptable to torture a baby for amusement. There are also lots of things that we admittedly do not know, but that we think we know what it would be to know them. Although I do not know how many feet tall the building that I live in is or how many pounds it weighs, I know what it would be to know these things and I have a good idea what I would need to do to acquire this knowledge. Knowledge is, however, much trickier than my discussion so far makes it seem. Consider this question: is knowing something merely believing something that is true? Compare two people, who when faced with the question, "What is the product of 17 and 19?" both answer "323." One, a skilled mathematician, says "323" because she got out a paper and pencil and did the calculations. The other did not make any mathematical calculations at all; he just said "323" in a parrotlike fashion because that number just happened to spring into his mind. The mathematician *knows* that 17 times 19 is 323, but the lucky guesser does not; at best, he has a mere belief that 17 times 19 equals 323, a belief that just happens to be right. This just shows that having a true belief is not enough to have knowledge. This, however, only tells us what knowledge is not, not what knowledge is (Gettier 1963).

There are many other problems associated with the concept of knowledge. Consider my *belief* that I am sitting in front of a computer wearing jeans and a T-shirt. I would say that I *know* that I am sitting in front of a computer wearing such clothing. But do I really *know* this? How can I be certain? Sometimes I dream that I am sitting in front of a computer wearing jeans and a T-shirt when in fact I am lying supine in my bedroom asleep and wearing just underwear. While having such a dream, if asked I probably would say, "I *know* that I am in front of a computer wearing jeans and a T-shirt," but I would be wrong—I am in a bedroom sleeping. If this is sometimes the case, it might also be the case at this very moment: I might well be dreaming *now*, dreaming that I am working on a computer when I am actually sleeping. So, what looked like knowledge (that is, my knowing that I am in front of this computer and my knowing that this room exists) is *not* in fact knowledge since for all I know none of these things is true (Descartes 1691). The branch of philosophy that examines knowledge is *epistemology*. Epistemology differs from metaphysics in that it concerns what we know; metaphysics does not concern what we know, but concerns the way the world is. In several places later, in the context of my discussion of sexual desire, I will say more about the contrast between metaphysics and epistemology.

So far I have given two examples of philosophical issues: personal identity and knowledge. What do these two issues have in common? In both instances, concepts that we take for granted, that we use every day in certain ways, are critically examined: are we right to use the concepts in the way that we do? what grounds do we have for using them in the common way? and so on. Further, these philosophical questions are about general and abstract concepts, and the purpose of these questions is to clarify these concepts and the various concepts related to them. Philosophy, then, is the critical examination of centrally important general concepts—such as knowledge, person, justice, right and wrong—for the purpose of clarifying the concepts and strengthening the foundations of human thought. In this book, I will be attempting to strengthen the foundations of human thought concerning sexual desire and sexual orientation and clarifying the concepts we use to think about them.

Note that the term "philosophy" gets used in colloquial talk in a way that is quite different than the way I use it here. I recently read a discussion of Newt Gingrich's philosophy for welfare reform, and I have seen a sign at my local grocery store that outlined the store's pricing philosophy. In cases such as these, the word "philosophy" is being used as a synonym for "strategy" or "policy." Not *any* sort of planned strategy or set of abstract rules count as philosophy in the sense I use it here. Food Mart's policy of providing its customers with the freshest produce at the lowest price is not a *philosophical* principle. And this is not just because of the narrowness of the principle. Philosophy can be done about relatively narrow topics, such as philosophy of mathematics, philosophy of economics, philosophy of sex, and even philosophy of food. What distinguishes philosophy from nonphilosophy and what would distinguish the fictional field of the philosophy of food from Food Mart's (nonphilosophical) pricing policies is the relative *depth* of the statements and questions that characterize philosophy as compared to nonphilosophy.

This much having been said about what the subject matter of philosophy is, what is the *method* of philosophy? How does one answer questions like, What is a person? What is knowledge? or What is a sexual orientation? Again, this is a tricky question. To begin, compare philosophy to some other academic disciplines. Philosophers, unlike many scientists, do not have laboratories. And although philosophers sometimes read texts written centuries ago, their relation to these texts is quite different from the way historians relate to the historical texts that they read. More than any other scholars, philosophers are like mathematicians with respect to their methods. How do mathematicians go about their work? Consider the mathematical question, Is there a highest prime number? First, the mathematician would develop a clear sense of what it is to be a prime number. So, for this example, the clear sense of the term would be that a number is prime if and only if it is a positive integer larger than one and evenly divisible only by one and itself. With this definition in hand, the mathematician would try to deduce as much as possible from this definition, by abstractly exploring its logical implications and the like. The mathematician would do all this, so to speak, from her armchair, with paper and pencil. No special equipment or venue is required. She would just try to think clearly and creatively, applying her other logical and mathematical knowledge to the problem before her. She would consider various proposals, for example, "1,021 is the largest prime number." First, she could test to see whether this number is prime. Discovering that it is, she could look for a prime number that is larger. But when she discovered that 1,031 is *also* prime, she would have determined that 1,021 is not the largest prime number. And, when she comes up with the thesis, for example, that there is no largest prime number, she needs to find an abstract proof for it that does not cite empirical evidence (that is, evidence obtained by observation or experimentation).

Now, the method of the mathematician is not exactly like the method of the philosopher (for example, there is no definite method of proof in philosophy while there does seem to be in mathematics), but there are many illuminating similarities. When I explained one of the central problems of epistemology under the guise of whether I know that I am really sitting in front of a computer at the moment, I was encouraging you to reflect on the concept "knowledge," to focus on what we take to be its definition and to see what follows logically from that. I did nothing out of the ordinary. I asked you simply to reflect on an everyday concept and to use your common sense. We did not need to run any laboratory experiments or consult any historical texts.

In a nutshell, the method of the philosopher involves taking a general, central, abstract concept or question and reflecting on it, challenging our assumptions about it, attempting to clarify the concept, and doing so using our common sense and our logical abilities. A philosopher considers counterexamples to the potential clarifications and answers, considers counterarguments to the arguments that favor one answer or definition over another, and considers how these answers fit with other philosophical theses. I will be exhibiting this method in various places throughout this book as I analyze sexual orientation and related concepts; I do so, for example, in chapter 1 with respect to the concepts of sex and gender.

Bertrand Russell, in his essay "The Value of Philosophy," said that philosophy is valuable because it can free those who study it from "the tyranny of custom" (Russell 1956, 157). Russell is suggesting that we have all been taught—both explicitly and implicitly—a whole host of things that we typically accept unquestioningly. "The tyranny of custom" refers to our unthinking acceptance of many things, from what counts as a just society and the degree of responsibility we have for our own actions to what counts as a sexual orientation and the degree of responsibility each of us has for our own sexual desires. Philosophy, according to Russell, can help free us from this unthinking acceptance by challenging our assumptions through critical examination. That is what I hope to do with regards to sexual orientation and sexual desire more generally: to challenge assumptions about these notions (as they occur in science, politics, theory, and everyday thinking) through critical reflection.

Some commentators on philosophy (from both inside and outside of the field) have claimed that philosophy has not made any significant progress since its inception thousands of years ago: the philosophical problems that puzzled Socrates and Aristotle, for example, remain unsolved. These commentators say philosophy has made no progress and has accomplished nothing except perhaps keeping some philosophers off the streets. I do not think this criticism rings true, but it does merit discussion. It is certainly true that some of the very same problems that philosophers worried about centuries ago are still very much with us today—the problems in epistemology and metaphysics that I discussed prviously are such examples. This does not, however, mean that philosophy has not made any progress with respect to these questions. Although it is true that the majority of philosophers would not agree on the answers to the long-standing questions of philosophy, to a certain extent, there is agreement about the range of answers that should be considered, about what would count as a good answer, and more importantly, there is some agreement as to what are the interesting questions.

Much of what is now considered science as well as many of the social sciences and humanities were once considered part of philosophy. Under the rubric of philosophy, Plato and Aristotle wrote about what we today call physics, biology, mathematics, astronomy, and a lot of other things that today we would not call philosophy. As an area of knowledge becomes more delineated, as the questions it asks become better defined and become more open to empirical testing, and so on, this area of knowledge will often break off from philosophy and become established as its own discipline, a discipline in which progress can be more concretely measured. A fairly recent example of this would be the emergence of psychology. Much of what we now call academic (as opposed to clinical) psychology was part of philosophy over a hundred years ago. Only recently has psychology established itself as its own discipline, with its own methods, explanations, and subject matter. This spawning of other disciplines is a significant kind of progress, although it does not lead to progress *internal* to philosophy. In fact, because the questions with the more definite answers are removed from the purview of philosophy, the field, when looked at just within its own boundaries, looks like it is *regressing* rather than progressing. There is, however, progress in terms of overall collective human knowledge. We know, for example, much more about how the human mind works today than we did two hundred years ago, thanks in part to the development of psychology. But if we are keeping score, philosophy should get some credit for that intellectual advancement. In fact, some people have called philosophy "the queen of the sciences" or "the master discipline" because of the role that philosophers play in establishing and providing foundations for other disciplines. I am not prepared to defend such a grand vision of philosophy here. I will, however, say that the picture of philosophy as contributing to the overall development of the tools, disciplines, and foundations for the progress of knowledge in general offers a promising answer to the charge that philosophy has failed to accomplish anything in two thousand years. I would defend the picture of philosophy that sees it playing a crucial role in the formation of new fields of inquiry (past and present). Partly for this reason, the method of philosophy is especially useful for this project as it involves two emerging fields of inquiry, lesbian and gay studies and the scientific study of sex.

## Coming Attractions

The remainder of this book is divided into three parts that concern, respectively, metaphysical, scientific, and ethical questions concerning sexual orientation. In part I, "Metaphysics," I explore the conceptual landscape related to sexual orientation and sexual desire, considering in particular what a sexual orientation is and whether the concept applies to people in cultures dramatically different from ours. This conceptual exploration provides a foundation for the discussions that follow. Most discussions of sexual orientation, whether scientific, legal, political, sociological, or historical, adopt what are presumed to be commonsense views about the various foundational questions related to sexual orientation and sexual desire. Such commonsense views, accepted unquestioningly, may lead to both practical and theoretical problems. In part II, "Science," I survey and critically examine scientific research on sexual orientation in order to understand more about the nature of sexual orientations and how people develop them. In part III, "Ethics," I consider the relevance of the scientific and metaphysical questions to ethical and legal questions relating to sexual orientation. I also consider the relevance of ethical issues to science and metaphysics.

The intended audience for this book is quite broad. I have tried to write this book in a way that my discussion of such diverse topics as endocrinology and epistemology will be readable and accessible to almost any interested reader. At the same time, I hope this book will be read by scientists, social scientists, and humanists interested in human sexuality and human nature; by people with an interest in social and political questions relating to things sexual; and by people who simply want to better understand their own sexual desires and those of others. In order to accommodate all sorts of readers, I try not to presume any specific knowledge of the subject, and I try to avoid using technical vocabulary and, if unavoidable, to define the terms I use. Because of my broad audience, portions of what follows may be quite familiar to some readers. Even for these readers, there are substantial portions of what follows that should engage them.

This book is meant to speak to people interested in sexual orientations and sexual desires. Lesbians, gay men, bisexuals, and transgendered people, because of their marginal status, may be more inclined than others to think about how sexual orientations develop and about legal and ethical matters concerning sexual orientations. Despite this fact, this book is not in any way directed only to lesbians, gay men, bisexuals, feminists, and their political allies. People of all sexual orientations, genders, political affiliations, and intellectual styles have reason to be interested in sex and sexual desires and will adopt various views on the issues discussed herein.

The next two chapters, which begin the metaphysics part of the book, lay the groundwork for much of the discussion that follows. Chapter 1 concerns the relationship between sexual orientation and the categories of sex and gender. A person's sexual orientation has something to do with his or her sex or gender and the sex or gender of the people to whom he or she is attracted. What is the difference between a person's sex and a person's gender? Which one is relevant to sexual orientation and how? In chapter 1, I introduce the concept of a person's *sex-gender,* which encompasses both a person's sex and a person's gender. This concept allows me to sidestep certain complicated questions about the metaphysics of sex and gender. Chapter 2 builds on chapter 1 and focuses on what a sexual orientation is. Together, these two chapters lay the foundation for the rest of the book.

# PART I
Metaphysics

# CHAPTER 1

# Sex, Gender,
# and Sexual Orientation

**M**uch of what we know about Socrates comes from dialogues that were written by Plato, a student of Socrates. In many of these dialogues, Socrates encounters an interlocutor who claims to know what some general concept is, for example, virtue, knowledge, justice. Through conversation, Socrates then engages this person in conceptual analysis about this concept. In doing so, he shows that this person does not know anything about the concept after all.

The idea behind conceptual analysis is that members of a culture or a multicultural society share an intuitive sense of what a concept means, but they have not bothered to articulate a definition of it. The process of conceptual analysis aims at making the meaning of a concept explicit. This involves trying to tease out a concept's meaning by considering candidate definitions of it and seeing how they fit with our intuitive sense of the concept's application. Sometimes this involves looking at day-to-day uses of the concept, and other times it involves trying to apply the concept to certain imaginary situations. It is important to note that conceptual analysis can often be revisionary. In trying to develop an analysis of a concept, I might discover a tension in how people determine to which things a concept applies. To take a simplistic example, if we thought that a fish is any animal that lives its life in water, and at the same time we thought that a whale lives its life in water but is a mammal, not a fish, then there would be a tension implicit in our taxonomic concepts for animals. Conceptual analysis can be revisionary in that it can provide a guide for eliminating this sort of tension. In the example of the whale, we would give up the view that all animals that live in water are fish.

In this chapter and the one that follows, I will be engaged in conceptual analysis concerning sexual orientation. In many contemporary cultures, sexual orientation is thought to be the most important aspect of a person's sexual tastes: in general, we are more concerned with whether a person is primarily attracted to men, women, or both rather than, for example, whether a person is primarily attracted to people of a certain hair color or of a certain personality type. While we can imagine cultures that are interested in aspects of people's sexual desires other than sexual orientation, we are much more interested in the sex or gender of the people to whom a person is primarily attracted and/or with whom a person is having sex. For this reason, sexual orientation seems an appropriate place to begin my study of human sexual desires. In fact, much of the book that follows will look at human sexual desires through the lens of sexual orientation. In the first part ("Metaphysics"), I try to develop a precise understanding of what a sexual orientation is and what its underlying nature is. I begin this process by conceptually analyzing sexual orientation.

To begin, a person's sexual orientation is in some way related to a person's sex or gender and the sex or gender of the people to whom that person is sexually attracted and/or with whom that person has sex. A successful conceptual analysis of sexual orientation will involve some discussion of sex and gender. It may seem obvious what the terms sex and gender mean, but it is actually more difficult than it might seem to say what a person's sex or gender consists of. In the present chapter, I engage in conceptual analysis of sex and gender and consider their relation to sexual orientation. In chapter 2, I turn to sexual orientation itself.

## Sexual Differentiation in Humans

People can be categorized as being of a particular sex on various grounds.* Perhaps the most basic way of categorizing a person by sex is in terms of chromo-

---

*John Money (1988, 28–29) mentions seven criteria for determining human (and mammal) sex: chromosomal sex, H-Y antigenic sex, gonadal sex, prenatal hormone sex, internal morphologic sex, external morphologic sex, and pubertal hormonal sex. Some of these criteria are discussed in what follows; for my purposes, I do not need to deal with all seven.

somal sex. Humans typically have twenty-three pairs of chromosomes, the units of genetic material. One chromosome from each pair comes from an egg and one comes from a sperm. The sperm and egg together produce a fertilized egg that may eventually produce a human being. One particular pair of a person's chromosomes are called the *sex chromosomes*. Typically, the egg contributes an X sex chromosome and the sperm contributes either another X sex chromosome or a Y sex chromosome. In most cases, a person of chromosomal sex XX develops into a female and a person of chromosomal sex XY develops into a male.

Not everyone, however, has two sex chromosomes. It is possible for a sperm or an egg to carry more than or fewer than the usual twenty-three chromosomes, for one of the forty-six chromosomes from the sperm or egg that produce a fertilized egg to be damaged, or for chromosomes to be unequally distributed during the stages of cell replication that occur soon after an egg's fertilization. If one of these things occurs, a person may have more than or fewer than two sex chromosomes. In some cases, this may have no noticeable physiological effects, while in others, it may lead to dramatic consequences. For example, there are people who have three X chromosomes; some of these people have impaired cognitive and/or reproductive capacities, but some have neither. In contrast, there are people who have *Turner's syndrome*, a condition in which the person has only an X chromosome (or two X chromosomes but one damaged). People with this condition develop as females but without ovaries, and as a result, they cannot produce eggs. They are also often rather short and may have webbed fingers or toes, heart defects, and other physical and cognitive impairments. The point is that a classification scheme for sex that aims to divide all people into two and only two categories—XX and XY—could not classify all human beings.

A possible alternative classification scheme for sex would group people together in terms of the presence or absence of a Y chromosome. According to this scheme, people with just an X chromosome as well as those with XX and XXX would be grouped together as one sex (female), while people with all other sex-chromosome configurations would be grouped together as the other (male). Although this scheme successfully classifies all human beings, it does not result in groupings that come close to our commonsense categories of sex. To see this, we need to consider other human characteristics that are related to sex in addition to sex chromosomes.

During the first six weeks after an egg has been fertilized and begins developing, there are no noticeable differences in the anatomy of XX and XY embryos (this is a shorthand way of referring to embryos that have XX sex chromosomes and XY sex chromosomes, respectively). Both types of embryos

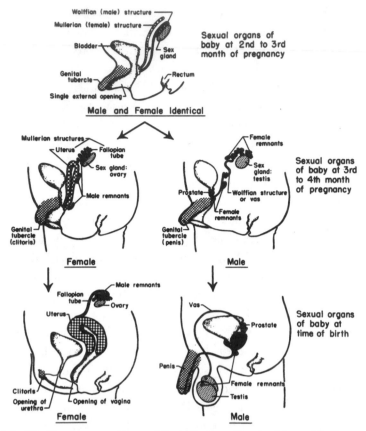

Figure 1-1. The Development of Internal Genitalia. From *Gay, Straight, and In-Between: The Sexology of Erotic Orientation* by John Money, p. 20. Copyright © 1988 Oxford University Press, Inc. Used by permission of Oxford University Press.

develop *undifferentiated* gonads as well as two sets of ducts: the *Müllerian ducts,* which have the potential to develop into the oviducts, the uterus, the cervix, and the upper part of the vagina, and the *Wolffian ducts,* which have the potential to develop into the vas deferens, the epididymis, the seminal vesicles, and the ejaculatory ducts (see Figure 1-1). As the fertilized egg begins to develop into a fetus, various anatomical differentiations occur. During the sixth week of embryonic development, due to the effects of a gene on the Y chromosome, most XY embryos begin to synthesize a protein known as the testis determining factor (TDF) protein that typically causes the gonads to begin to develop into testes. The testes then produce hormones, which have various effects, including the development of the Wolffian ducts into male-typical internal genital structures—including the seminal vesicles and the prostate gland—and the atrophy of the Müllerian ducts. In XX embryos, typically no TDF protein is synthesized, the Wolffian ducts atrophy, and female internal genital structures, namely the ovaries, the uterus, the oviducts, and the upper part of the vagina, develop.

The origins of *external* genitalia are rather different. Both male-typical and female-typical external genitalia begin with the very same structure, the undifferentiated gonads: the penis and the foreskin, on the one hand, and the clitoris and the clitoral hood, on the other, have their origins in the same embryonic structure. Typically, at about the eighth week of development, in XY embryos, a penis and scrotum are formed, while in XX embryos, a clitoris, labia, and the lower part of the vagina are formed (see Figure 1-2).

Not all embryos develop in the way that I have outlined. Some people, often called *true hermaphrodites,* have one ovary and one testis (that is, they have one male-typical and one female-typical internal genitalia). Others (*pseudohermaphrodites*) have either male-typical external genitalia and female-typical internal genital structures or female-typical external genitalia and male-typical internal

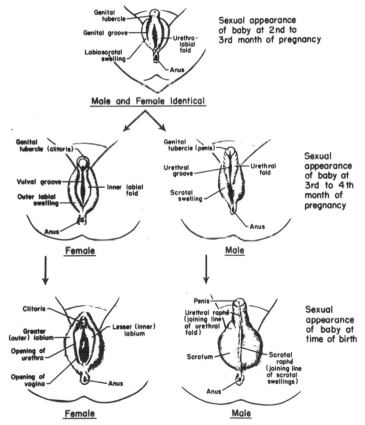

Figure 1-2. The Development of External Genitalia. From *Gay, Straight, and In-Between: The Sexology of Erotic Orientation* by John Money, p. 21. Copyright © 1988 Oxford University Press, Inc. Used by permission of Oxford University Press.

genital structures. Pseudohermaphrodites can have either XX chromosomes or XY chromosomes (or possibly some other chromosomal configuration). For example, a person with XX chromosomes who has a condition called *adrenogenital syndrome* will not produce a protein that plays a role in the development of female external genitalia. Such a person will have ovaries as well as having labial folds that fuse to form a scrotum (though an empty one) and a clitoris that is enlarged to form a penislike structure. A person with XY chromosomes who has a condition called *persistent Müllerian duct syndrome* will not produce the protein that inhibits the production of female internal genitalia. Such a person will have testes, a scrotum, a penis, and the internal genitalia typical for a male but will also have a uterus and fallopian tubes. One or both of the person's testicles may remain in the abdominal cavity rather than descending in the way that they typically do in males. The person with XX chromosomes and adrenogenital syndrome and the person with XY chromosomes and persistent Müllerian duct syndrome may well look morphologically quite similar, but according to the scheme of classification that divides people strictly in virtue of the presence or absence of a Y chromosome, they will be grouped apart—the first will be seen as a female, while the second will be seen as a male. This seems to be a problem for the classification scheme that groups people on the presence or absence of a Y chromosome.

There are other ways that either the external genitalia, the internal genitalia, or both may not conform to the arrangement that is typical for people with a particular configuration of sex chromosomes. I now turn to a different class of such cases than I have discussed so far. During postfetal development, especially at puberty, there are further sex differentiations that typically occur. Males typically develop facial hair, chest hair, and deeper voices, while women typically develop larger breasts and begin to menstruate. Such features are known as *secondary sex characteristics*. Not everyone develops the secondary sex characteristics typically associated with his or her chromosomal sex or genitalia, and people differ rather dramatically in the sorts of developments that occur. For example, some females develop facial hair and can even grow full beards, while some males may develop breasts and have little or no chest hair.

A person's sex can be identified with his or her chromosomal makeup, internal genital structures, external genitalia, secondary sex characteristics, or some combination of these (and other) characteristics. Depending on the context, different criteria may make more sense. In practice, a baby is identified as male or female at birth on the basis of external genitalia, although it is becoming more common to identify a baby's sex before birth by a procedure such as an amniocentesis or chorionic villus sampling that determines the chromosomal sex of a fetus (I will say more about these procedures in chapter 11). If, at birth or soon after, doctors detect an atypical configuration of sex-related characteristics—for example, "ambiguous" external genitalia—then they often perform some sort of "corrective" surgery to "disambiguate" the sex characteristics (Kessler 1990, 1998).

There are two tempting responses to the sort of problems with a straightforward classification scheme for sex that I have been describing. First, we might give up the implicit premise that there are simply two sexes and say that there are *three* sexes: male, female, and *intersex* (people who are in some way partly male and partly female or who are in between male and female—this group includes hermaphrodites and pseudohermaphrodites, as well as people with "ambiguous" genitalia, that is, external genitalia that are in between male-typical and female-typical genitalia). Second, we might hold on to the picture that there are two sexes by giving up the implicit premise that there is a clear-cut line between them. To better understand the difference between two options, I need to introduce some additional terminology.

Categories come in two different types—*continuous* or *discrete*—depending on the nature of the entities to which they apply. A category is discrete if any entity that falls into that category is as much a member of that category as every other member and if there is a clear-cut line between the category and rival categories. A category is continuous if there are various degrees of being a member of that category and if the category shades into rival categories. An example of a continuous category is baldness. Some people are completely bald, while others are only slightly bald. Further, there is a continuum between being bald and having a full head of hair. The category of bald people is thus a continuous category. An example of a discrete category is the category of pregnant people. A person either has a fertilized egg inside of her or she does not (although she may not know whether or not she is pregnant at a particular moment); there is no way to be more or less pregnant (although one's pregnancy can be further along than someone else's, but that is a different matter).

Returning to the category of sex, whether sex is a continuous or a discrete category depends on which sense of the word "sex" one is using. If sex is indexed to external genitalia, then sex is a continuous category since there are people who have "ambiguous" genitalia. This is the case with some hermaphrodites and pseudohermaphrodites as well other intersexed people. For example, due to certain atypical hormone levels, some embryos develop atypical external genitalia (namely a structure somewhere in between a penis and a clitoris) and some develop an atypical urinary opening; in XY embryos, such a genital structure is called a *penoclitoris* and the condition is called *hypospadias*, while in XX embryos, the structure is called a *clitoropenis* and the condition is called *partial urogenital fusion with clitoromegaly*. Unless they undergo surgery to alter their external genitalia, such people have *intermediate* external genitalia; this shows that if sex is indexed to external genitalia, then sex is a continuous category. In contrast, if sex is indexed to the presence or absence of a Y chromosome, then sex would be a discrete category. There are, as I have noted previously, problems with this account of sex as a general term since it does not really capture many of our intuitions about what sex many people are. Most of the other possible categories of sex (categories indexed to external genitalia, internal genitalia, chromosomal sex, hormonal sex) are continuous categories. This reveals a tension regarding the concept of sex; while our intuitive notion is that sex is a discrete category with two values, male and female, we must admit that various sorts of intersexed people exist and that sex seems to be a continuous category. From a scientific point of view, continuous categories are perfectly respectable, and many features of humans (for example, hair color, intestine length, and muscle strength) exist on continuums.

Some people claim that there are more than two sexes. Anne Fausto-Sterling (1993), for example, has argued (albeit with tongue in cheek) that many intersexed people (true hermaphrodites and pseudohermaphrodites) are really members of a distinct sex (or sexes). If sex is distinguished by internal and external genitalia, then there are more than two sexes. If we take Fausto-Sterling's proposal seriously, there are in fact five sexes, namely:

1. *males,* who have testes and a penis;
2. *females,* who have ovaries and a clitoris;
3. *true hermaphrodites* (herms), who have one ovary, one testis, and either a clitoris, a penis, a clitoropenis, or a penoclitoris;
4. *merms* (a kind of pseudohermaphrodite), who have testes and a clitoris (or at least some aspect of female external genitalia, for example, a penoclitoris);
5. *ferms* (another kind of pseudohermaphrodite), who have ovaries and a penis (or at least some aspect of male external genitalia, for example, a clitoropenis).

Similarly, if a person's sex is distinguished by sex chromosomes, then there are more than two sexes because one can have other chromosomal configurations, such as XXX, XXY, and X. The fact that there are quite a few people who, in various ways, do not fit straightforwardly into either the category male or female is supposed to show that there are more than two sexes.

This argument does not conclusively establish that there are more than two sexes. As I have noted above, if we categorize people in terms of whether they have any Y sex chromosomes, there would be only two sexes. Or we could categorize a person in terms of (past and future) reproductive capacities or potentialities. Can a person produce (or did the person have the potential to produce) sperm (or eggs)? The answer to either question is either yes or no; therefore a discrete two-sex categorization scheme can be developed on either of these grounds (that is, is the person a sperm producer or not? or is the person an egg producer or not?). If one of these pictures is embraced, then there would be two sexes and sex would be a discrete category. However, none of these pictures (the Y-chromosome picture, the sperm-producer picture, or the egg-producer picture) fits particularly well with our commonsense categories of sex—the first for reasons I have discussed above, the second because it counts infertile males as females, and the third because it counts infertile females as males. None of the evidence that supports the view that there are more than two sexes counts against the view that sex is a continuous category (that is, with male and female at either end of the continuum and with various intermediary forms existing between them). The continuum view is especially plausible given that there is significant variety among members of at least the last three of Fausto-Sterling's five categories. Rather than saying that there are more than two sexes, it may be more appropriate to say that sex is a continuous category. For my purposes, I do not need to decide how many sexes there are or whether sex is continuous or discrete.

### The Sex-Gender Distinction

Sometimes "gender" is used as a synonym for "sex." Often, however, the terms are used differently. Frequently, "gender" has come to be used for the roles, characteristics, and stereotypes associated with members of a particular sex, that is, a person's gender concerns a person's masculinity or femininity or some aspects thereof. A slogan for this way of using the terms "sex" and "gender" (adapted from Brown [1986, 313–314]) is that sex is "between the legs" and "under the shirt" as well as in the genes, while gender is in the culture. Following this usage, "male" and "female" are types of sex, while "man" and "woman" are types of gender, namely "man" and "woman" are the terms associated with the characteristics that a culture attaches to males and females. In a society where housecleaning and working as a nurse are typically associated with females, while driving a truck and playing football are typically associated with males, such practices would be characteristics of *gender* in that society. John Money (1955) seems to have been the first to distinguish between sex and gender in such a way that gender concerns how male-typical or female-typical a person's social presentation is. This usage is quite common today. For example, Supreme Court Justice Antonin Scalia recently adopted this usage saying that "the word 'gender' . . . connot[es] . . . cultural or attitudinal characteristics (as opposed to physical characteristics) distinctive to the sexes" (J.E.B. 1994, 157, note 1). I call this the *standard usage* of the terms "sex" and "gender."

In contrast, Suzanne Kessler and Wendy McKenna in their important book, *Gender: An Ethnomethodological Approach,* use gender more broadly than the standard usage (Kessler and McKenna 1978). They write:

> The term "gender" has traditionally been used to designate psychological, so-cial and cultural aspects of maleness and femaleness . . . [and the term] "[s]ex" generally designates the biological components of maleness and fe-maleness. . . . We . . . use gender, rather than sex, even when referring to those aspects of being a woman (girl) or man (boy) that have traditionally been viewed as biological. This will serve to emphasize our position that the ele-ment of social construction is primary in all aspects of being female or male, particularly when the term we use seems awkward (e.g., gender chromo-somes). (12)

Kessler and McKenna's usage fits nicely with the possibility that many of the characteristics typically thought to be associated with sex (understood in the standard sense) might turn out to be part of gender (understood in the stan-dard sense).

The standard usage of the terms "sex" and "gender" emphasizes that gender roles differ from society to society; for example, in some agricultural so-cieties, most of the farming is done by men, while in others it is done mostly by women. It is possible for a male who adopts the roles typically associated with females and who is treated by members of his society as a female typically is treated to be, in terms of gender, a woman. The parallel point is true for fe-males who adopt behaviors typical for males in a particular society. It is also possible for a society to have more than two genders. For example, in some Na-tive American cultures, there are males who play many of the roles that females in those cultures typically play (Whitehead 1993; Williams 1986). These males, known as *berdache,* marry men, do chores typically done by women, and so on, but they are known to be males nonetheless. Some scholars have argued that since these males adopt women's roles while still being recognized as males, they constitute a third gender. A society that also allowed for recogniz-able females to play roles typically associated with men, to marry women, and so on, might be said to have four genders.

Setting aside the question of how many genders a particular culture has, the standard usage of gender has the disadvantage that it implicitly "biologizes" characteristics typically associated with males and females. For example, in light of the apparent fact that in many different cultures more boys than girls engage in rough-and-tumble play, some people have argued that engaging in such play is associated with males in virtue of their biological makeup. This difference might, however, be cultural, not biological. Kessler and McKenna's alternative to the standard usage has the advantage of combating the presumption that the characteristics that we think are sex differences are biologically based.

For the purposes of this project, I do not want to commit myself to a particular account of what biological features, if any, distinguish males from females. Further, I do not want to be committed to the view that there must be two sexes and that the terms for these two sexes represent discrete categories. I am also not committed to the claim that, in all or most people, all bodily factors thought to be relevant to sex difference will point to the same sex. In fact, the existence of intersexed people seems to count against a simple picture of sex: their existence demonstrates that not all possibly sex-related bodily factors always point to the same sex. The existence of intersexed people also suggests either that there are at least three sexes—male, female, and intersex—or, more plausibly, that sex is a continuous rather than a discrete category or even that it is a cluster of continuous features. I also want to leave open the possibility that the term "sex" might not turn out to be a scientifically explanatory term, but rather that it might be replaced by several different terms (for example, terms associated with different sorts of internal genitalia or different sorts of external genitalia) that would provide more precision in talking about differences among people's bodies. Like Kessler and McKenna, I want to allow that our current views about what biological features distinguish males from females might be mostly wrong. To leave these various issues unresolved, I use the term *sex-gender* to encompasses both sex and gender as standardly used. Sex-gender includes all the characteristics (biological, psychological, cultural, etc.) that are supposed to distinguish males/men from females/women. Unless otherwise indicated, when I talk about sex and gender rather than sex-gender, I intend to use these terms in the standard way. Also, I use the terms "man" and "woman" as nouns associated with sex-gender and "male" and "female" as adjectives associated with sex-gender. Given that I want to avoid committing myself to the view that there are only two sexes, I try to avoid using the phrase "opposite sex" throughout.

Despite the fact that I have spilled a lot of ink over the sex/gender distinction and that I have bothered to introduce the rather infelicitous locution "sex-gender," I do not expect that much of what follows in this book will turn on which characteristic(s) of sex-gender, if any, will turn out to be a biological factor(s) that distinguishes males and females. With respect to my main focus on sexual desire and sexual orientation, I *provisionally* define sexual orientation as indexed to the sex-gender of the people a person is attracted to. In so doing, I steer clear of some of the sticky and unresolved questions about sex and gender that I have been focusing on in this section. I want to steer clear of these matters for now because my main concerns are sexual desire and sexual orientation, not sex and gender. It could be that the concept of sexual orientation involves a deep and irretrievable confusion about sex and gender. By using the notion of sex-gender, I hope to bracket this possibility in what follows.

## The Relationship Between Sex-Gender and Sexual Orientation

Although sex-gender and sexual orientation are clearly related, it is rather difficult to spell out how they are related (Calhoun 1994; Rubin 1984; Sedgwick 1990, 27–35). Various people have argued that, in most cultures of Western Europe and North American, lesbians are not women (Wittig 1993). The idea is that, in these societies, part of what makes a female count as a woman is being sexually, emotionally, and economically attracted to men, having sex with men, and entering romantic relationships with men. In these societies, lesbians—as females who are sexually attracted to females (or women), sexually active with females, and involved in relationships with females—are not women. Evidence of this might be the common notion in such societies that lesbians are not "real" women. If this view is right, lesbians would constitute a third gender, although they would still be females. This might be extended to an argument that gay men are not men. The parallel idea could be that what makes a male count as a man is being sexually and romantically attracted to women, having sex with them, and entering relationships with them. Gay males, because they lack many or all of these features, are thus not men. If this view is right, then gay men would constitute a fourth gender, although they would still be males.

Matters might even be more complex. It might be that *butch* lesbians—namely, lesbians who behave in male-typical ways and/or who are sexually attracted to women (but not to masculine females) and/or who play certain sexual roles that might be seen as male-typical—are members of a third gender, while *femme* lesbians—namely, women who behave in a female-typical fashion except for the fact that they are sexually attracted to females (although masculine ones) rather than males—would be counted as women (in terms of gender). Similarly, on this more complex view, males who are effeminate in terms of their appearance and/or their nonsexual behavior or males with a preference for being anally penetrated by men (*bottoms*) might count as members of a fourth gender, while masculine (*top*) gay men count as men (in terms of gender). This seems to fit with the culturally dominant view in some Latin American cultures in which men who anally penetrate men (and perhaps also have sex with women) are not seen as homosexual but rather are seen as particularly masculine, while males who are anally penetrated by other males are seen as homosexual and as feminine (Almaguer 1993; Alonso and Koreck 1993).

I am not saying that either of these accounts or any other accounts according to which there are four genders is the right account for our culture today or for any other culture past or present. For now, I am just trying to flesh out an account of what a society that had four genders might look like: in such a society, there would need to be four distinct social roles, some of which might be indexed to biological features that are supposed to be related to sex-gender differences.

Some people think that we live in a society in which sexual desires are not part of sex-gender, that is, in this society, lesbians and gay men qualify as women and men, respectively, in the same way that their heterosexual counterparts do. I am not sure what would settle the dispute as to whether being a heterosexual is part of what it is to be a woman or a man in this society, though many in this society seem to view lesbians and gay men as second-class women and men, respectively, rather than nonwomen and nonmen, respectively. Seeing lesbians and gay men as second class women and men preserves most of the insights of accounts that say lesbians and gay men are not women and men, respectively, without requiring a more complex gender ontology, that is, without saying there are four genders.

Matters are further complicated when we add the notion of a *gender identity* into the mix. A person's gender identity is his or her psychological sense of what his or her sex-gender is. Some people, although they have XY chromosomes and male-typical internal and external genitalia, have the feeling that they are "really" female; they feel that they are "females trapped in male bodies." Gender identity, the feeling of belonging to a particular sex-gender, is independent of a person's sexual orientation. There are men who feel that they are women who are nonetheless attracted to women. Such a man would say that he feels like he is a woman who is attracted to women and, hence, really a lesbian. Some people have such a strong sense that they are really trapped in a body of the wrong sex that they are willing to go through a long process of proving to a doctor that they believe this, followed by expensive and complicated sex-change surgery (Devor 1997; Hausman 1995). While a surgical procedure cannot change a person's chromosomal sex, it can remove internal genital structures, alter external genitalia, and, combined with hormone treatments, dramatically affect a person's secondary sex characteristics. A person who has undergone successful sex-change surgery will seem to most people to be a member of the sex towards which the surgery was directed.

On most accounts of what sex is (except, most notably, a chromosomal account of sex), successful sex-change surgery changes a person's sex and thereby brings a person's gender identity into accord with his or her sex. A person who has undergone such surgery is known as a *transsexual*. A woman who becomes a man is known as an *F-to-M,* and a man who becomes a woman is known as an *M-to-F.* A person who has undergone preliminary hormone treatments and is living in a manner typically associated with a person of the sex-gender that accords with his or her gender identity but who has not had surgery is known as a *preoperative transsexual* (*preop* for short). A person who is a transsexual or who feels that his or her sex differs from his or her gender identity, whether or not he or she has had or intends to have a sex-change operation, is known as a *transgendered person.* Some people include intersexed people under the term "transgendered person." I keep these notions distinct, although many intersexed people are also transgendered people because they have had surgery, often at a very young age, to alter their "ambiguous" external genitalia (Kessler 1998). If surgery to alter external genitalia is seen as changing a person's sex, then an intersexual person who has had such surgery but has a gender identity that is discordant from his or her surgically produced sex might, in virtue of this mismatch, be a transgendered person.

Transgendered people are distinct from people who, though they do not think that they are members of another sex-gender, like to wear clothes that are typically worn by members of another sex-gender. Such people are known as *cross-dressers.* Cross-dressers come in various forms, from women who like to wear men's ties to men who like to wear an entire ensemble of women's clothing from bras and girdles on up. What counts as cross-dressing can change dramatically over a short period of time and from place to place. It was rare and rather odd fifty years ago in North America for a woman to wear blue jeans or a man to have a pierced ear; on most college campuses today, many men have pierced ears and most women wear jeans.

It is important to realize that being a cross-dresser or a transgendered person is quite different from being a homosexual, although some transgendered people and cross-dressers are lesbians and some are gay men. It used to be the case that some people thought of all homosexuals as transgendered people (although these people would not have used the word "transgendered" and per-haps not the word "homosexual" either). Early thinkers about sexual orienta-tion such as Karl Heinrich Ulrichs (1994) and Magnus Hirschfeld (1914) saw lesbians and gay men (that is, the people who today would be called lesbians and gay men) as "inverts" or members of a "third sex" or an "intersex." All of these theories in a sense pictured gay men as having male bodies and female "souls" and lesbians as having female bodies and male "souls." Such theories might collectively be called *inversion models* of homosexuality because they see, for example, gay men as having inverted psychological constitutions, that is, female psychologies associated with male bodies. These accounts have to a certain extent been discredited, although, as I shall show in chapter 7, many contemporary scientific theories concerning sexual orientation still unques-tioningly accept something close to the inversion model of sexual orientation. Also, as I will discuss in chapter 4, it is not clear that people in the nineteenth century or earlier had sexual orientations in the sense that people do today. Per-haps the inversion models of sexual orientation of the nineteenth century were more applicable to the sexual interests of people of that century than to the sex-ual interests of people today.

I spent the previous section talking about sex and gender because of the connection to sexual orientation. Our idea of a homosexual is someone who has sex with and/or is attracted to people of the same sex-gender. Since my main interest in this book is sexual orientation, the central question concerning sex-gender is how it interacts with the notion of sexual orientation. As I men-tioned at the start, a person's sexual orientation is in some way indexed to his or her sex-gender and the sex-gender of the people he or she is sexually at-tracted to and/or sexually active with. Given the complexity of sex-gender and the possibility of there being more than two sex-genders or a continuum be-tween men and women, a simple picture of sexual orientation seems hard to preserve. Suppose, for example, that we adopt a *behavioral* account of what sexual orientation is, that is, an account that says a person's sexual orientation is determined by whether or not he or she has sex with people of the same sex-gender (more on this account in the next chapter). On this view, what sexual orientation is a person who has XY chromosomes, male-typical internal geni-talia, female-typical external genitalia and female-typical secondary sex charac-teristics, and has sex with and is attracted to males? Is this person a heterosex-ual woman, a gay man, or something else? Assuming sexual orientation has to do with a person's sex-gender and the sex-gender of the people he or she is at-tracted to and/or has sex with, if there are more than two sex-genders, then there will need to be more than two categories of sexual orientation (and this is just the beginning of this problem, as my discussion of bisexuality in chapter 2 will show). For example, if by a person's sex-gender we mean chromosomal sex, then what is the sexual orientation of a person with XXY chromosomes (that is, someone who has what is called *Klinefelter's syndrome*) who has sex with and is primarily attracted to people with XY chromosomes? What about a person with XX chromosomes whose only sexual partner has a single X chromosome? The prospect of a straightforward account of sexual orientation seems in serious trouble.

For my purposes, it is more important to develop an account of sexual orientation than an account of sex-gender. It is not obvious which of the many different things one might mean by the sex, gender, or sex-gender of a person is appropriate for use in talking about sexual orientation, although it initially seems that some such notion will be part of such an account. In chapter 2, I explore the notion of sexual orientation more extensively, allowing the notion of sex-gender to function as a placeholder for the various meanings of sex and gender. If I were engaged in a different project, I might proceed to engage in conceptual analysis and clarification of the notions of sex and gender. I might try to figure out which of the various accounts of what sex and gender mean would best capture the core meanings of these notions. I would also endeavor to understand and critique scientific research on sex and gender differences. My project in this book, however, concerns sexual desire and sexual orientation. For these purposes, it will suffice to have just surveyed the complexities of sex-gender.

# CHAPTER 2

# *What Is a*
# *Sexual Orientation?*

In Aristophanes' myth told in *The Symposium*, there are four sorts of human beings: males who are looking to become intertwined with other males, males who are looking to become intertwined with females, females who are looking to become intertwined with other females, and females who are looking to become intertwined with males. In a sense, these four groupings are in use today as categories of sexual orientation. Although we do not accept Aristophanes' mythological account of their origins, many of us do divide people into somewhat similar groups, namely, gay men, heterosexual men, lesbians, and heterosexual women, respectively (in some instances, bisexual men and bisexual women are added to the list).

Most people who talk about sexual orientation—from scientists to politicians, from gay rights activists to members of the religious right—use these groupings. Further, most people seem to have a clear idea what a sexual orientation is and they seem to be sure that every person fits into one of the four groups (except perhaps children, who may just have a nascent sexual orientation—in this regard, one hears talk of *prehomosexual* children). In fact, it is far from easy to spell out what a sexual orientation is partly because there are competing views about it. In this chapter, I try to develop an account of what a sexual orientation is. In doing so, I begin by looking at what a significant majority of people in North America and Western Europe mean by the term "sexual orientation." It is not that I think that this relatively small portion of the world's population necessarily uses the right concepts for thinking about sex and sexual desire. Rather, because of the influence of this term and the views associated with it, getting clear on what this group of people means by sexual orientation is crucial to understanding and evaluating, among other things, the science and the laws in societies that see human sexual desire in this way. By focusing on what such people (at least implicitly) believe is an important concept for our thinking about sex and sexual desire, I am not assuming that this way to think about sexual orientation is the right way. In fact, I will argue that it is probably not. In order, however, to assess this way of thinking about sexual orientation, I need to determine what sexual orientation means. In this chapter, I again use conceptual analysis; in doing so, I attempt to resolve or at least point out the many tensions in this concept. I proceed from commonsense pictures of the concept to more complex ones. Although I start simply and may seem to in some ways accept the commonsense view of what a sexual orientation is, by the end of this chapter, I will have called almost all of this picture of sexual orientation into question. If you have worries about the typical ways of thinking about sexual desire, I ask you to bear with me while I try to get clear on what the commonsense view of sexual orientation is. Once I have done so, I will turn to questioning the adequacy of this view. On the contrary, if you think it is obvious what sexual orientation is, in what follows, you will find that matters are far from simple.

As I discussed in the previous chapter, a person's sexual orientation seems to involve a person's sex-gender and the sex-gender of other individuals in relation to that person. Even bracketing the problems of what a person's sex-gender amounts to, there are many deep problems with characterizing what a sexual orientation is. In the first section of this chapter, I begin my conceptual analysis by asking whether a person's sexual orientation is indexed to his or her sexual behavior, to his or her gender identity, to his or her sexual fantasies, or to some combination of these (and other) factors. I argue that sexual orientation has to do with a person's sexual desires and the sexual activities in which he or she is disposed to engage. In the next section, I consider how many sexual orientations there are and how they are related to each other. The standard view says that there are just two sexual orientations—heterosexual and homosexual—and they are in some sense the opposite of each other (some commentators see this view as implicit in Aristophanes' myth). Another popular view sees sexual orientation as a continuum, a sliding scale ranging from exclusive heterosexuality to exclusive homosexuality with one or more positions in between the two. I will point to problems in both of these views of sexual orientation. Up to this point in the chapter, I will have focused on a person's sexual attraction to people in virtue of their sex-gender. In the third section, I consider whether this narrowness of focus is justified; perhaps there are other aspects of a person's sexual desires (for example, the race, height, or personality-type of the people a person is attracted to or the kind of sex that he or she wants to have) that warrant attention as well. My discussion thus far will have assumed that we know what a sexual behavior or sexual desire—as opposed to other kinds of behaviors or desires—is; in the next section, I consider whether this assumption is warranted. In the concluding section, I review the important questions that I have raised along with some of the answers I have given.

Before I proceed, I offer one caveat on my choice of the term "sexual orientation." In the 1970s, the term "sexual preference" was commonly used in the way that "sexual orientation" is commonly used today. Use of "sexual preference" was to a large extent abandoned because it was taken to imply that whether one was attracted to men or women was a choice. "Sexual *orientation*" was deemed preferable to "sexual *preference*" because "orientation" implies that a person's sexual desires are the result of deep features of a person's character, perhaps an innate, unchangeable feature. Throughout this book, I use "sexual orientation" rather than "sexual preference" (or some other synonym), but I do not do so because I am assuming that a person's sexual desires are the result of deep features of a person's character or that they are innate or unchangeable. Until I say (and argue) otherwise, I am neutral about the source and nature of sexual desires. I say otherwise in the part of this book devoted to scientific research on sexual orientation (part II). I think this usage of "sexual orientation" is justified partly because the term has now taken on its own life such that it no longer connotes the sense of the term that originally motivated the shift from "sexual preference."

## What Constitutes a Person's Sexual Orientation?

### The Behavioral View

Consider the following simple and straightforward account of what a sexual orientation is. One's sexual orientation is determined by the sex of the people that he or she has sex with: if one has sex with people of the same sex-gender, then one is a homosexual; if one has sex with people not of the same sex-gender, then one is a heterosexual. There are three features to this view. First, it focuses on a person's behavior as being determinate of his or her sexual orientation.

Second, it assumes that there are two and only two possible sexual orientations. Third, it focuses on whether the person is of the same sex-gender as that of the person's sex partners rather than whether the person's sex partners are men or women. All three features may, at first glance, seem part of our concept of a sexual orientation. The first feature has more to do with what a sexual orientation is, while the second and third features are about what sorts of sexual orientations there are. In this section, I focus on the first feature. I turn to the other features in the following two sections.

I call the view that a person's sexual orientation is indexed to his or her sexual behavior the *behavioral view* of sexual orientation.[1] The behavioral view of sexual orientation has the advantage of characterizing sexual orientations in a way that is objective and scientifically accessible. On this view, a person's sexual orientation is a matter of determining what sorts of sexual acts the person has performed. It may well be that these acts are in fact unknown to all but the person and his or her sexual partners, but they are in principle knowable. Facts of this sort are perfectly respectable, despite the possibility that there might be problems with *knowing* such facts (what philosophers call problems of *epistemological inaccessibility*). Similarly, statements about the far side of the moon and the status of the light in your refrigerator when the door is closed are reasonable despite their problems with epistemological accessibility. Especially for doing science, it might seem advantageous to be able to spell out what sexual orientation is simply in behavioral terms.

This account of what a sexual orientation is has connections with behaviorism, a popular psychological and philosophical view of the early twentieth century. According to this view, one can find out everything interesting about a person by observing her behavior.[2] Although this view has the advantage of making a person's psychology transparent to an observer (because an observer can see a person's behavior, which is all that there is to a person's psychology according to behaviorism), there are legions of problems with it. Most importantly, behaviorism allows that other people will typically be in a better position to assess my mental states than I am; it seems, however, that I have special access to at least a substantial part of my mental life. This problem with behaviorism is exemplified by the joke about the two behaviorists who meet on the street and greet each other by saying, "You're fine; how am I?" This joke, whether or not you find it funny, points to a serious problem for behaviorism: since an observer has as much if not more access to your behavior than you do, such an observer has as much if not more access to your psychology as you do. This, however, seems ludicrous. With respect to sexual orientation, the behavioral view is committed to the idea that anyone who can observe my sexual activity knows as much as I possibly could about my own sexual orientation. I seem to know more about my sexual orientation than an observer does because, in addition to my sexual behavior, I know what my sexual desires and my unexpressed feelings about sexual activities are. It will not help the behavioral view of sexual orientation to note that I can hide and/or repress my sexual desires. The behavioral view says that a person's sexual orientation is indexed to a person's sexual behavior. Allowing that a person's sexual orientation can be repressed admits the possibility that a person's behavior can be discordant with his or her sexual orientation. Given that this is a possibility, the behavioral view of sexual orientation is thereby undermined.

The behavioral account of sexual orientation runs into trouble in other ways as well. According to this view, one *acquires* a sexual orientation when one has sex for the first time; one does not have a sexual orientation if one has never had sex; and on this view, it is impossible for one's sexual orientation to be discordant with one's sexual behavior. Consider the case of Richard, who for as long as he can remember has been attracted to men, but because of social pressures, married Patricia and has never had sex with anyone but her. Further, Richard is only able to get aroused and have orgasms while having sex with Patricia if he fantasizes about having sex with men. According to the behavioral view of sexual orientation, Richard is a heterosexual, but according to an intuitive account, given his long-lasting sexual attraction to men, he is a homosexual. Or consider Mary, who, like Richard, has for as long as she can remember been attracted to men and has had lots of sexual fantasies about them. However, because she has been a devout Catholic all her life and a nun by profession, she has remained celibate. According to the behavioral view, she is asexual or she has no sexual orientation. In light of her attractions and fantasies, however, Mary seems to be a heterosexual. Further, suppose that after thirty years of celibacy, Mary finally has sex with Bernard. According to the behavioral view, by the very act of having sex with a man, Mary *becomes* a heterosexual. It seems, however, that given her rich fantasy life, Mary was a heterosexual well before Bernard came along. While committing a sex act with a man might confirm that she in fact likes having sex with men, Mary's first sexual act with another person does not *produce* her sexual orientation in the way the behavioral view entails it does. Due to these sorts of counterintuitive implications, the behavioral view seems in serious trouble.

It is worth stepping back for a moment to make a methodological point about my argument in the preceding paragraphs. Recall from the introductory passage to this chapter that I am undertaking a conceptual analysis of the notion of sexual orientation. Initially, it seems that a person's sexual behavior has a lot to do with his or her sexual orientation. For this reason, the behavioral account, which indexes sexual orientation to a person's sexual behavior, seems plausible. But when this view is examined more closely, it does not mesh with our intuitions about quite a few particular (and not extraordinary) instances of people and their sexual behaviors (for example, the cases of Richard and Mary considered above); it also fails to fit with more general ideas that we have about sexual orientation. These considerations suggest that sexual behavior, while it may be part of what determines a sexual orientation, is not its *only* determining factor. For this reason, I rejected the behavioral view of sexual orientation.

### The Self-Identification View

One reason why the behavioral view of sexual orientation runs into problems concerns its failure to take into account the fact that people have some privileged access to their thoughts and feelings in general and to their sexual desires, fantasies, and the like in particular. A view that gives weight to a person's own assessment of his or her sexual orientation is the view that I call the *self-identification view,* according to which one's sexual orientation is based on one's sense of what his or her own sexual orientation is. The self-identification view says that if someone really believes he or she is a heterosexual, then he or she is. This view avoids the objections that plagued the behavioral view. According to the self-identification account, a person can have a sexual orientation that is discordant with his or her sexual behavior. Richard, the monogamous married male I discussed above, would be a homosexual if he sees himself as gay despite the fact that he only has sex with women. This view, however, has the problem of not allowing for self-deception. It is possible for Richard to be a homosexual without him believing, even in his heart of hearts, that he is a homosexual. Consider, for example, the character of Roy Cohn (based on the 1950s American political figure of the same name) in the play *Angels in America* who says:

> Homosexuals are not men who sleep with other men. Homosexuals are men who know nobody and who nobody knows. Who have zero clout. I have clout. A lot. . . . [W]hat I am is defined entirely by who I am. Roy Cohn is not a homosexual. Roy Cohn is a heterosexual man . . . who fucks around with guys. (Kushner 1992, 45–46)

If Cohn actually believes what he says, according to the self-identification view, despite the fact that he has sex with men and is attracted to them, he is not a homosexual because he does not think of himself as one. It seems, however, possible for Cohn to be homosexual despite his denials and his belief to the contrary. (One might say the same thing about a Latin American man whose only sex with other men involves anally penetrating them and who considers himself a heterosexual despite his sexual behavior.) Similarly, it seems possible for a young person to be attracted to people of the same sex-gender without realizing it, perhaps because he or she lives in a society in which homosexuality is invisible and not talked about. Such a person would not have the concept of homosexuality or even the concept of having sex with a person of the same sex-gender available to him or her and, hence, would not be able to self-identify—even to himself or herself—as homosexual. Despite this, it seems possible that a person could be a homosexual if he or she has sexual desires and fantasies about people of the same sex-gender even though these desires are deeply repressed in his or her subconscious. This possibility makes sense, but the self-identification view does not allow for it.

### The Dispositional View

The self-identification view, then, does not seem to capture our notion of what a sexual orientation is. Its problems, however, seem less serious than those of the behavioral view. People are fairly reliable in reporting their sexual orientations, but in some cases, this can be trumped. A view that seems to incorporate the virtues of the behavioral and self-identification views but at the same time handles their vices is the *dispositional view* of sexual orientation. According to this view, a person's sexual orientation is based on his or her sexual desires and fantasies and the sexual behaviors he or she is disposed to engage in under ideal conditions. If a person has sexual desires and fantasies about having sex primarily with people of the same sex-gender and is inclined under ideal circumstances to engage in sexual acts primarily with such people, then that person is a homosexual. Conditions are ideal if there are no forces to prevent or discourage a person from acting on his or her desires, that is, when there is sexual freedom and a variety of appealing sexual partners available. In contrast to the behavioral view, the dispositional account of sexual orientation allows that people can have sexual orientations before they actually have sex. In contrast to the self-identification view, the dispositional view allows that, although people usually have some special insight into what their sexual orientations are, a person can deny and repress his or her sexual orientation. The dispositional view shares with the behavioral view the virtue of taking a person's behavior into consideration, although the dispositional view does so less directly: according to the dispositional view, certain sexual behaviors are relevant because they reflect a person's dispositions. For example, my behavior of eating ice cream when I am hungry and in the presence of ice cream is evidence of my disposition to eat ice cream as well as my desire to do so (unless, of course, ice cream is the only food available and I am starving, in which case it just shows that I do not have a strong aversion to ice cream). With respect to sexual orientation, the fact that, in general, Bill will have sex with men when he is horny and when there are interested and interesting men available reflects Bill's disposition to have sex with men. The dispositional view shares with the self-identification view the virtue of giving weight to one's sense of one's own sexual orientation—one does have a good sense of one's own sexual dispositions—although the dispositional view gives it less weight.

There is, however, a possible problem for the dispositional view: according to the dispositional view, to know one's sexual orientation, you need to know what one would do in various counterfactual situations. A counterfactual situation is a way that things might possibly have been (or be) but, in fact, were (or are) not:[3] for example, Lee Harvey Oswald's bullet might have missed John F. Kennedy (it didn't); the Yankees might have won the World Series in 1997 (they didn't); it might have been sunny today (in fact, it is cloudy). Some counterfactual situations are difficult to assess. What would the world be like if Oswald's bullet had missed? If the Yankees had won that series? The fact that it is difficult to know what to make of counterfactual situations is a potential problem for the dispositional view of sexual orientation. The dispositional view appeals to what a person would do sexually and how a person would feel erotically in certain counterfactual situations, but this might be difficult to assess. Would, for example, I mostly have sex with and/or be erotically attracted to males if I lived in a culture in which there was complete sexual freedom? Would, for example, you be more or less or equally attracted to females than you in fact are if you grew up and lived in a culture that had achieved maximal equality of the sexes? Would Socrates have been attracted to young men if he lived in a culture characterized by virulent homophobia? It is quite hard to assess such counterfactuals; I simply do not know what I would do or how I would feel in some counterfactual situations, especially ones that are quite different from the situations in which I have found myself. A defender of the dispositional view is likely to accept this point, but deny that it counts against this view of what a sexual orientation is. The dispositional view does index one's sexual orientation to what one would do and what one would want to do in certain counterfactual situations, and it is difficult to determine what one would do under circumstances that significantly differ from those in which one actually finds oneself. This partly explains, a defender of the dispositional view might point out, why it can take such a long time for a person to figure out what his or her sexual orientation is;[4] determining what one's sexual desires are under some future or ideal set of circumstances is not at all immediately transparent, but this does not mean that the dispositional view of sexual orientation is wrong.

The dispositional view is implicitly adopted by Alfred Kinsey and his collaborators in their landmark studies, *Sexual Behavior in the Human Male* (Kinsey, Pomeroy, and Martin 1948) and *Sexual Behavior in the Human Female* (Kinsey et al. 1953). The Kinsey researchers conducted two-hour interviews with thousands of men and women. Subjects were asked searching questions about their sexual experiences, sexual fantasies, and sexual desires. On the basis of these questions, each subject was placed on a "heterosexual-homosexual rating scale" that has come to be known as the *Kinsey scale*. As described by Kinsey:

> [T]he rating which an individual receives has a dual basis. It takes account of his overt sexual experience and/or his psychosexual reactions. In the majority of instances, the two aspects of the history parallel, but sometimes they are not in accord. In the latter case, the rating of an individual must be based upon an evaluation of the relative importance of the overt and the psychic in his history. . . . The position of an individual on this scale is always based upon the relation of the heterosexual to the homosexual in his history, rather than upon the actual amount of overt experience or psychic reaction. (Kinsey, Pomeroy, and Martin 1948, 647)

Future studies done by the Kinsey Institute, though not conducted by Kinsey himself, rated subjects on two distinct scales—"overt sexual experience" and "psychosexual reaction"—and then combined these two ratings in order to assign a person a sexual orientation (Bell and Weinberg 1978, 54).

The Kinsey view of sexual orientation is a dispositional picture of sexual orientation because it counts sexual behavior, sexual desires, and sexual fantasies as part of a person's sexual orientation. Further, it allows that these aspects of a person's sexual history may be discordant. In such cases, the placement of a person on the Kinsey scale is determined by the *relative importance* of the person's various behaviors and desires. Assessing this is tantamount to making a guess at a person's dispositions.

Recall that one criticism of the behavioral view of sexual orientation is that this account does not allow that you have special access to your own sexual orientation. The dispositional view of sexual orientation is supposed to avoid this problem, but a critic of this view might claim that it does not. Such a critic might say that if a person's sexual orientation has to do with a person's dispositions to engage in sexual acts and to have certain sexual desires and if a person might not know what his or her own dispositions are (perhaps because that person does not know what he or she would do in various counterfactual situations), then it follows that the dispositional view is committed to the possibility that a person may not know his or her own sexual orientation. Earlier, I presented this feature of the dispositional view as an advantage in that it partly explains why some people take a long time to realize what their own sexual orientation is. The criticism of the dispositional view is that it entails that most people will never have access to their own sexual orientations because most people do not know what they would do in counterfactual situations. Further, such a critic might point out that it is a result of the very same feature of the dispositional view that no one can know what anyone's sexual orientation is. Not only can't I not know what I would do under various counterfactual conditions, no one can know this, hence no one can know my sexual orientation.

Consider the case of Gerald, who is in fact sexually attracted to people of the same sex-gender, but who has never actually engaged in any sort of sexual activity with people of the same sex-gender and has completely repressed this desire, so much so that he would not under any circumstances admit, even to himself, that he is sexually attracted to people of his sex-gender. He does admit that he feels a certain kind of warmth towards men and that, in certain contexts, he gets an erection because of this warm feeling. He does not, however, think of this feeling—and the erections that are sometimes associated with it—as sexual. If he were interviewed by a Kinsey researcher, he would not be classified as having a history of even incidental homosexual desire or behavior. The critic of the dispositional view would note that, by assumption, Gerald has homosexual attractions; the critic thereby claims to have established that the dispositional view is wrong.

I think this criticism of the dispositional view of sexual orientation is mistaken, but for an interesting reason. Recall the distinction between metaphysical and epistemological questions from the introduction. Metaphysical questions concern the way the world is, while epistemological questions concern what we can know about the world. You might, for example, never be able to tell for sure if the light in your refrigerator goes off when you are not looking at it. Whether you can know this is an epistemological question. This is different from the metaphysical question of whether in fact the light is on or off at a particular moment. With respect to sexual orientation, the objection to the dispositional view that I just sketched focuses on the epistemological question of whether one can know for sure what a person's (one's own or someone else's) sexual orientation is. This epistemological question is different from the metaphysical question I am considering, namely what a person's sexual orientation consists of. The dispositional view of sexual orientation might be the right account of sexual orientation even if it is committed to the view that one's sexual orientation is hard to discern in certain contexts (even for oneself) and is perhaps impossible to know with certainty. Even allowing that the dispositional view has associated epistemological problems, it may well be the case that the sort of careful questioning involved in studies like Kinsey's is typically quite good at determining a person's sexual orientation.

Recall that I am engaged in conceptual analysis concerning sexual orientation. According to the dispositional view, a person's sexual orientation is constituted by his or her dispositions to engage in certain sexual acts. I think that there is something right about this account of sexual orientation; however, insofar as I have described it, the account offers only a partial analysis of our notion of sexual orientation. Sexual orientation has to do with a person's sexual desires and behaviors with respect to other people *in virtue of their sex*. In the next section, I turn to this further feature of our notion of sexual orientation. In so doing, I begin to deal with some of the worries raised in this section.

## The Dimensionality of Sexual Orientation

### The Binary View

One standard form of our traditional notion of sexual orientation sees people as dividing up into exactly two mutually exclusive types of sexual orientations, heterosexual and homosexual. I call this the *binary view* of sexual orientation. This view is implicitly accepted in many scientific, political, legal, and day-to-day discussions about sexual orientation. According to this view, a person's sexual orientation is like a simple light switch with two settings, on or off; in the case of sexual orientation, the two settings of the switch are heterosexuality or homosexuality. In terms that I discussed in the previous section, the binary view, although it is compatible with both the behavioral and the dispositional views of a sexual orientation, sees sexual orientation as a discrete category rather than a continuous one. Because the binary view is committed to a discrete view of sexual orientation, it faces a serious problem that results from the existence of people who are (at least apparently) bisexual, that is, people who are attracted to both men and women, are sexually active with both males and females, and/or who identify (at least to themselves, but in many instances, to others) as bisexual.

Some of those who accept the binary view of sexual orientation, especially—

as I will show in chapter 7—scientists interested in developing a theory of the origins of sexual orientation, seem to appreciate that there are "genuine" bisexuals but go on to ignore them for the purpose of developing their theories. Strict advocates of the binary view of sexual orientation try to explain the existence of apparent bisexuals by insisting that such people are *really* either heterosexual or homosexual and that their behaviors (and/or dispositions) to the contrary are to be seen as merely *situational* homosexuality or heterosexuality, in other words, as sexual behaviors resulting from particular sorts of situations that encourage behavior (or at least a desire for it) that is discordant with a person's actual sexual orientation. Single-sex institutions such as prisons or boarding schools are canonical sites of situational homosexuality. Two canonical contexts for situational *hetero*sexuality are prostitution and marriages in which at least one spouse is trying to hide his or her homosexuality (Ross 1983). No doubt there are cases of people who engage in sexual behaviors that, all else being equal, are sexually unappealing to them. Put a person in a situation in which there are no particularly desirable sexual partners available and, after enough time in such a situation, this person may well be willing to have sex with someone who is less desirable than his or her ideal sexual partner (Posner 1992, 111–180). The truth of this does not establish that *every* person who has (or desires to have) sex with both men and women is *necessarily* appropriately described as merely a situational heterosexual (and hence really a homosexual) or a situational homosexual (and hence really a heterosexual). Neither does the fact that some people who identify as bisexual at one point in their life later identify as either heterosexual or homosexual. In fact, there seems to be strong evidence that many people are neither exclusively heterosexual nor exclusively homosexual. In the face of such evidence, the binary view seems false.

My point here is a somewhat revisionary one within the project of conceptual analysis concerning sexual orientation. In various contexts, many people (for example, many of the scientists doing research on sexual orientation) think of sexual orientation as binary even though they might acknowledge that some people are bisexual. Such people have a contradictory picture of sexual orientation; they think people are either gay or straight, but at the same time they allow that a particular individual might be bisexual. By rejecting the binary view of sexual orientation, I am taking a step toward developing a coherent account of sexual orientation. My conceptual analysis is revisionary because I am showing that there is, on reflection, good reason for people to reject the binary view of sexual orientation despite its seeming plausibility. This point parallels the position discussed in chapter 1 that denies that sex should be seen as a discrete category with just two possible values, male and female.

### The Bipolar View

In their extensive interviews, the Kinsey researchers found a significant number of men and women with histories of both "heterosexual and homosexual experiences and/or psychic responses" (Kinsey, Pomeroy, and Martin 1948, 639; Kinsey et al. 1953, 469–472). From this, they determined that "the heterosexuality or homosexuality of many individuals is not an all-or-none proposition" (Kinsey, Pomeroy, and Martin 1948, 638). To deal with this, the Kinsey researchers developed a "classification [scheme] . . . based on the relative amounts of heterosexual and of homosexual experience or response in each [individual's] history" (639) known as the Kinsey scale. This scale rates individuals on the basis of both sexual experience and sexual desires as follows:

0. exclusively heterosexual with no homosexual
1. predominately heterosexual, only incidental homosexual
2. predominately heterosexual, but more than incidental homosexual
3. equally heterosexual and homosexual
4. predominately homosexual, but more than incidental heterosexual
5. predominately homosexual, only incidental heterosexual
6. exclusively homosexual with no heterosexual (638–641)
X. no social-sexual contacts or reactions (656)

The Kinsey scale is commonly referred to as a "seven-point scale" (see Figure 2-1) for categorizing sexual orientation; the X category is often neglected, perhaps because few men over the age of sixteen—less than 2 percent of all adult men in the United States—fell into this category, fewer than any other Kinsey rating (654). A considerable number of women fell into this category (between the ages of twenty to thirty-five, about 15 percent of unmarried females, about 2 percent of married females, and over 5 percent of previously married females) (Kinsey et al. 1953, 474), which pushed Kinsey to more fully articulate this category in his female volume. He writes:

> [I]ndividuals are rated as X's if they do not respond erotically to either heterosexual or homosexual stimuli, and do not have overt physical contacts with individuals of either sex in which there is evidence of any response. . . . It is not impossible that further analyses of these individuals might show that they do sometimes respond to socio-sexual stimuli, but they are unresponsive and inexperienced as far as it is possible to determine by any ordinary means. (472)

Figure 2-1. The Kinsey Scale. From Kinsey (1948).

It might be that today, as opposed to the 1940s and 1950s, the number of Kinsey Xs is even smaller, but at least conceptually, it is important to recognize this category, even though from the Kinsey-scale perspective it is literally off the scale.

Kinsey's insight in developing the heterosexual-homosexual rating scale parallels my reason for rejecting the binary view of sexual orientation. The model of sexual orientation that Kinsey developed in place of the binary view is a version of what I call the *bipolar view* of sexual orientation. A bipolar view sees sexual orientation as *continuous:* each person's sexual orientation falls somewhere on a one-dimensional scale between two extreme poles—exclusive homosexuality and exclusive heterosexuality—on the basis of his or her relative attraction to men and women. This view of sexual orientation can be compared to a dimmer switch that can make a light exhibit various degrees of brightness between completely on and completely off.

The simplest version of the bipolar view involves a three-point scale, namely heterosexual, bisexual, and homosexual. In terms of switches, an appropriate analogy would be a hair-dryer switch that has three distinct settings: off, low, and high. Recalling my distinction between discrete and continuous categories (introduced in chapter 1), one might wonder why the simplest version of the bipolar view of sexual orientation is a continuous picture rather than a discrete one, albeit a discrete view in which there are three rather than two possible sexual orientations. The relevant difference between continuous and discrete categories is that a continuous category involves, at least implicitly, an *ordering* among the entities that it categorizes. For example, in the case of the hair dryer, the settings—off, low, and high—are ordered by how much air the hair dryer blows out—respectively, none, some, and a lot. To make the contrast between continuous and discrete categories clearer, contrast the hair-dryer switch (an analogy for a continuous categorization scheme with three values) with an analogy for a discrete categorization scheme with three values, namely, a switch on some radios with three settings: off, AM, and FM. There is no sense in which AM is in between FM and off. (If you aren't familiar with this sort of radio, another analogy for a discrete three-value category would be the switch on some ovens with three settings: off, bake, and broil.) A biological example of a discrete category with more than two values is human blood type: there are four possible blood types (A, B, AB, O), and there is no straight-forward sense in which these blood types can be placed in a particular order.

Insofar as the bipolar view sometimes replaces the binary view of sexual orientation in political, legal, scientific, and everyday talk about sexual orientation, it is the simplest version of the bipolar view that people implicitly hold. It is this simple version that seems implicit in the following quote from an Attic Greek writer about the Greek god Zeus who, like the writer himself, was sexually attracted to both men and woman: "Zeus came as an eagle to god-like Ganymede, as a swan came he to the fair-haired mother of Helen. So there is no comparison between the two things: one person likes one, another likes the other; I like both" (quoted in Boswell 1992, 168–169). In a similar vein, the title of one of sexologist John Money's books is *Gay, Straight, and In-Between* (Money 1988). Both Money's title and the quotation about Zeus implicitly evoke a three-point bipolar scale of sexual orientation.

Although it avoids the problem that the binary view of sexuality has with bisexuality, the bipolar view has a different problem with bisexuality. According to all versions of the bipolar view, a person who is placed on the middle of the bipolar continuum representing sexual orientation—that is, a bisexual—has an equal amount of sexual attraction for and/or sexual behavior with men and women. A Kinsey 3, who falls in the middle of the Kinsey scale, is characterized as follows:

> Individuals who are rated 3's stand midway on the heterosexual-homosexual scale. They are about equally homosexual and heterosexual in their overt experience and/or psychic reactions. In general, they accept and equally enjoy both types of contacts, and have no strong preferences for one or the other. Some persons are rated 3's even though they may have a larger amount of experience of one sort, because they respond psychically to partners of both sexes, and it is only a matter of circumstance that brings them into more frequent contact with one of the sexes. (Kinsey, Pomeroy, and Martin 1948, 641)

A problem with the Kinsey scale as well as all other bipolar classification schemes is that they lump together people who, although they are erotically inclined to both men and women, have very different sexual desires with respect to men and women. Consider three different characterizations of people (in terms of their sexual dispositions) who would be considered bisexuals on the bipolar view (Kinsey 3s):

a. Individuals who are *strongly* attracted to people of the same sex and *strongly* attracted to people of the other sex.

    b. Individuals who are *moderately* attracted to people of the same sex and *moderately* attracted to people of the other sex.

    c. Individuals who are *weakly* attracted to people of the same sex and *weakly* attracted to people of the other sex.

Individuals in these three groups seem to have significantly different sexual dispositions (whether or not they have different histories of actual sexual behavior), but they are all grouped together as bisexuals. As such, the bipolar scale collapses these three different forms of sexual desire into one category, although it is not obvious that they belong in the same category. To put the point another way, bipolar classification schemes implicitly accept that degree of attraction to men varies inversely with degree of attraction to women. Weak attraction to women does not, however, entail strong attraction to men. Someone can be both strongly attracted to women and strongly attracted to men or weakly attracted to men and weakly attracted to women.

    This criticism of the bipolar view can be phrased more technically. The bipolar view of sexual orientation is *one-dimensional*, but the existence of at least three different ways a person can come to be considered a bisexual— (a), (b), and (c)—suggests that sexual orientation is *multidimensional*. The problem with the bipolar view is not the number of categories on the scale— three in the case of the simplest version; seven in the case of the Kinsey scale— but rather the number of dimensions that the scale uses.

### The Two-Dimensional View

The criticism that the bipolar view of sexual orientation is only one-dimensional when it should be multidimensional parallels a critique of the traditional view of masculinity and femininity. The traditional view sees masculinity and femininity, defined in terms of conformity to gender stereotypes, as opposite sides of a scale, that is, if a person is strongly masculine, he or she is necessarily weakly feminine, and vice versa. Working independently, psychologists Sandra Bem and Janet Spence have pointed out that there is something seriously wrong with this traditional view of masculinity and femininity (Bem 1974; Bem 1977; Spence, Helmreich, and Stapp 1974; Spence, Helmreich, and Stapp 1975). They suggest that masculinity and femininity should be seen as independent sets of traits; somebody can have a high (or low) degree of masculinity and at the same time have a high (or low) degree of femininity. This conflicts with the traditional model of gender characteristics, according to which high masculinity entails low femininity and high femininity entails low masculinity. The Bem-Spence critique extends naturally to the issue of sexual orientation; contrary to the bipolar view (which says sexual orientation is one-dimensional), sexual orientation might be *multidimensional*. That a person is highly attracted to people of the same sex-gender does not necessarily imply that the same person is not also attracted to people of a different sex-gender, and vice versa.

Psychologist Michael Storms argues for what I call a *two-dimensional* view of sexual orientation—with one dimension representing the degree of attraction to people of the same sex-gender and the other dimension representing the degree of attraction to people of a different sex-gender—in order to characterize accurately the variety of sexual orientations (Storms 1979; Storms 1980; Storms 1981). He supports this view with the finding that, on average, bisexuals are as attracted to their own sex-gender as exclusive homosexuals are and as attracted to people not of the same sex-gender as exclusive heterosexuals are. The bipolar view presupposes that attraction to members of the same sex-gender varies inversely with attraction to members of the other sex-gender. Storms's data suggest, however, that this is not the case. Many bisexuals are as much attracted to people of all sex-genders as *monosexuals*—people who are primarily attracted to members of one particular sex-gender, that is, heterosexuals and homosexuals—are to one particular sex-gender.

The two-dimensional view of sexual orientation can be represented by a grid with two bipolar scales as the axes. One version of a two-dimensional view of sexual orientation might connect two Kinsey-style seven-point scales perpendicularly to each other with, for example, the vertical axis representing amount of homosexual desire and activity and the horizontal axis representing amount of heterosexual desire and activity (see the axes labels in Figure 2-2). On this view, a person's sexual orientation can be represented by an ordered-pair of numbers, each between zero and six, representing respectively the degree of homosexuality and the degree of heterosexuality. A Kinsey 6 would be placed in the upper-left corner of the grid—a (0, 6)—and someone represented as a Kinsey 0 would be placed in the lower right—a (6, 0). Whereas a one-dimensional view like the Kinsey scale places bisexuals of types (a), (b), and (c) on the same place on the scale (namely, 3) and places people who might be called *asexuals* off the scale (in the X category), the two-dimensional view allows the three types of bisexuals to be distinguished and makes room for asexuals. Type (a) bisexuals—those who are strongly attracted to both males and females— would be placed in the upper right corner of the grid (6, 6), type (b) bisexuals would be placed in the middle of the grid (3, 3), and type (c) bisexuals would

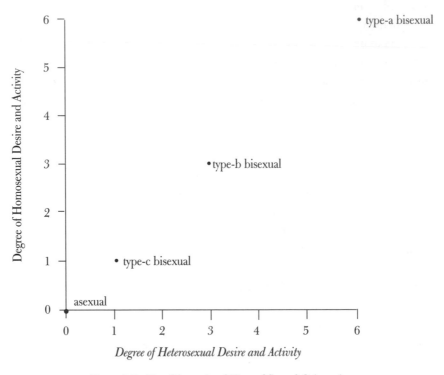

Figure 2-2. Two-Dimensional View of Sexual Orientation

be placed just a bit outside of the lower left corner (1, 1), just above and to the right of asexuals (0, 0) (see Figure 2-2).

I have highlighted two advantages of the two-dimensional view of sexual orientation: it distinguishes among different types of bisexuals, and it incorporates people whom Kinsey excludes from his rating scale (the Xs). The second point may seem somewhat superficial. If Kinsey wanted to include asexuals on his scale, he could have consistently grouped the Xs with the 3s. Kinsey 3s are defined as people who are "about equally homosexual and heterosexual in their overt experience and/or psychic reactions" (Kinsey, Pomeroy, and Martin 1948, 641) and "they accept and equally enjoy both types of contacts, and have no strong preferences for one or the other" (641). Asexuals satisfy both of these requirements, although they do so in virtue of having no strong sexual desire at all. Kinsey Xs are close to (c)-type bisexuals, that is, individuals who are weakly attracted to people of the same sex and weakly attracted to people of the other sex (Figure 2-2 brings this out visually). Kinsey had grounds for not placing asexuals on his scale because the scale is supposed to rate people on the amount of sexual response and experience and these people have little (if any) such response or experience. But since there is a continuum between asexuals and (c)-type bisexuals, it seems arbitrary to leave the asexuals off the scale. The two dimensional view avoids this problem placing the asexuals at (0, 0), signifying that they are not attracted to men or women (see Figure 2-2).

This way of describing the advantages of the two-dimensional view of sexual orientation over the Kinsey bipolar view underestimates the virtues of the two-dimensional view. The Kinsey version of the bipolar view not only collapses quite distinct ways of being a 3; it does the same with people it places in all of the categories of sexual orientation. A woman (call her Barbara) who is strongly attracted to men and has had lots of sex with men as well as being moderately attracted to women and has had some sex with women might be a 2 on the Kinsey scale. She would share this category, however, with a woman (call her Hillary) who is somewhat attracted to men and has had lots sex with them and is slightly attracted to women and has had some sex with them. On the two-dimensional view, Barbara would be a (6,4) while Hillary would be a (3, 2) (see Figure 2-3). Just as I rejected the binary view of sexual orientation in the face

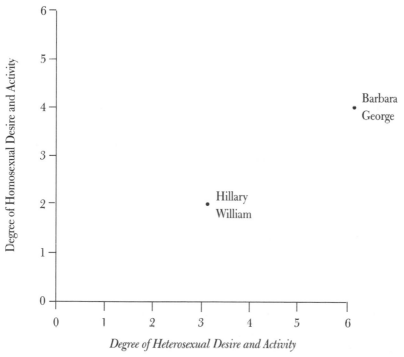

Figure 2-3. The Homo-Hetero Version of the Two-Dimensional View of Sexual Orientation

of evidence of the existence of bisexuals as a revisionary turn in my conceptual analysis of sexual orientation, a similar fate befalls the bipolar view in the face of the existence of various kinds of bisexuals. A two-dimensional view seems to fit better with the varieties of human sexual desires.

One issue for the two-dimensional view of sexual orientation is that there is no principled reason for labeling the axes of the grid "homosexual desire" and "heterosexual desire" as opposed to "attraction to women" and "attraction to men." The first way of labeling the axes (used by Storms and exhibited in Figures 2-2 and 2-3) groups gay men and lesbians together and heterosexual men and heterosexual women together. The male versions of Barbara and Hillary—respectively, a man (call him George) who is strongly attracted to and has had lots of sex with women and who is moderately attracted to and has had some sex with men and a man (call him William) who is somewhat attracted to and has had some sex with women and is slightly attracted to and has had a bit of sex with men—appear in the same places on the chart as, respectively, Barbara and Hillary do (see Figure 2-3). In other words, on the first way of labeling the axes, a person is placed on the chart independent of whether he or she is a man or a woman. This way of labeling the axes focuses on the sameness or difference of the sex-gender of the person and the sex-gender of his or her desired sexual partners (I call this the *hetero-homo version* of the two-dimensional view of sexual orientation). In contrast, the second way of labeling the axes would group gay men and straight women together—both groups are attracted to men—and lesbians and straight men together—both are attracted to women (see Figure 2-4). This way of labeling the axes focuses on just the sex-gender of the person's desired sexual partners (I call this the *male-female version* of the two-dimensional view of sexual orientation). The *second* way of labeling the axes (the male-female version) fits nicely with inversion models of homosexuality. Recall that inversion models see, for example, lesbians as people with female bodies and male souls and thus group lesbians and heterosexual men together (both are "really" men). It is not easy to determine a priori which of the two versions of the two-dimensional picture better represents sexual orientation. Before I discuss this further, I will step back and say something about what is at stake here.

Recall that the primary advantage of the bipolar view over the binary view is that the bipolar view seemed to better describe the actual "geography" of sexual orientation. Some people seem to be heterosexual, some seem to be homosexual, and some seem to be bisexual. The binary view of sexual orientation does not capture this aspect of sexual orientation. The two-dimensional view has similar advantages over the bipolar view; it also seems to better

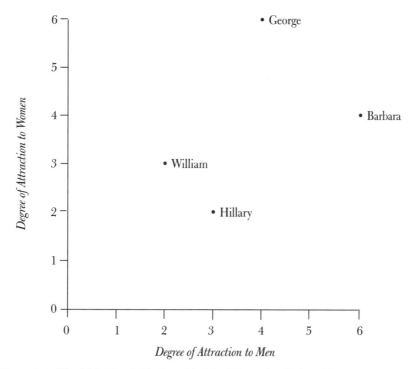

Figure 2-4.  The Male-Female Version of the Two-Dimensional View of Sexual Orientation.

describe the varieties of sexual orientation that exist. Which of the two versions of the two-dimensional view—the hetero-homo version and the male-female version—provides a better picture of sexual orientation is, however, a different sort of question. Among the differences between the binary and the bipolar view and between the bipolar and the two-dimensional view were the relative number of different types of sexual orientations they allowed for. In contrast, both the hetero-homo version and the male-female version of the two-dimensional view allow for the same number of types of sexual orientations. The difference between the two versions of the two-dimensional view, rather, is the relative closeness of the various sexual orientations. The hetero-homo version says that gay men are more like lesbians (because both of them are attracted to people of the same sex-gender); the male-female version says that gay men are more like heterosexual women (because both of them are attracted to men).

To better appreciate the differences between these two views, look back at Figure 2-3; it shows the sexual orientations of Barbara—a woman who is strongly attracted to and has had lots of sex with men and who is moderately attracted to and has had some sex with women—and Hillary—a woman who is somewhat attracted to men and has had lots of sex with them and who is slightly attracted to women and had had some sex with them. Barbara and Hillary are both Kinsey 2s on the bipolar view, but are (6, 4) and (3, 2), respectively, on the hetero-homo version of the two-dimensional view. Note that the male versions of Barbara and Hillary—George, a man who is strongly attracted to and has had lots of sex with women and who is moderately attracted to and has had some sex with men, and William, a man who is somewhat attracted to and has had some sex with women and is slightly attracted to and has had a bit of sex with men—would be placed in the same spot on the homo-hetero version of the two-dimensional picture as their female counterparts. But now contrast Figure 2-3 with Figure 2-4 that shows the very same individuals on the male-female version of the two-dimensional view. While Barbara and Hillary remain in the same places they were in Figure 2-3, George and William move to different places in Figure 2-4. This shows the difference between the two versions of the two-dimensional view.

For the purpose of developing an account of what sexual orientation is, it is not obvious that I need to decide between the two versions of the two-dimensional view. There is a sense in which both versions correctly describe the closeness of the various sexual orientations: gay men are like lesbians in that both are attracted to people of the same sex-gender and gay men are like heterosexual women in that both are attracted to men. One version is better than the other only if we look deeper, that is, to the causes of why people have the sexual orientations that they do. Suppose, contrary to fact, that the inversion model of sexual orientations—which says that gay men have male bodies and female souls and that lesbians have female bodies and male souls—were right. If this were the case, then, although it would still be true that gay men are like lesbians in that both are attracted to people of the same sex-gender, the male-female version of the two-dimensional picture of sexual orientation would be preferable to the hetero-homo version because the male-female version correctly identifies *why* gay men and heterosexual women are similar in terms of sexual orientation, namely, in the case of the inversion theory, they are similar because gay men are "really" women. I am not, at the moment, concerned with why people have the sexual orientations they do, but rather with what a sexual orientation is. Given this interest, the differences between the two versions of the two-dimensional version are not important. The difference between these two pictures of sexual orientation will, however, matter when I turn in chapters 5 through 8 to theories of why people have the sexual orientations that they do. For purposes of developing a consistent and powerful account of sexual orientation that fits to a considerable extent with our intuitions, the two-dimensional account of sexual orientation, however the axes are drawn, seems like a good choice, better at least than the more popular binary or bipolar views of sexual orientation.[5] In the next section, I consider the limitations of the two-dimensional view by discussing aspects of human sexual desire other than sexual orientation.

## Sexual Interests

A person's sexual orientation is just one part of a person's general sexual desires or sexual interests. In this section, I sketch a fuller account of sexual interests and consider the way that sexual orientations fit into them. In the previous section, I suggested that a person's sexual orientation is a location on a two-dimensional grid that represents his or her sexual dispositions, determined by assessing his or her sexual desires and sexual behavior, with respect to the sex-gender of the people to whom he or she is attracted. But what if, as I considered in chapter 1, there are more than two sex-genders? If, say, transgendered or intersexed people constitute a third sex-gender (or a third and fourth sex-gender, respectively), where on the two-dimensional grid do we locate such a person who is attracted to men and where do we locate men and women who are especially attracted to intersexed or transgendered people? We might well require a third axis to represent the attraction to members of the third sex-gender. On such a three-dimensional view of sexual orientation, a person's sexual orientation would be represented by an ordered *triple* of numbers, for example, each between zero and six, with the first axis representing degree of attraction to men, the second representing the degree of attraction to women, and the third representing the degree of attraction to people of the third sex-gender (assuming, for the sake of simplicity, the male-female-intersex version of the three-dimensional view). Or, if there are four sex-genders, it would be easy to articulate (though not to draw) a four-dimensional view of sexual orientation in roughly the same fashion. Although they would be easy to articulate, three- and four-dimensional views of sexual orientation seem so complex that any reasonable way to avoid having to embrace them is worth considering.

John Money has a view of sexual orientations that seems to deal with the potential complexities of integrating intersexed and transgendered individuals into a view of sexual orientation. Money's proposed solution to these complexities focuses on *morphology* (the structure of bodies). He writes:

> [A homosexual] . . . is one who has the potential to fall in love only with someone who has the same body sex—the same genital and body morphology—as the self. For a heterosexual, the morphology must be that of a person of the other sex. For the bisexual, it may be either.

It is not necessary for the body sex of the partner to be in agreement with the chromosomal sex, the gonadal sex (testicles or ovaries), or the sex of the internal reproductive anatomy. For example, [an M-to-F] sex-reassigned transsexual with the body morphology transformed to be female in appearance is responded to as a woman—and vice versa in [an F-to-M] . . . .

[A person with XX chromosomal sex who has a] penis and an empty scrotum . . . [and who grows up to have] a fully virilized body and mentality, both [of which are] . . . discordant with the genetic sex, the gonadal sex, and the internal sexual structures, . . . who falls in love with a . . . [genetically] normal woman is regarded by everyone as heterosexual, and so is his partner. The criterion of their heterosexuality is the sexual morphology of their bodies and the masculinity or femininity of their mentality and behavior, not the sex of their chromosomes, gonads, or internal organs. (Money 1988, 12–13, some parenthetical phrases omitted)

Money's account, at least on the surface, has the advantage of simplicity: his account seems to make clear what a sexual orientation is, and he attempts to handle various difficulties that transgendered and intersexed people pose for a straightforward account of sexual orientation without the complexities that result from adding additional dimensions to the view of sexual orientation. There are, however, problems with his suggestion.

The core of Money's account of sexual orientation focuses on the body morphology of the sorts of people with whom a person can fall in love. Even leaving aside some problematic features of Money's account—for example, the prominence he gives to "falling in love" in his account of sexual orientation (sexual desire and love, though perhaps related for many people, are conceptually distinct)—it is not clear that Money's focus on "genital and body morphology" will do the work he thinks it can. Implicitly, Money counts as male everyone who has a penis and a scrotum, whether or not these structures result from surgery and regardless of the person's chromosomal makeup. One problem with this is what to make of a person with XY chromosomes and male-typical internal genitalia who lacks male-typical external genitalia, for example, because of a war injury. It seems that we would want to count this person as man, but Money's view does not allow us to do so. In his defense, we might note that Money says he is interested in "genital *and body* morphology" (12, emphasis added). This two-part criterion, however, only makes matters worse. If body morphology is distinct from genital morphology, then the two can be discordant—someone might have a male-typical genital morphology and a female-typical body morphology (for example, an F-to-M who had limited or no hormone treatment).

A related problem for Money concerns the use he makes of the word "same": how similar do two bodies have to be to count as being of the same morphology? Of course, everyone has somewhat different genital and body morphology—breast size, amount of chest hair, penis or clitoris size, for example, vary significantly from person to person. Money seems to think that body morphology can be neatly divided into two distinct groups in terms of morphology. Although Money wants to allow for a continuous, bipolar view of sexual orientation (hence his title *Gay, Straight, and In-Between*), he seems wedded to rejecting a continuous view of sex-gender. In fact, it is his implicit insistence on a discrete (that is, noncontinuous) view of sex that undergirds his bipolar view of sexual orientation. Money's insistence on a discrete view of sex-gender seems odd because he is a prolific chronicler of hermaphrodites, pseudohermaphrodites, and other transgendered and intersexed people. If anyone should recognize the continuity of the category of sex-gender, John Money should. But when he tries to develop an account of human sexual orientation, the presumption in favor of a one-dimensional (bipolar) view is so strong that he is forced to embrace discrete categories of sex-gender.

The above quotation from Money does, however, leave room for an alternative reading of his view of sexual orientation, one not based on a discrete view of sex gender. He says that the criterion for sexual orientation is "the sexual morphology of . . . bodies *and the masculinity or femininity of . . . mentality and behavior*" (13, emphasis added). The reference to mentality and behavior seems to move Money towards a focus on *gender* rather than *sex* (as these terms are typically understood), to the social overlay onto the body rather than to the body itself. Even if our bodies do not fit into two discrete types, male and female, our culture can still force us into culturally constructed binary categories. The problem for Money is that sexual orientation then falls into the study of culture, not the study of anatomy and physiology (where he wants it to be). If gender becomes part of his focus, the very problems that an account like Money's is supposed to avoid reappear: are there two, three, or four genders in our culture? are lesbians women? and so on. The straightforward one-dimensional view of sexual orientation that Money wants to retain is undermined when it is linked to gender. Money's view of sexual orientation does not solve the problems one might have hoped it would.

There is a further problem with Money's attempt to build an account of sexual orientation on top of a morphological account of sex. People's preferences relating to body morphology vary dramatically, and they do so independent of their sexual orientations. There are heterosexual men who are attracted to boyish or androgynous women, lesbians who are attracted to very masculine women, both gay and heterosexual men who are attracted to trans-gendered people, and lesbians who like to be "phallicly" penetrated. This variety among people's sexual tastes for body and genital morphology is just the tip of the iceberg with regards to the variety of human sexual tastes.

To start exploring just below the tip of the iceberg, consider a problem raised by reflecting on an essay by Pat Califia. Califia (1994) describes herself as a lesbian who likes, on occasion, to have sex with gay men. Simply calling her a (2, 6) on either two-dimensional scale (two because she is occasionally attracted to men and six because of her strong attraction to women) seems to miss an important feature of her sexual desires, namely, that the men she is moderately and occasionally attracted to gay men, never straight. Similarly, some gay men describe themselves as interested only in "straight" men. Consider the following personal ad: "Handsome, twenty-five year old man, six feet tall, 170 pounds, wants to meet good-looking straight men, aged twenty to thirty, for hot times and maybe more." Since such an ad is presumably placed by a man looking for a sexual relationship with another man, by "straight," he must presumably mean that he is looking for men who act straight, look straight, and perhaps even self-identify as straight, even though they have sex with other men (my earlier example of the Roy Cohn character comes to mind). Money's view of sexual orientation, which focuses on the body morphology a person is attracted to, ignores this dimension, namely the sexual orientation of the people a person is attracted to. Perhaps we need to develop a *four*-dimensional view of sexual orientation with the axes representing, respectively, attraction to heterosexual men, attraction to gay men, attraction to heterosexual women and attraction to lesbians. On this view, Califia's sexual orientation might be represented by (0, 4, 3, 6), while the sexual orientation of the "gay" man attracted to "straight" men might be represented by (6, 3, 0, 1). This four-dimensional view of sexual orientation might seem to have affinities with seeing lesbians and gay men as a third and fourth gender (or third and fourth sex), but the affinity is only superficial. On the four-dimensional view currently under discussion, heterosexual women, heterosexual men, lesbians, and gay men are types of what might be called *sexual object choice* rather than types of sex-genders; they are represented as the groups of people to whom a person might be sexually attracted, not as instances of categories of people who are attracted to certain sorts of people.

There is a serious danger here of an explosion of dimensions. If a person's sexual orientation is supposed to encompass the sorts of people that he or she is attracted to beyond just the person's sex-gender, then sexual orientation encompasses much more than four dimensions. People have a wide range of sexual tastes. Some people are attracted to people of certain age ranges, people

of certain body types, of certain races, of certain hair colors, of certain personality types, of certain professions, as well as to people of a certain sex-gender
and/or a certain sexual orientation (Sedgwick 1990, 22–27; Suppe 1984,
394–397). This is perfectly compatible with our intuitions about human sexuality. We have no problem allowing that some people are sexually interested in
quite specific human attributes. We can recognize someone as a "leg man," as
someone who "has a thing for redheads," or as someone who "goes for the
Robert Redford type." Gay men involved in the gay community have a large
vocabulary for talking about distinctive sexual desires (Frye 1992, 115): a
person might, for example, be a "snow queen" (a person especially attracted to
Caucasian men), a "rice queen" (a person especially attracted to Asian men), a
"chicken hawk" (a person especially attracted to young boys), a "prune queen"
(a person especially attracted to older—hence wrinkled—men), or a "size
queen" (a person especially attracted to men with large penises).

People are not only sexually interested in certain sorts of people, some also
have quite specific interests in certain sorts of sexual acts, certain venues for sex,
certain frequencies for having sex, or for sex with certain sorts of entities. Some
people are especially interested in oral sex. Some people are particularly interested in having sex in public places, for example, in Woody Allen's movie
*Everything You Ever Wanted to Know about Sex (But Were Afraid to Ask)*, there
is a character who is sexually uninterested in her newlywed husband unless they
have sex in a public setting (Allen 1972). In the same movie, Gene Wilder
plays a man who is sexually attracted to, falls in love with, and has sex with a
sheep. In some cases, we have a special term for people with a sexual interest
that involves something other than a particular object choice, for example, a
nymphomaniac (a person who wants to have sex with great frequency), an exhi-
bitionist (a person who enjoys public nudity or having sex in public), or a sadist
(a person who is sexually aroused by causing pain). In the 1970s, in certain
contexts, gay men used a somewhat elaborate set of symbols known as the
"hanky code" to indicate the sorts of activities in which they wanted to engage.
For example, a light blue handkerchief indicated an interest in oral sex, a dark
blue handkerchief indicated an interest in anal sex, and a black handkerchief
indicated an interest in "heavy" sadomasochistic activities. Whether you
displayed your handkerchief in your left or right back pocket indicated the
specific role you wanted to take in the particular activity, for example, a dark
blue handkerchief in the left pocket indicated that you wanted to play the
insertive role in anal sex, while the same color handkerchief in the right pocket
indicated an interest in being anally penetrated.

My point here is that we recognize that people can be sorted into all sorts
of groups in virtue of their sexual interests; why include only a narrow range of

sexual interests (namely just the sex-gender that a person is sexually attracted to) under the heading of sexual orientation? Why focus on this feature of a person's sexual desires as the crucial one? Why not include the vast collection of other dimensions along which people differ in terms of what they are sexually interested in? We are unable to picture a graph with so many axes, but we can represent a wider range of sexual interests on a table that would represent the whole gamut of a person's sexual desire (see Table 2-1). This table shows, for example, that Tom is a heterosexual man with an interest in shy, small, blond, white women and that Bill is sexually attracted to a type of transgendered person, namely to men who present themselves as women, especially when they are drag queens or hustlers. This figure could be made even more complex by assuming that each entry in a column was a point on a bipolar continuum or a two-dimensional grid.

Table 2-1 represents a broadening of my scope. The binary, bipolar, and two-dimensional views have in common a focus on the sex-gender of the people who are the objects of sexual desire. Talk of people who are sexually interested in others in virtue of characteristics besides or in addition to sex-gender has the potential to cause trouble for Money's view as well as the other views of sexual orientation articulated above.

An important insight made by some practitioners of the interdisciplinary field of lesbian and gay studies is that the concepts of homosexual and heterosexual as representing types of people are relatively new concepts, dating only back to the late nineteenth century. This is not equivalent to denying that people throughout history and across all cultures have engaged in both homosexual and heterosexual acts. The claim, rather, is that only beginning in the late nineteenth century did people begin to think that one's sexual orienta-

Table 2-1. Representation of a Broader Range of Sexual Interests

| Dimension of Sexual Interest | Tom | Dick | Harry | Bill |
|---|---|---|---|---|
| Genital sex | female | male | no preference | male |
| Gender | woman | man | no preference | woman |
| Race | white | Latino, Asian | no preference | no preference |
| Body size | small | small | large | no preference |
| Hair color | blond | dark | red | no preference |
| Personality-type | shy, quiet | aggressive | "bitchy" | no preference |
| Profession | no preference | working class | no preference | female impersonators and hustlers |
| Venue | bedroom | public rest rooms, parks | no preference | no preference |

tion—namely, the sex-gender of the people one is attracted to—indicates something about the sort of person one is. I will have more to say about this and related claims in the next two chapters.

Sexual orientation is not unique in this respect. According to some scholars, in the late nineteenth century, people began to focus on other aspects of a person's sexual interests as revealing something deep about his or her character (Foucault 1977; Hacking 1986b). For example, the German psychiatrist Richard von Krafft-Ebing, whose medical writings were among the most important of the late nineteenth century, wrote about homosexuals in the same vein as he wrote about fetishists, masochists, and sadists (Krafft-Ebing 1965).

Scientists doing research on sexual desire and most of us in this culture who reflect on human sexual desire think that our commonsense categories of sexual orientation—heterosexual, homosexual, and bisexual—are the most important categories to be used in the scientific study of sex. Other categories of sexual desire, like fetishist, sadist, leg man, or snow queen, are thought to be less important or perhaps insignificant for the science of human sexuality. A person's sexual orientation is only a part of a person's sexual desires or *sexual interests*. A person's sexual desires include the things (people, acts, venues, and so forth) to which a person is erotically disposed. Sexual desires can vary along a huge number of dimensions: the sorts of sexual acts in which a person likes to engage; the venues in which one likes to engage in them; the sorts of entities (humans, animals, inanimate objects) with which she likes to do them; the age, color, size, number, personality, and so forth, of people, animals, or objects with which she likes to do them; and so on. Some people have quite particular sexual interests, for example, a person (like Tom, from Table 2-1) might primarily be interested in having sex in a bedroom with a person not of the same sex-gender who has blond hair, light skin, a small build, and a shy personality. A person's sexual *orientation* is only a narrow part of a person's sexual interests, namely the sex-gender of the people with whom a person is disposed to have sex. The categories of sexual orientation organize people in a particular way in virtue of their sexual dispositions. People can be categorized in a countless number of other ways in terms of their sexual interests; in fact, in other cultures and in other eras, people are and have been categorized differently (Greenberg 1988). Whether societies that have categorized people in terms of their sexual desires in ways radically different from the way our society does are simply mistaken in their uses of these categorization schemes or whether scientists who think they can apply the categories of sexual orientation to people in all other times and places are the ones who are mistaken is the central question discussed in the next two chapters. For now, I leave this as an open question.

## Having Sex

Thus far, in engaging in conceptual analysis about sexual orientation and sexual desire more generally, I have been assuming a notion of what it is to have sex. In this section, I consider whether that notion is reasonable. I begin by considering an essay by Marilyn Frye (1992) that concerns a 1983 study of the sexual behavior of heterosexual, lesbian, and gay couples (Blumstein and Schwartz 1983). According to this study, gay male couples have the most sex of all three types, heterosexual couples have the next most sex, and lesbian couples have the least. Something seemed suspicious about these results to Frye, particularly when she discovered that the study says heterosexual married couples reported that, on average, it takes them about eight minutes to have sex (Frye 1992, 110). She writes:

> If the havings of sex by heterosexual married couples did take on the average eight minutes, my guess is that in a large number of those cases the women did not experience orgasms. My guess is that neither the women's pleasure nor the women's orgasms were pertinent in most of the individuals' counting and reporting the frequency with which they "had sex." (112)

This analysis suggests that the picture of what it is to have sex that the people surveyed in this study had in mind involves primarily the risings and fallings of penises. Frye suggests that the idea of having sex is a paradigmatic *phallocentric* concept.

The general question that Frye points to, at least implicitly, concerns what counts as having sex. There are many different notions of what it is to have sex. There are even variations on how sex might be indexed to penises. If a man gets an erection and his penis gets inside of a vagina or an anus, but he does *not* have an orgasm, have he and the person whose orifice he has penetrated had sex? What if his penis gets inside of his sexual partner's mouth? If he gets an erection and has an orgasm, but his sexual partner does not in any way come in contact with his penis, have they had sex or has he just masturbated in the presence of another person? Does masturbation (whether in the presence of another person or not) count as sex (Fortunata 1980)?

The problem is compounded as the examples are multiplied. In "Are We Having Sex Now or What?" Greta Christina (1992) considers a variety of tricky cases. Initially, Christina saw herself as having had sex if she had a man's penis in her vagina. But as she became more sexually experienced, she began to question this deceptively straightforward picture of having sex. When have two women had sex? If one of them has an orgasm? When there is genital contact between them? Does that mean that a gynecologist has had sex with her patient when she touches the patient's vulva as part of a routine examination? Christina offers the following story: while working as an erotic dancer in a peep show, she saw a man masturbating while watching her from inside a glass booth. She crouched down in front of the booth and began to masturbate as well. The two of them watched each other through the glass while they both reached orgasm. Have they had sex? What if there was no glass wall between them? What if they were not at the peep show but in Christina's bedroom but they still did not touch?

If I were primarily interested in developing an account of what counts as a sexual behavior as opposed to a nonsexual one, I might try to engage in a conceptual analysis of the notion of "having sex." Certainly, there would be lots of contradictions to ferret out. We have the concepts of "phone sex" and "cyber sex"—which sound as if they count as a way to have sex, but it seems as though they should not count as having sex—and the concept of "mutual masturbation" (when two people manually stimulate each other's sexual organs)—which sounds like it does not count as a way to have sex, but it seems as though it should. Or I might try to simply finesse the problem by somewhat arbitrarily defining what counts as having sex. This might be a reasonable solution to Frye's problem (so long as I am careful not to define what counts as having sex in a phallocentric fashion) if my object of study were sexual behavior. My interest here is in sexual orientation, and having rejected the behavioral view of sexual orientation (see the first section of this chapter), I need to be concerned with sexual *desires* as well as sexual behavior. In the context of sexual desires, Frye's problem becomes how to distinguish between a sexual desire and a nonsexual desire. Just as there is a problem distinguishing between genital contact that counts as sexual and genital contact that does not (for example, genital contact in the context of a gynecological examination), so too there is a problem distinguishing between sexual and nonsexual desires. For example, sometimes the desire for a kiss can be sexual and sometimes it can be nonsexual (a desire for a kiss from one's parent or child would be a nonsexual desire for a kiss while a desire for a kiss from one's lover would be sexual desire).

While this is not the place to develop a detailed account of the distinction between sexual and nonsexual (I will have some more to say on this in chapters 6 and 10), I need to say something here about this distinction. For now, I want to claim that a desire is sexual insofar as it involves (in the appropriate way) the *arousal* of the person who has the desire and that a behavior is sexual insofar as it involves (in the appropriate way) the arousal of at least one of the participants in a behavior. By arousal, I do not mean the various physiological manifestations of arousal (for example, having blood flow to one's penis or clitoris), but to the *psychological* state of being aroused. This psychological state may be caused by different ideas or events in different people and may cause different bodily and psychological reactions in different people, but there is some abstract property or set of properties that mark off states of arousal from other states; it is such properties that are indicative of sexual versus nonsexual desires and behaviors. Consider the contrast between having your vagina touched by a sexual partner and by your gynecologist. The first case is considered sexual and the second not insofar as having a sexual partner touch your vagina arouses you (and/or your partner) but having your gynecologist touch your vagina does not arouse you (or your gynecologist). If either you or your gynecologist is in fact aroused by the vaginal touching, then the touching would be sexual. Although this account is sketchy and, as yet, undefended, I hope that it seems plausible, both on its own and as the beginning of an answer to the problem that I take from Frye's article.[6]

## Conclusion

My goal in this chapter has been to examine what a sexual orientation is and to understand this concept in the context of human sexual desires more broadly understood. I have suggested that a person's sexual orientation has to do with his or her sexual dispositions towards people in virtue of their sex-gender. In this chapter, I have been concerned with what the relationship is between a person's sexual orientation and his or her behaviors and desires, how many kinds of sexual orientations there are, what counts as having sex or having a sexual disposition, and how sexual orientation differs from (but fits with) sexual interests in general. In discussing these issues, I have begun to develop some answers—most notably, I have shown that a person's sexual orientation is only a part of a person's overall sexual interests and have argued that a person's sexual orientation crucially involves his or her dispositions and desires. In doing so, I have defended the dispositional view of sexual orientations while pointing to problems with the binary and bipolar views of sexual orientation. I have also left several matters unresolved. In subsequent chapters, I return to these matters. Among the unresolved matters is whether and to what extent sexual orientation, compared to other sexual interests, is especially important in understanding human nature. I lay the foundation for answering this question in the next chapter. I begin to build on this foundation in the chapters that follow it.

# CHAPTER 3

# *Human Kinds*

In the previous chapter, I showed that people can be classified in terms of their sexual interests in various ways. We can divide people into heterosexuals and homosexuals, and we can divide them using Kinsey's categories. We can also divide people into those who are attracted to blondes and those who are not, people who like to have sex outdoors and those who do not, people who have had the plurality of their sexual activities with a person named John and those who have not. Intuitively, some of the ways that we can divide people in terms of their sexual desires are clearly arbitrary while others do not seem arbitrary. Are sexual orientations merely arbitrary groupings, or do they refer to something "deep" about human nature? This is an overly simple way of asking a question that is central to lesbian and gay studies as well as scientific research on human sexual orientation (although many scientists do not acknowledge this is an issue). The question is typically seen as having two answers: *essentialism* and *constructionism*. As a first pass, essentialism is the view that sexual orientations are deep categories of human nature, while constructionism is the view that they are not. This is a simplification of a rather complex issue. In the next two chapters, I develop a more sophisticated approach to this issue.

Among scholars, many historians, anthropologists, sociologists, literary theorists, cultural studies scholars, and lesbian and gay studies scholars accept constructionism, while most scientists doing work on sexual orientation, along with some humanists and social scientists, accept essentialism. People give various reasons for taking a stand on this issue. The debate is thought to be related to a variety of important scientific, social scientific, ethical, and political questions. According to essentialists, since sexual orientations are deep properties of humans, scientific research into the origins of heterosexuality and homosexuality is legitimate, as is historical research into whether a historical figure was a heterosexual or homosexual and anthropological research into the status of homosexuals in other cultures. Various people have argued that scientific and/or social scientific research is relevant to lesbian and gay rights and related ethical and political issues.[1] If they are right, and given that essentialism is relevant to scientific research, the debate between essentialism and constructionism is also relevant to ethical and political issues. In contrast, constructionists think it is a mistake to look at an individual as having a sexual orientation unless that person lives in a culture that believes people have sexual orientations. Constructionism, if true, has significant ramifications for historical, scientific, sociological, philosophical, anthropological, and psychological studies of sexuality that assume the objects of their investigations are natural rather than merely social entities. If this scientific and social scientific research has political and ethical implications, so too does constructionism. The debate between essentialists and constructionists about sexual orientation is thus important to our scientific understanding of sexual orientation, and a prima facie case can be made for its relevance to ethical and political questions concerning sexual orientation.

The distinction between arbitrary and nonarbitrary ways of dividing people into categories is widely applicable. People can be divided up in terms of their age, their blood type, their HIV status, their height, the month in which they were born, the zip code in which they live, and so on. Some of these divisions sort people into deep categories of human nature, while others clearly do not. What distinguishes deep categories from arbitrary ones? In the present chapter, I try to articulate in a clear fashion what a deep category of human nature is. Although there is intrinsic interest in clarifying the distinction between arbitrary and deep categories of human nature, my main purpose in doing so is to make sense of the debate between essentialism and constructionism about sexual orientation. In chapter 4, I use the distinction between arbitrary and deep categories that I articulate in the present chapter to inform the debate between essentialism and constructionism about sexual orientation. Clarifying this distinction is not an easy process. At times, I will be talking about issues that seem to have little to do with sexual orientation. In the several chapters that follow this one, these seeming detours will prove crucial to grounding the discussion of the science and metaphysics of sexual orientation and sexual desire more generally.

## An Extended Analogy

Imagine that you find yourself in the (imaginary) country of Zomnia. Zomnia is a place much like the one in which we live, but the human inhabitants of Zomnia are, unlike us, deeply interested in very particular details of each other's sleep habits. Specifically, Zomnians are concerned with whether people sleep on their backs or on their stomachs: people who sleep on their backs are called "backers" and people who sleep on their stomachs are called "fronters." The majority of people in Zomnia are thought to be fronters, and until recently there was explicit and prevalent discrimination against people known or suspected to be backers. I say "suspected" because most people who sleep on their backs do not publicize this fact and because most Zomnians think that they can tell a backer by sight. Backers, so the folk wisdom goes, have very rigid posture and are typically quick-tempered and have aggressive personalities. Scientists, psychiatrists, and others in Zomnia are interested in what makes some people have one "sleep orientation" rather than the other. Some think that whether or not one is a backer is genetically determined, others think it is shaped by whether or not one's family members or other adult role models are backers, and others think it has to do with one's diet during puberty. Recently, some Zomnians have started to publicly identify themselves as backers and have started forming groups designed to combat discrimination against them, dispel myths about them, and form a community of kindred spirits. These self-styled "out-of-the-closet" backers (in Zomnian terms, "out-of-the-bedroom" backers) have been partially successful: their community organizing has affected public perceptions as well as academic research. To give two examples, first, historians in Zomnia have become concerned about the sleep positions of historical figures and claim to have evidence that certain important figures in Zomnian history were backers and, second, art historians have discovered previously unrecorded paintings that contain positive portrayals of people sleeping on their backs. The backer movement has also had the political effect of bringing attention to antibacker laws and practices; in fact, there is now a legal movement to attain equal rights for all Zomnians, regardless of their sleep orientation.

Now imagine that you were a visitor to Zomnia: what would you have to say about the importance that Zomnians place on sleep positions? My reaction would be to tell them that their practice of grouping people into backers and fronters is laughable at best, their practice of discriminating against people on the basis of their sleep habits is morally wrong, and their scientific theories that concern the "etiology" of "backerhood" are pseudoscientific. None of this would involve denying that some people (both inside and outside of Zomnia) tend to sleep on their backs and others on their stomachs. My claim had better not involve anything of this sort because people do, of course, have such tendencies—I, for one, usually sleep on my stomach, but some people sleep on their backs (not to mention the insidious groups consisting of those that sleep on their sides or of those who sleep in different positions on different occasions). What I would want to claim (and I bet you would too if you visited Zomnia) is that there is something seriously *inappropriate* about the categories "backer" and "fronter" and the use to which Zomnians put them. It is not only that Zomnians, by discriminating against backers, are behaving in ways that are *morally* inappropriate. Moral matters aside, I would want to claim that the Zomnian categories are both *scientifically* and *metaphysically* inappropriate. What I mean by "scientifically and metaphysically inappropriate" will become clearer later in this chapter; for now, I will broadly sketch what I mean. Implicit in the Zomnian use of the terms "backer" and "fronter" is a view of human nature according to which a person's sleep orientation is a deep and important fact. When I claim that these categories are inappropriate, I am saying that the Zomnians are committed to a theory of human nature that is mistaken: it is a mistake to think that there are groups of people that fit into these categories in virtue of natural and objective facts.

My claim here is a stronger one than, for example, the view discussed in chapter 1 about the categories of sex-gender that are indexed to external genitalia. According to that view, the existence of intersexuals shows that a binary view of sex-gender—defined in terms of external genitalia—was mistaken and that what is needed in its place is a more fine-grained view of sex-gender—either there are more than two sex-genders or sex-gender should be seen as a continuous category. With respect to sleep orientation, I am making a more radical claim. I am not claiming that we need more fine-grained categories of sleep orientation, for example, that we need to add the category of "sider" (a person who sleeps on his or her side) or the category "switcher" (a person who alternates between various sleep positions). Rather, I am claiming that there is something deeply mistaken about the very notion of grouping people in virtue of their sleep orientation.

Suppose that in an article in a Zomnian newspaper or scientific journal I made the claim that sleep orientations are scientifically and metaphysically mistaken categories. How might a Zomnian respond? One likely Zomnian response would be a *scientific* defense of the categories of sleep orientation. According to this response, the difference between backers and fronters is a deep difference that is present in Zomnian culture but that has its basis in every human's psyche and/or physiology. Whatever the exact details of how people develop differences in sleep orientation, people have these differences. The

Zomnian response might then cite various scientific studies done in Zomnia to establish the appropriateness of the categories of sleep orientation. This response to my criticism is designed to show that sleep orientations are metaphysically appropriate, useful, and not mistaken.

The *form* of this response to my criticism of the Zomnian sleep orientation categorization scheme seems fine; it is the *content* that seems implausible. What seems wrong to me (and I suspect to you as well) about the Zomnian worldview is that Zomnians have a mistaken picture of human nature. They seem committed to the view that a person's preferred sleep position reflects some deep and essential feature of that person's character. It is this claim that I want to deny. I can imagine that my anti-Zomnian position *might* be wrong. It is *possible* that their theory of human nature is right and that the position in which one sleeps is an important feature of one's psyche, but I am willing to bet the Zomnians are wrong.

There is another way that a Zomnian might respond to my criticism of the practice of categorizing people by their sleep orientation, namely to give what might be thought of as a *sociological* defense of these categories. This response would admit that I am right or, at least, that I might be correct in saying that the categories "backer" and "fronter" are inappropriate for science because they do not correctly describe human nature. This sociological response would, however, defend the Zomnian categorization scheme by saying that the categories of "backer" and "fronter" are real categories *socially* speaking. My criticism, this response says, denies the lived experience of people who are backers in spite of social pressures pushing them towards being fronters. The categories of sleep orientation may not be appropriately applied to any people in North America or Western Europe, but they do apply to the people of Zomnia. The life of a Zomnian is dramatically affected by whether members of Zomnian society consider him or her a fronter or a backer. The social expectations of Zomnian culture are internalized into the psyche of each individual Zomnian. People may not be born with a particular sleep orientation, but in the context of Zomnian society, they develop them, as surely as a child brought up in an English-speaking country learns to speak English. Given this, the sociological defense against my argument would conclude that the categories "backer" and "fronter" are, contrary to my observations, scientifically and metaphysically appropriate for use in Zomnia.

There may be something correct about this sociological response. The categories of sleep orientation may well fit with the social reality of Zomnia. Although, from the Zomnian point of view, the categories may not be arbitrary, I would argue that these categories are *merely* social. Every category that we can express is social in a certain sense because the only way it can be expressed is through language or some other socially mediated apparatus. All categories that we use are social in this sense. Some categories, however, also pick out a scientific property, concept, or the like. Such categories are *more than merely* social. In the next section, I will shed more light on the idea I am trying to convey when I talk about a "merely social category." For now, you can take my claim to be that sleep orientations will not play an explanatory role in any scientific laws or correlate with anything significant about human nature.

My position about backers and fronters is akin to the position constructionists take about sexual orientation. I deny that the Zomnian categories of sleep orientation apply to people in all cultures, and I deny that these categories will play a role in any scientific explanation. Further, I claim that people in Zomnia fit these categories only in virtue of social facts. Constructionists about sexual orientation deny that our categories of sexual orientation are universal categories, they deny that these categories will play a role in any scientific explanation, and they claim that people in our culture fit into these categories (insofar as they do) in virtue of social facts. If you find my position about Zomnia plausible (or at least sensible), you should find constructionism about sexual orientation at least sensible (and perhaps plausible). The analogy is not supposed to be an *argument* in favor of constructionism about sexual orientation; rather, it is supposed to be the beginning of a charitable account of constructionism, a position that lots of people have a hard time understanding.[2] In the rest of this chapter, I will attempt to flesh out constructionism about sexual orientation as well as its rival view, essentialism about sexual orientation. Although I will consider various arguments for both positions in this chapter, I will not attempt to settle this dispute about the nature of sexual orientations here. That will be the task of several of the chapters that follow.[3]


## Natural Kinds

In the previous section, I offered an extended analogy designed to make constructionism about sexual orientation—and more generally, the debate about the nature of sexual orientations—more plausible. I now want to develop a more precise characterization of constructionism about sexual orientation and its primary alternative, essentialism about sexual orientation. The debate between essentialism and constructionism, once it has been appropriately distinguished from various other questions, can be best understood as related to a set of issues in philosophy of science and metaphysics (see the introduction for discussion) concerning *natural kinds*. I begin this section by surveying some of the philosophical questions concerning natural kinds. In the following section, building on the work of Ian Hacking (1984; 1986a; 1986b; 1990; 1991; 1992), I extend my discussion of natural kinds to kinds of human beings and describe how we can tell whether a group is a natural kind or a merely social kind. In chapter 4, I use this idea of *natural human kinds* as a lens for understanding constructionism and essentialism about sexual orientation.

### Natural, Artifactual, and Empty Kinds

To begin simply, I shall use the word "group" to refer to any collection of things, using the word "thing" quite abstractly to include properties and groups as well as physical objects. Examples of groups include (a) the group consisting of all tennis balls, (b) the group consisting of all concepts described by words with exactly five letters, (c) the group consisting of all the states in the United States, and, more abstractly, (d) the group consisting of all groups that can be described in less than twenty words (note that [d] has the interesting feature of including itself as a member). Some groups are small, for example, (e) the group of all buildings taller than 110 stories high, (f) the group of things named Ethel, and (g) the group of prime numbers between seventy and eighty. Other groups are quite large, for example, (h) the group of all the electrons in the universe, (i) the group of all real numbers (that is, the group of numbers that can be expressed using a single decimal point and the numerals, possibly preceded by a minus sign), and (j) the group of all organisms that are currently alive. Typically,[4] a thing is either a member of a group or not. George Washington is not in group (j)—since he is not currently alive—and not in group (i)—since he is not a number. In contrast, my neighbor's dog Ethel is in group (j)—since she is currently alive—and in group (f)—due to her name. Groups can be infinitely large—for example, group (i)—or empty—for example, (l) the group consisting of people taller than nine feet or (m) the group of women who have been president of the United States. Groups can also be quite arbitrary in their membership—for example, (n) the group consisting of my left thumb, the number seventeen, the third floor of the Empire State Building, and all the words on page forty-five of the latest edition of *People* magazine.

Intuitively, some groups are distinctly *non*arbitrary in their membership. One particularly interesting type of nonarbitrary group is the type of group that coheres in nature independent of human intervention and that is governed by a common set of laws (by which I mean laws of nature, not laws in the legal sense). Such groups are the "real divisions" of the world. They play a role in explaining why the world is the way it is in terms of its structure and behavior. For example, (h), the group of all electrons, is one such group. Certain scientific laws govern all electrons and have done so since before humans existed. Further, there are scientific laws that make use of electrons as a group and rely on the properties that all electrons have in order to explain, for example, why certain chemical elements interact in the way that they do. Groups that are nonarbitrary in this way are called *natural kinds*. Words that refer to natural kinds (called *natural-kind terms*) provide the linguistic tools for scientifically categorizing the world and its furniture.

Philosophers have long debated what the properties of natural kinds are and whether natural kinds exist. In fact, in the Middle Ages Erasmus reported that roughly this debate led to violence among advocates of the various positions: "They wrangle with one another till they are pale, till they take to abuse and spitting and sometimes even fisticuffs" (Armstrong 1989, 6). Because of the various controversies surrounding natural kinds, it is hard to come up with a clear account of what they are, even though the notion of a natural kind is an intuitive one. Some people describe natural kinds as the groups that things are divided into when the world is seen from a god's-eye point of view, but this is at best metaphorical. Another metaphor for natural kinds—used by Plato and Aristotle, among others—is that they are the groups that enable us to "cut nature at its joints."[5] Here the idea is that natural kinds divide nature into the groups that provide its underlying structure, the way bones give bodies their underlying structure.

Natural kinds can be contrasted with what might be called *nonnatural kinds* (sometimes called *nominal kinds*), namely groups of things that do *not* play a role in scientific laws and explanations. Some of these nonnatural groups may be arbitrary in a strong sense, for example, (n)—the group consisting of my left thumb, the number seventeen, the third floor of the Empire State Building, and the words on page forty-five of *People*—while others may play an explanatory role in other realms besides science, for example, (c)—the group consisting of all the states in the United States. Group (c) will not play an explanatory role in physics, chemistry, or biology, but it might play a role in answering legal or political questions. While nonnatural kinds may be significant in various ways, they do not cut to the underlying structure of nature, and they do not match the explanatory categories of nature.

To begin to understand natural kinds, consider some groups that are typically thought to be natural kinds and some that are not. The following groups are typically considered to be natural kinds: apples, pine trees, gold, water, hearts, horses,[6] electrons, and hemoglobin. The following groups are typically considered *not* to be natural kinds: chairs, streets, teddy bears, fake gold, diet soft drinks, breakfast cereals, televisions, and concepts described by words with five letters.

The groups in the list of things *not* typically considered to be natural kinds make up only a significant subset of kinds—called *artifactual kinds*— that are not natural kinds. An artifactual kind, roughly, is a group of things that have a common property only in virtue of human intentions. What diet soft drinks have in common is a particular sort of connection to human intentional activity. Even if, by some amazing coincidence, a liquid identical in chemical composition to Diet Pepsi was produced by a natural spring, it would not be a diet soft drink until humans discover it and interact with it in certain ways. In contrast, an undiscovered chemical element is still an element whether or not humans ever interact with it (Keil 1989, chapter 3, especially 47–51).

Another significant sort of kind that is not a natural kind but is also not an artifactual kind (at least not in a straightforward sense) would be a kind that was thought to play a role in scientific explanations, but that in fact does not. An example of this is *phlogiston*. Until the late 1700s, scientists thought that phlogiston was an element found in high concentrations in substances that burned while exposed to air. Air that had absorbed a lot of phlogiston would not support further combustion and was not suitable for living creatures to breathe because air was supposed to remove phlogiston from the body through respiration (Conant 1950). We now know that there is no such substance as phlogiston. What were at one time thought to be scientific laws made use of phlogiston, but these laws have been rejected. Phlogiston was thought to play an explanatory role in scientific theories, but in fact it does not. There is no single substance that has the properties attributed to phlogiston. Phlogiston is an empty group. I will call such groups *empty kinds* because nothing in this world properly fits into these kinds.[7]

I have now introduced three different kinds of kinds: natural, artifactual, and empty. I want to pause to compare and contrast them. To begin, what is the difference between an *artifactual* kind (like chairs) and an *empty* kind (like phlogiston)? The difference is that there are things that fit into an artifactual kind, while there are none that fit into an empty kind—for example, there are chairs (I am sitting on one), but there is not any phlogiston. In this sense, *natural* kinds are like *artifactual* kinds because just as there are things that fit into artifactual kinds, there are things that fit into natural kinds—for example, there are electrons, and there are chairs. The *difference* between natural kinds and artifactual kinds is that the existence of an artifactual kind, but not the existence of a natural kind, has to do with intentional human intervention (or the intentional intervention of other creatures[8]); if there were no human intervention, there would be no artifactual kinds. Philosophers sometimes make this point by saying natural kinds have the property of *mind independence*, that is, natural kinds are natural kinds independent of any human intentions or the intentions of other creatures. In contrast, artifactual kinds are *mind-dependent*. In this sense, empty kinds are like natural kinds: just as natural kinds are natural kinds independent of human intervention, empty kinds are empty kinds independent of human intervention. Humans invented the word "phlogiston," but nothing humans can do or could have done could make it true that phlogiston exists.

This last point may not be obvious. The following example may help. Suppose that some scientist decided to use the word "phlogiston" for the stuff we call oxygen. If this were the case, would phlogiston thereby exist? Does this example refute my claim that nothing humans can do or could have done would make phlogiston exist? The answer to both of these questions is no. Here is why: when I ask whether there is anything humans could have done to make it the case that phlogiston exists, I use the word "phlogiston" in the way it is *in fact* defined, not the way it *might have been* defined. As it is *in fact* defined, phlogiston does not include oxygen; as it is *in fact* defined, phlogiston does not exist.

This same point can be made by considering a question attributed to Abraham Lincoln. Lincoln is purported to have asked the following (rather odd) question: "If we called a dog's tail a leg, how many legs would a dog have?" There are two tempting answers to his question: "four" and "five." This is because there is an ambiguity in the question. Lincoln might be trying to get at the question, How many legs does a dog have? (although he is asking the question in an intentionally tricky way), or he might be trying to get at the question, How many legs would you *say* a dog had if by the word "leg" you meant to include both what we in fact count as legs and what we in fact count as tails? (this is an even trickier question than the first one). The first reading of Lincoln's question asks about dogs in terms of our *actual* words for talking about the world. This question is meant to bring out the point that even if we used the words "dog" and "tail" differently than the way we actually use them, dogs would still have *four* legs (this is because the question is asked and the answer is given using our *actual* meaning of "leg," not some other definition). The second reading of Lincoln's question asks what we would say about dogs if our words meant something different than they in fact mean. People who use the word "leg" to refer to tails and legs (using these words in the way they are *actually* used) would say that dogs have *five* legs.

There is the same potential for confusion when I ask whether there is something someone might have done to make phlogiston exist. I am *not* asking whether there would be something that we would refer to by the word "phlogiston" if by the word "phlogiston" we meant something other than we in fact mean. Rather, I am asking whether anyone could have made it be the case that phlogiston existed (given the actual meaning of the word "phlogiston"). The answer, given what we in fact mean by phlogiston, is no. This is just another way of making the point that phlogiston is an empty kind. This leads to a related point: the question of whether a kind is a natural kind, an empty kind, or an artifactual kind (that is, what "kind" of kind it is) is a *metaphysical* question (a question about the way the world is) rather than an *epistemological* question (a question about what we know about the world) or a *semantic* question (a question about the meaning of words).

To summarize, I have so far made three main points about the similarities and differences among natural, empty, and artifactual kinds:

1. Natural kinds play a role in scientific laws and explanations, while empty kinds and artifactual kinds (which are both sorts of nonnatural kinds) do not.
2. Natural and artifactual kinds both have things that actually fit into them (for example, there are electrons and there are chairs), while empty kinds do not.
3. An artifactual kind is an artifactual kind in virtue of human intervention, while a natural kind and an empty kind are, respectively, a natural kind and an empty kind independent of human intervention.

### Do Natural Kinds Exist?

Having discussed some of the different kinds of kinds, I now turn to perhaps the most important philosophical question about natural kinds, namely whether natural kinds exist. Some thinkers, called *nominalists* (sometimes they are called *antirealists*, but I reserve this term for a more general use), say that there are no natural kinds.[9] According to nominalism, the only feature that all members of a kind have that distinguishes them from all other entities is that we group them together into a kind. So, for example, the only thing that entities we call "horses" have in common that distinguishes them from all other things is that we call them horses. This might seem a crazy view—and, in a way, it is, but sometimes what seem like crazy views are philosophically respectable. Against this view, you might be tempted to say that what distinguishes horses from other things is that they have four legs, a mane, and people ride on their backs; that does not, however, distinguish horses from, say, donkeys. Even if you get more precise in describing the external features of horses and the activities that they engage in, you would still face problems picking out all and only horses. A three-legged horse with no mane that is too weak to support a person on his back is, for example, still a horse. Similarly, a robot horse might have many of the external features that a horse has and might be able to engage in many of the activities that horses do, yet still not be a horse. To distinguish horses from all other entities, you need to get at some basic "horseness." Only by doing this can you delineate the group of horses in a way that, as Plato would say, cuts nature at its joints. Nominalists deny that our words for groups can refer to groups that cut nature at its joints. Or, as some versions of nominalism might state it, the only thing that horses have in common that distinguishes them from all other entities is that we call them horses. In a nutshell, nominalists hold that "the classification of . . . [things] into kinds is solely 'the workmanship of [human] understanding'" (Boyd 1991, 130).

A limited version of nominalism's central claims are, in a sense, obviously right about empty kinds, for example, phlogiston. The only property that all the stuff that was called phlogiston has in common that distinguishes it from everything that was not called phlogiston is that the stuff called phlogiston was called phlogiston by scientists in the early 1700s. Nominalism is, however, a *general* thesis—it says that all kind terms are in a sense like the term "phlogiston." According to nominalism, there are no natural kinds, not even the kinds that we think are natural kinds. Nominalism is thus a radical thesis.

Whereas nominalists deny that there are any natural kinds, *realists* hold that there are natural kinds. Scientific realists hold that natural kinds exist, and in particular, the natural kinds that do exist are the ones that our sophisticated scientific theories predict exist. They further hold that the existence of these natural kinds in no way depends on the fact that we have theories about them. According to scientific realists, electrons, for example, exist and are among the basic features of the "furniture" of the world. Our word "electron" refers to electrons, but even if we did not have a word for electron and did not understand anything about the internal structure of atoms, electrons would still exist. In fact, electrons existed long before humans existed, and they would have existed even if humans never came into existence. The same is true, scientific realists would say, about most other terms of science (Leplin 1984).

There are other versions of realism about natural kinds besides scientific realism—for example, *naive realism,* which says that our commonsense categories (sometimes called *folk categories*), rather than scientific groups, are the kinds that actually exist in nature, and *promiscuous realism* (Dupré 1993) (sometimes called *pluralism*), which says there are many different ways of dividing the world into natural kinds that are equally real and legitimate. For my purposes, the differences among the various versions of realism are not important; in what follows, I will focus on scientific realism (and, henceforth, unless I say otherwise, when I use the term "realism," I mean to refer to *scientific* realism).

### Do Natural Kinds Have Essences?

Thus far, I have avoided spelling out a precise definition of natural kinds. I have avoided this because of the contentious issues lurking here. Some people have argued that a natural kind must be individuated by an *essence,* namely a set of features intrinsic to objects of this kind. So, for example, gold is a natural kind because it is individuated by having the atomic number 79 (the atomic number of an element is the number of protons that an element has in its nucleus). Philosophers traditionally call this view of natural kinds *essentialism,* but to avoid confusion with essentialism about sexual orientation (where the term is used with a somewhat different meaning), I will call this view about natural kinds *essenceism.* According to essenceism, a kind is a natural kind if and only if all and only members of that kind share an intrinsic property (or a set of intrinsic properties). For example, the essence of gold is having the atomic number 79. According to essenceism, gold is a natural kind because all members of the group gold have that atomic number (the "all" condition) and everything that has the atomic number 79 is gold (the "only" condition).

Some philosophers have argued that essenceism is false because there are perfectly respectable natural kinds that do not have essences (that is, whose members do not have intrinsic properties in common). These philosophers argue that natural kinds are defined by a *cluster* of relevant causal conditions rather than by "all and only" conditions (Boyd 1991; Dupré 1993, 42–46; Wilson 1999). According to this view, a thing is a member of a specific kind if it satisfies some number of the relevant conditions for being such a kind. When conditions in the cluster can be satisfied independent of human intentions, such natural kinds are capable of functioning in scientific laws and scientific explanations and doing the other things that natural kinds can do. Among the proffered examples of natural kinds that do not have essences are earthquakes, species, and diseases (Boyd 1991; Dupré 1993; Wilson 1999). While some philosophers have argued that scientific realism is false because there are no kinds that have true essences, these examples suggest that even if there are no natural kinds with essences, there might still be natural kinds. These examples are not definitive, but they do shift the burden of proof. They indicate that an argument is needed to show that the real divisions of nature must be distinguished by essences and that, in the absence of such an argument, it is plausible that some natural kinds are *cluster properties*. Given this, it is possible to be a scientific realist—that is, to believe that there are natural kinds—while denying that natural kinds have essences. In other words, scientific realism is compatible with the falsity of essenceism.

Having explained what a natural kind is and how this notion relates to certain questions in metaphysics and philosophy of science, in the next section, I consider how natural kinds apply to groups of humans. This will help make sense of essentialism and constructionism about sexual orientation. Building on the distinction between natural kinds and merely social kinds, I will distinguish between *natural* human kinds and merely *social* human kinds and show that *essentialism is the view that sexual orientations are natural human kinds* and *constructionism is the view that sexual orientations are merely social human kinds*.

## Natural Human Kinds

Just as things can be sorted into various groups, people, since we are things (in the general sense of the term), can also be sorted into groups. Examples of groups of people are (p) registered members of the Democratic Party, (q) matriculated students at Ivy League schools, (r) people with blood type AB, (s) people with XY sex chromosomes, (t) experts on the migratory habits of birds, and (u) convicted felons. Ian Hacking (1984, 1986a, 1986b, 1990, 1991, 1992) introduced the notion of a *human kind* to talk about groups of people. Expanding on this notion, I use the term *natural human kind* for a natural kind that applies to people, in other words, a human kind that plays a certain sort of role in scientific explanations and laws. Examples of natural human kinds include groupings of people by blood type—for example, (r) all people with blood type AB—and groupings of people by genetic structure—for example, (s) all people with XY sex chromosomes. Group (r) is a natural human kind because it plays a role in laws about what sorts of people a person can donate blood to and receive blood from—for example, a person with blood type AB can receive transfusions of red blood cells from a person of any blood type. Similarly, (s) is a natural human kind because it plays a role in laws about the development of fetuses—for example, a person with an XY chromosome will typically develop a penis during fetal development.[10]

Also, just as there are many ways that things can be grouped that are not natural kinds, there are many ways people can be grouped that are not natural *human* kinds. Examples of such nonnatural human kinds include (p) registered members of the Democratic Party, (q) matriculated students at an Ivy

League schools, (t) experts on the migratory habits of birds, and (u) convicted felons. I call these nonnatural human kinds *social human kinds*. (It might be clearer to call these *merely social* human kinds because, for reasons discussed in the section above, *all* kinds—hence all human kinds—are in a sense social; for the sake of brevity, I do not bother with the extra word "merely.") Such human kinds do not refer to groups that exist in nature; rather, these groups have a social existence—they are created and sustained by human intentions. Like artifactual kinds, social human kinds come into existence at particular moments; they did not exist before humans created them. Take, for example, an artifactual kind like gloves. Gloves came into existence at a particular time, in virtue of human intentions to create them: someone got the idea of making something to cover the hand. Gloves and the concept "glove" resulted from this idea (Hacking 1986b, 78). Some human kinds are like this as well. At some particular time, the idea of a felony was developed. Convicted felons and the concept "convicted felon" resulted from this (Foucault 1977). Hacking argues that the same is true of people with multiple personalities and the concept of "multiple personality" (Hacking 1995).

To better appreciate the distinction between social human kinds and natural human kinds, compare the following generalizations:

i. People with XX chromosomes are more likely to have higher levels of the hormone estrogen in their bloodstream than are similarly aged people with XY chromosomes.

ii. People who were matriculated students at Ivy League schools are more likely to be registered members of the Democratic Party than are similarly aged people who did not.

Note (i) involves natural human kinds, while (ii) involves social human kinds. Further, (i) is a reasonable candidate for a scientific law, while (ii) is not. One distinctive sign of the difference between (i) and (ii) is that the kinds involved in (ii)—namely, (p) registered Democrats and (q) Ivy Leagues graduates—are applicable only to people in particular cultures at particular times, while the kinds involved in (i)—namely people with XX chromosomes, (s) people with XY chromosomes, and people with high estrogen levels—are applicable to people in any culture.

Natural human kinds have the feature that it is *possible* for a person in any culture to fit into them; social human kinds lack this feature. To see this, note that it makes sense to ask, for example, what sex chromosomes Joan of Arc had in a way that it does not make sense to ask whether she was a registered

Democrat or whether she went to an Ivy League college. To put the general point another way, a group is a natural human kind if it is *applicable* to people in all cultures. When I say this, I am not saying that a natural kind in fact *applies* to any person in all cultures, for example, that (s) is a natural kind of course does not mean that everyone has XY chromosomes. Further, saying that a group is a natural kind if it applies to all cultures does not mean that there is at least one person in every culture to whom the kind applies. That (s) is a natural kind does not mean that there is someone in every culture that has XY chromosomes. We can imagine that there could be a group of people in which everyone has either XX chromosomes or XXY chromosomes. That nobody in this group has XY chromosomes does not mean that XY is not a natural human kind; it would still be *possible* for a kind to be able to be applied there.[11] The kind (s) is *applicable* even if it does not in fact apply to anyone there. To better understand the distinction between a concept being applicable to a culture and a concept in fact applying to a culture, suppose that at a particular time and in a particular culture there is only one person was has blood type AB. The kind (r) is both applicable and in fact applies in this culture. If the person dies, (r) no longer in fact applies to anyone in this culture, but (r) is still applicable there.

Attempting to treat merely social human kinds as if they are natural human kinds is a serious conceptual mistake. If I put (ii) forward as a scientific law, I am committed to the claim that the groups (p)—Ivy League graduates—and (q)—registered Democrats—are natural human kinds. In fact, (p) and (q) are social human kinds. The mistake that I am implicitly making when I assert that (ii) is a scientific law is that *every* person—for example, Joan of Arc—is a candidate for being in group (p) and for being in group (q). However, only people in certain social contexts are possible candidates for being in these groups; this is what makes them social human kinds. Trying to put people from other social contexts into such groups is to mistake a social human kind for a natural human kind.

Sometimes it is not obvious whether a particular claim involves this sort of mistake. Richard Mohr made roughly this point in discussing constructionism about sexual orientation. In the context of discussing the appropriateness of the concept "yuppie" as an analogy for constructionism about sexual orientation (Stein 1990, 342–343), Mohr writes that the "range of applicability" of "yuppie"

> depends on how one defines [it] . . . . If one defines "yuppie" in such a way
> that in the very definition there is an essential reference to Volvos or VCRs or
> "thirtysomething," then necessarily the term can apply only to the modern

era. On this account, it is question-beggingly true that yuppies did not exist in Attic Greece. If, however, one defines yuppies as middle-aged effete money-grubbing conspicuous consumers, then we have something that at least in theory could be applied to other eras and places; it has at least the possibility of being instantiated in different cultures because definitionally it is culturally neutral. It is a concept that could be instantiated in, say, the oligarchs of Plato's *Republic* 8. Now it looks like "yuppie" is not in fact transcultural—not, that is, occurring in all cultures. For there are no middle-aged, effete money-grubbing conspicuous consumers in hunting-and-gathering tribes. Still, "yuppie" so defined is at least a candidate for being transcultural, for it is defined in such a way that we can look in other cultures to see whether it picks anything out there, whether it is there denoting. (Mohr 1992b, 237–238)

The relevance of this for the present discussion is that whether someone is mistaking a social human kind for a natural human kind depends on how the kind involved is being used. If, for example, yuppie is defined in a way that makes reference to VCRs and other culturally specific entities, then asking whether Socrates was a yuppie involves mistaking a social kind for a natural kind. I say this is a *narrow* interpretation because the range of applicability is narrowed by reference to culturally specific properties. If yuppie is defined *widely*, that is, in a way that does *not* refer to objects and properties that are culture specific, yuppie might well be a natural kind, and thus it would make sense to ask whether Socrates was a yuppie. That some terms can be read either widely or narrowly does not undermine the distinction between natural human kinds and social human kinds. Instead, it suggests that, with respect to some particular human kinds, it will be difficult to determine whether they are social or natural human kinds.

There is whole class of human kinds that is potentially difficult to classify as either natural or social. As an example, compare (i) and (ii) with the following generalization:

iii. Poor people tend to have a lower life expectancy than rich people.

Is "poor people" a natural human kind or a social human kind? The answer is not obvious. It is not clear, for example, if there were rich or poor people in cultures where there was no money. Cavemen and hunter-gatherer societies, for example, probably did not have rich or poor people. Even the *wide* sense of yuppie may not apply to people in such societies. If that is the case, then (iii) is not a law, like (ii), it is at best a generalization that is limited to certain cultures.

The issue here is related to a general question that concerns philosophers and theoretically minded social scientists, namely whether there are laws in the social sciences (sociology, economics, anthropology, history, and so forth) (Rosenberg 1988). The question of whether there are laws in the social sciences is too big to tackle here. Instead of attempting to resolve this question, I shall leave open the possibility that there are some laws and associated natural human kinds in the social sciences and the possibility that there are laws and associated natural human kinds in some of the social sciences but not in others. Even if there are natural kinds in the social sciences, this does not mean that all generalizations about humans made within the social sciences will be lawlike. In science, a law that involves a grouping that turns out not to be a natural kind will not be an actual law. "Nothing burns in air that has absorbed a great deal of phlogiston" is not a law because phlogiston is not a natural kind. Similarly, a generalization about humans that involves social human kinds will not be a law. "All witches float" is not a law—despite what a character in the movie *Monty Python and the Holy Grail* says—because witches do not constitute a natural human kind. Even if it is hard to determine whether some human kinds are natural or social kinds, the conceptual distinction between these two types of human kinds is clear, intuitively plausible, and important for science and metaphysics.

Finally, just as there are empty kinds—ways of grouping entities that are or were supposed to be natural kinds, but that fail to match the way nature actually is grouped—there are also empty *human* kinds, that is, ways of grouping people that are or were supposed to be natural human kinds, but that fail to match with the way nature actually groups people. An empty human kind is a grouping that does not in fact apply to humans. As an example, consider the concept of a hysteric woman. The idea that there are some people, especially women, who suffer from a particular condition called "hysteria" dates back to early Egyptian culture and continued to the middle of the twentieth century. The symptoms of this condition included uncontrollable outbursts as well as various bodily symptoms, most typically spasms, paralysis, swelling, blindness, and deafness. Originally thought to be caused by a "wandering" womb, hysteria came to be seen as a specific neurotic illness affecting primarily, but not exclusively, women. Many women were diagnosed as having hysteria when they actually had some unidentified illness or were depressed, tired, or nervous (Micklem 1996). Today, most people do not think that hysteria is an actual medical or psychological condition. Just as phlogiston is an empty kind, hysteric is an *empty human kind* because there are no hysterics (and because there cannot be any). Other examples of empty human kinds are witches and warlocks, namely women and men, respectively, with particular sorts of supernatural powers. These are empty human kinds, I would argue, because people with such supernatural powers simply do not (and cannot) exist.[12]

## How To Tell What Kind of Kind a Kind Is

Having introduced the notions of natural human kinds, social human kinds, and empty human kinds, I can now talk about Zomnia in more precise terms. Working through this example will set up the discussion of essentialism and constructionism about sexual orientation in chapter 4. At the beginning of this chapter, I said that if I were to travel to Zomnia and encounter the cultural practices surrounding sleep positions and sleep orientations, I would say that the Zomnian categories of sleep orientation are inappropriate both metaphysically and ethically. I can now make my metaphysical claims more precisely. Simply put, I claim that Zomnians mistakenly assume that sleep orientations are natural human kinds. My claim involves two parts, first, that Zomnians implicitly accept the view that sleep orientations—that is, backer and fronter— are natural human kinds and, second, that this view is mistaken—sleep orientations are not natural human kinds. The second part of my claim commits me to one of two possibilities: sleep orientations are *either* empty kinds *or* social kinds. Sleep orientations would be empty kinds if no one in Zomnia or elsewhere is actually a backer or a fronter. Sleep orientations would be merely social human kinds if people fit these categories in virtue of social forces that are not generalizable to cultures outside of Zomnia.

As I noted, most Zomnians would disagree with my assessment. They would agree with the first part of my claim—they would agree that they think sleep orientations are natural human kinds—but they would disagree with the second part of my claim because they think their beliefs about sleep orientations are correct. What would settle this dispute between the Zomnians and me? How would we determine whether or not sleep orientations are natural human kinds? First, we would have to make sure that we were using the words "backer" and "fronter" to mean the same thing. Second, some sophisticated cross-cultural scientific (and possibly social scientific) research would need to be done on sleep positions, the dispositions that underlie them, and the origins of these dispositions. I discuss both of these steps in turn.

The terms "backer" and "fronter" can be defined widely or narrowly. Just as a narrow definition of yuppie involves VCRs and Volvos, a narrow definition of sleep-orientation terms would involve Zomnia-specific facts about backers and fronters: culturally specific stereotypes about them, cultural artifacts associated with them, social attitudes towards them, and the like. Wide definitions would focus on sleep positions and/or the disposition to sleep in particular positions. One wide definition of sleep orientation (the behavioral view of sleep orientation) is that a backer is someone who sleeps on his or her back more than 50 percent of the time he or she spends sleeping. This definition is *applicable* to people in any culture (even in a culture where all people sleep on their stomachs; the categories would still be applicable even if no one in fact is a backer). A fairly sophisticated wide definition of "backer" would be a person who is disposed, all else being equal, to sleep on her back rather than on her stomach (this is a dispositional account of sleep orientations). Defined widely, sleep orientations would be applicable to all cultures, while defined narrowly, it would not. For sleep orientations to even be candidates for being natural human kinds, they must be defined widely rather than narrowly. By definition, narrowly defined categories appeal to culture-specific characteristics, hence they are inappropriate candidates for natural human kinds.

For a group to be a natural human kind, it is required that the group be defined widely. Being defined widely is not, however, enough to guarantee that a group will be a natural human kind. That sleep orientations can be defined widely does not, however, establish that sleep orientations are natural human kinds. Even though the wide definition of "backer" might be applicable to people in other cultures, it may well be the case that there are no scientific laws in which the categories of sleep orientation, widely defined, play a role; it may well be the case that the categories of sleep orientation, widely defined, might have no explanatory role in the sciences or the social sciences. Even if the Zomnians and I were to agree upon a wide definition for sleep orientations, this would not settle the dispute between us about the metaphysical appropriateness of sleep orientations, namely it would not settle the matter of whether sleep orientations are natural human kinds. If "fronter" is defined as someone who usually sleeps on her stomach (a wide and a behavioral definition), then I would count as a fronter since I usually sleep on my stomach. A Zomnian could point to me and others like me in this culture and claim to have thereby established that sleep orientations are natural human kinds since they are applicable across cultures. There is, however, a problem with this behavioral definition of sleep orientations. I may be a fronter in the wide sense, but I may have nothing interesting in common with fronters from Zomnia except for the behavior of sleeping on our stomachs. I might sleep on my stomach because when my sleep preferences were developing, bright light shined into my bedroom window and, in order to avoid the light, I slept with my eyes facing into my pillow and thus on my stomach. In Zomnia, many fronters (defined behaviorally) might sleep on their stomachs because of social sanctions to which people who sleep in other positions are subjected. Their sleep patterns, even if they are similar to mine, were shaped in a different way than my sleep patterns. This deeper sort of commonality is required to establish that fronters are natural human kinds. Giving a wide definition of "fronter" and then providing examples of people in various cultures who fit it does not establish that it is a natural human kind. Such evidence shows only that there are certain basic behavioral (and/or dispositional) similarities between people in various cultures. This does not, however, establish that there are natural human kinds associated with the people who have these similarities. More evidence is required.

In order to show that a group is a natural human kind, there needs to be evidence that the group plays an explanatory role in a scientific (or social scientific) law. The sort of evidence that is needed is empirical evidence, that is, evidence obtained by observation or experimentation. If cross-cultural studies indicate that, for example, backers, defined in dispositional terms, developed certain conditions of the spine that made them quick tempered or if such studies indicate that there are certain genetic, neuroanatomical, or cognitive psychological differences between backers and fronters that transcend cultural differences in how backers versus fronters are treated, then there would be grounds for thinking that sleep orientations were natural human kinds. Evidence that these differences between backers and fronters were found in cultures where people were not thought to have sleep orientations (cultures like those in contemporary North America, for example) or where sleep orientations had very different cultural connotations than they do in Zomnia would be especially persuasive. In the face of this sort of empirical evidence, I would begin to be persuaded that my original assessment of the metaphysical appropriateness of sleep orientations was mistaken. Social explanations would be ill-suited to explain the existence of lawlike generalizations related to sleep orientations in cultures where these categories have not been articulated. If the same scientific generalizations about sleep orientations apply to people in Zomnia, in the United States, and, for example, in Mongolia, then I would be quite impressed. This would be significant evidence that sleep orientations are natural kinds; my view of human nature would have to be modified to incorporate this new information.

On the other hand, what sort of evidence would persuade a reasonable Zomnian that sleep orientations are not natural human kinds? First, insofar as Zomnians have articulated scientific (or social scientific) theories of how people in general develop sleep orientations, one might try to show that these theories collapse when they are applied to people in other cultures. Second, one might

articulate and defend theories of how people in Zomnia develop sleep orientations according to which sleep orientations are social human kinds, not natural
human kinds. Zomnians might be persuaded by these theories if, for example,
they account for the changes that are occurring in Zomnia as the social conditions for backers change. Third, one might show that the view that sleep orientations are natural human kinds is in tension with other well-established theories of human nature. Finally, in association with this other evidence, one might
point to the paucity of other societies that divide humans on the basis of sleep
orientations. As I have argued above, this sort of cultural evidence is not decisive; in combination with other sorts of evidence, it may be persuasive.

## Conclusion

In this chapter, I have articulated the concept of a natural human kind and
shown how this concept plays a role in our thinking about human nature and
how we understand it. In the next chapter, I use the conceptual tools and the
hypothetical examples I have developed here to make sense of essentialism and
constructionism about sexual orientation, the central metaphysical issue about
human sexual orientation. I shall show that essentialism is the view that sexual
orientations are natural human kinds and constructionism is the view that
sexual orientations are merely social kinds.

# CHAPTER **4**

# *Essentialism and Constructionism about Sexual Orientation*

In chapter 3, I developed the notion of a natural human kind and used this notion to characterize the situation in the imaginary country of Zomnia. The example of Zomnia is an extended analogy for the debate between essentialism and constructionism about sexual orientation. This debate is at the foundation of scientific, social scientific, and humanistic studies of sexual orientation. Many people (essentialists, constructionists, and others) also think that this debate is relevant to legal and ethical questions concerning sexual orientation. In the present chapter, I turn to this foundational debate about sexual orientation with both the analogy to Zomnia and the notion of a natural human kind in hand. I begin by returning to Aristophanes' myth.

## Interpreting Aristophanes' Myth

In his speech in the *Symposium* that I discussed in the introduction, Aristophanes talks about the three different types of people defined by the type of person he or she was longing for.

> The man who is a slice of the hermaphrodite sex . . . will naturally be attracted by women . . . and the women who run after men are of similar

descent . . . . But the woman who is a slice of the original female is attracted by women rather than by men . . . while men who are slices of the male are followers of the male. (Plato 1935b, 191d–e)

A natural interpretation of this myth is that Aristophanes is talking about heterosexual men, heterosexual women, lesbians, and gay men, respectively, and that he is arguing that sexual orientation is an important, inborn, and defining feature of a person (Boswell 1989; 1992, 163–164). For example, the historian John Boswell said that the "manifest and stated purpose [of Aristophanes' speech] is to explain why humans are divided into groups predominantly of homosexual and heterosexual interest . . . [and it] is strongly implied that these interests are both exclusive and innate" (Boswell 1989, 25).[1] This reading of the myth is based on the view that the same categories of sexual desire are applicable to both us and to the Greeks. This interpretation, which I call the *universalizing interpretation,* depends on the appropriateness of applying our categories of sexual orientation to people living in Athens around the time of *The Symposium.*

There is, however, an alternate interpretation of Aristophanes' myth, which I call the *localizing interpretation.* Some scholars have argued that Aristophanes' speech is not about sexual orientation at all. This alternative reading draws support from historical evidence that the Greeks thought about people's sexual interests in a quite different way than we do. In Attic Greece, a person's social status—that is, whether the person was a citizen or noncitizen, a slave or a free person, an adult or a child, a woman or a man—was important to how the culture viewed his or her sexual interests. In terms of law and social custom, a citizen was allowed to penetrate but not be penetrated by a noncitizen (noncitizens included all slaves, all children, all women, and foreigners) and was not allowed to penetrate or to be penetrated by another citizen. Thus, the important categories of sexual desire revolved around a person's civic status and whether he wanted to penetrate or be penetrated. This historical evidence is supposed to indicate that Aristophanes and his contemporaries could not have used anything like our categories of sexual orientation because these categories simply did not exist in their vocabulary or their culture. According to this view, it is anachronistic to interpret Aristophanes as talking about heterosexuals, lesbians, and gay men because this interpretation projects into his mind notions he could not possibly have had. It would be anachronistic in almost the same way as interpreting someone in Attic Greece as talking about telephones or computers.

The argument against interpreting Aristophanes' myth as being about gay men, lesbians, and heterosexuals (that is, against the universalizing interpretation) is supported by a more detailed examination of Aristophanes' speech. Since each pair of lovers, regardless of their sexual desires, originally came from the same globular human, the two lovers should be of the same age. Nothing Aristophanes explicitly says about the putative heterosexuals and lesbians contradicts this, but what he says about the putative gay men does. To return to Aristophanes' speech where I left off in the introduction:

> [M]en who are slices of the [original] male are followers of the male, and show their masculinity throughout their boyhood by the way they make friends with men, and the delight they take in lying beside them and being taken in their arms. . . . And . . . when they themselves have come to manhood, their love in turn is lavished upon boys. They have no natural inclination to marry and beget children. Indeed, they only do so in deference to the usage of society, for they would just as soon renounce marriage altogether and spend their lives with one another. (Plato 1935b, 191e–192b)

Age difference seems to be a crucial factor among men who love men in Attic Greece—when they are young, they desire adult men; when they are adults, they desire boys. Someone who wanted to argue that Aristophanes' speech does not refer to homosexuals in our sense of the term might point to this age factor as support for the localizing interpretation: an age difference of this sort is not crucial for contemporary gay men and does not play a role in our conception of male homosexuality (Halperin 1990, 20). In fact, if the concept that Aristophanes is talking about refers to any contemporary concept it would, on this view, be closer to the contemporary concepts of a "boy-lover" or a "pederast" than to the contemporary concept of a gay man.

Supporters of the universalizing view might admit that the social institutions of Attic Greece provided structures that supported the *transgenerational* or *age-asymmetric* form of homosexuality and that, as a result of these social structures and forces, homosexual desire in Attic Greece was primarily expressed in the transgenerational form.[2] In our society, there are different social structures and forces; as a result of these social structures, people who experience homosexual desire typically (approximately as often as their heterosexual counterparts) end up desiring relationships and sexual contacts with people roughly of the same age as each other (the *egalitarian* form of homosexuality). On the universalizing view, there are homosexuals and heterosexuals in both contemporary times and in Attic Greece, but these types of people may express their sexual desires in different ways in different eras. As Richard Mohr (1992b, 233) put it, "[T]he form and salience of each conceptualized sexual mode may vary from culture to culture . . . [b]ut the concept 'homosexual' is there in each case."

Aristophanes can, on this view, still be interpreted as talking about heterosexuals, lesbians, and gay men, even though he is talking about social structures for expressing homosexual desire that seem foreign to us.

The general point is that just because there are different social structures surrounding some human phenomenon in the past and the present does not necessarily mean that the two phenomena are different. Consider the example of pregnancy. In earlier times, people thought about pregnancy in ways very different from how we do today. Many people in Attic Greece believed that men were solely responsible for the material production of offspring; they thought that each sperm contained a small human being inside of it. Women, on this view, were just incubators who enabled sperm to develop into human beings; while men provided the seed, women provided the fertile soil and the nutrients for the seed (Needham 1959). The fact that the Greeks believed this does not mean that women in Attic Greece did not produce eggs in their ovaries that, when fertilized by sperm, developed into fetuses and babies. Even though the Greeks had a dramatically different understanding of the cause of pregnancies than we do today, and even though pregnancy had a quite different meaning in their culture than it does in ours, pregnancy then and now is the same physiological phenomenon. I can say with confidence that a woman in Attic Greece became pregnant when an egg was fertilized by a sperm and became attached to the wall of her uterus.

Similarly, with respect to sexual orientation, someone who favored the universalizing interpretation would reply to the localizing interpretation of Aristophanes' speech in a way that parallels the points I made about pregnancy: just because homosexuality took a different form and was understood differently in Attic Greece does not mean that our categories of sexual orientation fail to apply to people there. Our contemporary medical and biological categories apply to them; why should our sexual-orientation categories fail to do so? Further, a friend of the universalizing interpretation might say that the localizing interpretation takes Aristophanes' myth too literally. Aristophanes did not really believe that there were once globular humans with four arms, four legs, and the like. The crucial ideas that his myth was supposed to convey were that (a) two lovers, whether they are of the same sex-gender or not, have a very strong wish to be together; (b) that some people have such desires for people of the same sex-gender, while other people have it for people not of the same sex-gender; and (c) people have these varied desires from an early age. To focus on the fact that the lovers must be of the same age if they are truly "offspring" of the same globular human is to take the myth too literally.

A friend of the localizing interpretation might reply to this line of argument by admitting that *some* of our categories are appropriate to apply to people from Attic Greece—perhaps pregnancy is among them; sexual orientation, however, is not. The difference between us and the Greeks is not just that we have a different terminology for sexual orientation; we also live our lives in different ways. Attic Greeks and people from contemporary Western cultures have different *forms of desire*. Among Westerners, the most important characteristics of a person that determine whether one is attracted to another person is the other person's sex-gender, while for the Greeks age and social class were of greater or equal importance. Sexual desire is simply not experienced in the same way by Attic Greeks and people in contemporary Western societies.

The question of how Aristophanes' speech in *The Symposium* should be interpreted is connected to the debate between essentialists and constructionists. Essentialists think that everyone, regardless of his or her culture, has a sexual orientation. According to essentialists, heterosexuals, homosexuals, and perhaps bisexuals are natural human kinds. Just as there are such kinds of people in our culture, there are also such kinds of people in other cultures. The universalizing interpretation of Aristophanes' speech—according to which he is talking about heterosexuals, homosexuals, and bisexuals—thus fits nicely with essentialism about sexual orientation.

In contrast, constructionists think that sexual orientations are *not* natural human kinds but are merely social human kinds. Recall from chapter 3 that it does not make sense to try to apply the Zomnian terms "backer" and "fronter" to people in Attic Greece or contemporary North America because the Zomnian categories of sleep orientation are (or at least seem to be) merely social kinds. Similarly, constructionists say that it does not make sense to try to apply the terms "heterosexual," "homosexual," or "bisexual" to other cultures such as Attic Greece. Constructionists admit that there were people in Attic Greece who had sex with people of the same sex-gender—they even admit that there were people who had sex *primarily* with people of the same sex-gender—but they deny that this entails that there were homosexuals in our sense of the term in Attic Greece. To apply our sexual-orientation terms to another culture, we need to have evidence that people in that culture had sexual orientations in roughly our sense of the term. In fact, say constructionists, there is good reason to think few, if any, people in any cultures before the mid-1800s had sexual orientations.

What then is the relationship between the essentialism-constructionism debate on the one hand and an interpretive question like the one about Aristophanes' speech in *The Symposium* on the other? If the universalizing interpretation of Aristophanes' speech is right and the speech was about lesbians, gay men, heterosexual men, and heterosexual women, then this shows that we share our categories for thinking about sexual orientation with the people of Attic Greece. This alone does not show that essentialism about sexual orientation is true. A person who believes that witches are a natural human kind would not establish the truth of this belief by showing that people in another culture, say the colonists of Massachusetts in the 1600s, used "witch" in the same way they do and had the same beliefs about witches that they do. Contemporary believers in witches could have the same category as the colonists, but this would not prove that witches are a natural human kind. To take another example, I would be no more convinced that sleep orientations are natural human kinds if the Zomnians were able to establish beyond a shadow of a doubt that some other culture also used the categories "backer" and "fronter."

Although the truth of essentialism is not established by showing that the Greeks used the same categories of sexual orientation as we do, the Greeks' use of the categories is suggestive evidence for essentialism. If almost every culture divides people up into the same categories, this suggests, but does not establish, that these categories capture some truth about human nature. Showing that Attic Greece has the same categories of sexual orientation as we do goes *some* way towards supporting essentialism. Recall that at the end of chapter 3, in the context of discussing what it would take to show that sleep orientations are natural human kinds, I said that social scientific evidence could be relevant. The same sort of claim applies here: historical and anthropological evidence about other cultures may provide some support for essentialism about sexual orientations.

If, however, Aristophanes was *not* talking about lesbians, gay men, heterosexual women, and heterosexual men, this does not establish the truth of constructionism about sexual orientation either. No one in Attic Greece talked about blood types, but—then and now—the categories of blood type still pick out natural human kinds. That most cultures lack a concept does not establish the truth of constructionism with respect to this concept. A culture might not have the concept, but the people in that culture might still fit it. If not, we could fairly easily eliminate genetic traits like, for example, colorblindness: simply wipe out all discussion of color blindness from textbooks and never tell any children about it. Over time, there would be no one alive who knows about color blindness and the condition would simply disappear. This is of course absurd: colorblindness exists even without the concept. With regards to sexual orientations, even if Aristophanes was not talking about heterosexuals, lesbians, and gay men, constructionism is not thereby established.

Just as the truth of the universalizing interpretation of Aristophanes' speech does not establish the truth of essentialism (it only provides suggestive evidence for it) and the truth of the localizing interpretation does not establish the truth of constructionism, the truth of essentialism does not entail the truth of the universalizing interpretation and the truth of constructionism does not entail the truth of the localizing interpretation. I will briefly explain both of these claims. First, suppose that essentialism is true and sexual orientations are natural human kinds. It is perfectly consistent with this that the Attic Greeks lacked these categories and, hence, that Aristophanes was not talking about homosexuals and heterosexuals in *The Symposium*. If essentialism is true, then there were homosexuals, heterosexuals, and bisexuals in Attic Greece, but it would be possible that the Greeks lacked the appropriate concepts for talking about these natural human kinds. A parallel point can be made about eggs, the structures by which women contribute genetic material to their offspring: it is perfectly consistent with the fact that most women in Attic Greece produced human eggs that the Greeks lacked a concept of a human egg.

Further, suppose that constructionism is true and that sexual orientations are not natural human kinds. It is consistent with this that the Greeks might still have the same categories of sexual orientation that we do. Phlogiston is not a natural kind, but medieval European cultures had roughly the same concept of phlogiston as did residents of Massachusetts around the time of the American revolution. It is of course not a coincidence that medieval Europeans and American colonists shared the same concepts for talking about combustion and related processes; the Americans inherited their scientific belief system from the medieval Europeans. The point is that two (or more) cultures can have the same concept even if the concept does not refer to a natural kind; it might be that one culture got the concept from the other, or it might just be a coincidence that they share the same concept.

The debate between essentialism and constructionism has often been equated with the debate over how various cultures categorize people in terms of their sexual desires. It is easy to see why this has happened. Our access to the sexual orientation of people in cultures that no longer exist (like Attic Greece) is dramatically limited—we cannot observe their sexual behavior, and we cannot ask them about their sexual desires. Our access is limited to their writings, their art, their laws, and the like. This limitation on our knowledge of other cultures should not, however, cause us to confuse what is at issue between essentialism and constructionism. *Even if the Greeks lacked our categories of sexual orientation, sexual orientations might still be natural human kinds; even if the Greeks had our categories, sexual orientations still might not be natural kinds.*

Having indicated what the debate between essentialists and constructionists is not, I turn to what the debate between essentialists and constructionists actually is. I will also say more about the intellectual context of this debate, why it is important, and why certain arguments that are supposed to settle it fail to do so. I conclude by articulating my own views on this debate.

## The Intellectual Background

Historians and theorists interested in sexuality disagree about the development of our contemporary categories of sexual orientation. David Halperin (1990, 155, note 2) attributes to Karl Maria Kertbeny in 1869 the coining of the word "homosexual" (actually, the German equivalent of the word) and attaches significance to this event;[3] others (Boswell 1989, 1992) argue that the concept that the word refers to has been circulating for centuries. For now, I am not concerned with the historical question of when these categories were developed. Rather, I am concerned with whether humans in general have sexual orientations, that is, whether sexual orientations are natural human kinds. This question could only be formulated once the categories of sexual orientation had been articulated.

As the categories of sexual orientation began to circulate, essentialism gained a foothold. In general, as people become aware of a medical or scientific category, they almost inevitably come to think that there are people to whom these terms apply. Doctors and scientists—for example, Magnus Hirschfeld (1914) and Richard von Krafft-Ebing (1965)—who put forward theories of the origins of homosexuality implicitly accepted essentialism about sexual orientation. The accounts of the causes of homosexual desire and behavior they gave require that homosexuals are natural human kinds. This does not mean that they thought that homosexuality was necessarily innate. In fact, many early thinkers thought that homosexuality could be "cured," but still thought that homosexuals had a medical condition, in virtue of which scientific laws applied to them. As I will argue in the next section, essentialism about sexual orientation is compatible with environmental theories of how sexual orientations develop.

Constructionist views about sexual orientation were formulated in response to essentialism. Someone had to articulate the thought that sexual orientations are in effect natural human kinds before someone bothered to claim that sexual orientations are in effect merely social human kinds. Early constructionist sentiments were expressed by Kinsey and his collaborators when they wrote that people should not be "characterized as homosexuals and heterosexuals" (Kinsey, Pomeroy, and Martin 1948, 656); they were discouraging people from thinking that sexual orientations were natural human kinds. More recently, starting in the early 1970s, some of the rhetoric of the gay liberationist movement seemed implicitly to embrace constructionism. The notion of "bringing out the homosexual in everyone" (Wittman 1997, 388) suggests that it is a mistake to divide people into homosexuals and heterosexuals: if everyone has a gay side, then heterosexuals and homosexuals are empty human kinds. More explicit versions of constructionism about sexual orientation were formulated by academic theorists starting at about the same time. Using the tools of labeling theory (a theory that focuses on the effects of being labeled a deviant and of internalizing this label), the sociologist Mary McIntosh (1968) argued that homosexuals are created through social processes that emerge at a certain time in history. Although McIntosh did not explicitly make the same claim about heterosexuals, she would presumably accept that they are also created by social processes—although different processes than those that create homosexuals—and the internalization of the labels that they produce. Other theorists, working within different disciplinary frameworks and making different sorts of arguments, reached conclusions similar to McIntosh's.[4] Such theorists pointed to the contemporary emergence of sexual orientations and argued (though not using these words) that sexual orientations are not natural human kinds. As I discussed at the start of chapter 3, the debate between essentialists and constructionists is still unresolved, as is the question of its relevance. In the subsequent sections of this chapter, I clarify this debate and carve out a position on it.

## Why the Debate Does Not Reduce to the Nature-Nurture Debate

The debate between constructionism and essentialism is commonly confused with the issue of whether people have the particular sexual orientation they do in virtue of their genetic makeup (*nativism*) or their environment (*environmentalism*). As typically discussed, the issue between nativism and environmentalism (sometimes called the *nature-nurture debate*) is based on a false dichotomy—this is true not just with respect to nativism and environmentalism *about sexual orientation*, but to nativism and environmentalism *in general* as well. No human trait is strictly the result of genetics or strictly the result of environmental factors; all human traits are the result of both. There are genetic and neurological factors that affect even the most seemingly environmental traits, like what a person's major will be in college. On the other hand, environmental factors contribute to the development of even the most seemingly genetic traits, like eye color—if I had not gotten enough of certain sorts of vitamins and minerals at crucial times, my eyes would be a different color than they are, even though my genes would be the same. Despite the fact that every human trait is affected by *both* genetic and environmental factors, there does seem to be some variance in degree—that my eyes are hazel and that my blood type is B are more tightly constrained by genetic factors than that my major in college was philosophy and that I associate the word "tree" with tall, leafy plants found in forests. I have genes that make it almost certain that my eyes will be hazel, but I do not have genes that make it almost certain that I will major in philosophy—I do not even have genes that make it almost certain that *if* I live in a culture where there are colleges that offer philosophy degrees, I will major in philosophy. The nature-nurture debate about sexual orientation, properly understood, concerns where sexual orientation fits on the continuum between eye color on the one hand and college major on the other. (I will have more to say on these issues in chapters 5, 7, and 8.)

Many people assume that if essentialism is true, then sexual orientation is strongly constrained by genes, and if constructionism is true, then sexual orientation is primarily shaped by the environment. This is not the case. In general, it is possible for a group to be a natural human kind without it being the case that one fits into that group in virtue of one's genes. For example, being (or having been) a biological mother (in the sense of being a person who has given birth) is a natural human kind, but whether or not one is a member of either group is *not* genetically determined (even though one's genes do play an important role in whether or not it is biologically possible for a person to be a mother).

Essentialism about sexual orientation could still be true even if some environmental theory of how sexual orientations develop is true (see chapter 8). For example, if a person's sexual orientation is connected to his emotional interactions with his parents or with the nature of his first sexual encounter, then sexual orientations could still be natural human kinds. If, once the environmental factors have had their effects, a person has a naturalistically determinate sexual orientation and his or her brain instantiates a particular psychological state in virtue of which he or she is a heterosexual or homosexual, then certain scientific laws apply to this person. If such a theory is right, then sexual orientation would be a natural human kind, but it would not be primarily genetic. This shows that *natural human kinds need not have a genetic basis.*

The same example will suffice to show that if sexual orientation is shaped primarily by environmental factors, the truth of constructionism does not necessarily follow. According to some environmental theories of sexual orientation, sexual orientation is not innate, but constructionism would be false because, in virtue of its psychological basis, sexual orientation would be a natural human kind. The simple connections commonly thought to hold between the nature of the categories of sexual orientation and the cause of sexual orientation do not in fact hold: *essentialism does not entail nativism* and *environmentalism does not entail constructionism.**

The commonly held view that there is a connection between the essentialism-constructionism debate and the nature-nurture debate about sexual orientation is not, however, completely wrong. If sexual orientations are innate, then constructionism about sexual orientation is false and essentialism is true. Suppose that a person's sexual orientation is primarily determined by genetic factors. In this case, sexual orientations are innate. In virtue of the genes that I am positing as responsible for sexual orientation, there are natural human kinds associated with sexual orientations; sexual orientations appear in scientific laws involving these genes. If this is the case, then constructionism is false.[5] Additionally, other nativist accounts of sexual orientation, if true, establish essentialism about sexual orientation. Note, that for reasons developed earlier in this section, essentialism can be true even if nativism is false. According to some environmental theories of sexual orientations, essentialism is true but sexual orientations are not innate.

That the truth of nativism entails the truth of essentialism does not in itself constitute an objection to constructionism. It just makes clear that constructionism and essentialism are *empirical* theses, that is, they are claims that can only be established by observation and/or experimentation. In particular, essentialism and constructionism are empirical theses that are related to whether sexual orientation is innate: if nativism is true, then constructionism is false and essentialism is true. Relatedly, the truth of constructionism entails that nativism about sexual orientation is false; if sexual orientation is not a natural human kind, then it cannot be innate.

Given what I said in chapter 3 about natural kinds and natural human kinds, nothing I said in the preceding paragraph should be surprising. Whether a group is a natural kind depends on whether it is involved in various

---

*A similar argument shows that *voluntarism* (the view that people choose their sexual orientation) does not entail constructionism (and vice versa) and determinism does not entail essentialism. That my choices do not determine my sexual orientation does not entail that genetic factors do; there are *social* forms of determinism as well as genetic. For example, in some societies, being a member of a certain socioeconomic class is not a matter of a person's choice, but being a member of such a class is not a natural human kind. Although class might be a merely social kind, it might still be determined. Further, various versions of essentialism are consistent with the view that you can make choices that have an effect on your sexual oriention. See chapter 9 for more on voluntarism, determinism, and sexual orientation.

scientific laws, and it is an *empirical* question whether a group is involved in scientific laws. With respect to Zomnia, my claim that fronters and backers are not natural human kinds is an empirical claim; it is true or false depending on contingent facts, that is, facts about the world and the people who inhabit it that might have been otherwise. If, for example, it turned out that it is genetically determined that particular people sleep on their backs while others do not, then the Zomnian theory would be right and I would be wrong. What I need to do to show that the Zomnians are wrong is to prove that there are no natural human kinds associated with sleep positions. This is clearly an empirical project. At the end of chapter 3, I discussed the sort of evidence that is relevant to this empirical project. The same kind of evidence is relevant to the debate between essentialism and constructionism. In chapters 5 through 9, I consider in depth the empirical evidence relevant to determining whether sexual orientations are natural human kinds.

## "What Is a Sexual Orientation?" Revisited

In order to settle whether sexual orientations are natural human kinds, we need to clarify what we mean by sexual orientation, and we need to be sure that we have a wide definition of sexual orientation, that is, a definition of sexual orientation that has the potential to be applicable to various cultures because it does not refer to culture-specific properties. Although "homosexual" can be defined narrowly—by making reference to gay pride marches, rainbow flags, domestic partnership legislation, and other contemporary cultural notions that connect to homosexuality—there are problems with using this narrow definition in some contexts. Since there were no gay pride marches, rainbow flags, or domestic partnership laws associated with homosexuality in Attic Greece, the term "homosexual"—in this narrow sense of the term—could not even possibly apply to anyone from that culture. In the next several paragraphs, I consider problems with the narrow definition of sexual orientations in the context of whether sexual orientations are natural human kinds.

Some people want to say that the presence in all cultures of homosexual behavior and/or people with sexual desires for people of the same sex-gender is enough to establish the truth of the claim that our categories of sexual orientation are natural human kinds (Ruse 1988, 15–18; Weinrich 1987b, chapter 5). If the homosexuals are people who engage in sexual acts with people of the same sex-gender, then it follows that homosexuals existed in every culture because in every culture there are men who had sex with men and women who had sex with women. Although this sort of behavioral view of sexual orientation gives rise to a wide definition of sexual orientation, it is a mistake to simply focus on the sex of the people with whom a person engages in sex to determine their sexual orientation. As I argued in chapter 2, the dispositional view of sexual orientations is preferable to the behavioral view of sexual orientations; the focus should be on the sex-gender of the people to whom a person is sexually attracted, not simply the sex-gender of the people (if any) with whom a person has actually had sex. In particular, the question is whether it is right, for example, to say that Socrates was a homosexual in the sense that he had an underlying preference to have sex with men rather than women. This is a wide definition of sexual orientation.

Merely offering a dispositional (and wide) view of sexual orientation does not solve the debate between essentialism and constructionism, though some people have suggested that it does. Richard Mohr (1992b, 241) offers one such definition—a homosexual is a person who has "the desire for sexual relations with members of one's own biological sex"—as does Michael Ruse (1988, 18)—a homosexual is a "person whose erotic yearnings and fantasies are directed towards his/her own sex and whose activities are influenced by such yearning." Although Mohr's and Ruse's definitions are wide enough to be candidates for playing a role in scientific (or social scientific) explanations (although both definitions are rather vague[6]), their wideness does not prove that sexual orientations are natural human kinds. Even granting that every person in any culture has sexual desires and sexual tastes (asexuals aside), it does not follow that there are interesting generalizations that can be made about people who have specific sexual interests in people of the same sex. This is what needs to be the case for the categories of sexual orientation to be natural human kinds. Simply defining sexual orientations in a way that they are applicable to people in all cultures does not prove that they are natural human kinds (chapter 3). Arguments and evidence are needed to establish essentialism or constructionism. Ruse and Mohr both think they have given strong arguments for essentialism, but they have in fact failed to move beyond simply offering a wide definition of "homosexual." They fail to provide an argument that "homosexual," so defined, refers to a natural human kind.[7] While it is crucial to define the categories of sexual orientation in a wide enough manner that they are applicable to other cultures—something some constructionists fail to do, thereby stacking the deck in favor of constructionism (Mohr 1992b)—merely defining the categories of sexual orientation widely does not establish essentialism (or constructionism, for that matter); more argument or evidence is required.

## Some Arguments for Constructionism

I will now consider some arguments for constructionism. These arguments may seem appealing at first glance, but I shall show that they are unsatisfactory. I consider both *positive* arguments for constructionism (that is, arguments that attempt to establish constructionism directly) and *negative* arguments for constructionism (that is, arguments that attempt to establish constructionism by pointing to problems with essentialism). In the next section, I turn to a series of unsatisfactory arguments for essentialism.

### Argument from Cultural Variation

Some constructionists think that all they need to do to establish constructionism is to demonstrate that other cultures conceptualize human sexual desires in ways different from ours. They might point out that homosexuality takes many different forms in different cultures or that many cultures lack anything like our categories of sexual orientation. The existence of a wide range of cultural variation is supposed to show that sexual orientations do not exist in other cultures and thus that it is a mistake to think sexual orientations are natural human kinds.

The argument from cultural variation does not, however, show that constructionism is true. Cultural variation is perfectly consistent with the existence of underlying natural human kinds. Recall my earlier example involving the claim that the Attic Greeks had a different picture than we do of how reproduction occurred. Presumably, early Native American cultures had other different pictures of how human reproduction worked. There is, no doubt, over history and across cultures a great variety of theories of how human reproduction occurs. This cultural variation does not prove that reproduction occurred in different ways in different cultures; it just shows that reproduction means different things in different places. In fact, we are perfectly justified in believing that reproduction occurred in precisely the same way throughout the existence of the human species. With respect to sexual orientation, the fact that other cultures have other ways of thinking about human sexual desire and other ways of grouping people in virtue of their sexual interests does not prove that sexual orientations are not natural human kinds, but it also does not prove that they are merely social human kinds.

### Argument from Different Forms of Desire

A more sophisticated argument that some constructionists make points to another kind of cultural variation. According to this argument, it is not just that different cultures have different ways of thinking about sex and sexual desires;

different cultures *produce* different forms of sexual desire and different types of people. On this view, different ways of thinking about sex, sexual desire, and related matters produce dramatically different kinds of desires in people that in turn make their lives qualitatively different. The sorts of sexual lives that people live in some other cultures are so dramatically different from ours that the way we describe sexual activities in our culture cannot possibly describe their cultures. That there are various "forms of life" associated with sexual desire in various cultures is supposed to show that people in other cultures do not have sexual orientations. If people in other cultures are not possible candidates for being heterosexuals or homosexuals, then essentialism about sexual orientation is false.

It is certainly true that people in different cultures have radically different ways of looking at sex and sexual relationships and have different ways of expressing and experiencing sexual desire and sexual pleasure. However, only the most extreme essentialist would disagree with this. What most essentialists *would* disagree with is arguing from the fact that different societies have different ways of thinking about and experiencing sexual desire to the conclusion that, in such societies, there are no homosexuals or heterosexuals. To show that the argument based on different forms of life also fails, consider a (completely contrived) example involving epilepsy. Suppose that an anthropologist studying various societies' conceptions of epilepsy showed that different cultures had vastly different views of this condition and thereby constructed it differently. Suppose that Attic Greeks thought that epileptic fits were caused by Zeus to demonstrate his power; and that in medieval times, epileptics were thought to be possessed by the devil; and that in certain Native American cultures, epileptics were thought to have special powers and their fits were thought to be causally connected to rainstorms. Some cultures construct institutions and attitudes around epilepsy as a spiritual phenomenon (such as these three), whereas others construct institutions and attitudes around the epileptic condition as a disease (as our society does). A great diversity of social structures around this condition is perfectly compatible with the fact that epileptics are a natural human kind because epilepsy involves irregularities in neurotransmitters caused by certain genetic configurations. Even if societies conceive and construct epilepsy in quite different ways and, as a result, epileptics in different cultures conceptualize and experience epilepsy in different ways, an epileptic is still a natural human kind. The different forms of life argument for constructionism thus fails.

### Argument from Antirealism

I turn now to an evaluation of another positive argument for constructionism. Recall from chapter 3 my discussion of whether natural kinds exist. In that discussion, I introduced nominalism, the view that there are no natural kinds. If nominalism is true, it follows that there are no natural *human* kinds and, thus, that sexual orientations are not natural human kinds. The position that there are no natural human kinds is part of a general philosophical view known as *antirealism* (although it goes by other names as well). Antirealists, roughly, deny the existence of a reality that exists independent of perceptions and conceptualizations of it. As a result, antirealists do not believe in the existence of laws of science or natural kinds, and more generally, they do not believe that there are objective truths.* People are antirealists for various reasons, among them that all beliefs are mediated by language and culture and that all observations are necessarily based on some undefended theory. These two claims— that all our beliefs and observations are mediated by implicit assumptions and that these assumptions are undefended—lead antirealists to the conclusion that nothing can be proven, that no one can justifiably believe anything, and further, that there are no objective truths. (*Skepticism* is the view that we have no good reason to believe that there are laws of science or natural kinds or objective truth; the skeptic abstains from taking a position on whether realism or antirealism is true. Skepticism is an *epistemological* thesis; antirealism is a *metaphysical* thesis.) The impossibility of objective truth entails that there are no laws of science and no natural kinds. From this, it follows that our categories of sexual orientation cannot refer to natural human kinds. I call this the antirealist argument for constructionism.

I have two things to say about this argument. First, as an argument for constructionism about sexual orientation, the antirealist argument amounts to throwing out the baby with the bath water. The bath water is composed of the categories "heterosexual" and "homosexual," which the constructionist wants to say do not refer to natural kinds, while the baby is the rest of our categories. Constructionism about sexual orientation says that sexual orientations are not natural human kinds, but it also implicitly says that there are some natural kinds, perhaps being a proton or being a person with blood type B. If antirealism is true, then there is nothing special about sexual orientation; sexual orientations are, at best, merely social kinds (or they might be empty kinds), but the same is true of *all* groups that we think are natural kinds—for example, having a Y chromosome or being a proton would either be social kinds or empty kinds as well. Constructionism is an interesting position *about sexual orientation* only if some version of realism is true. Antirealism may be an inter-

---

*So defined, antirealism is a *wider* claim than nominalism. All antirealists are also nominalists, but some nominalists might not be antirealists. For example, someone who believed in some truths but denied that there are natural kinds would be a nominalist, but *not* an antirealist.

esting position in metaphysics in general (Putnam 1987; Rorty 1979), but it says nothing particular about sexual orientation. More than being like throwing the baby out with the bath water, using a general antirealist argument to establish constructionism is like (beware of falling metaphors) using an atomic bomb to kill a fly—an atomic bomb will kill a fly, but it will take almost everything else with it, including most of the reasons one might have had for wanting to kill the fly in the first place. Constructionism is the claim that sexual orientations are not natural human kinds; this is only an interesting claim if there are other categories that *do* refer to natural kinds. The antirealist argument for constructionism attempts to establish constructionism by arguing that there are no natural human kinds at all. This is too high a price to pay to establish constructionism about sexual orientation.

Second, taken as a general claim in metaphysics, antirealism is a highly problematic thesis. I here only sketch some of my reasons for thinking this. To begin, if there are no natural kinds, then there can be no explanation for the apparent and abundant regularities of nature. Consider just a few random regularities of nature: the sun has risen every day in the past; all samples of copper conduct electricity; and primates die when they have no air to breathe. Each of these regularities cries out for an explanation. If antirealism is true, there can be no explanations of these regularities because there are no scientific laws and no natural kinds. We think, however, that such regularities can be explained. This suggests that there is something wrong with antirealism. Further, antirealism is self-refuting. Anyone who claims that there are no absolute truths is open to a question about what sort of claim she is making. If her claim that there are no absolute truths is supposed to be an absolute truth itself, then her claim is self-refuting—if it is true, it cannot be true—and thus false (Mackie 1964; Stein 1996, 216–221). If her claim is merely the expression of an opinion, then the claim is not self-refuting, but it is not particularly interesting; if her claim is just a mere opinion that is not even supposed to be true, why should anybody else be interested in it? As a general claim, antirealism is false; as a mere opinion, it is not especially interesting.[8] Antirealism is, I think, an untenable philosophical position. More importantly, as an argument for constructionism about sexual orientation, it is impotent.

### Argument from the Simplicity of Essentialism

I now turn to *negative* arguments for constructionism, namely arguments that attempt to establish constructionism by arguing against essentialism. First, some constructionists have argued that essentialists are committed to giving an overly simplistic account of sexual orientation. Essentialism, these critics argue, is committed to the view that there is some single property that everyone of a particular sexual orientation must have. They then argue that there is no such property and hence that essentialism is false and constructionism is true.

This argument against essentialism is tantamount to saying that essentialism is committed to essenceism. Recall from chapter 3 that essenceism about a category is the claim that the particular category has an essence and that having this essence constitutes a necessary and sufficient condition for membership in that category. For example, having two parts hydrogen and one part oxygen is the essence of water; for something to be water, it is required that it be made of two parts hydrogen and one part oxygen (the *necessary* condition); if something is made of two parts hydrogen and one part oxygen, then it is thereby water (the *sufficient* condition). With respect to sexual orientation, *essentialism about sexual orientation does not entail essenceism about sexual orientation.* Some essentialists about sexual orientation are, however, also essenceists about sexual orientation. For example, someone who thinks that all forms of homosexuality are caused by the size of the INAH-3 region of the hypothalamus is both an essentialist and an essenceist about sexual orientation. An essentialist does not, however, need to accept this theory or any other essenceist theory; an essentialist can hold that sexual orientation is a cluster property, namely, that sexual orientation is a natural human kind, but there are no necessary and sufficient conditions for having a sexual orientation. This position is consistent with it being the case that our categories of sexual orientation apply to people in other cultures. If this were the case, then essentialism about sexual orientation would be true while essenceism about sexual orientation would be false. For now, I have shown that some essentialists are essenceists, but not all of them are. In other words, *one can accept that sexual orientations are natural human kinds without being committed to the view that sexual orientations have essences.*

As I will show in subsequent chapters, many versions of essentialism about sexual orientation that have been proposed seem to be essenceist theories as well: they posit specific naturalistic properties—for example, the number of cells in the INAH-3 region of the hypothalamus or the level of a particular hormone in the bloodstream—associated with a person's sexual orientation. These theories cannot be refuted as a group just because they embrace essenceism. The negative argument for constructionism attempts to defeat all such theories with a simple abstract wave of the hand against essenceism about sexual orientation. Such general arguments against essenceism will not refute essentialism for two reasons. First, as I have shown, essentialism does not require essenceism. Second, particular essenceist (or essentialist) theories of sexual orientation—such as the one that involves the INAH-3 region of the hypothalamus—since they are empirical, cannot be defeated without specific examination. I turn to such examinations in chapters 5 through 9.

## Some Arguments for Essentialism

### Argument from Involuntariness

I turn now to some initially appealing arguments for essentialism, arguments that, ultimately, do not succeed. First, many people in our society (especially men) experience their sexual orientation as a fixed and determinate fact about themselves. "For as long as I can remember, I have always been attracted to other men" is a common refrain among gay men. Some thinkers have tried to parlay this common experience into an argument for essentialism. The thought is that such a deep feeling, one maintained in the face of especially negative social attitudes, must be closely linked to a person's biology or psychology in such a way that sexual orientations are natural human kinds. Andrew Sullivan, a former editor of the *New Republic,* has made roughly this argument. Sullivan argues for the conclusion that constructionism is false on the basis of the premise that "for the overwhelming majority of [homosexual] adults, the condition of homosexuality is as involuntary as heterosexuality is for heterosexuals [and] . . . is evident from the very beginning of the formation of a person's emotional identity" (Sullivan 1995, 17).[9]

As I argued earlier, the truth of nativism about sexual orientation does entail the truth of essentialism about sexual orientation; if some genetic factor causes an innate sexual orientation, then this would support the view that sexual orientation is a natural human kind. But the fact that many lesbians and gay men in our culture experience their sexual orientation as involuntary does not in any way establish the truth of nativism about sexual orientation or, for that matter, of any essentialist theory of sexual orientation. Let me explain why.

There are serious problems with the argument that moves from a person's sense that his sexual orientation is determined at an early age to the conclusion that essentialism about sexual orientation is true. First, people are not reliable at discovering the *source* of something as complex as their own sexual dispositions simply through introspection. Self-examination is a notoriously misleading way to do science (Lyons 1986; Stein 1996, 158–161). Just because you think that your sexual orientation was not a choice, that it has been the same since birth, and so on, does not mean that it is so. (I develop this argument at greater length in chapter 8).

Second, it is a mistake to base a generalization about all people on the experience of some people in a rather limited set of cultures. While it may be true that many people in our culture experience their sexual orientation as determined at an early age and as not a matter of choice, this is not necessarily the case in other cultures. Vera Whisman (1996) suggests that many nonheterosexuals in this culture actually experience their sexual orientations as choices. For the argument from involuntariness to establish essentialism, one would need to begin by showing that everyone across all cultures views one's own sexual orientation as determined. Even restricted to this culture, this seems not to be the case in general. Various studies have suggested that women experience their sexual orientations as more fluid than men do (see chapter 5). Even if, contrary to what I have said, the involuntariness of sexual orientations were a good argument for essentialism, the argument would show that men's sexual orientations are natural human kinds, but not that women's sexual orientations are. This is an odd result to say the least.

Third, even if most people think that their sexual orientations are involuntary, this still does not show that one's sexual orientation is innate, and hence this does not establish the truth of essentialism. Consider the property of being a member of a certain economic or social class. One can have a sense of being born a member of a class, of not having a choice about what one's class is (especially in cultures with highly stratified class systems), and so on, but being a member of a certain class is not a biological or an innate property; in fact, it is a paradigmatic example of a socially constructed property. Just as one might have the sense of not being able to choose to be a member of any social or economic class, even though membership in such a class is a cultural artifact, so too one might experience one's sexual orientation as determined and determinate, yet sexual orientation might still be a merely *social* human kind, *not* a *natural* human kind.

### Argument from Cultural Universality

Some people have tried to defend essentialism about sexual orientation without appealing directly to how people experience their sexual orientations. Instead, they cite historical, anthropological, and related evidence for the claim that homosexuals and heterosexuals exist in all cultures. The best explanation for the universality of sexual orientation, they say, is the truth of essentialism. If the various sexual orientations were not natural human kinds, then the universality of sexual orientation would just be an incredible coincidence. Given the incredible odds against such a coincidence, essentialism is almost surely true

(Boswell 1980, 1989, 1992; Mohr 1992b; Ruse 1988). Perhaps the quickest version of this argument comes from Michael Ruse: "[I]t is surely the case that in all societies (across time and space) there are some individuals with more or less exclusively homosexual inclinations. . . . This . . . is . . . a factual claim and thus needs evidence" (Ruse 1988, 17). In a single paragraph, he then goes on to cite some evidence from the work of John Boswell to show "in full detail that right through the ages from Ancient Greece to the Renaissance, there were men and women who were recognized as having a . . . homosexual orientation" (18).

There are several problems with this line of argument. As we saw earlier in my discussion of *The Symposium,* constructionists can agree with the historical and anthropological evidence cited by essentialists but disagree with their interpretation of it. Where essentialists see homosexuals and heterosexuals, constructionists may see people with sexual dispositions quite different from homosexuals and heterosexuals of today. Here, the "width" of the categories of sexual orientation is crucial (recall my discussion in chapter 3). Homosexuality in Attic Greece was typically of the transgenerational form (that is, there was typically a significant age or status difference between same-sex sexual partners), while homosexuality in contemporary North America more closely fits the egalitarian form (that is, same-sex partners are typically of roughly the same age and often of the same status). If "homosexual" is defined narrowly as referring to the egalitarian form common in contemporary culture, then there were few if any homosexuals in Attic Greece. If "homosexual" is defined more broadly, then at least a stronger case for cross-cultural similarity can be made. But the problem with a wider definition is that it might be too broad. This is one of the problems with the behavioral view of sexual orientation. There is no *conceptual* problem determining whether a person had sex with a person of the same sex (setting aside the problems—discussed in chapter 2—of defining what it is to have sex and what it is to be of certain sex). One of the problems with the behavioral view is that it might count as homosexuals some people who are not really homosexuals. The behavioral view would count as homosexual a man who is almost exclusively interested in sex with women but has sex with men in the context of an extended stay in an all-male prison. This definition of "homosexual," while it is wide enough to be applied to other cultures, counts some people as homosexuals who are not homosexuals.

The problem with the cultural universality argument for essentialism can be usefully understood in light of the example of Zomnia. A Zomnian theorist could point to the sleep behaviors of people in other cultures (like, for example, my behavior of sleeping primarily on my stomach) and claim that the categories of sleep orientation apply to me and people like me. In light of this sort of evidence, the Zomnian might claim that sleep orientations are natural human kinds. But showing that sleep orientations apply to people in other cultures does not thereby establish that they are natural kinds. Similarly, showing that sexual orientations, defined behaviorally, apply to people in other cultures, does not thereby establish that they are natural kinds.

### Argument from the Ubiquity of Sex Drive

Several essentialists defend their position by appealing to the existence of a basic sex drive. For example, as part of his critique of constructionism, Richard Mohr argues that "homosexual behavior may be genetically driven like the drive to eat or to sleep" by appealing to the fact that "sex drive appears to be relevantly like such biological needs as eating and sleep, in that it occurs independently of one's acts and intentions" (Mohr 1992b, 229). Similarly, Simon LeVay supports his belief in "the existence . . . of homosexuality" (by which he means essentialism) by saying that "[s]exual attraction is an aspect of consciousness; it is directly experienced, like hunger, thirst, seeing the color red, taking fright, loving one's mother, and countless other aspects of our mental life" (LeVay, 1996, 56). Both Mohr and LeVay miss the point. Even if we grant that there is a biologically based sex drive, this does not in any way establish that sexual orientation is a natural human kind any more than it establishes that being attracted primarily to people with red hair is a natural human kind. What is at issue between essentialists and constructionists is not whether there is a sex drive, but whether there are natural human kinds associated with a person's preferences with respect to the sex-gender of his or her sexual partner. Showing that people have a sex drive does not establish essentialism. It is consistent with constructionism about sexual orientation that all people have a sex drive. Constructionists deny that there are natural human kinds associated with sexual orientations; Mohr and LeVay conflate the existence of a sex drive and the existence of natural human kinds associated with having a sex drive of a particular type.

## Conclusion

The debate between essentialism and constructionism about sexual orientation is a debate about whether sexual orientations are natural human kinds and, hence, whether sexual orientations will function in scientific laws and scientific explanations. Understanding this debate is a necessary precondition for answering metaphysical, scientific, and ethical questions about sexual orientation.

We live in a culture in which one's sexual orientation is an important fact about a person, a fact that seems deep and open to scientific explanation. Essentialists about sexual orientation try to build on this fact about our culture to argue for the claim that heterosexuals and homosexuals are natural human kinds. In contrast, constructionists deny that our categories of sexual orientation refer to natural human kinds. They say the same things about our categories of sexual orientation that I say about the Zomnian categories of sleep orientation. The big difference between the Zomnian categories of sleep orientation and our categories of sexual orientation is that Zomnia is made-up while our culture is real. No one is interested in figuring out whether or not backers and fronters are *really* natural human kinds. Lots of people are, however, interested in figuring out whether or not homosexuals and heterosexuals constitute natural human kinds; the debate between essentialists and constructionists is real, and it is contentious. Earlier I argued that this is an empirical debate. If we want to determine whether sexual orientation is best understood with the standard tools of scientific scrutiny, we need to determine whether homosexuals and heterosexuals are natural human kinds and whether they can figure in scientific laws and scientific explanations. How can this be done?

Think about what would be involved in definitively proving to a Zomnian that sleep orientations are not natural human kinds. It might be useful to introduce them to other cultures, past and present, that do not have their categories of sleep orientation. While exposing them to other ways of thinking about people might be suggestive, such evidence will not ultimately be convincing. It is open to a Zomnian to say that other cultures are not advanced in their understanding of human nature. An advanced science would, a Zomnian might say, discover that backers and fronters are bona fide natural human kinds and would provide a scientific account of how people develop their sleep orientations. To really convince a Zomnian that sleep orientations are not natural human kinds, we would need to refute their scientific theories and point to general problems that would face any theory that sees sleep orientations as natural human kinds.

The same evidentiary situation holds with respect to sexual orientation. To establish constructionism, one must refute specific scientific theories that see sexual orientations as natural human kinds and point to general problems that would face *any* such theory. In contrast, to establish essentialism, one must defend a specific scientific theory in which sexual orientations are seen as natural human kinds. Either way, empirical questions need to be answered. In an attempt to make progress on the debate between essentialism and constructionism, I turn in part II ("Science") to various scientific theories relating to human sexual orientation. I begin by discussing in detail what I call the emerging scientific research program concerned with sexual orientation. In chapter 5, I present the recent biological research concerning sexual orientation in a positive light. In chapters 6 and 7, I criticize the assumptions and methodology of this research program. In chapter 8, I consider experiential theories of the development of sexual orientation. I will argue that the empirical questions relevant to the debate between essentialists and constructionists are not at all settled. Whether sexual orientation is a natural human kind is, I will argue, an open question.

# PART II
Science

# CHAPTER 5

*The Emerging Scientific
Program for the Study
of Sexual Orientation*

## Why Science?

Since the late 1800s, scientists, physicians, and mental health specialists have
been interested in how people develop sexual orientations. In pursuing this
interest, these researchers have typically studied gay men; occasionally, lesbians;
to a lesser extent, bisexuals; and, to a much lesser extent, heterosexuals.
Initially, the special interest in homosexuality was connected to the desire to
cure or eliminate what was seen as a sexual perversion, an interest some recent
studies explicitly deny. Whatever their motivations, the studies of sexual orientations done in the last one hundred or so years vary dramatically in their
motivations, methodological approaches, disciplinary foundations, working
hypotheses, and general conclusions. One could write an entire book detailing
the history of this research (Bullough 1994; Irvine 1990; Robinson 1989).
Although I will occasionally make points about this history, my main focus in
the next three chapters is to consider biological theories of sexual orientation
that contemporary thinkers take seriously. I discuss psychological or experiential theories of sexual orientation in chapter 8. In the next section of this
chapter, I discuss the distinction between biological and psychological theories
of sexual orientation.

Contemporary scientific theories concerning sexual orientation warrant attention for several reasons. First, science has proven a great source of insight into many diverse questions. Comparing what the Attic Greeks knew with what we know today, one discovers great disparity. Collectively, we know a lot more about the world and about the creatures who inhabit it. Much of what we know today that the Greeks did not know comes from the development of and advancement within the natural sciences; compared to the Greeks, we have more detailed and accurate theories in the physical sciences; and we know more than the Greeks about human nature, both physically and psychologically. Humans live longer and have a higher quality of life due in part to the maturation of the medical sciences and discoveries in such basic sciences as biology and chemistry. If we want to understand human sexual orientation and sexual desires, it seems reasonable to look to science. This is not to say that science will have all the answers, but given its success in other realms and the claims it makes with regards to human sexuality, scientific research warrants close examination.

Second, in the past few years, several scientific studies have been published that have begun to reshape the paradigm for scientific research on sexual orientation. These studies appeared in top scientific journals, are widely cited, and they seem to have the potential to come together to form a systematic research program. Three main pieces of this emerging research program are the neuroanatomical work of Simon LeVay (1991); the heritability studies of Michael Bailey, Richard Pillard, and their collaborators (Bailey and Pillard 1991b; Bailey, Pillard, and Agyei 1993); and the genetic linkage studies done by Dean Hamer, Angela Pattatucci, and their collaborators (Hamer et al. 1993; Hu et al. 1995; Pattatucci and Hamer 1995). These studies are widely interpreted as indicating that sexual orientations are strongly biologically based and that the biological basis is inborn or determined at an early age. The scope and prestige of this research program—which I will sometimes refer to as the *emerging scientific program for the study of sexual orientation* or some variation of this—at least suggests that science is making progress with respect to sexual orientation. In the present chapter, I pay particular attention to the work of these three research teams.

Third, scientific research on sexual orientation seems to fit well with the intuition, shared by many people, that sexual orientations are not the result of choice. The sense that people do not choose their sexual orientation suggests to many people that sexual orientation requires a genetic or biological explanation. The emerging research program and the studies that are its backbone fit with this intuitive sense about sexual orientation. That such studies fit with many people's intuitions about their own sexual orientations also suggests that the emerging research program is worth considering.

Fourth, studies of sexual behavior and desires of animals suggest that, in some ways, animals exhibit sexual behaviors and preferences that are, in significant ways, similar to human sexual behavior and sexual orientation. Models of human sexual orientation have been articulated in fruit flies (Ferveur et al. 1995), ferrets (Baum et al. 1990), finches (Adkins-Regan and Ascenzi 1987), and various other nonhuman animals (Nadler 1990; Vasey 1995). That human sexual orientation may be amenable to such a wide variety of animal models suggests that human sexual orientation is, to a significant extent, open to biological study.

Fifth, biological theories of sexual orientation fit especially well with evolutionary theory, which plays an important explanatory role in biology and in giving an account of human nature more generally. At the center of evolutionary theory is the theory of natural selection. This theory explains the origin of the species by focusing on the relative reproduction success of organisms. As such, natural selection holds great promise for giving an account of human biological and psychological mechanisms that relate to sex. Some have attempted to articulate an evolutionary theory of sexual desires (Buss 1994), and many scientists and other thinkers interested in sexual orientation see evolutionary theory as playing an important role in their research project (Hamer and Copeland 1994, 180–186; LeVay 1996, 188–193; McKnight 1997; Posner 1992, 85–110; Ruse 1988, 130–149). These evolutionary explanations will, however, seem as much science fiction as science unless such accounts can be paired with plausible stories of the mechanisms that underlie human and perhaps nonhuman animal sexual desires. Accounts of the evolution of such mechanisms, accounts of the biological mechanisms in humans, and studies of sexual behaviors and desires in nonhuman animals potentially have mutually supporting relationships. We can better understand human sexual desires from an evolutionary perspective if we understand the sexual lives of other animals. We are better positioned to understand the biological mechanisms of human sexual desire if we understand the mechanisms that underlie nonhuman animals' sexual behaviors. If there are plausible accounts of the selective advantage of certain sorts of mechanisms underlying sexual desire, this would lend support to biological accounts that explain sexual desires by appeal to such mechanisms. If scientists can articulate plausible accounts of the mechanisms underlying human and nonhuman sexual desire, then this would support evolutionary accounts that appeal to such mechanisms. For now, I just note that among the reasons for examining the emerging scientific research program is that it has the potential to mesh nicely with evolutionary theory.

Sixth, whatever their merits, recent studies of the development of sexual orientations have garnered a great deal of positive attention in the media and among the general public. Scientific research on sexual orientation has been reported on the front pages of newspapers across America and on the covers of the most widely read weekly news magazines (for example, Gelman 1992). In addition, a growing number of people in the United States, and many people in other countries, now believe that human sexual orientation is biologically based (Berke 1998; Ernulf, Innala, and Whitam 1989; Inglehart 1990, 194, Table 6-8). This is in contrast to what most people believed in 1970 when "environmental" theories of homosexuality were more popular (Klassen, Williams, and Levitt 1989, 186–171).[1] The fact that many people believe them does not mean that these theories are true. That many people believe these theories does, however, count as a reason to examine them closely.

Seventh, many people have argued that the truth of certain scientific theories concerning sexual orientation has interesting and important ethical, legal, and political implications. In particular, the scientists doing this research think that their work has the potential to make the case for lesbian and gay rights (LeVay 1996, 231–254). For example, Michael Bailey and Richard Pillard, writing on the op-ed page of the *New York Times* wrote, "Science is converging on the conclusion that sexual orientation is innate. [Such a conclusion] . . . is good news for homosexuals and their advocates" (Bailey and Pillard 1991a). Enthusiasm about such scientific research is not restricted to scientists. Some lesbian and gay rights advocates maintain that by bolstering the claim that sexual orientation is not chosen, the biological evidence will enhance society's tolerance of homosexuality, making a variety of social and political goals more easily attainable (Bawer 1993; Sullivan 1995). In particular, studies of animal sexual behavior are often seen as relevant to ethical questions. For example, some people have claimed that if most animal species engage in same-sex sexual activity, then this will show that homosexuality is "natural." Whether the scientific arguments have such implications is among the topics of chapter 10. The initial plausibility of such scientific arguments justifies the concern with scientific research on sexual orientation.

Finally, as I argued in the previous chapter, scientific research on sexual orientation is relevant to the debate between essentialists and constructionists. If there is a particular biological basis for homosexuality and heterosexuality, then, in virtue of this, homosexuality and heterosexuality are natural human kinds and essentialism is true. If essentialism is true, it would make sense to talk about lesbians, gay men, and heterosexuals in other cultures. If essentialism is false, we might need other terms for talking about the sexual desires of people in other cultures. Also, the debate between essentialism and constructionism may prove to be relevant to ethical questions independent of the relevance of scientific research to such questions.

As a specific example of the value of looking at the current scientific research, suppose, as LeVay and Hamer suggest in a coauthored article in *Scientific American,* that a specific portion of a particular chromosome in men (the q28 region of the X chromosome) codes for a set of proteins that leads a certain region of the human hypothalamus (the INAH-3 region) to develop in a way that in turn leads a person to develop into either a gay man or a heterosexual man (LeVay and Hamer 1994). If correct, their suggestion would provide a quite specific account of the biological basis of sexual orientation. Further, if their suggestion—or something like it—is right, this might have far-reaching consequences. Their theory would provide new insight into human nature, especially into the basis of complex behavioral traits and psychological mechanisms and their evolution. The theory would fit with the widely held intuition that sexual orientations are determined. The theory would establish the truth of essentialism and legitimate talk of homosexuals and heterosexuals in historical and anthropological research. And, by showing that people do not choose their sexual orientations, the truth of such a theory might have significant ethical, legal, and political implications. Given the various reasons for being interested in sexual orientation and in sexual desires more broadly construed, there are several strong reasons for examining the scientific theories.

In the present chapter, I describe the important contemporary scientific theories of sexual orientation in generally positive terms. I put the emerging scientific program in historical context, I try to explain why it is plausible, and I survey the scientific evidence in support of the emerging research program. In chapter 6, I examine animal models of human sexual orientation and consider the evolution of human sexual desires. In chapter 7, I turn to a critical examination of the emerging research program with a focus on its methodological and theoretical assumptions. My conclusion in both chapters 6 and 7 is that the evidence in favor of the emerging research program is weak.

## What Makes a Theory a Biological One?

Before I describe contemporary biological theories of sexual orientation, I will discuss what sorts of claims these theories make. To say that sexual orientation is biologically based is an ambiguous claim; there are various senses in which it is trivially true that sexual orientation is biological. Everything psychological is biologically based. I am the sort of entity that can have a sexual orientation, while my computer and a one-celled organism are not. Why? The biological/psychological structure that makes me a human—rather than a computer or an amoeba—makes it possible for me to have a sexual orientation. This is not a terribly interesting claim. The same sort of claim is true with respect to having a favorite type of music. My computer and a single-celled organism cannot have a favorite type of music. Even though my preference for classical music seems a paradigmatic example of a learned trait, there is a sense in which my musical preferences are biologically based as well. Sexual orientation is at least biologically based in the sense that musical preferences are; even if sexual orientation were primarily caused by environmental factors, it would still be biological in this sense. When discussing proposed alternatives to biological theories of sexual orientation, John Money (1988, 50) wrote that "the postnatal determinants that enter the brain through the senses by way of social communication and learning are also biological, for there is a biology of learning and remembering." Any even vaguely plausible theory about how people develop sexual orientations (even one that sees social factors as playing a crucial role in determining a person's sexual orientation) is a biological theory in this sense. The emerging scientific research program on sexual orientation must be making a stronger claim than that sexual orientation is biologically based in this sense.[2]

The central claim of the emerging research program that studies sexual orientation is that a person's sexual orientation is inborn or determined at a very early age and, as a result, is "wired into" his or her brain. However the details are worked out, the claim is that sexual orientation is biologically based in some strong sense of the term. As William Byne (1994, 50) put it, "The salient question about biology and sexual orientation is not whether biology is involved but how it is involved." The studies that have enabled the scientific research program concerning sexual orientation to emerge have in common a thesis about how biology is involved in sexual orientation: *a person's biological makeup at birth or at an early age* determines *or strongly* constrains *his or her sexual orientation,* in particular, it determines (or strongly constrains) whether a person is attracted primarily to men or women. This is an interesting and nontrivial claim. It is important to keep in mind that this is the claim at the heart of the emerging research program concerned with sexual orientation. In this chapter, I present evidence for this claim. In chapters 6 and 7, I critically examine this evidence and its theoretical underpinnings.

To get clearer on what this claim involves, consider some other human characteristics with respect to the degree that they are biologically based.

Consider first a person's eye color, a trait that (tinted contact lenses aside) is about as biologically based as can be. This does not, however, mean that a person's eye color is completely and unalterably determined by one's genes. There are various links between one's genes and one's eye color. Genes code for patterns of protein synthesis. Proteins lead to the development of things like hormones, other proteins, and, ultimately, eyes. The appropriate proteins will be synthesized only given certain environmental conditions (such as the availability of various chemical compounds in the body). Further, these proteins will lead to the development of eyes only given appropriate developmental conditions. If a developing human fetus fails to get water, certain vitamins and minerals, and so on, it will fail to develop eyes of the color typically associated with the genes that the fetus has; in the face of severe lack of the appropriate compounds, an infant might fail to develop functional eyes. The point is that a gene or a set of genes for eye color do not as straightforwardly lead to actual eye color as one might have thought. In spite of this, because a person's eye color is coded for in a person's genes, which strongly dispose that person to develop a certain eye color, eye color is biologically based.

Consider next a person's musical tastes (which might include whether one prefers classical music to country music or, more generally, loud and cacophonous music to soft and melodic music) or a person's favorite television show. These characteristics of humans are quite different from eye color with respect to the degree to which they are biologically based: a person's musical tastes seem weakly biologically based. Biology does, however, have something to do with musical taste. An amoeba cannot have musical tastes or a favorite television show. Further, biological differences between individuals do contribute in some way to their different tastes in music and television shows. For example, people who have genes for especially good hearing might be more likely to appreciate certain kinds of music (perhaps more subtle or intricate kinds). The connection to genes is much less direct and the contributions of the environment are much more significant in the case of musical tastes than in the case of eye color.

With these two simple examples, we can imagine a continuum representing the contribution of biological factors to a trait. Eye color and blood type would be at one end (representing *strongly* biologically based) and favorite television show and taste in music would be at the other (representing *weakly* biologically based). In the middle would be something like biceps circumference. The size of one's biceps is similar to the color of one's eyes in that one's genes have quite a lot to do with both; however, postnatal environmental factors can have a greater impact on biceps size than on eye color. If I lift heavy objects, frequently, my biceps will get bigger. Although biceps size is malleable, there are constraints, and some people are just genetically better suited than others to develop large biceps. The debate about the extent to which sexual orientation is biologically based is, roughly, a debate about where sexual orientation falls on this continuum, that is, whether sexual orientation is more like eye color, biceps size, or musical tastes. The emerging scientific research program sees sexual orientation as more like eye color than musical taste or biceps size.

To do more to flesh out what it means for something to be biological, it is useful to contrast three models of the role genes and other biological factors might play in sexual orientation (Byne 1996; Byne and Parsons 1993). According to the *permissive model,* genes or other biological factors influence neuroanatomical structures on which experience inscribes sexual orientation, but biological factors do not directly or indirectly determine sexual orientation. It is consistent with this view that genetic factors constrain the period during which experience can affect a person's sexual orientation. Various genetic and biological factors make it possible for our experiences with various kinds of music to shape our musical preferences. While genetic and other biological factors surely play a role in making it possible for humans to have musical preferences and may well constrain the ways in which experience shapes musical preferences, such factors probably do not determine, either directly or indirectly, a person's particular musical preferences. Something like the permissive model correctly describes the development of musical preferences.

Contrast the permissive model with the *direct model,* according to which genes, hormones, or other biological factors directly influence the brain structures that underlie sexual orientation. According to the direct model, the neurological structures responsible for the direction of a person's sexual attraction towards men or women develop at a very early age as a result of a person's genes or other biological factors. Most researchers working in the emerging research program on sexual orientation favor the direct model. Typically, when they say that sexual orientation is biologically based, they mean to be endorsing the direct model of sexual orientation. A version of the direct model is LeVay and Hamer's suggestion that the q28 region of the X chromosome codes for a set of proteins that causes the INAH-3 region of the hypothalamus to develop so as to determine a person's sexual orientation (LeVay and Hamer 1994).

Finally, the direct and the permissive models can be contrasted with the *indirect model,* according to which genes code for (and/or other biological factors influence) temperamental or personality factors that shape how a person interacts with one's environment and one's experiences of it, which, in turn, affects the development of a person's sexual orientation. On this view, the same gene (or set of genes) might predispose to homosexuality in some environments, to heterosexuality in others, and have no effect on sexual orientation in others. An example of such a theory is Daryl Bem's "experienced-based developmental" theory of sexual orientation (Bem 1996a). According to Bem's theory, biological factors code for childhood personality types and temperaments (aggressiveness, willingness to engage in physical contact, and so on). In *gender-polarized societies* like ours—that is, in societies where there are significantly different gender roles typically associated with men and women—these different personality and temperament types get molded into gender roles, which in turn play a crucial role in the development of sexual orientation (I discuss Bem's theory in chapter 8).

It is important to keep in mind that there are rival theories of how biology plays a role in shaping sexual orientation. For this reason, I return to this tripartite distinction several times throughout the course of this book. Although most scientists whose research is part of the emerging scientific program embrace the direct model, their experimental results, even taken at face value, are, I shall argue in chapter 7, also consistent with the indirect model. In what follows, as I am introducing the emerging research program, I focus on theories that fit the direct model. My focus in turn is articulating scientific studies that look for the origins of sexual orientation in bodies, families, and genes.

## Looking for Sexual Orientation in Bodies

In this section, I consider explanations of the development of sexual orientations that involve the human body. I begin by discussing studies that focus on the body types of gay men and lesbians compared to heterosexuals. I then consider studies that concern hormone levels. Finally, I consider studies that focus on neuroanatomical features of the brain, paying particular attention to Simon LeVay's hypothalamus study.

### External Body Types

Karl Heinrich Ulrichs, a nineteenth-century German writer and one of the first modern writers concerned with people ordinarily attracted to people of the same sex-gender, in one of his earliest works, compared lesbians and gay men (he used the terms *uringins* and *urings*, respectively) to hermaphrodites. Hermaphrodites have some physical features typically associated with one sex-gender and some physical features typically associated with the other. The comparison that Ulrichs made between hermaphrodites, on the one hand, and lesbians and gay men, on the other, seemed appropriate because he thought sexual attraction to women was necessarily a male feeling (even if it was felt by a person with the body of a woman) and sexual attraction to men was necessarily a female feeling (even if felt by a person with the body of a man). Viewed in this way, lesbians and gay men had the physical features of one sex-gender and the sexual instinct of the other. According to the commonly held view of the time, a person's sexual instinct resides in his or her soul; lesbians and gay men were, according to Ulrichs, the result of hermaphroditism of the soul (Kennedy 1988). While not everyone believed that sexual orientation was based in the soul, the view that homosexuality is a form of hermaphroditism has dominated scientific thinking about homosexuality. Some researchers thought that this hermaphroditism would be present in the external features of the human body while others thought that the indications of homosexuality would be found in the body in the amount of certain substances or the size and shape of certain organs, particularly the brain.

In the context of this theoretical background, the bodies of lesbians and gay men were examined in great detail. The German researcher Magnus Hirschfeld, for example, thought that there would be physical differences between lesbians and heterosexual women and between gay men and heterosexual men that included, for example, differences in height, weight, musculature, skeletal structure, distribution of fat throughout the body, amount and location of hair, and pitch and intonation of the voice (Herrn 1995; Hirschfeld 1914). One of Hirschfeld's students, Arthur Weil, claimed that the ratio of shoulder width to hip width differed significantly between heterosexual and homosexual men (Weil 1921). In the United States, one of the more interesting studies concerning physical differences was conducted by the Committee for the Study of Sex Variants in the late 1930s and reported by George Henry (1941). Researchers conducted extensive psychological interviews of "sex variants" and examined their bodies in great detail, giving special attention to their external genitalia (Terry 1990).

There were, however, various methodological problems with studies that claimed to identify external physical differences between heterosexuals and homosexuals. Two of the most serious problems have to do with the possible social sources of these physical differences and with biases in the sample populations studied. At the time when most of these studies were done, few lesbians and gay men were open about their homosexuality. Many of those who were part of these studies had been arrested or were placed under the care of a psychiatrist or physician because of their sexual behaviors or inclinations. Others came to the attention of doctors and scientists because they presented themselves as wanting to change their sexual desires and/or behaviors. This pool of homosexual subjects probably was not representative of all lesbians and gay men. (In chapter 7, I argue that contemporary studies of sexual orientation face a similar problem.) In fact, those lesbians and gay men who were part of these studies were probably more than likely to have the physical characteristics stereotypically associated with lesbianism and male homosexuality respectively. This would skew the results of these studies in favor of finding physical differences between heterosexuals and homosexuals. This might have happened when, given cultural presuppositions, women with facial hair, deep voices, and muscular builds were more likely to be suspected of being lesbians than women who lacked these attributes. Partly for these reasons, such women were also more likely to have doubts about their own sexual orientation. As a result, they were more likely to come to the attention of doctors and scientists interested in homosexuality and thereby were disproportionately represented in the studies of physical differences. Studies with a subject pool biased in this way would provide scientific reinforcement of cultural stereotypes associated with homosexuality. The research done by the Committee for the Study of Sex Variants (Henry 1941) is somewhat of an exception to this account of the source of subjects. The eighty subjects were recruited through social networks in the bohemian New York City neighborhoods of Harlem and Greenwich Village (Terry 1997).[3] Interestingly, compared to other studies done at the time, the results of this study were particularly contradictory and inconclusive with respect to the physical signs of homosexuality; this was the case even though this study, like most early studies, did not examine any heterosexuals as an experimental control group.

In any event, more comprehensive studies (Allen 1958; Freund 1963) found no interesting bodily differences between heterosexuals and homosexuals (of either the "feminine" or "nonfeminine" sort). Even if, as some recent studies (Blanchard and Bogart 1996; Bogart and Blanchard 1996; Hall and Kimura 1994) suggest, there are in fact external physical differences, this might not show that sexual orientation is primarily biological; the differences might be due to primarily social factors. For example, because homosexuality was viewed negatively by much of society, homosexuals might disproportionately suffer from chronic depression or other psychological conditions that could have an impact on one's physical health and one's long-term physical condition. This might explain the scientific and medical conclusion that there were external physical differences between homosexuals and heterosexuals.

### Hormones

Studies that look *inside* the body for differences associated with sexual orientation are perhaps more sophisticated. These include theories that focus on levels of hormones or other bodily substances (for example, menstrual fluid or sperm) in the bloodstream, sex glands, or urine and theories that focus on the size and structure of parts of the central nervous system, especially the brain. Experimenters throughout much of the twentieth century claimed that lesbians had higher levels of testosterone and lower levels of estrogen in their menstrual fluid, urine, and bloodstream than heterosexual women and that gay men had lower levels of testosterone and higher levels of estrogen in their urine and bloodstream than heterosexual men. Even before the "sex hormones" (for example, testosterone and estrogen) were isolated, some scientists believed that there were differences between heterosexuals and homosexuals in the structure and/or the secretions of the sex glands. These hypotheses led to attempts to "cure" gay men (and, to a lesser extent, lesbians) of their sexual orientation through various surgical and hormonal treatments, including castration and in some cases the implantation of another man's testicle (LeVay 1996, chapter 5; Murphy 1992).

Attempts to cure people of their homosexuality based on theories involving internal bodily differences continued in North America and Western Europe until the late 1970s and they continue today in some countries in other regions. This is still the case despite the lack of any concrete evidence that such techniques can effectively change anyone's sexual orientation. In fact, most gay men who have been treated with testosterone to change the object of their sexual desire experienced an increase in their sex drive without any change in its object.

The failure of attempts to cure homosexuality in this way does not conclusively prove that there are no hormonal differences associated with differences in sexual orientation. It is possible that there might be hormonal or other similar internal differences between heterosexuals and homosexuals that cannot be changed by externally increasing hormone levels. Or it might be that these differential hormone levels are not the *cause* of homosexuality, but rather are the *effects* of other differences that determine a person's sexual orientation. Neither of these possibilities seems to be the case. Of the twenty-five studies of adult hormone levels and sexual orientation reviewed by Heino Meyer-Bahlburg (1984), twenty found no significant difference between gay and straight men. Although three studies did find that heterosexual men had higher testosterone levels than gay men, two found exactly the opposite correlation.

Even these results do not, however, amount to the final word on hormonal differences. Some researchers believe that although adult hormone levels are not correlated with sexual orientation, there will still be important hormonal differences between homosexuals and heterosexuals. In the last twenty years, several laboratories working in this paradigm published evidence that gay men exhibit what were considered to be female-typical positive feedback responses when injected with estrogen. In women, a hormone known as the Luteinizing hormone (LH) plays a crucial role in the menstrual cycle and the release of mature eggs from the ovary; LH is released at high levels in response to high levels of estrogen in the bloodstream. In men, LH typically plays a role in the synthesizing of testosterone. Some researchers claimed that gay men experience a surge of LH following exposure to estrogen (Dörner et al. 1975; Gladue, Green, and Hellman 1984). This sex difference relating to hormones was supposed to provide support for the view that the brains of gay men are in some way female-typical because hormone response patterns are mediated by the brain. More carefully executed studies in other laboratories have not, however, been able to replicate the findings that relate to LH secretion (Gooren 1986; Hendricks, Graber, and Rodriquez-Sierra 1989). Moreover, the suggestion that gay men might have female-typical feedback responses to estrogen is highly suspect on theoretical grounds. In humans and other primates, the brain mechanism regulating LH secretion appears to be the same in both sexes rather than taking two sexually distinct forms as it does in rodents. Although males and females (nonhuman and human animals) do have different patterns of LH secretion, this is because they have difficult levels of androgen and estrogen in circulation, not because they have differently organized brains. This claim applied to humans is supported by an ingenious experiment by Louis Gooren (1986) in which the LH secretions of transsexuals (both F-to-M and M-to-F transsexuals and both preoperative and postoperative transsexuals) were studied. Preoperative F-to-M transsexuals responded to estrogen injections as women typically do and postoperative F-to-M transsexuals responded as men typically do. The same findings held with respect to M-to-F transsexuals. These results support the claim that LH response is determined by levels of circulating hormones rather than the organization of the brain. If there is no sex-gender difference in the human brain mechanism to begin with, then this evidence cannot be used to argue that gay men have female-typical brains.

Contemporary advocates of hormonal accounts of sexual orientation say that the hormonal difference between heterosexuals and homosexuals involves *prenatal* hormone levels rather than adult hormone levels. The prenatal differences are supposed to have a different organizational effect on the brains and bodies of gay men and lesbians as compared, respectively, to heterosexual men and women. The prenatal hormone theory cannot be tested as straightforwardly as the theory that homosexuals have atypical hormone levels as adults. Testing the prenatal theory would require subjects to be followed for decades so that their sexual orientation as adults can be considered in light of their hormone levels before birth. Despite this, the prenatal theory does have some initial plausibility. This plausibility comes from two main sources: laboratory experiments on rodents and "natural experiments," which occur when a developing embryo or fetus is exposed to an atypical level of a certain hormone.

In rodents, hormonal exposure in early development exerts organizational influences on the brain that determine the balance between male- and female-typical patterns of mating behaviors displayed in adulthood. The question is how similar humans are to rodents. While humans and rodents are both mammals and while their brains have some regions that seem similar in form and function, the sexual behavior of humans and rodents is rather different. However, the similarities do perhaps lend a certain initial plausibility to the analogy from prenatal hormonal influences on rodents to prenatal hormonal influences on humans. In chapter 6, I discuss rodent models of human sexual orientation and raise serious worries about their applicability to humans.

The other significant evidence in favor of the prenatal hormonal theory of human sexual orientation has to do with natural experiments: conditions like congenital adrenal hyperplasia (CAH), a condition of some people with XX sex chromosomes in which male-typical levels of androgens are released into the bloodstream. In most cases, such levels of androgen cause these individuals to be born with variant (or ambiguous) genitalia (Kessler 1998). In the past, many of these intersexuals were reared as men; more recently, they are raised as women and are given hormone therapy and surgery is performed on their external genitalia to make them more female-typical in appearance and structure. The observation about individuals with CAH that is relevant to the prenatal hormone theory is that, compared to women who do not have this condition, a greater percentage of women with this condition report sexual desire for other women. In a couple of the studies of women with CAH, about half of them as adults reported both homoerotic and heteroerotic attraction and fantasy (Ehrhardt, Evers, and Money 1968; Money, Schwartz, and Lewis 1984). In other CAH studies, however, this effect was much smaller (Mulaikal, Migeon, and Rock 1987) or not present (Lev-Ran 1974). Even setting aside the equivocal nature of these results, this evidence is far from conclusive for several reasons. First, subjects with CAH are not good models of lesbians since as a group lesbians have female-typical external genitalia. Second, a prenatal theory is not required to explain the increase in homosexual desire among women with CAH. Women born with atypical genitalia are likely to have been treated atypically by their parents, family, and peers. Further, such women are more likely to have concerns about their gender given the role that genitalia play in our notions of gender. Both of these factors are likely to affect the relative percentage of CAH versus non-CAH women who report sexual desire for people of the same sex-gender (Byne and Parsons 1993). The very same sort of problems arise with respect to the support that other natural experiments—for example, various forms of androgen insensitivity whereby a person with XY chromosomes is unable, for one of various reasons, to respond to androgen and, hence, fails to develop male-typical genitalia—provide for the prenatal hormone theory. Although LeVay (1996, 126), in summarizing his discussion of hormonal theories, says there is "evidence that prenatal hormones do play a role in the establishment of sexual orientation, but the exact nature and strength of this role remains to be established," most other commentators disagree, saying that the evidence that prenatal hormones play a role in the development of homosexuality is, at best, inconclusive (Bailey 1995; Banks and Gartrell 1995; Byne 1995; Gooren 1995).

A more robust hypothesis about internal bodily signs of sexual orientation has to do with the brain. Rather than seeing homosexuality as hermaphroditism of the soul, the American psychiatrist James Kiernan saw it as resulting from "hermaphroditism of the brain" (Kiernan 1892). The early German sexologist Richard von Krafft-Ebing modified this hypothesis, talking about hermaphroditism not of the entire brain but of just the "psychosexual centers" of the brain (Herrn 1995; Krafft-Ebing 1965). There remains some question as to what these "psychosexual centers" are and whether these regions are in fact sexually dimorphic. Among the most potentially illuminating current research strategies concerning sexual orientation pick up where these hypotheses leave off. The research discussed in the next two subsections adopt precisely these strategies.

### Brains

In a discussion article about current research on sexual orientation in the leading journal *Science*, sex researcher Dick Swaab (an apt name for a scientist studying sex!) is quoted as saying that the difference between homosexuals and heterosexuals is "in the brain, not in the heart" (Barinaga 1991). There is a sense in which sexual orientation must be in the brain because everything psychological is in the brain. Swaab seems to be suggesting somewhat more, namely that sexual orientation, in virtue of being in the brain, must be biologically based. In a sense, this too must be right because everything psychological must be biologically based, as I discussed in the previous section. All this is uncontroversial, but the same sort of claim is true for a countless number of other properties. Consider the fact that I like classical music more than country music. This fact about me must also be in the brain (how could it possibly be "in," say, the heart or the ear when neither of these places is a site of cognitively mediated processes?), and in virtue of being in my brain, it must also be biologically based. When Swaab says that sexual orientation is "in the brain," he must want to make a stronger claim than that my preference for classical music is in the brain. Rather, he must be claiming that there is a *special place* in the brain for sexual orientation. On this view, the contrast between musical preferences and sexual orientation is that musical preferences would presumably be stored somewhere in the general purpose section of the brain, while sexual orientation has a specifically reserved place in the brain (for a discussion of the distinction between general-purpose versus specialized [modular] brain mechanisms, see Jerry Fodor [1983]).

This is a tricky claim. To help make better sense of it, consider an analogy involving human language ability. Initially, you might think that we learn how to speak a language in much the same way we learn how to play chess or drive a car with standard transmission, that is, we are taught—partly by example, partly by explicit rules, and partly by trial and error. Over the past several decades, Noam Chomsky and others have persuasively argued that language learning is significantly different from many other kinds of learning; linguistic knowledge, he argues, is primarily innate and, at root, genetic (Chomsky 1986; Pinker 1994). According to Chomsky, there are universal principles that are genetically programmed in us as humans that dramatically restrict the range of possible languages we can learn. There is of course variation among languages (Japanese is different from Spanish), but this variation is constrained by the structure of mental mechanisms in the brain. The debate between *nativists* about language (like Chomsky) and their opponents is not over whether language is innate, but rather is over whether the innate components of our linguistic knowledge are specific to language or whether they are instances of the general knowledge that is involved in learning almost anything. Everyone, even the most extreme nonnativist, agrees that some innate capacities are involved in learning a language (otherwise, a tennis shoe or an amoeba could acquire a language). At the other end, even the most extreme nativist would agree that the environment makes some contributions that go beyond our innate capacities (whether a child learns to speak Portuguese rather than Swahili is determined by the environment in which she grows up). The debate about language is over *how much* is contributed by the innate stuff rather than by the environment and *what form* this contribution takes. The nativist says that quite a lot of our linguistic knowledge is innate and, further, that this innate knowledge is *language specific* rather than due to general-purpose learning mechanisms. The nonnativist says that quite a lot is environmental and/or the result of general learning mechanisms.

Returning to sexual orientation, Swaab's claim that sexual orientation is in the brain can be construed as similar to Chomsky's claims about language.[4] Everyone agrees that there must be something innate, genetic, and "in the brain" about a person's sexual orientation because humans, but not amoebas or tennis shoes, have sexual orientations. At issue between Swaab and his allies, on the one hand, and their opponents, on the other, is what the form of the innate contribution to sexual orientation is as well as how much of sexual orientation is innate and how much comes from the environment. One way to show that there are specific brain mechanisms involved in developing a sexual orientation would be to locate the place in the brain responsible for sexual orientation in particular. If sexual orientation is in the brain in this sense, then there ought to be differences in the brains of heterosexuals and homosexuals. Some current research on sexual orientation takes precisely this form.

The idea of looking in the brain for differences among groups of humans has a long history. The nineteenth century, for example, was the heyday of *craniometry*, the "science" devoted to the measurement of the skull and its contents, and its various subfields, including phrenology. Craniometrists found gross differences between the heads of people of different sexes, different races, classes, professions, ages, sexual tastes, and so on (Gould 1991). Current research on differences in the brain is based on much more refined measurement techniques than those used by craniometrists.[5]

### LeVay's Study of the Hypothalamus

In 1991, Simon LeVay, a neuroanatomist, published a study of the size of a particular cell group in the anterior region of the hypothalamus (LeVay 1991). LeVay did not choose this particular region of the hypothalamus at random; he had some reasons for looking where he did. The hypothalamus, a small region of the brain slightly smaller than a golf ball, is located on either side of the brain's third ventricle, one of the fluid-filled spaces in the brain (see Figure 5-1, p. 136), and "plays a key role in sex, diet, cardiovascular performance, control of body temperature, stress, emotional response, growth and many other functions" (LeVay 1993, 39). As small as the hypothalamus is, it is too large an area to expect to find specific neuroanatomical differences. One cannot simply get a hold of a bunch of hypothalami and start randomly looking around for differences—there are just too many differences between individuals. LeVay had to find a way to narrow his search. As the hypothalamus contains various functional

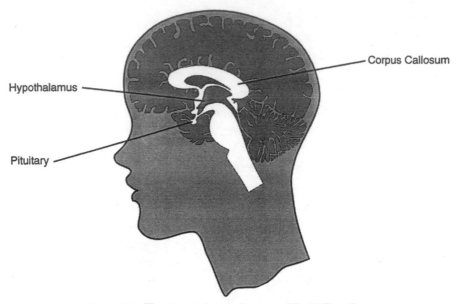

Figure 5-1. The Hypothalamus. Courtesy of Dr. William Byne.

cell groups (or regions) that have different functions and can be studied separately. LeVay's idea was to focus on areas of the hypothalamus that are thought
to be different between men and women (see Figure 5-2).

Recall my chapter 1 discussion of the development of sex differences in
fetuses. Some embryos, most typically those with XY sex chromosomes,
synthesize a protein known as testis determining factor (TDF). Typically, TDF
leads to the development of male internal genitalia, including the testes, which
produce, among other things, testosterone. Many scientists believe that testosterone levels during particular critical periods of fetal and infant development
have important effects on the organizational structure of parts of the developing
brain. In particular, many believe that beyond a certain early point in fetal
development, the human brain exhibits significant sex-gender dimorphism,
that is, men tend to have one sort of brain and women tend to have another.
The extent to which the human brain is sex-gender dimorphic is, however,
quite controversial. At a gross level, there is a debate about whether men have
larger brains than women once compensation for the overall difference in body
size has been made (Fausto-Sterling 1993, 13–60). Also controversial is the
claim that specific regions of the brain are sex-gender dimorphic (Byne 1995).

Given that there are various bodily differences that exist between men and
women, it is not surprising that there will be some brain differences between
them as well. Whether there are any larger-level regional differences between

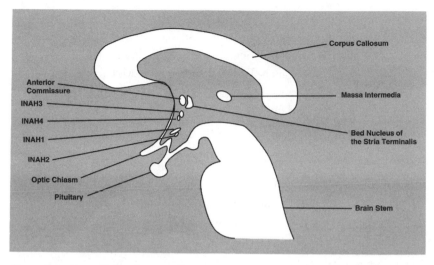

Figure 5-2. Some Brain Regions That Might Be Associated with Sexual Orientation. Courtesy of Dr. William Byne.

men and women and exactly which regions are sexually dimorphic is quite controversial. Laura Allen and her collaborators reported two cell groups in the anterior hypothalamus (INAH-2 and INAH-3) as well as parts of the corpus callosum, the stria terminalis, the amygdala, and the anterior commissure (see Figure 5-2) that differ in size in men and women (Allen and Gorski 1990; Allen and Gorski 1991; Allen, Hines, and Shryne 1989). For the most part, these results have not been replicated (Byne 1995; Fausto-Sterling 1993, 13–60). Taking just one of these regions as an example, consider the corpus callosum. The corpus callosum is a region of the brain that connects the two hemispheres of the brain. In 1982, a research team reported that an area of the corpus callosum (the cross-sectional area of the splenium) was larger in women than in men (de Lacoste-Utamsing and Halloway 1982). This study is frequently cited as an example of sex-gender dimorphism in the brain, despite the fact that some forty studies done using a variety of techniques have been unable to establish any significant sex-gender difference in this region (Byne 1995; Witelson 1991). In general, while no sex-gender dimorphism in the human brain has been uncontroversially identified, it is not unreasonable to expect that some such sex-gender difference will eventually be identified.

Starting from the assumption that there is sex-gender differentiation among human brains, LeVay decided to look for *sexual-orientation* differentiation in some of the areas of the hypothalamus that seem to exhibit sex-gender differentiation. He reasoned as follows: given that most people who are primarily attracted to women are men and most people who are primarily attracted to men are women, in order to discover where sexual orientation is reflected in the brain, we should look in parts of the brain that are structured differently for men and women. Further, although the evidence for sex-gender differentiation in the human brain is controversial, there is fairly strong evidence for sex-gender differences in the brains of some mammals. Perhaps surprisingly, we know more about the brains of various mammals than we do about our own brains. This is because the people who make the relevant determinations have decided that experiments that are not morally permissible to run on humans *are* permissible to run on most other mammals (Singer 1990).

Looking at research on sex differences in animals' brains, LeVay (1991) noted that the rodent hypothalamus contains a number of cell groups (also known as nuclei) whose size varies with sex. Several of these structural sex differences seemed relevant to sexual orientation, like the differences in the regions responsible for mating behaviors and the regulation of hormones. The best studied of these sex differences was first described in the rat, where it was designated as the sexually dimorphic nucleus of the preoptic area of the hypothalamus (SDN-POA). Four different nuclei in the human brain have been described as possibly corresponding to the rat's SDN-POA. The four nuclei of the human brain have been designated as the first through the fourth interstitial nuclei of the anterior hypothalamus (INAH-1, INAH-2, and so forth).

With this research in mind, LeVay set out to examine the four INAHs for structural differences that relate to sexual orientation. Given current technology and the size and location of the hypothalamus, in order to examine this region, a brain has to be immersed in a chemical compound for a couple of weeks, thinly sliced, dissected, immersed again, sliced again, mounted on slides, dried, and then examined under a microscope (LeVay 1991, 1035). To examine the INAHs in the relevant way, LeVay had to study portions of human brain tissue that are accessible only after the person has died. A research scientist in LeVay's position would typically be able to get access to brains for these sorts of studies. For his project, however, LeVay needed more than just a random collection of brains; in order to look for differences in sexual orientation, he had to know the sexual orientations of the people associated with the brains he was studying. Unfortunately, LeVay could not simply ask the person his or her sexual orientation because the person to whom the brain belonged was dead. As a result of the AIDS pandemic, it is possible to locate brains from people whose self-reported sexual histories are to some extent part of their medical records. (In fact, LeVay got the idea for his study following the death from AIDS of his male lover. Knowing that it is as yet technologically impossible to study minute neuroanatomical structures of a living human brain, but that it is rare to know much about the sexual history associated with cadaver brains typically available for research, and realizing the disproportionate impact AIDS has had on gay men, LeVay saw in AIDS a unique opportunity to study the brains of gay and bisexual men.)

LeVay examined forty-one brains: nineteen of them from men who died of complications due to AIDS and whose medical records suggested that they had been exposed to HIV, the virus that causes AIDS, through sexual activity with other men; six of them from men of undetermined sexual orientation who also died of AIDS and who LeVay presumed were heterosexual; ten of them from men of undetermined sexual orientation who died of causes other than AIDS and who were also presumed to be heterosexual; and six of them from women all of whom were presumed to be heterosexual, one who died of AIDS and five who died from other causes (see Table 5-1). LeVay found that, on average, the INAH-3 of the homosexual men were significantly smaller than those of men of undetermined sexual orientation and about the same size as those of the women (see Figure 5-3). This seems to suggest that gay men's INAH-3 are in a sense "feminized." Although LeVay rather cautiously concluded that "the results do not allow one to decide if the size of INAH-3 in an individual is the cause or consequence of that individual's sexual orientation, or if the size of INAH-3 and

Table 5-1. LeVay's Subjects

| Sex | Presumed Sexual Orientation* | Cause of Death | Risk Factors[†] (for AIDS) |
|---|---|---|---|
| Male (35) | heterosexual (16) | AIDS (6) | IV drug use (6) homosexual sex (0) |
| | | other (10) | not applicable |
| | bisexual (1) | AIDS (1) | not reported |
| | | other (0) | |
| | gay (19) | AIDS (19) | IV drug use (3) homosexual sex (19) |
| | | other (0) | |
| Female (6) | heterosexual (6) | AIDS (1) | not reported |
| | | other (5) | not applicable |
| | lesbian (0) | | |

*Source:* LeVay 1991.

*The presumed sexual orientation of the subjects was determined in the following manner: for women, subjects were all presumed heterosexual; for men with AIDS, subjects were grouped according to membership in risk group for HIV infection as indicated on their medical records; if the patient indicated he had engaged in same-sex sexual activity, then he was presumed to be homosexual; otherwise, he was presumed to be heterosexual. All men who died of causes not related to AIDS were presumed to be heterosexual (as part of their medical records, two of these explicitly denied homosexual activity).

[†]Subjects who died of causes related to AIDS were included in the study only if they had in their medical records an indication that they belonged to at least one AIDS "risk group." In three cases, there was an indication that the subject belonged to two risk groups (homosexual men and IV drug users).

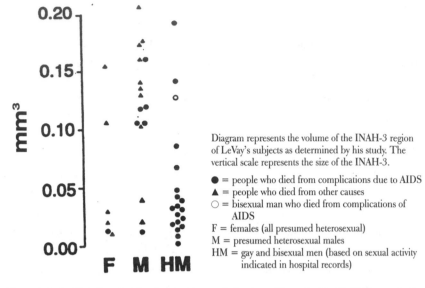

Figure 5-3. LeVay's Results. Reprinted with permission from Simon LeVay, "A Difference in the Hypothalamic Structure Between Heterosexual and Homosexual Men," *Science*, vol. 253, August 30, 1991, p. 1036. Copyright © 1991 American Association for Advancement of Science.

sexual orientation covary under the influence of some third unidentified variable," he also said that his study illustrates that "sexual orientation in humans is amenable to study at the biological level" (LeVay 1991, 1036). In media interviews after the publication of his study, he made even stronger claims; he said, for example, that the study "opens the door to find the answer" to the question of "what makes people gay or straight" (Gelman 1992). In chapter 7, I consider (among other things) whether LeVay is justified in reaching these conclusions by examining both his theoretical assumptions and his research methodology. Presently, I will describe other studies that, like LeVay's, are central to the emerging research program for the study of sexual orientation.

## Looking for Sexual Orientations in Family Trees

### Heritability

Compared to Plato, we now know a great deal about why living things have the traits that they do. Inside of every one of our cells, each of us has an elaborate chain of DNA that constitutes our genetic code. My genes provide something like a recipe for how to make my body. There is mounting (albeit contested) evidence than many complex behavioral traits are genetic or at least strongly influenced by our genes. The Human Genome Project, which started in 1990, is a multibillion-dollar, fifteen-year research project to identify what traits each piece of our genetic material codes for. For example, the genetic contribution to eye color is primarily due to quite specific regions of some specific human chromosomes. Isolating the role that a portion of genetic material plays is, however, a complex task. The links between a gene and a trait are indirect and complex. A gene directs a particular pattern of RNA synthesis that in turn specifies the production of a particular protein, which under the right conditions plays a role in the production of a particular trait or traits. For some traits, a connection like this can be isolated with a reasonable degree of certainty.

There are less direct ways to get evidence concerning the genetic basis of a trait besides isolating a specific portion of genetic material that codes for it. One straightforward way to test to see if a trait is genetic is to study twins. Identical twins (in technical terms, such twins are called *monozygotic* twins, meaning "from the same egg") have the same genes. Fraternal twins, though like identical twins in that they are carried in the same womb and born one immediately after the other, are only as genetically related as any two nontwin biological siblings (these twins are *dizygotic* twins, meaning "from two different eggs"). Differences between identical twins must be due to differences in their environment (either prenatal or postnatal), not their genes. This does not, however, work in the other direction: if identical twins have the same trait, one cannot infer that this trait is genetic. For example, both members of most pairs of identical twins in the United States know the words to the "Star Spangled Banner," but this does not show that knowing the "Star Spangled Banner" is genetic. Concordance (that is, being the same with respect to a trait) among identical twins (or among biologically related siblings in general) with respect to a trait does not show that the trait is genetic because most identical twins (and most siblings) are raised in the same environment; they thus share genetic *and* environmental factors, either of which can explain why they have the same trait. For this reason, studies of twins separated at birth (since identical twins separated at birth are influenced by the same genetic factors but by at least somewhat different environmental factors) and studies of adopted siblings raised together (since they are influenced by the same environmental factors but by different genetic factors) are among the most useful studies for providing information on the genetic basis of traits.

A related strategy is to show that a trait runs in families. This is not as simple as it may seem. Compare two traits: having ten fingers and having red hair. Suppose that we did not know whether either of these two traits is genetic and that we tried to ascertain whether they are by determining whether they run in families. We might do this by finding people who have a trait and then determining whether his or her siblings also have that trait. Suppose that we got the following results: if a person has red hair, then there is a 25 percent chance that a sibling of this person will also have red hair; and if a person has ten fingers, then there is a 99 percent chance that this person's sibling will also have ten fingers. What do these numbers alone tell us? They do not tell us that the number of fingers a person has is more strongly genetic than hair color. To begin to assess this, we need to know the base rate of a trait, namely, the frequency a trait appears in the population. We know that a person is in general more likely to share a genetic trait with his or her relatives than with a person chosen at random. This effect is stronger the more rare the trait is. Most of the world's population has ten fingers while only a small percentage has red hair. Given the base rate, the fact that a significant number of the siblings of people with red hair also have red hair provides rather good evidence that having red hair is genetic.

Even knowing the base rate and the extent to which a trait runs in families does not allow us to determine whether a trait is genetic. To see this, consider the trait of knowing the words to the "Star Spangled Banner." The base rate for this trait might well be the same as the base rate for having dark hair and it might run in families to the same extent. But knowing the "Star Spangled Banner" is clearly not genetic, while having dark hair is. The point is that knowing the base rate and the extent to which a trait runs in families is not enough to determine whether a trait is genetic.

To quantify the heritable factors affecting whether a trait is inherited, scientists have developed a technical concept that makes use of the concordance rate within families and the base rate. *Heritability* is the ratio of genetically caused variation to the total variation. In equation form

$$\text{heritability of a trait} = \frac{\text{genetic variance among individuals with the trait}}{\text{total variance among individuals with the trait}}$$

where total variance = genetic variance + environmental variance

The heritability of a trait represents the extent to which such a trait was caused by genetic factors. Heritability can be determined using the base rate of a trait in the population and the likelihood that the sibling of a person with a trait will also have this trait.[6] A trait's heritability is, however, importantly different from whether a trait is genetically determined. Heritability has to do with the extent to which differences among people with regards to a characteristic (hair color, for example) are in any way caused by genetic differences between them. The notion of heritability captures *some* aspects of our intuitive sense of genetic causation, but it fails to capture others.

Consider one example. Although having ten fingers is a paradigmatic example of a trait that is genetically determined, the heritability of number of fingers is in general quite *low*. Having more than or fewer than ten fingers is typically due to environmental factors that are usually not correlated with genetic factors. Most cases of not having ten fingers (though not all) are due to problems in fetal development (a fairly common cause of which was the sleeping pill thalidomide) or to accidents (a fairly common cause of which is carelessly cutting a bagel). Take all the people with fewer than ten fingers and divide them into those that have fewer than ten fingers due to genetic factors (call this group g) and those that have fewer than ten fingers due to nongenetic factors (call this group n). The heritability of having fewer than ten fingers is the number of people in g divided by the total number of people with fewer than ten fingers (g + n). Since far more people have fewer than ten fingers because of nongenetic causes, the heritability of this trait—g/(g + n)—will be low (Block 1995, 103). Although having ten fingers seems like a paradigmatic example of a trait that is genetically determined, it is also a trait with quite low heritability. This shows that heritability is a rather complicated concept.

Consider the following contrived example that further articulates some of the complexities involved with the notion of heritability (Block 1995; Jencks et al. 1972). Suppose there is a country—call it Brickland—where everyone with red hair gets hit over the head with the brick several times a day. This will no doubt affect the cognitive development and intellectual abilities of red-haired people living in Brickland. Given these circumstances, the siblings of people with stunted mental faculties are also likely to have stunted mental faculties in virtue of the fact that the siblings of people with red hair are also likely to have red hair. In such a society, having stunted mental faculties is caused by the effects of being repeatedly hit over the head; in virtue of the role that hair color plays in this result and due to the fact that hair color is heritable, having stunted mental faculties is also heritable. So in Brickland having stunted mental faculties would be highly heritable. In other countries in which stunted mental faculties are caused by factors that are randomly distributed across the population, heritability will be very low.

This example brings out two important features of heritability. First, the degree to which a trait is heritable is contingent on features of the environment. Having stunted mental faculties would be highly heritable in Brickland, moderately heritable in some places, and not very heritable in others. Second, a trait can be heritable because of either *direct* or *indirect* causes. In Brickland, having stunted mental faculties is highly heritable due to *indirect* genetic causes while having red hair (leaving aside people who dye their hair red) is highly heritable due to *direct* genetic causes. High heritability is thus consistent with *both* the direct model (according to which genes or other biological factors influence the brain structures that mediate sexual orientation) *and* the indirect model (according to which genes or other biological factors influence temperamental or personality factors that shape a person's interaction with his or her environment, which, in turn, affects the development of a person's sexual orientation). That a trait is highly heritable may be *either* the direct result of a person's genes (as in the case of hair color), in which case the high heritability is due to *direct heritability,* or it may be the result of how certain genetic factors interact with a person's environment (as in the case of having stunted mental faculties in Brickland), in which case the high heritability is due to *indirect heritability* (Block and Dworkin 1974a, 479–482), also known as *reactive heritability* (Tooby and Cosmides 1990). Further, this discussion highlights the difference between showing that a trait is heritable and showing that a trait is genetically determined. A trait can be heritable yet *not* genetically determined (for example, having stunted mental faculties in Brickland), and a trait can be genetically determined but *not* heritable (having ten fingers in most contexts). With this explanation of heritability in hand, I turn to studies that attempt to show that sexual orientation is heritable.

### Kallman's Twin Study

It has long been hypothesized that homosexuality runs in families (Herrn 1995; Hirschfeld 1903). The first study that attempted to test this hypothesis using twins was done in the 1950s by Franz Kallman (1952a; 1952b). The twin portion of Kallman's study included eighty-five *target subjects* (that is, the subjects initially selected for the study; the *nontarget* subjects are the family members of the target subjects), of whom forty had an identical twin and forty-five had a fraternal twin. (The other portion of Kallman's study included a larger sample and involved looking at the sex ratio among siblings of homosexual men.) Kallman reported that *100* percent of the identical twins were concordant for sexual orientation (that is, the identical twin of *every* gay target subject in his study was also gay) as were 15 to 42 percent (depending on whether only exclusive or nearly exclusive homosexuals—Kinsey 5s and 6s— were counted as homosexual or whether anyone who had engaged in any homosexual activity would count as a homosexual—Kinsey 1s, 2s, 3s, 4s, 5s, and 6s) of the fraternal twins and approximately the same percentage[7] of the nontwin siblings. From these results, Kallman concluded that sexual orientation was primarily genetic.

The problems with Kallman's study are legion. First, his homosexual target subjects were mostly men who were under psychiatric care, in prison or other correctional facilities, or receiving assistance from charitable agencies, although some of them (he does not say what percentage) were recruited "through direct contacts with the clandestine homosexual world" (Kallman 1952a, 287). As such, they in no way constituted a reasonable cross-section of the homosexual population or the general population.

Second, there is no indication of how Kallman determined the *zygosity* of his subjects, that is, how he determined whether a twin of a target subject was an identical or a fraternal twin. This is not a trivial matter. Simply looking at a particular target subject and his same-sex twin is not an accurate method for determining whether they are identical or fraternal twins, that is whether they are genetically identical or not. In fact, it is not clear in many instances in this study whether Kallman had *any* information on the zygosity of the twins of target subjects except what the subjects told him. Given that *only* 21 percent of Kallman's subjects were "diagnosed as sufficiently adjusted, both emotionally and socially" and all of them were, by his own admission, "distrusting research subjects" (293), there is no particular reason to trust his assessment that a particular pair of twins was identical or fraternal. Even the more recently developed questionnaires for assessing zygosity are only 90 percent accurate. (In contrast, the most advanced biological testing methods, for example, blood-group testing and DNA "fingerprinting" are accurate well over 90 percent of the time.)

Third, there is no indication of how Kallman determined the Kinsey ratings of his target subjects. It is not at all clear whether he used the same testing procedure for rating each subject or whether he used some combination of looking at the subjects' psychiatric records; asking subjects to rate themselves; making an assessment on the basis of the subjects' answers to questions about their desires, fantasies, and behaviors; and doing so on the basis of full sexual histories.

Fourth, there is no indication of how Kallman assigned Kinsey ratings to nontarget subjects. Did he interview the siblings of the target subjects? If so, did he assess their sexual orientation in the same manner as he did the sexual orientation of target subjects? If not, did he trust each target subject to assess the sexual orientation of his twin? Whatever his method for assessing the sexual orientations of nontarget subjects, many of them were "unclassifiable." In fact, 42 percent of the fraternal twins were unclassifiable. How reliable can his data for the fraternal twins be in light of this? In fact, one cannot help but question the veracity of his data when it is noted that less than 8 percent of his identical twin subjects were unclassifiable (one-fifth of the percentage of fraternal twins who were unclassifiable). The complete concordance for sexual orientation among the identical twins of target subjects seems far too perfect to be genuine.

The frustrating lack of details for Kallman's study aside, there are two fundamental problems with interpreting this twin study that are worth considering. To assess the results of such a twin study, one needs to know the base rate of the trait being studied (that is, the percentage of people in the general population with that trait). Kallman (289) mentions two figures from Kinsey (1948): *37 percent* of all men admit to at least some overt homosexual experience between adolescence and old age and *10 percent* of all men are more or less exclusively homosexual for at least three years. To make any inferences about the genetic basis of a trait from twin studies, one must make use of a good estimate of the base rate of this trait. Kallman does not make much use of the Kinsey figures that he mentions, probably because they do not fit well with his results. Only 4 percent of the fraternal twins of Kallman's target subjects are exclusively homosexual (Kinsey 5 or 6) compared to Kinsey's figure of 10 percent of the general population, and only 15 percent of the fraternal twins of Kallman's target are homosexual or bisexual (Kinsey 2 through 6) compared to Kinsey's figure of 37 percent of the general population. Kallman fails to offer an explanation of why the fraternal twins of his gay target subjects should have a rate of homosexuality that is less than the rate in the general population.

Even setting this worry aside, it is not clear that Kallman's data show anything about the genetic basis of sexual orientation. If his goal was to tease out the effects of genetic factors from the effects of environmental ones, Kallman's data are of little use. How many of the environmental factors are shared by two identical twins (assuming they are raised together)? By two fraternal twins? Clearly there are *some* shared environmental factors, but there are some *unshared* ones as well. Is there a significant difference between the amount of unshared environmental factors between fraternal compared to identical twins?

Typically, twin studies assume that there is not a significant environmental difference between identical twins and fraternal twins. The *equal environments assumption* says that a pair of identical twins and a pair of fraternal twins share the same amount of environmental factors. Everyone agrees that identical twins share all their genes and fraternal twins share approximately 50 percent. The equal environments assumption holds that all pairs of roughly same-aged siblings (whether they are identical twins, fraternal twins, nontwin siblings, or adoptive siblings) of the same sex-gender have the same amount of shared environment, in other words, the equal environments assumption entails that a pair of identical twins share no more environmental factors than a pair of fraternal twins do. This assumption is crucial to interpreting twin studies as providing evidence relevant to the development of sexual orientation.

Various commentators (for example, Lewontin, Rose, and Kamin 1984) have argued that, in general, parents and others treat identical twins more alike than they do fraternal twins. This similar treatment might be part of the explanation of the higher concordance rate among identical twins. I will just give two illustrative examples. First, identical twins tend to look very similar while fraternal twins may look quite different. Since one's physical appearance has a lot to do with how people (even one's parents) will treat one (especially in primary and secondary school, but so too in almost all other aspects of our lives), how one looks will have a significant impact on one's environment, especially with respect to the sexual possibilities available and with respect to one's erotic self-image. In virtue of the effects of physical appearance, identical twins are likely to share more of this significant aspect of the environment than other sorts of same-aged, same sex-gender sibling pairs. Second, and more generally, people shape their environment in many ways (both conscious and unconscious). Some of the ways people shape their environment are connected to their genetic makeup. As a result, identical twins will shape various aspects of their environments in similar ways, more so than fraternal twins will. The high concordance rate among identical twins might have much to do with environmental factors that identical—but *not* fraternal—twins share, much more so than Kallman allows. If the equal environments assumption is not right, a higher concordance rate for identical twins compared to fraternal twins might be due to environmental rather than genetic factors.

Even if Kallman could have given a justification for the equal environments assumption, this would not have allowed him to isolate *direct* genetic effects as opposed to *indirect* genetic effects. These sorts of twin studies do not provide any information about the developmental mechanisms behind the traits they study. A twin study that showed that a trait was highly heritable for a given population would not provide any evidence for thinking that the trait was the result of a direct genetic cause as opposed to an indirect one. (Recall that having stunted mental faculties in Brickland is highly heritable even though the primary cause of having stunted mental faculties is having been hit over the head with a brick.) More recent studies avoid this problem either by only claiming that sexual orientation runs in families or by using more sophisticated techniques to try to tease out genetic from environmental factors.

## Recent Studies

Several recent studies suggest that sexual orientation runs in families (Bailey and Pillard 1991b; Bailey, Pillard, and Agyei 1993; Pillard 1990; Pillard and Weinrich 1986). These studies show that a same sex-gender sibling of a homosexual is more likely to be a homosexual than a same sex-gender sibling of a heterosexual; more simply, the brother of a gay man is more likely to be gay than the brother of a straight man and the sister of a lesbian is more likely to be a lesbian than the sister of a heterosexual woman. These studies do not establish that sexual orientation is genetic because most siblings, in addition to sharing a relatively high percentage of their genes (nontwin siblings typically share about 50 percent of their genes), share many environmental variables. My sister and I, for example, in addition to sharing approximately 50 percent of our genes, also shared a similar childhood environment: we were raised in the same house, attended the same elementary school, ate many of the same meals, watched many of the same television shows, and had many of the same adult role models. For these reasons, disentangling genetic and environmental influences requires studies that include adopted siblings or studies of twins separated at birth.

Adopted siblings share roughly the same environmental factors that biologically related siblings do,[8] but adopted siblings share only as many genes as a person chosen at random from the population at large.[9] Comparing biologically related siblings to adopted ones may help us better understand the relative importance of genetic versus environmental contributions to a person's development. If adopted siblings share a trait as often as biologically related siblings do, this would suggest that the trait is more environmental than genetic; if adopted siblings differ in a trait more often than biologically related siblings, this would suggest the trait is more genetic than environmental. Identical twins raised separately offer a different path to the same sort of conclusions. Identical twins share all of their genes, but if they are raised in different environments, they are likely to share only about as many environmental factors as two people chosen at random. Conversely, if twins separated at birth share a trait less frequently than biologically related siblings raised together, this suggests that the trait is more environmental than genetic. If twins separated at birth share a trait more often than biological siblings raised together, then this suggests that the trait is primarily genetic.

Researchers working with the Minnesota twin registry—which has nothing to do with the baseball team with a similar name—have done various studies of twins separated at birth (Bouchard et al. 1981). The registry has, however, only six recorded cases of identical twins separated at birth in which at least one of the siblings is reported to be homosexual (Eckert et al. 1986). Two of these cases involved men and four involved women. Three of the four pairs of identical twin sisters separated at birth were discordant for sexual orientation, that is, one was heterosexual, the other was a lesbian (or bisexual); the fourth pair of twins was made up of a lesbian and a woman who had engaged in sex with other women until the age of twenty-nine, at which point she got married to a man and was exclusively heterosexual for nineteen years. Even if we count this last pair as concordant, this study results in only a 25 percent concordance rate for being a lesbian. Of the two pairs of identical twin brothers separated at birth, one pair was concordant and the other pair consisted of a man, who had sex with men and women until the age of nineteen but had been exclusively homosexual for the next sixteen years, and his brother, who had sex with men and women until the age of twenty but had been exclusively heterosexual for the next fifteen years. Researchers labeled the first of these homosexual but said that they could not classify the second. They concluded that the concordance rate for being a gay man was at least 50 percent.

This study is clearly plagued by a small sample size and by unclear and seemingly unreasonable criteria for assessing sexual orientation. More generally, studies of twins separated at birth are subject to additional concerns. Crucial to using this sort of method for studying the roots of a human trait or behavior is the assumption that twins separated at birth are raised in significantly different environments. Without this assumption, this method will not allow the effects of shared genes and the effects of a shared environment to be disentangled. It is, however, often not the case that identical twins who had been separated are raised in significantly different environments. In fact, studies based on the Minnesota twin registry have been criticized because they assume that the twins raised separately are raised in quite different environments when, in fact, they may be raised in quite similar environments (Billings, Beckwith, and Alper 1992; Horgan 1993). Sometimes they are raised by different relatives, sometimes they are raised in the same geographical region, and sometimes the adoption agency or biological family members in charge of their placement try to place each of the twins in environments like that of their biological parents (in terms of race, ethnicity, religion, class, and so on). Some of these twins, although raised in separate homes, may have had contact with each other during childhood (some even attended the same schools) or had contact as adults before they took part in the twin study. Further, identical twins, even if reared apart, may share somewhat similar environments in virtue of their physical appearance, especially if there is something distinctive about it.

The twins, since they have identical genes, may in some way create similar environments for themselves. Suppose, for example, that two identical twins who are both especially short are raised in separate environments. Both of them may be subject to the same sort of teasing by their peers and be similarly constrained in certain physical endeavors. These experiences may shape them in similar ways, and despite being raised separately, they might develop similar personality traits as a result of their similar experiences. Finally, those twins who take part in such studies usually volunteer to do so, often as a pair. As such, they may constitute a skewed sample of identical twins, or they may have some interest (psychological or otherwise) in finding similarities with their "long-lost" twin.

Heritability studies involving twins raised together but that also include an adoption component are not hindered by the small sample sizes and some of the other problems affecting studies of twins separated at birth. Two such heritability studies done by Michael Bailey and Richard Pillard assessed sexual orientation in identical twins, same sex-gender fraternal twins, same sex-gender nontwin biological siblings, and similarly aged unrelated adopted siblings (Bailey and Pillard 1991b; Bailey, Pillard, and Agyei 1993). The idea behind these studies is as follows: if sexual orientation is genetic, first, all identical twins should have the same sexual orientation and, second, the rate of homosexuality among the adopted siblings should be equal to the rate of homosexuality in the general population (see the first two rows of Table 5-2). If, on the other hand, identical twins are as likely to have the same sexual orientation as adopted siblings of the same sex-gender, this suggests that genetic factors make very little contribution to sexual orientation.

Bailey and Pillard's study of men (Bailey and Pillard 1991b) and their study of women (Bailey, Pillard, and Agyei 1993) are in some ways similar to Kallman's, although they are much more sophisticated. In both of Bailey's studies (the two are almost identical in design), subjects were recruited through ads placed in gay publications that asked for homosexual or bisexual volunteers with twin or adoptive siblings of the same sex-gender. Volunteers were encouraged to reply to the ad "regardless of the sexual orientation" of their siblings. Once recruited, the testing of the subjects was more objective and more systematic than in Kallman's study. The twins were asked to fill out a questionnaire to determine (to a 90 to 95 percent degree of accuracy) whether they are fraternal or identical twins (Nicols and Bilbro 1966). Target subjects were interviewed either in person (62 percent of the subjects in the male study; 34 percent in the female study) or by phone (38 percent of the subjects in the male study; 64 percent in the female) and asked to rate their own sexual orientation (combining fantasy and behavior) on a Kinsey scale and to identify the sexual

Table 5-2. Comparison of Concordance Rate for Idealized Traits and Homosexuality Among Different Kinds of Siblings from Bailey and Pillard's and Kallman's Twin Studies

| | Identical Twin (%) | Same-Sex Fraternal Twin (%) | Same-Sex Nontwin Biological Sibling (%) | Same-Sex Similarly Aged Adopted Sibling (%) |
|---|---|---|---|---|
| Trait for which all variation is genetic | 100 | 50 | 50 | 10* |
| Trait for which all variation is environment | 10* | 10* | 10* | 10* |
| Male homosexuality (Kallman) | 100 | 15 | ≈ 15[†] | no data |
| Male homosexuality (Bailey) | 52 | 22 | 9 | 11 |
| Female homosexuality (Bailey) | 48 | 16 | 14 | 6 |

*I am, for the basis of illustration, supposing that the base rates of the traits involved are 10 percent.

[†]Kallman does not give his data on nontwin siblings because they are incomplete but says the concordance rate for nontwin biological brothers "do not differ significantly."

Note: For these studies, I report the percentages of siblings who rated from 2 to 6 on the Kinsey scale (that is, who were bisexual or homosexual).

*Source:* The first set of results for male homosexuality comes from Kallman 1952a. The next two sets of results (for male and female homosexuality respectively) come from Bailey and Pillard 1991b and Bailey, Pillard, and Agyei 1993.

orientation (heterosexual, homosexual, or bisexual) of their relatives. Target subjects were then asked for permission to contact their twin or adoptive siblings. Of the male target subjects with identical twins, 93 percent gave such permission, as did 87 percent of those with fraternal twins (in the female study, 93 percent of the twins—fraternal and identical combined—gave permission) and 63 percent of those with adoptive siblings (80 percent in the female study). When permission was granted to contact siblings of the target subjects, the siblings were mailed a written questionnaire in which they were asked (among other things) to place themselves on the Kinsey scale in terms of the sexual behavior and fantasies (during adolescence and adulthood), to identify their sexual identity, to say how exciting or disgusting they found, respectively, the idea of sex with a man and sex with a woman, as well as, for twins, to answer questions related to zygosity. Completed questionnaires were obtained for 74 percent of the relevant siblings of the male target subjects and 82 percent of the female target subjects.

If researchers were unable to obtain a completed questionnaire from a relative, they used the target subject's assessment of his or her sibling's sexual orientation so long as the target subject was "virtually certain" or "certain" of this assessment. They were thus able to classify the relevant siblings for 97 percent of the male and 96 percent of the female target subjects in terms of sexual orientation. They also asked target subjects about the sexual orientation of their nontwin biological siblings, but they made no attempt to contact these relatives.

The results for Bailey's two studies are summarized in the fourth and fifth rows of Table 5-2. In both of these studies the concordance rates for identical twins is substantially higher than for fraternal twins. Looking at the last row, for example, 48 percent of the identical twins of lesbians were themselves lesbians, 16 percent of the fraternal twins were lesbians, 14 percent of the nontwin biological sisters were lesbians, as were 6 percent of adoptive sisters. The higher concordance rate is *consistent* with a genetic effect because identical twins share all of their genes, while fraternal twins, on average, share only half of their genes. Note also that the concordance rates for both types of twins are higher than the concordance rates for adopted siblings; this is also consistent with a genetic effect.

Like Kallman's study, this twin study requires the equal environments assumption, namely, the assumption that there is not a significant environmental difference between identical twins and fraternal twins. Bailey and Pillard make two points in defense of this assumption (Bailey and Pillard 1995). First, they cite two studies (Kendler et al. 1993; Plomin, DeFries, and McClearn 1990) that report that for certain traits—for example, psychiatric illnesses—there does not seem to be a difference in the effects of parental treatment of identical twins between parents who make an effort to treat their identical twins differently and those who make an effort to treat their identical twins the same. These studies have only limited relevance to concerns about the equal environments assumption because they test the effects of parent's intentional and conscious treatment of their twin children. The relevant objection to the equal environments assumption need not say anything about this aspect of parental effects on their child's environment (most of which will be unintended, unconscious, and indirect). Second, Bailey and Pillard note that although the equal environments assumption has not been directly tested, it does not contradict existing evidence that might bear on it. On this point, they are right. This does not, however, really answer the plausible hypothesis that identical twins will share more environmental factors than fraternal twins because, for example, identical twins have the same physical characteristics, which means that they are more likely to be treated similarly than fraternal twins. In light of the fact that identical twins are likely to have more environmental traits in common than fraternal twins, the burden of proof rests with those who use the equal environments assumption as a fundamental part of their research methodology for studying sexual orientation. Without the equal environments assumption, it is difficult to know how to interpret Bailey's results for the concordance rates for homosexuality.

Setting aside worries about the equal environments assumption, compare the last row of Table 5-2 with the first two. This difference suggests that sexual orientation is significantly heritable. It also suggests that the environment also plays a significant role in the development of sexual orientations. Further, although Bailey's results are consistent with sexual orientation having a significant genetic basis, it does not show that the genetic basis is a direct one. Sexual orientation might have only an indirect connection to genes, roughly like having stunted mental capacities in Brickland. While Bailey and his collaborators are careful not to say that their studies prove that sexual orientation is genetic (although their first study's title, "A *Genetic* Study of Male Sexual Orientation," is somewhat misleading on this point), they do say that their studies show that "genetic factors are important in determining individual differences in sexual orientation" (Bailey and Pillard 1991b, 1093). These results seem significant, but they do not, in contrast to studies like LeVay's, even potentially suggest a causal mechanism for how people develop sexual orientations. Looking for the causes of sexual orientation in families seems to have promise, but studies other than heritability studies are required to find the mechanism by which sexual orientations are distributed in families. In the next section, I discuss just such a study.

### Looking for Sexual Orientation in the Genes

In the early part of the century, geneticist Richard Goldschmidt (1916) hypothesized that homosexuals might be people whose bodies do not match their sex chromosomes. According to this theory, which was accepted by various thinkers in the early part of the twentieth century, including Magnus Hirschfeld (Herrn 1995, 38), gay men have female-typical sex chromosomes and lesbians have male-typical sex chromosomes. This theory was disproved in the 1950s (Pare 1956), but its disproof is *consistent* with the existence of genetic differences between heterosexuals and homosexuals. In fact, some people have interpreted the recent heritability studies as suggesting that such genetic differences probably do exist. Perhaps the most complex study that plays a central role in the emerging scientific research program for the study of sexual orientation attempts to locate these genetic differences. Such a study, if successful, has the potential to link studies that suggest that differences in sexual orientation are found in bodies and those that suggest that sexual orientations run in families. If sexual orientation has a genetic basis, then this might explain both the bodily differences associated with sexual orientations and the fact that sexual orientation runs in families.

### Hamer's Pedigree Analyses

Building on research like Bailey's, Dean Hamer and his colleagues attempted to locate the portion of the human genome that is responsible for sexual orientation (Hamer et al. 1993). Hamer's study involved two main stages: pedigree analyses and a linkage study. First, Hamer conducted two *pedigree analysis* studies, studies of how a trait is spread out among members of an extended family. In the first pedigree analysis, seventy-six gay men were recruited from Washington, D.C., area AIDS-related clinics and gay organizations and interviewed about their sexual orientation and the sexual orientation of their relatives. Hamer assessed each of his subject's sexual orientation on the basis of self-ratings of his own sexual orientation and, in some cases, on the assessment of at least one of his relatives. Whereas Bailey simply asked subjects their sexual orientation in a way that combined various aspects of their sexual desire, Hamer asked some of his subjects a detailed series of questions about their sexual histories and current sexual practices, and he also asked them to rate themselves on Kinsey scales representing various aspects of their sexual histories (Hamer and Copeland 1994, 234–243). At least one relative of twenty-six of these men (a total of forty-six relatives altogether) was also interviewed to determine the reliability of the initial subjects' assessment of their relatives' sexual orientations; these assessments were judged to be quite reliable. The analysis of this data indicated that brothers of gay men were more likely than any other male relative to be gay and that maternal uncles (brothers of the subject's mother) and the sons of maternal aunts (sons of sisters of the subject's mother) were much more likely to be gay than a man chosen at random from the general population. In contrast, fathers and male paternal relatives (men on the subject's father's side of the family) were no more (and in some cases less) likely to be gay than a randomly chosen man.

In the second pedigree analysis, thirty-eight families with at least two homosexual brothers were recruited through advertisements in D.C. and Baltimore area gay publications. Two families from the first study were also included. Further, there were restrictions on the families that were allowed to be involved in the second study: only families with no bisexuals, with no more than one lesbian, and no gay men among the fathers or sons (if any) of the gay brothers were allowed to be part of the study. Hamer's idea was to select families that were especially likely to have the gene connected to male homosexuality if such a gene existed; families with two gay brothers are more likely to have such a gene than families with one or no gay brothers. Hamer defended this procedure as follows:

> Assume that being gay could be caused either by a gene or an environmental factor. Assume also that the gene is on the X chromosome, that it's operative only in men, and that two percent of the general [male] population is gay. Now suppose the gene and the environmental factor are equally prevalent. In that case, fifty percent of a random sample of gay men should have the "gay gene," but fifty percent will not. On the other hand, . . . in a group of gay brothers, ninety-seven percent will carry the "gay gene" and only three percent will lack it. Thus the gene has been enriched by a factor of two [from fifty percent to ninety-seven]. (Hamer and Copeland 1994, 107)

The second pedigree analysis yielded the same pattern of distribution of homosexuality within the families of gay men that was found in the first pedigree analysis.

This distinctive pattern of the distribution of male homosexuality in the families of the gay subjects suggested to Hamer that homosexuality in men might be a trait that is inherited from one's mother (a maternally linked trait), like color blindness. Why this seemed likely to Hamer requires a bit of explanation. Take a simple human trait like eye color. There are various rival traits, called *alleles*, that exist for this feature. Alleles are two or more genetic sequences that occur in the same place in chromosomal material and that code for rival traits. The alleles for human eye color include a blue allele, a brown allele, and so on. Roughly, the difference between a person with green eyes and one with hazel eyes is a difference in their genetic code in a particular portion of some particular chromosome. At most, two alleles for the same feature can be present in a single organism—one allele from the organism's father and one from its mother. If a person has the same allele from each parent, then she will exhibit the trait associated with that allele. If, for example, I inherit an allele for blue eyes from my father and an allele for blue eyes from my mother, I will have blue eyes, and I will be said to be *homozygous* for eye color. If a person has one allele from one parent and a different allele from the other parent, she will be *heterozygous* for that trait. In the case of individuals who are heterozygous for a trait, the *dominant* allele will be exhibited and the *recessive* trait will not be. For example, the allele for brown eyes is dominant while the allele for blue eyes is recessive. This means that if I inherit an allele for blue eyes from my father and an allele for brown eyes from my mothers, I will have brown eyes—the dominant allele trumps the recessive one. A person who is heterozygous typically exhibits only the trait associated with the dominant allele but can pass on to an offspring either of the two alleles that she got from her parents. For example, even if I have brown eyes, I can still pass genes coding for blue eyes to my offspring so long as I am heterozygous for eye color (in particular, so long as I have an allele for brown eyes and one for blue eyes); whether my offspring will actually exhibit blue eyes depends on what allele he or she inherits from his or her other biological parent.

The details of genetic inheritance get more complex when we turn to traits that are coded for on the X chromosome. As I explained in chapter 1, most humans have two sex chromosomes, one from their biological mother and the other from their biological father. Most men have XY sex chromosomes, while most women have XX sex chromosomes. For traits that are coded for on the X chromosome, a typical man will necessarily exhibit the trait coded for on the X chromosome that he gets from his mother because he gets a Y chromosome, not an X chromosome, from his father. The gene for color blindness, for example, is carried on the X chromosome, so a man whose mother passes on to him an X chromosome that carries a genetic sequence for color blindness will almost certainly exhibit that condition. This is true whether the trait in question is dominant or recessive. Women, since they have two X chromosomes, will exhibit a trait coded for by genes on the X chromosome only if they are homozygous for that trait (that is, only if both parents pass the trait on to them) or if the trait is dominant. Assuming that a trait is recessive and coded for by genes on the X chromosome, men will be more likely to get this trait than women. A man will have such a trait whenever he gets an allele coding for the trait from his mother. A woman can only get such a trait when she gets a gene coding for the trait from her mother and a gene coding for the trait from her father. Since it requires an additional event for a woman to get such a trait than it does for a man, men are more likely to get this trait than women are. Color blindness is recessive and is coded for on the X chromosome. As a result, men are much more likely to be color blind than women. However, women are much more likely than men to pass on the gene for color blindness to their offspring; in fact, a man cannot pass the gene for color blindness to his son because men contribute a Y chromosome to sons and color blindness is carried on the X chromosome. Traits like color blindness are called X-linked traits; as a result of being X-linked, such traits are distributed in different ways in men and women.

When Hamer looked at the distribution of male homosexuality in his pedigree analysis, he noticed that the pattern of distribution looked like an X-linked trait (Hamer and Copeland 1994, 91–104); see Table 5-3 for the numerical details. Maternal male relatives of gay men (that is, men on the mother's side of the family) were much more likely to also be gay than paternal (father's side) male relatives. (See Figure 5-4 for some family trees that display this pattern.) This pattern is the same pattern that would be exhibited with respect to color blindness. Hamer thus formed the hypothesis that a gene connected to homosexuality is carried on the X chromosome.

### Hamer's Linkage Study

Recall that to test the hypothesis that there is a gene for homosexuality, Hamer created a pool of subjects that seemed to be enriched for the gene he was looking for. Having created a pool, Hamer obtained DNA samples from the two gay brothers in each of the families and, if available, from their mother. These samples were then analyzed using a method called *linkage analysis* to see if there was any particular portion of the X chromosome that was identical in the pairs of brothers at an unexpectedly high frequency (Hamer and Copeland 1994, 112–122; LeVay 1996, 178–188). Linkage analysis is a technique for narrowing the location of a gene for some trait. Scattered throughout the human genome are various DNA *markers* that can be detected through laboratory tests of a person's cells. Using these markers, which are like signposts, scientists can determine the likelihood that two people have the same genetic

Table 5-3. Results of Hamer's Pedigree Analysis

| Relationship to Gay Men | 1st Pedigree Analysis (% Who Are Also Gay) | 2d Pedigree Analysis (% Who Are Also Gay) |
|---|---|---|
| Father | 0 | 0* |
| Son | 0 | 0* |
| Brother | 13.5 | 100* |
| Maternal uncle | 7.3 | 10.3 |
| Paternal uncle | 1.7 | 1.5 |
| Maternal cousin, aunt's son | 7.7 | 12.9 |
| Maternal cousin, uncle's son | 3.9 | 0 |
| Paternal cousin, aunt's son | 3.6 | 0 |
| Paternal cousin, uncle's son | 5.6 | 5.4 |

*Sample was selected to achieve these numbers (that is, only families with gay brothers and no gay fathers or sons were allowed in the study).
*Source:* Hamer et al. 1993.

## Family Tree A

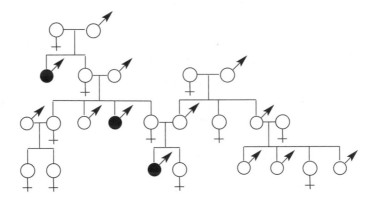

## Family Tree B

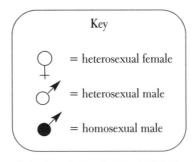

Key

○ = heterosexual female

○⤴ = heterosexual male

●⤴ = homosexual male

Figure 5-4. Sample Family Trees Exhibiting X-Linked Trait

code in some particular stretch of DNA. Suppose that A and B are two such markers and that each has two forms (respectively, $a_1$ and $a_2$ and $b_1$ and $b_2$). If A and B occur close to each other on the same chromosome, then they can be useful for linkage analysis. Suppose that two individuals, Mary and Martha, both have form $a_1$ of marker A and form $b_2$ of marker B. It follows, for reasons having to do with how genetic material is combined and passed on, that Mary and Martha are likely to have the same genetic material in between the two markers. The closer the markers are to each other, the more likely this is. If Mary and Martha are sisters (and not identical twins), they are even more likely to have the same genetic material in between the two markers. If one of their parents has the same form of both markers and the other parent has neither form of either marker, then it is even more likely that both of them inherited the identical sequence of genetic material between A and B from the first parent.

Using this sort of linkage analysis, Hamer found that a higher than expected percentage of the pairs of gay brothers had the same genetic sequences in a particular portion of the q28 region of the X chromosome (82 percent rather than the expected 50 percent). In other words, he found that gay brothers are much more likely to share the same genetic sequence in this particular region than they are to share the same genetic sequence in any other region of the X chromosome. Given the indication from the pedigree analysis that sexual orientation is coded for on the X chromosome, Hamer's study suggests that the q28 region is the particular place where this difference is inscribed. This study does *not*, contrary to popular belief, identify any *particular* genetic sequence associated with homosexuality. Rather, it found that within most pairs of homosexual brothers, the brothers had the same genetic sequences in this quite specific portion of the X chromosome. When Hamer is at his most precise, he says that his study shows that "at least one subtype of male sexual orientation is genetically influenced" (Hamer et al. 1993, 321). In less technical contexts, Hamer is less careful. For example, in his book, *Science of Desire*, he talks of "gay genes" and even uses the phrase in the book's subtitle (Hamer and Copeland 1994).

Compared to LeVay's study, Hamer's study (like Bailey's studies) has the advantage of having the potential to offer more than a mere correlation with sexual orientation. Hamer's study has a further virtue: it offers a concrete genetic proposal. Bailey and Pillard's results have to do with the heritability of sexual orientation while Hamer's results seem to count towards a specific genetic basis for sexual orientation. In this way, the three studies can be seen as building on one another. LeVay points to a neuroanatomical correlation with male sexual orientation, Bailey suggests that sexual orientation is heritable, while Hamer seems to have isolated a specific genetic region that codes for homosexuality and hence could provide a direct genetic explanation of the heritability of sexual orientation. As such, Hamer's study potentially unifies neurological studies like LeVay's and heritability studies like Bailey's.

## Women in the Emerging Paradigm

Most of the studies in the emerging research paradigm focus primarily or exclusively on sexual orientation in men. Some researchers working in this program think that sexual orientation in men and women will have the same or roughly the same explanation. For example, LeVay, by hypothesizing that INAH-3 will be larger in lesbians than in heterosexual women (LeVay 1991, 1035), indicates that he thinks that sexual orientation in men and women will be given the same sort of scientific explanation. While explaining all sexual orientations with the same mechanism has its virtues (Bem 1996a, 320), there are some indications within the emerging research program that women's and men's sexual desires are to be explained differently.

Some of the most prominent studies in the emerging program that concern sexual orientation in women suggest that homosexuality in women runs in families, although the evidence that this is due to genetic rather than environmental factors is weaker for women than for men (Bailey and Benishay 1993; Bailey, Pillard, and Agyei 1993; Pattatucci and Hamer 1995). The studies conducted by Hamer's research group suggest that the factors that cause homosexuality in men and those that cause homosexuality in women are partially overlapping and partially distinct (Hamer et al. 1993; Pattatucci and Hamer 1995, 417). This is based on evidence that lesbians have more gay brothers than would be expected from a random sample (but a lower percentage of gay brothers than lesbian sisters) and that gay men have more lesbian sisters than would be expected from a random sample (but a lower percentage of lesbian sisters than gay brothers).

Other studies have attempted to provide further evidence that women's sexual orientation is to be explained differently in women than in men. A recent study by McFadden and Pasanen (1998) concerned *otoacoustical emissions,* weak sounds produced by the inner ear. In particular, they studied such emissions produced in response to a brief sound (a click). Earlier studies by the same research team found a sex-gender difference in the emissions produced in response to these clicks, namely, women produced stronger emissions than men (McFadden, Loehlin, and Pasanen 1996). With regards to sexual orientation, the study reported that nonheterosexual women produced weaker emissions than heterosexual women but stronger emissions than men while finding no differences between heterosexual and homosexual men (although bisexual men produced somewhat stronger emissions than either gay men or heterosexual men) (McFadden and Pasanen 1998). The researchers interpreted these results as showing that "different processes may underlie homosexuality in males and females" (2712).

Many researchers working within the emerging research program think that the conclusion that sexual orientation in men and sexual orientation in women are distinct biological phenomena requiring different biological explanations is supported by studies of sexual desires that point to differences between men and women with respect to sexual orientations and desire. Among these reported differences are that women are more likely than men to be bisexual (Bailey and Benishay 1993; Bailey, Pillard, and Agyei 1993; Kinsey, Pomeroy, and Martin 1948; Kinsey et al. 1953; Pattatucci and Hamer 1995; Rust 1992), that for women sexual orientation is more fluid than for men, that in men sexual desire is more linked to physical appearance and sexual variety than in women, and that sexual desire for women is more linked to emotional attachment to particular people (Bell and Weinberg 1978; Blumstein and Schwartz 1990; Symonds 1979; Weinrich 1987b). Richard Pillard nicely articulated a common view within the emerging research program on women's sexual desires when he said:

> Women's sexuality is different from men's. . . . [W]omen are much more flexible in their sexual orientation—they don't as often label themselves as gay or straight. Usually when you ask that question of men, at least men over the age of thirty or thirty-five, a few will say they're bisexual but most will say they're gay or straight; they dichotomize. Women often will say, "Well, it depends on who I'm with, on what sort of relationship I'm having. . . ." And they'll often have had relationships that are lesbian and relationships that are heterosexual. . . . You might want to call more women bisexual, which we end up doing [in Bailey, Pillard, and Agyei 1993], but I think women's orientation is really much more complicated than men's sexual orientation. I think it's really a harder thing to study in the quantitative way that we've been doing. (Stein 1993)

Many researchers within the emerging research program try to give a sociobiological or evolutionary psychological account for these differences, focusing on the different "mating strategies" of men compared to women (Buss 1994). Men and women have different reproductive systems, and they have evolved different psychological mechanisms in association with them. Men pass on their genes through sperm, and they have loads of sperm to spread around: sperm are cheap, easily produced, and easily replaced. According to one estimate, men produce about twelve million sperm per hour (19). Women, in contrast, pass their genes on through eggs. Compared to sperm, eggs are hard to produce and a woman can produce only a small number of them in her lifetime, approximately four hundred (19). Further, a woman's time investment in the development of an offspring is necessarily more than a man's. A woman carries the fertilized egg in her womb and spends a great deal of time and energy providing the right sort of environment for that egg to develop into a newborn human. A woman needs to devote nine months of her reproductive energy to the development of one egg. During that time, a man could fertilize hundreds of eggs. These and other biological differences are, in the hands of sociobiologists and evolutionary psychologists, used to explain a wide range of differences between men and women in terms of sexual desires (such as why men have more sexual partners than women, why women are more nurturing than men, and why women, in general, are more likely to be attracted to older men than men are to be attracted to older women) (Buss 1994; Pinker 1997; Symonds 1979). I discuss evolutionary accounts of human sexual desire in chapter 6. I mention them here as part of my discussion of how the emerging research program thinks about sexual orientation in women as compared to men, but also to exemplify the role that sociobiology and evolutionary psychology play in the emerging research program.

## Summary

The evidence in favor of the truth of some sort of biological theory of sexual orientation seems, at least initially, rather strong. Although it may be hard to fit studies that claim to find sexual orientation differences in the distribution of ridges on fingerprints (Hall and Kimura 1994) or in the response of the inner ear to clicks (McFadden and Pasanen 1998) into a general and plausible biological story, at least the major biological theories of sexual orientation fit together rather nicely. If the q28 region of the X chromosome underlies all or most instances of male homosexuality, it could explain why Bailey and Pillard found the heritability patterns that they did. This same region might code for proteins that lead to a certain pattern of development in the INAH-3 region of the hypothalamus and thereby fit with LeVay's results (LeVay and Hamer 1994; Stein 1993). The emerging research program offers the potential for a unified theory of human sexual orientation. The considerations I have discussed thus far suggest that a research program for the biological study of sexual orientation is emerging. Several different laboratories have been doing work that many people think points to a strong biological basis for sexual orientation. Taken together, the neuroanatomical, the heritability, and the genetic research summarized above seem to point towards the direct model, according to which genes influence the brain structures that underlie sexual orientation. This concordance of results from a variety of research techniques is a telltale sign of the development of a coherent and sophisticated scientific research program. Despite these results, in the next two chapters, I turn to a critical evaluation of this program. I will argue that the appearance of a sophisticated and coherent research program is deceiving.

# CHAPTER 6

*Animal Models
and Evolutionary
Accounts in the Emerging
Research Program*

**M**uch of the emerging scientific research program concerning sexual orientation depends on or in some way appeals to animal models of sexual orientation. Animal research has many practical advantages over research on humans; using animal models simplifies the study of sexual orientation in many ways. In general, animal models have played a major role in the development of vaccines, medications, and the advancement of our general understanding of the human body and its functioning. Especially given the ethical constraints on using human subjects in research, animal studies are an important tool for the scientist. Animal models of sexual orientation seem plausible because organisms in various animal species, including many species of mammals, engage in sexual acts with conspecifics (that is, organisms of the same species) of the same sex (Beach 1979; Denniston 1980; Vasey 1995; Weinrich 1982). From fruit flies to sheep, from seagulls to our nearest primate relatives, same-sex sexual behavior has been observed and offered as in some way analogous to homosexuality in humans. That animals exhibit same-sex sexual desires and sexual orientations seems to provide some sort of a clue to the evolution of human sexual mechanisms. Some human traits have clear-cut

*[handwritten margin note: What about environmental factors since everyone acknowledge their role in pollution, food in the womb... those are different w/ humans than w/ animals.]*

correlates in animals, many of which are evolutionary hand-me-downs to humans. For example, the eye as it exists in humans is not that much different from the eye in chimps and even pigs. Studying the eye in these other species gives us insight into the adaptive function of the human eye. Other human traits are more recent evolutionary developments, such as our ability to learn and use language. If there are good animal models of human sexual orientations, then this suggests a certain direction for our evolutionary theorizing about human sexual orientation.

The interest in animal models of human sexual orientation is not only motivated by scientific interest in how humans develop sexual desires. Many people think that the existence or nonexistence of homosexuality in animals will determine whether homosexuality is natural or nonnatural. I discuss the ethical relevance, if any, of the presence of same-sex sexual activity in nonhuman animals in chapter 10. In this chapter, I consider its *scientific* relevance with particular attention to four animal models of human sexual orientation.

As an example of how studies in the emerging research program make use of animal models of sexual orientation, consider LeVay's neuroanatomical study. LeVay draws on animal research both as a justification for studying a particular region of the hypothalamus and for interpreting his results as establishing a biological basis for sexual orientation. In the second paragraph of his *Science* article, LeVay writes: "A likely biological substrate for sexual orientation is the brain region involved in the regulation of sexual behavior. In nonhuman primates, the medial zone of the anterior hypothalamus has been implicated in the generation of male-typical sexual behavior. Lesions in male monkeys impair heterosexual behavior without eliminating sexual drive" (LeVay 1991, 1034). Also, in his final paragraph, he cites studies that point to sexual dimorphism in the rat brain to support interpreting his results as showing that INAH-3 size influences sexual orientation in humans (1036). Animal research thus plays a role in providing evidence that is supposed to support the direct model of the role of biological factors in the development of sexual orientations in humans.

Like LeVay, many practitioners of the emerging research program appeal in one way or another to animal models of human sexual orientation. Many also appeal to evolutionary explanations of human sexual desires in connection with their research (Hamer and Copeland 1994, 180–186; LeVay 1996, 188–193; Pillard 1997, 237–238; Weinrich 1987b, 310–336). This is not surprising for at least two reasons. First, if biological factors underlie sexual orientation, then there must be an explanation of their development. Evolutionary theory is in the business of offering explanations for the development of biological traits. In particular, evolutionary theory promises explanations of the development of differences between humans and nonhuman animals. In this chapter, I consider animal models of human sexual orientation as well as evolutionary explanations of human sexual orientations.

## Fruit Flies

In a recent book written for a general readership, Chandler Burr, a journalist, talks about sexual orientation in fruit flies (*Drosophila melanogaster*) (Burr 1996a, 29–35). He discusses research that is supposed to have identified the cause of "homosexuality" in "gay" fruit flies. Such talk is not, however, merely the stuff of pop science. An article published in the distinguished scientific journal *Science* also talks about "sexual orientation" in *Drosophila*—in fact, the title of the article specifically mentions "sexual orientation in male *Drosophila*" (Ferveur et al. 1995). Both LeVay and Hamer touted the significance of this fruit fly study (Barinaga 1995) showing that practitioners of the emerging research program have embraced the fruit fly model of sexual orientation. Burr describes the discovery of a single gene—dubbed "fruitless" (also known as "fru" and "fruity")—that is supposed to control male-male "courtship" behavior in fruit flies. According to Burr (1996a, 34), the behavior exhibited by fruit flies with the fruitless gene is "a dramatic example of homosexuality in animals." What Burr is actually discussing amounts to a dramatic example of how some of the biological literature on animal sexual behavior (and some of the biological literature that cites it) is guilty of extreme anthropomorphism.

In the study of fruit fly "sexual orientation" published in *Science,* male fruit flies were subject to a process that researchers call "genetic feminization," whereby flies were genetically altered so that the portions of their brains responsible for odor detection developed as such brain regions typically develop in females of the species (Ferveur et al. 1995). Flies altered in this fashion will "court" both males and females of the species (that is, such flies will attempt to initiate the activities that typically precede sexual reproduction or attempts at it). There are several other fruit fly mutations that affect courting behavior, including several variants of the fruitless mutation (Hall 1994). In chapter 2, I suggested that human sexual orientation is a complex psychological trait that is not reducible to sexual behavior. For reasons I discuss below, studies of fruit flies are irrelevant to understanding human sexual orientation, that is, they are no more relevant to understanding human sexual orientation than they are to any other complex psychological property of humans.

Fruit flies cannot be said to have desires or to experience attraction in ways even remotely like how humans have desires and experience attraction. Whatever mechanisms underlie the mating activities of flies are *reflexes* because the only behaviors that creatures like flies are capable of are reflexes. Human sexual response is in some sense animalistic and some features of it are reflexes, but human sexual response is not completely reflexive. Rather, human sexual responses are cognitively mediated, by which I mean that human sexual desire is intimately intertwined with our thinking processes. Flies do not have the relevant thought processes; in fact, they are at best borderline cognitive systems. Although flies may act in such a way that seems to reflect a desire, so too do inanimate objects; thermostats, for example, behave *as if* they want to keep the temperature of a room stable even though thermostats do not have desires. Simply put, flies do not have beliefs and desires. This is a quite serious objection to the view that flies have sexual orientations in anything like the sense that humans do and, thereby, the view that flies can be useful models of human sexual desire.

A defender of the relevance of flies to understanding human sexual orientation might argue as follows: flies, like humans, come in two sexes—male and female—and, like humans, reproduce sexually rather than asexually (single-celled organisms, for example, rather than mating, reproduce by splitting in half and producing two identical "offspring"). The idea is that human sexual reproduction and fruit fly sexual reproduction have something deep in common: both have the ability to reproduce sexually. The various species that reproduce sexually can be grouped into an abstract natural kind that can play an explanatory role in scientific explanations that apply across a wide range of species. I call such a group an *interspecies natural kind*. There are important scientific generalizations that can be made about the process of sexual reproduction that apply to humans, fruit flies, and the sexually reproducing species that, taxonomically speaking, are in between them. Given this, it is also possible to delineate a group of organisms that engage in roughly the same behaviors that are involved in sexual reproduction in their respective species but with members of the same sex. This group includes male fruit flies that try to "have sex with" other male fruit flies as well as humans who engage (and desire to engage) in various forms of sexual behavior with people of the same sex-gender. These organisms from various species can be grouped together as homosexual in virtue of their sexual behavior. The idea is that the group of organisms that engage in same-sex sexual activities constitutes an interspecies natural kind. The defender of the relevance of flies to human sexual orientation would conclude that it makes sense to talk about homosexual fruit flies and homosexual humans and to use the former as a model for the latter.

This line of thought is quite problematic. Studies of fruit flies do not have any particular relevance to human sexual orientation. The proposed interspecies natural kind groups together human homosexuals and flies who engage in same-sex behavior by adopting a very narrow *behavioral* definition of homosexuality. In chapter 2, I argued that the behavioral view of sexual orientation (for humans) was mistaken. Most animal models of sexual orientation, but especially any models that include fruit flies, are behavioral models. Behavioral similarities are not likely to demarcate any interspecies natural kinds that include human sexual orientations.

Consider the following example from a realm other than sexuality. Referring only to organisms' behavior, one could describe a group that includes organisms of various species. For example, one might use the term "soldiers" for those organisms who have primary responsibility for protecting a group of organisms of the same species against life-threatening attacks. One might include worker ants, the leaders of lion packs, certain alpha chimps, and humans in the military. There might be some reasonable behavioral criteria for calling some but not other organisms "soldiers" in this sense of the term. Although such a grouping can be described, it remains highly unlikely that this interspecies grouping will constitute an interspecies natural kind. This interspecies collection of soldiers is not likely to play a role in any scientific laws about the behavior of all (or most) species because the underlying mechanisms that lead to soldier behavior among ants, lions, chimps, and humans are quite different. Given the huge range of environments in which soldiering behaviors occur, the various roles that such behaviors play, and the various forms such behaviors take, it is highly unlikely that such behavioral similarities will stem from an interspecies natural kind. The same points apply to attempting to describe an interspecies natural kind relating to homosexuality, especially since the fruit fly model of homosexuality crucially involves the sense of smell. Even granting that smell is involved in human sexual desires, it is crazy to equate odor-discriminating abilities in flies to sexual orientation in humans.

The proposed interspecies natural kind that will encompass gay humans, "gay" fruit flies, and other "gay" critters is even worse off than my objections so far suggest. In humans, it is possible to distinguish sexual behaviors from nonsexual behaviors that look outwardly the same, but it is not possible to do so for fruit flies. Any contact between two *Drosophila* of the same sex that makes use of an organ involved in sexual reproduction counts as homosexual. If we make use of this criteria for humans, we must count a female gynecologist touching the vulva of one of her patients, a male urologist touching the penis of one of his patients, and perhaps even wrestling between people of the same sex-gender as homosexual behavior. The problem is that any sort of criteria that might be proposed for picking out sexual behavior, courtship behavior, or homosexual behavior in fruit flies will be completely ill-suited for humans. Many aspects of human sexual behavior are intentional, cognitively mediated (even if they are unconscious), and nonreflexive, whereas no aspect of fruit fly behavior has any of the properties.

This problem is, in a way, an interspecies version of what in chapter 2 I called "Frye's problem," that is, the problem of drawing a line between sex acts and nonsex acts. Frye's problem is a difficult one for humans, but it seems potentially tractable. The *interspecies* version of Frye's problem is whether there is a single set of criteria that can be articulated that apply to animals from fruit flies on up to humans and that will distinguish between sex acts and nonsex acts in a way that fits with reasonable intuitions for humans (for example, that matches our intuitions that gynecological examinations typically do not count as sexual) while applying to species as different from humans as fruit flies.

Relatedly, there is a problem with what distinguishes males from females in fruit flies and how this fits with what distinguishes males from females among humans and other creatures (this is roughly the interspecies version of some of the issues I discussed in chapter 1). This problem of sex differentiation is underscored by fruit flies bred for studies like the one in *Science* (Ferveur et al. 1995). In this fruit fly study, the flies in question are engineered "intersexual" flies. According to the scientists who created them, they have "feminized" genes and brains but are still males. In one article, these intersexual flies are referred to as "*mainly* male" (Greenspan 1995, 74). Despite this, their sexual activity towards other males (who may or may not be feminized) is still considered homosexual behavior. It is not clear, however, whether fruit flies that have what might be called "female mating centers" in their central nervous systems should count as homosexual when they attempt to have sex with males (especially when they also attempt to have sex with females). Who is to say that the genetic feminization of fruit flies results in "male homosexual" flies rather than "transsexual heterosexual" ones? I am not suggesting that fruit flies are better models for transsexuality or intersexuality than they are for homosexuality. Rather, I am noting that the existence of the proposed interspecies natural kind for homosexuality that is supposed to apply to species as divergent as humans and flies is unproven partly because what counts as female and male and what counts as a sex act are unclear and unarticulated. This, in addition to my earlier point that fruit flies do not have desires and intentions—mental states that are required for having a sexual orientation—shows that the fruit fly is an inappropriate model for human sexual orientation. Simply put, when it comes to human sexual orientation, fruit flies are a fruitless (groan) analogy.

## Seagulls

Although the comparison with fruit flies is perhaps "the most dramatic example" of a poor animal model for human sexual orientation, some of the very same worries that arose with fruit flies apply to attempts to model human sexual orientation on the basis of the sexual behavior of other animals. In another article published in *Science,* George and Molly Hunt reported on female-female pairings among seagulls found in various islands off the coast of Southern California (Hunt and Hunt 1977). They discovered that about 10 percent of seagull nests had twice the number of eggs as expected. As they investigated the cause of this, they determined that these nests were tended by pairs of female seagulls rather than by the male-female pairs that tended most seagull nests. The female pairs had "courted" each other and together defended a territory in the ways that male-female pairs usually do. A small percentage of these female pairs engaged in "mounting and attempted copulation" (1466) activities typical in male-female pairs. The significant difference between the female-female pairs and the male-female pairs was, not surprisingly, the number of offspring they produced. A female seagull can produce an egg on her own, but a male is required to fertilize it. There were more offspring and a much higher percentage of fertile eggs in the nests of the male-female pairs compared to the nests of the female-female pairs; however, the female-female pairs did have *some* offspring, which means that at least one of the females in the pair had sex with a male of the species.

In 1993, Simon LeVay's Institute of Lesbian and Gay Education organized a boat trip in search of these "lesbian" seagulls. Their hope, it seems, was to use the existence of lesbian seagulls as a way to show that homosexuality is natural. Their well-meaning goal did not ensure success; they failed to find any evidence of lesbian seagulls (LeVay 1996, 202). The explanation for the apparent appearance of these "lesbian" seagulls in the 1970s and their subsequent disappearance seems, as the Hunts hypothesized in their original article, due to the percentage of males in the seagull population (Fry 1993). The idea is that if a female seagull cannot find a male to pair with, it is adaptive for her to find other ways to raise chicks. In this case, some females adopt a two-pronged strategy of attempting to find a male seagull to fertilize her eggs while trying to find another female to share the responsibilities of tending a nest and protecting the surrounding territory.

Suppose this story is true. Are these "lesbian" seagulls thereby good models for human homosexuality? Although birds certainly have greater cognitive capacities than flies, it is not clear whether seagulls have the cognitive architecture required for desires and intentions; after all, the expression "bird brain" means "stupid" for a reason. Further, with fruit flies, we only have behavioral evidence: we know the "lifestyle" of the seagulls in question, but we know nothing of their desires and preferences (insofar as birds have such mental states). Given that the favored hypothesis is that the same-sex behavior of these females is due to the paucity of males, not the desire for females, the relationship between the two female seagulls is, if we must anthropomorphize, more like the relationship between two single mothers who decide to be housemates to share the expenses and duties involved in child rearing than it is like that of a lesbian couple who decide to coparent. Even granting that it is possible to distinguish what is sexual from nonsexual for birds, only in some cases does the relationship between two female seagulls seem sexual. The bottom line is that although researchers who want to use the seagull as a model for human homosexuality do not face all the problems that those who want to do so with fruit flies (for example, it is clear that the putative "lesbian" seagulls are female), there are still so many differences between human sexual orientation and pair-bonding in seagulls as to render the analogy between them useless. (Their scientific value aside, lesbian seagulls have been immortalized in a song— called "Lesbian Seagulls"—from the movie *Beavis and Butthead Do America.*)

## Rats

Although some researchers working in the emerging scientific program for sexual orientation do mention fruit flies and seagulls, far more important and more frequently cited as a model of sexual orientation are rodents. Almost every biological study of sexual orientation mentions rodents at least in passing, and some like LeVay (1991) use the rat model of sexual orientation as a linchpin. Rodents are remarkably similar to humans in terms of neuroanatomy, body chemistry, and reproductive systems. Their cognitive systems are much closer to ours than are those of flies or seagulls. Further, research on rodents has particular promise because they are small and easy to maintain, they reproduce quickly, there is a large supply of laboratory rodents available for study, and their anatomy and physiology are fairly well understood. However, just because the rodent makes an appropriate and convenient model for humans in some ways does not mean that the rodent is a good model for studying human sexual orientation. In fact, extrapolating from behaviors in rodents to psychological phenomena in humans is problematic.

According to some researchers and many popular accounts, a male rat

Figure 6-1. Rat Lordosis. The rat being mounted (the one on the right) is displaying lordosis. On the standard view of rat "sexual orientation," if both rats are male, the rat displaying lordosis is homosexual, while the other rat is heterosexual. If both rats are female, the rat displaying lordosis is heterosexual, while the other rat is homosexual. If the rat displaying lordosis is a female and the other rat is a male, they are both heterosexual. Finally, if the rat displaying lordosis is a male and the other rat is a female, it is unclear what their sexual orientations are.

that is castrated at birth and subsequently shows a sexually receptive posture called *lordosis* (meaning curvature of the spine) when mounted by another male is homosexual. (Figure 6-1 shows a rat in lordosis.) This posture is typically displayed by female rats to "invite" a male rat to have sexual intercourse with her. This receptive posture, however, is little more than a reflex for females and castrated males. In particular, a neonatally castrated male will assume lordosis if a handler strokes its back. Further, while the male who displays lordosis when mounted by another male and the female who mounts another female are counted as homosexual, the male that mounts another male is considered heterosexual and escapes scientific scrutiny and labeling, as does the female that displays lordosis when mounted by another female. In this laboratory paradigm, sexual orientation is defined in terms of specific behaviors and postures. In contrast, in the human case we typically count both a man who penetrates and a man who is penetrated (as well as a man who engages in or desires to engage in various acts that do not involve penetration at all) as gay. Sexual orientation in humans is defined not by the motor patterns of copulation (that is, what "position" one takes in sexual intercourse), but by one's pattern of erotic responsiveness and the sex-gender of one's preferred sex partner. That this is the case becomes even clearer in light of the fact that the *dispositional* view, not the behavioral view, is the right picture of human sexual orientation.

    LeVay's study of the hypothalamus has, for example, been interpreted as evidence that INAH-3 has something to do with sexual orientation. Much of this speculation, as well as LeVay's initial decision to look at this part of the hypothalamus, is based on the assumption that INAH-3 is homologous to a region of the rat's hypothalamus known as the *sexually dimorphic nucleus of the preoptic area* (SDN-POA, for short) (LeVay 1991, 1034). The function of the rat's SDN-POA has, however, eluded researchers for over a decade and a half: although the size of the SDN-POA correlates positively with the amount of mounting behavior displayed by males, it can be totally destroyed on both sides of the brain without any discernible effect on mounting behavior (Arendash and Gorski 1983). Despite this, various researchers have been interested in showing that one of the INAH regions is roughly equivalent to the SDN-POA in rats. However, not all species that are closely related to humans and rats are known to have regions like the SDN-POA or INAH-3; for example, attempts to find a homologue of SDN-POA in mice have failed (Bleier, Byne, and Siggelkow 1982).

Compared to fruit flies and seagulls, rats may seem to provide a fairly promising model for humans. It is reasonable—though not uncontroversial—to think that rats have desires and intentions, which are prerequisites for having a sexual orientation. Further, it may be possible to develop an account of what counts as a sexual act for a rat that is roughly parallel to such an account for humans. However, the way that rat sexual behavior is currently studied and understood is radically different from how we understand human sexual orientation. The sexual desires of rats are assessed by observing their sexual behavior. Homosexuality in rats is equated with lordosis (sexual posture) rather than sexual desire. Further, the putative homosexual rats are hormonally and neurologically altered in a way that human homosexuals are not. There are, then, serious problems with the way that rats are typically used as a model for human sexual orientation (Byne 1995; Byne and Parsons 1993, 231; Fausto-Sterling 1995).

Some researchers acknowledge the problem of equating behaviors in rodents with sexual orientation, and they employ a variety of strategies to assess sexual-partner preference in rats (Bakker et al. 1993; Brand et al. 1991; Brand and Slob 1991; Matuszczyk, Fernandez-Guasti, and Larssen 1988). A typical version of such a study involves giving rats the chance to press one of two levers that will allow them to spend time in the company of either a male or a female rat. Male rats who have been castrated, hormonally manipulated, or neuroanatomically altered choose to spend more time with male rats than female rats and initiate sex more often with the male rats than with the female rats. These rats are claimed to be homosexuals in the sense that they have an underlying homosexual preference, not just that they happen to engage in same-sex sexual behavior. Studies like these—of rats and of other nonhuman animals such as hamsters (Johnson and Tiefer 1972) and ferrets (Baum et al. 1990)—are supposed to reveal organisms' underlying desires rather than just their behaviors.

While studies designed to reveal underlying sexual desires are more interesting than those that focus simply on mounting behavior, even these studies may have little to do with human sexual orientation. In order for a male rat that is chromosomally typical to behave as a female rat typically does with respect to either partner preference or receptive posturing, he must be exposed to extreme hormonal abnormalities that are unlikely to occur outside the neuroendocrine laboratory. First, he must either be castrated at birth (or soon after), depriving him of androgens, or particular androgen-responsive regions of his brain must be destroyed (Goy and McEwen 1980). Then, in order to activate the display of female-typical behaviors and preferences, he must be injected with estrogen in adulthood. Because gay men and lesbians have hormonal profiles that are indistinguishable from those of their heterosexual counterparts (see chapter 5), it is difficult to see how this situation has any bearing on human sexual orientation. Even those studies that attempt to assess rat sexual desires rather than simply their behavior suffer from the same problems as do most other studies of rat sexuality. Further, it is not obvious whether they actually overcome the problems faced by fruit fly and seagull models of human sexual orientation. As yet, it has not been shown that rats constitute a good model of human sexual desire or sexual orientation.

## Nonhuman Primates

Primate models of human sexual orientation are prima facie far more promising than nonprimate models. Various of our primate "cousins" are neurologically, anatomically, and genetically quite similar to us. For example, humans share over 98 percent of our genetic code with both the common chimpanzee (*Pan troglodytes*) and the pygmy chimpanzee or bonobo (*Pan paniscus*); as a species, we diverged (evolutionarily speaking) from these two chimpanzee species about six to eight million years ago, a short span of time from the evolutionary time frame (Diamond 1992). Also, it is the nonhuman primates who are the most likely candidates among the entire animal kingdom for having desires and intentions.

Further, nonhuman primates are more like humans in terms of sexual practices than any other group in the animal kingdom. In particular, some nonhuman primates frequently engage in *recreational* sex (sex for fun or making friends rather than for procreation) (Waal 1989). While this suggests that they will be good models for human sexual desire, it also creates a potential problem. Many nonhuman primates engage in mounting and *presenting*—the display of sexually receptive positions, in other words, adopting a posture that seems to say "mount me"—for seemingly nonsexual purposes. For example, members of some primate species will mount and/or present when they are reunited with a friend or family member after a long period of separation. Such possibly functional and nonsexual mounting and presenting also occurs for purposes of appeasement, aggression, and reassurance. It is, thus, hard to distinguish between sexual and nonsexual behaviors and desires, especially between *nonsexual but sexlike acts*, on the one hand, and *nonreproductive yet actual sex acts*, on the other. It is even more difficult to distinguish between the desire to engage in nonsexual sexlike acts and the desire to engage in nonreproductive sex acts.

Some have tried to make the distinction between sexual and nonsexual acts by focusing on persistent genital stimulation and sustained sexual arousal. For example, Ronald Nadler in his survey of studies of homosexual behavior in nonhuman primates distinguishes sexual from nonsexual behavior by the presence of:

> *persistent genital stimulation* (i.e., more than perfunctory) and *sexual arousal*, in at least one of the individuals involved . . . [where] sexual arousal is usually inferred from certain physiological and behavioral responses, especially, but not limited to, those responses that have been identified . . . as components of the species-typical pattern of reproductive behavior. (Nadler 1990, emphasis added)

Call this the *arousal view* of what counts as sexual for nonhuman primates. Others have gone in the opposite direction and included as sexual behavior all genital contact regardless of its apparent social function (Vasey 1995). Call this the *genital view* of what counts as sexual for nonhuman primates.

There are rationales for both the arousal view and the genital view of what counts as sexual in human behaviors. Humans sometimes engage in behaviors that look sexual but in fact are not, for example, gynecological examinations. Neither the gynecologist who inserts his or her finger into the vagina of a patient nor the urologist who touches the penis of his or her patient is (typically) engaging in a sexual act. One of the reasons why these acts do not count as sexual is because neither of the people involved are aroused. This seems to count in favor of the arousal view. But humans engage in sex in a variety of contexts for various social functions. Regardless of its function—to earn money,

to advance socially or professionally, to appease someone—most genital stimu-
lations are counted as sexual. This counts in favor of the genital view.

The fact that it is hard to distinguish sexual from nonsexual acts in
nonhuman primates is not a strong objection to using such primates as a model
for human sexual desire and sexual orientation. In fact, roughly the same
problem exists for humans. An interesting example of this is discussed in
George Chauncey's article concerning the U.S. Navy's attempt to discover and
eliminate a male homosexual subculture that existed near its base in Newport,
Rhode Island (Chauncey 1989). In order to investigate "the gang" (as they
were known) of homosexual men that congregated around the Newport
YMCA, the Navy recruited volunteers from among the enlisted men to infiltrate
the gang and collect evidence concerning their activities. These decoys were
expected, as part of their infiltration, to have sex with members of the gang.
The decoys accomplished their mission, and several gang members and other
men who fraternized with gang members (including some local clergymen)
were brought to trial. At the trial, when the decoys were cross-examined by
lawyers for the defendants (gang members and those associated with them), the
motives of the decoys were brought into question. The following exchange
between a lawyer for one of the defendants and one of the decoys is especially
interesting:

Q:  You volunteered for this work?
A:  Yes, sir.
Q:  You knew what kind of work it was before you volunteered, didn't
    you?
A:  Yes, sir.
Q:  You knew it involved sucking and that sort of thing, didn't you?
A:  I knew we had to deal with that, yes, sir.
Q:  You knew it included sodomy and that sort of thing, didn't you?
A:  Yes, sir.
Q:  And yet you were quite willing to get into that sort of work.
A:  I was willing to do it, yes, sir.
Q:  And so willing that you volunteered for it, is that right?
A:  Yes, sir, I volunteered for it.
Q:  You knew it included buggering other fellows, didn't you?    (306)


The lawyer seems to be pushing the genital view of what counts as sexual. The
decoys were having sex because they willfully engaged in genital stimulation.
On this view, the decoys are as homosexual as the gang members; they are as

guilty of committing the crime of sodomy as the gang members, and the Navy is guilty of encouraging the decoys to commit sodomy.

Some of the decoys tried to defend themselves by adopting, at least implicitly, the arousal view of what counts as sexual.

> One decoy protested that he had never responded to a pervert's advances: "I am a man . . . The thing was so horrible in my sight that naturally I could not become passionate . . . ." Another, less fortunate decoy had to plead, "Of course a great deal of that was involuntary inasmuch as a man placing his hands on my penis would cause an erection and subsequent emission. That was uncontrollable on my part. . . . It is a physiological fact." (306–307)

The less fortunate decoy is granting that there was genital stimulation, but he seems to be denying that there was genuine arousal and implying that it would be wrong to count his acts as sexual or homosexual.

The example of the Newport investigation suggests that humans and nonhuman primates are similar when it comes to determining what counts as sex. Both the genital view and the arousal view of sex are plausible for humans and other primates. Frye's problem of demarcating the sexual from the nonsexual (chapter 2) is not a uniquely human problem.

Whatever it is that counts as sex for nonhuman primates, it is clear that there is a great range of sexual behaviors among the various nonhuman primate species. Vasey's systematic survey of the primatological data found that homosexuality is widespread among the higher primates (that is, the anthropoid suborder of primates including monkeys, apes, and humans) but mostly absent among the lower primates (the prosimian suborder of primates including the lesser-known lemurs and bush babies) (Vasey 1995). Vasey enumerates some thirty-three anthropoid primate species who engage in some homosexual behavior and twelve who do so on a regular basis. Among these species, there is a wide range of contexts in which homosexual behavior occurs and, when it does occur, the behavior takes a multitude of forms and fulfills a wide variety of social functions. In the case of using the nonhuman primate as a model for understanding human sexual behavior, it is not at all clear what we should infer from the application of this model because of the huge variance among the sexual behavior of the various primate species.

Even if we were able to focus on a particular nonhuman primate (or a set of nonhuman primate species), there remain some potential problems for modeling human sexual desire. Many discussions of sexual behavior among nonhuman primates do not distinguish between biological bases of same-sex sexual behavior and of sexual behavior generally. Although there is clearly a great deal of same-sex sexual activity among many nonhuman primates, it is not clear that there are any species of nonhuman primates that exhibit anything like *exclusive* homosexuality, especially exclusive homosexuality among hormonally and chromosomally typical male and female nonhuman primates. Most nonhuman primates that engage in same-sex sexual activity also engage in extensive sexual activity with conspecifics not of the same sex. Given the seeming *bi*sexuality of most nonhuman primates that engage in same-sex sexual activity, it is not clear how such animal models will help us understand human sexual orientation, even if it helps us to understand human sexual behavior generally. For example, although studies of chimps might lead us to believe that certain regions of the hypothalamus are involved in sexual desire, such studies could only be suggestive of the biological bases of same-sex desire in humans.

Finally, although nonhuman primates are clearly better models than nonprimates for studying the complex cognitive processes involved in human sexual desire, there are still important differences between humans and other primates and these very differences may be crucial in developing an account of human sexual orientation. In particular, humans have—and nonhuman primates lack—the ability to learn and use complex languages, we have multifaceted cultures, and we can engage in abstract planning and reasoning processes. Whether these differences are enough to disqualify even other primates as models of human sexual orientation remains to be seen (Adkins-Regan 1988, 345). In any event, if any species will be good models of human sexual orientation, it seems that nonhuman primates will be. Unfortunately, the few studies of sexual orientation in nonhuman primates have not been especially illuminating.

Same-sex sexual activity occurs among many species from flies and finches to ferrets and Francois' leaf monkeys, and it takes almost as many forms. Given present knowledge, no species is an ideal model of human sexual orientation. Sexual orientation involves complex cognitive, emotional, social, psychological, and perhaps linguistic properties that nonprimates and perhaps nonhumans lack. Even nonhuman primates lack some complex cognitive processes that humans have. While these differences do not necessarily mean that only humans can have sexual orientations, such differences between humans and other primates may be so significant as to prevent primates from being a useful model of human sexual orientation. Before we can determine which animals are, given these constraints, the best model for human sexual desire, we need to have a better understanding of human sexual desire and behavior. When we are trying to understand the sexual behaviors and desires of other animals, we need to be careful not to project unjustifiably onto other animals assumptions about what sex and sexual desire are for humans. For example, we should not begin by assuming that animal species can be sorted into sexual orientations—some species of animals (that is, some nonhuman primates) might be bisexual and some might be primarily heterosexual but engage in situational homosexual behavior. We must be skeptical of how scientists use nonhuman animals to support their favored theories of how humans develop sexual orientations. It is important to remember that sexual behavior is subject to a great deal of selective pressure over the course of evolution; as a result, the mechanisms underlying sexual behavior are among the most likely to change as species branch off from each other. The extent to which human sexual desires and orientations can be usefully understood from the point of view of evolutionary theory is the subject of the next section.

## The Evolution of Human Sexual Orientations

The sexual behaviors of animals are subject to evolutionary explanations. We have already encountered such a story in the context of the "lesbian" seagulls. Female-female pair-bonding in seagulls was explained as an adaptive strategy for a female who, in the face of a shortage of males, did not find a male with whom to pair and instead paired with another female, while at the same time looked for a male to fertilize her eggs. One possible evolutionary story is that if one were a female bird that cannot find a male bird to both fertilize one's eggs and share child-care duties, then one should try to find a female bird to nest with and various males to fertilize one's eggs. Female birds with neuroanatomical structures that lead them to adopt this strategy rather than, for example, the strategy of taking care of their chicks by themselves, will leave more offspring under conditions in which there are fewer males than females. In many instances, animal sexual behaviors as well as other behaviors can be usefully explained from the evolutionary perspective. Thinkers in the tradition of sociobiology and evolutionary psychology have argued that all or most human behaviors can be given evolutionary explanations (Barkow, Cosmides, and Tooby 1992; Pinker 1997; Wilson 1975; Wilson 1978). I now consider the extent to which such explanations are useful to explaining human sexual behavior and the mechanisms that underlie it.

### Evolution, Natural Selection, Sociobiology, and Evolutionary Psychology

Before Charles Darwin articulated the theory of natural selection, the origins of species and the development over time of traits were mysteries that required positing a powerful and intelligent designer to explain their emergence. The

theory of natural selection—and evolutionary theory, of which it is a part—
explains these phenomena solely by appeal to natural forces. The power of
natural selection is that it explains the appearance of design without appealing
to a designer. The three major components of natural selection are variation,
selection, and retention. According to Darwin, variations are not predesigned
to perform certain functions. Rather, those variations that perform useful functions are selected, while those that do not are not selected. Natural selection is
responsible for the appearance that useful variations occur in such a way that it
seems there is intentional progress in evolution. In the modern theory of evolution, genetic mutations provide the blind variations (blind in the sense that
variations are not influenced by the effects they have and the likelihood of a
mutation is not correlated with the benefits or liabilities that mutation would
confer on the organism), the environment provides the filter of selection, and
reproduction provides the retention. Fit between organism and environment is
achieved because those organisms with features that make them less fit do not
survive in competition with other organisms that have features that enable them
to flourish or at least survive (Sober 1984; Williams 1966).

As an example of the power of evolution and natural selection, consider
the human eye. The eye has many interacting parts, each of which is intricately
designed. Together, these parts enable their possessor to see with great precision and efficiency. William Paley used the amazing complexity and power of
the eye as evidence for the existence of an all-knowing, all-powerful creator of
life (Paley 1802). Darwin, in contrast, explained the evolution of such a
complex structure without an intentional designer (Darwin 1859). Natural
selection is able to explain how minutely small modifications to a structure are
retained; it does so on the basis of how well these modifications improve the
functioning of the structure. Selection on the basis of merit is required for
random mutations to lead to the production of complex structures like the
human eye. The chances are infinitesimally small that some other noninten-
tional force could produce a structure that can do all the things that an eye can
do—for example, focus an image, control incoming light, respond to the presence of edges, and react differentially to colors. Such an unlikely arrangement
of biological matter could come into existence in the right place to perform
such specific and special functions only through a process involving selection
on the basis of how well this collection of stuff performs functions, that is,
through the process of natural selection (Dawkins 1986).

Given the power of natural selection, it is not surprising that some people
have tried to use evolutionary theory to explain human behaviors. Sociobiologists, in particular, attempt to explain all human behavior using evolutionary

theory (Wilson 1975, 1978). The idea is that behaviors that increase an organism's reproductive success will be selected for and flourish and those that decrease it will be selected against and disappear. The theory of natural selection can explain some human behaviors: some of our psychological mechanisms no doubt evolved through reproductive pressures. For example, some researchers have argued that the psychological mechanisms underlying our linguistic ability evolved through natural selection (Pinker 1994, 332–369; Pinker and Bloom 1990). Sociobiologists, however, believe that *all* human behaviors, even cognitively mediated ones, can be explained in this fashion. One example they give of how this might work involves the presence in most cultures of an incest taboo—that is, a legal or social prohibition of sex between siblings—and the fact that most individuals have an aversion to sex between siblings. The offspring, if any, that result from sex between siblings are, because of the genetic similarity of their parents, much more likely that other people to exhibit recessive traits, which are often nonoptimal and can sometimes be fatal. Sociobiologists argue that organisms that have psychological mechanisms than make them more likely to have sex with their siblings will have decreased reproductive success (Wilson 1978, 36–39; for a critique of how sociobiologists theorize incest, see Kitcher 1985, especially 342–350). The sociobiologist wants to use explanations of this form to explain such diverse human phenomenon as religious beliefs (Wilson 1975, 559–562), and aesthetic judgments (Wilson 1978, 169–194).

Sociobiology has been criticized for making a direct leap from genes to behavior (Cosmides and Tooby 1987). For example, sociobiologists might talk about natural selection selecting for or against genes for adultery or homosexuality (Wilson 1975, 555; 1978, 144–146). This sort of talk clearly involves dramatic oversimplification. Natural selection involves selection for genes, but the connection between genes and behavior is quite complex; at a minimum, the connection is mediated by the process of development (the process through which genes, in the presence of certain environmental factor, will produce embodied organisms) and by the mind (genes do not cause desires and behavior; genes cause certain mental mechanisms to develop, which in turn engender certain sorts of desires and behaviors). Focusing on the role of the mind, behaviors are not selected by natural selection; rather, genes are selected that lead to the development of mechanisms that cause behaviors (more precisely, genes produce proteins; which in turn produce neurons, hormones, and the like; which lead to the development of mechanisms that cause behaviors). Sociobiology is not the right approach for developing an understanding of mental mechanisms; rather, *cognitive science* (the scientific study of thinking)

informed by evolutionary considerations—known as *evolutionary psychology*—
is (Barkow, Cosmides, and Tooby 1992; Pinker 1997; Tooby 1988; Tooby and
Cosmides 1987).

### The Evolution of Homosexuality

The continued existence of homosexuality, according to some thinkers, poses a
potential problem for sociobiology and evolutionary psychology. Sociobiology
and evolutionary psychology explain human behavior and psychological mechanisms in terms of reproductive success. What could be harder to explain in
terms of reproductive success than a mental mechanism that leads individuals to
strongly desire sexual activity that does not lead to reproduction? The theory of
natural selection holds that, all else being equal, a mutation that leads to a small
change in the visual system, which in turn causes worse eyesight, will be eliminated from the gene pool through natural selection. Similarly, the sociobiologist
says that a mutation that leads to cognitive mechanisms that increase the likelihood that a person will desire or engage in sex with his or her sibling, which will
increase potentially fatal recessive traits, will be eliminated. A mutation that
increases the chance a person will be a homosexual should, it seems, have a
similar fate. The continued existence of homosexuality in significant numbers
poses a problem for this story (see chapter 7, for a discussion of the percentage
of lesbians and gay men in the population). As the emerging scientific program
is committed to seeing sexual orientation as being strongly biologically based, it
needs to deal with this tension between the continued existence of homosexuality and the central role played by reproductive success in evolutionary theory.
Some sociobiologists have developed accounts of the continued existence of
homosexuality (McKnight 1997; Ruse 1988, 130–149; Wilson 1975, 555;
1978, 144–147), and some practitioners of the emerging scientific program
have endorsed such accounts (Hamer and Copeland 1994, 180–186; LeVay
1996, 188–193; Weinrich 1987b, 310–336). These accounts, some of which
date from the early days of sociobiology, divide into two general strategies for
dealing with the problem of the continued existence of homosexuality.[1]

The first strategy is to show that homosexuality in some way contributes to
the overall good of the community and thereby contributes to the reproductive
success of the family or group to which the lesbian or gay man belongs.
According to one of the more popular versions of this strategy, homosexuality is
selectively advantageous because gay men and lesbians (directly or indirectly)
help their siblings raise their children. In this way, gay men and lesbians pass
on their genes through their nephews and nieces (McKnight 1997, 124–162;
Ruse 1988, 134–149; Weinrich 1987b, 318–336; Wilson 1978, 144–147).

This evolutionary account of the continued existence of homosexuality is a version of a perfectly reasonable evolutionary story known as *kin selection*. Kin selection stories can explain how traits that seem to be reproductively *dis*advantageous to an individual organism can in fact be reproductively advantageous. Notably, kin selection stories provide an evolutionary explanation of altruistic behavior (Dawkins 1976; Wilson 1978, 149–168). An organism displays altruistic behavior when it sacrifices its own well-being for the well-being of another. A bird is behaving altruistically if it screeches to warn other birds of the approach of a predator because it risks its life by drawing attention to itself. If behaving altruistically is genetically based, as sociobiologists claim, it seems that the gene for altruistic behavior will die out after a few generations. The thought is that birds who are genetically disposed to screech in the face of predators are more likely to be eaten by such predators before they have a chance to reproduce than are the ones who remain silent and just fly the coop when they see a predator. Over time, it seems, the forces of natural selection will lead to the extinction of screechers and other creatures with genes for altruistic behavior. Kin selection is a response to the problem that altruism persists despite the selective pressures against it. Flocks with screechers in them will survive better in the face of predators than flocks with no screechers. Screechers contribute to the overall fitness of the flock, which typically includes many of the screechers' relatives. A screecher typically helps its siblings, offspring, cousins, nephews, and nieces to survive and reproduce, although it may die in the process. A screecher's genes, which include the gene for screeching, get passed on through its kin. The odds that his kin will actually survive to reproduce are increased because the genes they have inherited are for the mental mechanisms that cause screeching behavior.

The kin selection story about homosexuality is of the same general form: gay men and lesbians, by foregoing offspring of their own, are free to help raise and care for their siblings, the offspring of their siblings, and for other relatives. The claim is not that lesbians and gay men are consciously thinking about the benefits to their siblings, nephews, and nieces when they forgo reproductive sex by looking for opportunities to engage in sexual activity with people of the same sex-gender. Rather, their genes have given them psychological mechanisms that underlie sexual desires for people of the same sex-gender. Given these desires, gay men and lesbians are much less likely to produce offspring. The thought is that the time they would devote to child care if they had their own children would be devoted to the care of their siblings, nephews, and nieces. Given the extra attention family members of gay men and lesbians would get, these family members would have increased reproductive success and more copies of their genes would get out into the gene pool. Included in their genes would be the genes that underlie the desire for people of the same sex-gender in their lesbian and gay family members. This way the genes that lead to homosexuality would get passed on to future generations, not (primarily) through the offspring of lesbians and gay men, but through their family members (I discuss a structurally similar sociobiological account known as *parental manipulation* in chapter 8).

Another version of this story involves *group selection* rather than kin selection. According to this story, gay men and lesbians devote themselves to the arts and other activities that require aesthetic abilities instead of rearing children. The people in these communities benefit from these artistic pursuits by having better, more productive lives. Like the flock with screechers in it, a community with artists will be better than one without them (Posner 1992, 303–304; Whitam and Dizon 1980). It serves the community to have some lesbians and gay men who can focus their time on projects that benefit the entire community rather than devote their time to child rearing. Both the kin selection and the group selection story provide an account of how the mechanisms that underlie homosexuality are selectively advantageous.

The second strategy for explaining the continued existence of homosexuality is to claim that homosexuality is associated with some other trait that provides increased reproductive success. Homosexuality, on this view, is a *piggyback trait*—genes for homosexuality are retained in the gene pool not for intrinsic reasons (as suggested by the kin and group selection stories), but for coincidental ones. As an analogy, sociobiologists often give the following example. There is a genetic sequence that codes for immunity to malaria. The same genetic sequence has the effect of increasing the chance that its possessor will develop sickle-cell anemia, a serious blood disorder that is typically fatal. In environments in which malaria is a serious health risk, the advantage of immunity to malaria is worth the increased risk of sickle-cell anemia. Sickle-cell anemia is not selected for; it rides on the back of the selective advantageousness of immunity to malaria. Applied to sexual orientation, the idea is that homosexuality is associated with another trait or traits that lead to reproductive success (Hutchinson 1959; Kirsch and Rodman 1982; McKnight 1997, 64–123; Ruse 1988, 130–149; Wilson 1975, 555). For example, there might be a gene for psychological mechanisms that produce men who are especially appealing to heterosexual women as mates such as "sensitive" heterosexuals. If this gene were in some way associated with psychological mechanisms that led to male homosexuality and if being a sensitive heterosexual were selectively advantageous, then male homosexuality would remain in the gene pool because it rides piggyback on sensitive heterosexuality.

Here are the details of one way that this might work (McKnight 1997,

64–123; Ruse 1988, 130–149). Suppose that $H$ and $h$ are two alleles—rival traits that can appear in a particular place on a chromosome—and that $H$ is dominant and $h$ is recessive (see chapter 5 for a brief account of some of this terminology). Suppose that a person who gets an $H$ from one parent and an $h$ from the other—an $Hh$ heterozygote (someone who got a different allele from each parent)—typically develops psychological mechanisms that lead him to become a sensitive heterosexual, that is, a man who is attracted to women, who romantically courts them, who is faithful, and a good father. Suppose that a man who gets an $H$ from each of his parents—an $HH$ homozygote (someone who got the same allele from each parent)—is a "nasty" heterosexual, that is, he is attracted to women, but is unromantic, rude, promiscuous, and a bad father. Finally, suppose that a man who gets an $h$ from each of his parents—an $hh$ homozygote—typically develops psychological mechanisms that lead him to be sensitive, romantic, good with children, *but* attracted to men. Given what I have supposed so far, it is reasonable that most heterosexual women would prefer, all else being equal, to mate with sensitive heterosexuals, namely $Hh$ heterozygotes. If this is the case, it seems plausible that, as a result, sensitive heterosexual men will have more offspring than either nasty men or gay men and be more likely than either to pass on their genes to future generations. A parent can, however, pass on to an offspring only one allele for each chromosomal slot. This means that sensitive men will pass on an $H$ half of the time and an $h$ half of the time. Assuming that these two alleles are roughly equally distributed among women, 50 percent of the next generation will be $Hh$, but 25 percent will be $HH$ and another 25 percent will be $hh$. If this story or one somewhat like it is right, homosexuality will continue to be present in the gene pool even if it is not selectively advantageous. According to this story, genes that typically lead to homosexuality remain in the gene pool on the back of genes that typically lead to being a sensitive heterosexual.

An evolutionary account of homosexuality need not embrace one of the particular stories about kin selection, group selection, or piggyback selection that I have described. There are other versions of both of these stories that have been (or could be) articulated. Whichever story one embraces, however, the question is how plausible that story is and what evidence there is for it.

### The Evolution of Heterosexuality

The kin selection, group selection, and piggyback selection accounts and most other sociobiological and some evolutionary psychological stories assume that we have a good evolutionary explanation of heterosexuality but that we lack one for homosexuality. The idea, presumably, is that heterosexual acts can produce offspring, while homosexual acts cannot; therefore, heterosexuality is the most selectively advantageous sexual strategy. On this account, the desire to have sex with people of a different sex-gender has greater selective advantage than the desire to have sex with people of the same sex-gender. In general, evolutionary explanations of this form are perfectly good explanations: one can explain why members of a species have one trait rather than an alternative if the trait they have enables them to leave a greater number of descendants than the alternative trait would (in other words, if the trait gives them greater selective advantage). The sociobiological account of the incest taboo took this form. The incest taboo is almost universal, sociobiologists argue, because people who desire sex with their siblings will have decreased reproductive success compared to those who do not.

Sexual activity has various uses, only one of which is reproduction; if the study of animal sexual behaviors shows anything, it shows this (Vasey 1995; Waal 1989). Further, the existence of kin selection, group selection, and piggy-back selection—whether or not any versions of these are the right accounts about the evolution of the mechanisms that underlie homosexuality—show that it is possible for a trait to be passed on to future generations even if it does not increase the number or quality of its possessor's offspring (Sober 1984, 20–31 and 97–102; Stein 1996, 175–186). In light of these two points, it is not clear that *exclusive* heterosexuality is the most selectively advantageous sexual behavior (McCaughey 1996; Stein 1994, 274–275). Some sort of bisexuality, for example, might be a better strategy. For a man, it might be selectively advantageous, in addition to having sex with women, to have sex occasionally with men. Nonhuman primates engage in all sorts of sexual activity for nonreproductive purposes; exclusive heterosexuality in humans (and nonhuman primates) might be disadvantageous because it limits the nonreproductive uses of sex to only half the population. Perhaps, it is selectively advantageous for a woman to use nonreproductive sex as a way to form alliances with both men and women in the hope that these women and men will also befriend her children and help in various ways to preserve their well-being. Perhaps, for various reasons, it is selectively advantageous for men to have reproductive sex with women and various forms of nonreproductive sex with men and women for purposes of alliance formation, violence avoidance, and sexual gratification. Perhaps women, believing that men are basically nonmonogamous, prefer that the men who are their sexual partners have sex with men rather than with other women because sex with other women, but not with men, could produce offspring that would draw their mate's time and energy from her offspring, whom she might want him to help raise. If women had such a preference, bisexuality might be a selectively advantageous trait for men.

Alternatively, perhaps sexual plasticity is the best evolutionary strategy for humans (Futuyma and Risch 1983–1984; Seaborg 1984). A person is sexually plastic if his or her sexual desires are somewhat malleable, depending on certain features of the environment. It might be selectively advantageous for sexual desires to be somewhat flexible, at least early on in life. This way, social factors can play a role in determining a person's sexual orientation, sexual desires, and sexual behaviors. The advantages and disadvantages of various sexual acts in a particular environment can play a role in the development of sexual orientations. In various places in previous chapters, I have discussed the varied sexual characters of different cultures from Attic Greeks and Native Americans to contemporary Latin Americans and North Americans. Given the various sexual environments into which a human might be born, it would be useful to allow the environment to have some role in shaping sexual desire. In light of cultural variability, genes that lead to sexual inflexibility might not be selectively advantageous.

I am not here claiming that humans have genes that code for psychological mechanisms that, in many environments, lead to bisexuality or sexual plasticity. My claim, rather, is that, from an evolutionary perspective, adaptive stories can be told for almost any psychological mechanisms underlying sexual behaviors, desires, and orientations. If we are in the business of trying to understand the evolutionary origins of human sexual desires, we should not just assume that we have an evolutionary explanation of heterosexual sexual activity and desire. Further, there is no particular evidence that lesbians and gay men contribute to the reproductive success of their siblings or to the benefit or detriment of the community at large any more or less than heterosexuals do (Futuyma and Risch 1983–1984). Similarly there is no particular evidence that homosexuality rides on the back of the selective advantage of some other trait (Dickemann 1995).

In a book on the evolution of different mating strategies for men and women, David Buss said, after reviewing some evolutionary accounts of homosexuality, that "no current evidence exists to support . . . these theories. The [evolutionary] origins of homosexuality remain a mystery" (Buss 1994, 61). While I agree with Buss, I would go further and argue that there is no evidence to support the claim that a person's sexual orientation is caused by the same psychological mechanism in every person. Most sociobiologists and some evolutionary psychologists assume that homosexuality and heterosexuality are each a single type of sexual desire caused by a single gene or psychological mechanism (Kitcher 1985, 247–251). This assumption is unjustified, for reasons I will further develop in the chapters that follow, especially chapter 8.

For now, consider the example of celibacy. In most societies, there are some people who are celibate for significant parts of their adult lives, for example, nuns, workaholics, people in solitary confinement, and people who cannot enjoy some aspects of sex due to a physical ailment. It would seem a mistake to lump everyone who is or has been celibate for a significant portion of his or her adult life into one kind and try to find a gene for the psychological mechanisms that underlie his or her celibacy. In other words, being a celibate is not a natural human kind.

The practitioners of the emerging research program claim to have evidence for thinking that sexual orientations are natural human kinds or that each sexual orientation is a single trait. If we knew that the size of a person's INAH-3 or some gene in the q28 region of the X chromosome determined a person's sexual orientation, then we would have good reason to look for an evolutionary explanation for these biological factors. It would also be useful for such research if we understood the sources of sexual desires in our evolutionary ancestors and in our other primate species, just as it helps us understand the evolution of the capacity for human language to explain how our linguistic capacity emerged in the course of evolution from our closest primate cousins. In the next chapter, I evaluate whether the emerging research program has this sort of evidence, namely, evidence that at birth or an early age biological factors determine or strongly constrain the formation of a person's sexual orientation later in life (the direct model of the role of biological factors in the development of sexual orientations). Without strong evidence from the emerging research program, we have just as much reason to believe that experiential and cultural forces, rather than biological and evolutionary forces, play a considerable role in determining sexual orientation. This would not contradict evolutionary theory even though it would count against a strong version of sociobiology. As Jerome Barkow, in a book on evolutionary psychology, admitted, "The process of cultural evolution may shape even sexuality, tied tightly though it is to fitness. . . . [O]ne can still be a good evolutionist and still concede that there is considerable distance between genes and culture" (Barkow 1989, 363).

## Conclusion

The emerging scientific research program concerning sexual orientation depends in substantive ways on animal models and evolutionary theories of human sexual orientation and behavior. In this chapter, I have argued that there is no clear nonhuman model for human sexual orientation. When one looks to the animal world, even to nonhuman primates, one finds multiple configurations of sexual behaviors and desires, not a single model for under-standing human sexual desires and orientations. I have also argued that proposed evolutionary accounts of human sexual orientation do not confirm any aspect of the emerging research program. If we had strong reasons for believing a particular account of the development of human sexual orienta-tions, then evolutionary theory might be able to tell a plausible natural-selec-tion story of the development of this trait. Without some account of the nature of human sexual orientations and some plausible theory of how sexual orienta-tions develop, the stories that sociobiologists tell about the development of sexual orientations are simply stories.

I am not claiming that the failure to find a particularly informative model of human sexual orientation in animals and the consequent failure to provide a particularly plausible evolutionary story about human sexual orientations undermine the emerging research program. Rather, there should be a syner-getic relationship between the emerging research program, on the one hand, and research on sexual orientation in nonhuman animals and research from the perspective of sociobiology and evolutionary psychology, on the other. Insofar as the emerging research program is well supported, there is good reason to look for animal models, animal precursors, and evolutionary accounts of human sexual orientations. If, however, the emerging research program is unsupported, there is little reason for thinking that evolutionary and animal research on sexual orientation has more promise than does evolutionary and animal research designed to shed light on being celibate, a yuppie, or a coffee drinker.

# CHAPTER 7

# *Critique of the Emerging Research Program*

**C**hapter 5 was primarily devoted to a positive articulation of the emerging research program for the scientific study of sexual orientation with particular attention paid to three different biological studies that constitute the backbone of this program. In that chapter, I presented the emerging program and the evidence that supports it in a fashion similar to the way researchers doing work in that program might. In the current chapter, I adopt a critical stance towards the emerging research program. In particular, I examine the methodologies for the three studies and their theoretical underpinnings, especially the assumptions they make about what a sexual orientation is. I focus on these three studies not only because they are cited positively by almost every researcher doing work in the emerging program, but also because these studies are typical of the empirical research program in their methodology and their assumptions. My goal in this chapter is not simply to criticize scientific research on sexual orientation; rather, it is to tease out and evaluate its unquestioned assumptions. Evaluating its assumptions is a precondition for strengthening the foundations of this research program, although my critical examination does not guarantee that the research program will in fact be strengthened. It might instead lead to the conclusion that scientific research on how humans develop their sexual desires can progress only if it is dramatically reconceptualized.

My critical examination of the emerging scientific research program focuses on the underlying assumptions of these studies. I begin by looking at who the subjects of these studies are. If an experiment makes use of a subject pool that is in some way biased, this gives rise to doubts about the conclusions based on it. I then examine how the sexual orientations of the subjects are determined. If subjects are assigned to sexual orientations in problematic ways, this also gives rise to doubts about conclusions based on such studies. Relatedly, I look at implicit and undefended assumptions that studies in the emerging research program make about sexual orientation. Here I revisit some of the issues I discussed in chapter 2 about what a sexual orientation is and in chapter 4 about whether sexual orientations are natural human kinds. I argue that many of the studies accept without argument a quite particular picture of sexual orientation; such a picture may skew the results of such studies. For example, many studies in the emerging research program unquestioningly accept the inversion assumption, according to which lesbians and gay men are seen as sex-gender inverts. Although this is a culturally salient assumption, it is scientifically unsupported. As this assumption infiltrates much of the emerging research program, a crucial premise of the program remains unjustified. I also consider whether the design of the various studies is adequate to support the direct model of how sexual orientations develop. I argue that, even setting aside the other methodological objections that I raise, there is no convincing evidence that biological factors are a direct cause of sexual orientation. In general, I argue that the studies that are the backbone of the emerging research program are far from conclusive and that the strong claims frequently made on behalf of this program are overblown. I also offer some positive suggestions for better research design for the study of human sexual orientations and human sexual desires more generally.


## Who Is in the Studies?


Recall Kallman's twin study (Kallman 1952a, 1952b) discussed in chapter 5. One of the criticisms that I made of this study concerned the problem of sampling bias: Kallman's homosexual target subjects were mostly men under psychiatric care in a correctional facility or in a hospital. I argued that it was a mistake to make generalizations about all homosexuals based on such a sample. I had a similar worry about early studies that examined the bodies of lesbians and gay men for signs of their sexual orientation (Weil 1921), namely, that given the cultural assumptions about gender atypicality, it is likely that the people who ended up as subjects in these studies of gay men and lesbians had bodily characteristics that were atypical for their sex-gender. Studies that are part of the emerging scientific research program must select a subject pool to study; one worry about these studies is that they too suffer from a *sampling bias,* that is, that the subject pools used in these studies are in some ways atypical.

Consider first Bailey's twin studies (Bailey and Pillard 1991b; Bailey, Pillard, and Agyei 1993). The target subjects in these studies were recruited through ads placed in lesbian and gay newspapers. Only qualified subjects (that is, gay men and lesbians with a twin of the same sex-gender or an adopted sibling) who read such newspapers (or have friends who read such newspapers who would think to draw their attention to such an ad) have the *opportunity* to volunteer for such studies. Only a subset of those who have this opportunity to volunteer eventually take advantage of it by actually volunteering. It might be that those subjects who read gay newspapers and then decide to volunteer for such studies are in some way atypical (although they are, no doubt, more typical of the general population than Kallman's subjects). Only people who would be found through this method and who would be willing to volunteer to talk about their homosexuality, their families, and the like are represented in this study.

Bailey and Pillard (1991b, 1094) discuss the potential problems with sampling bias and admit that a study with a random subject pool would be preferable. However, they make several points in defense of their study. They distinguish between two ways that the data might be biased due to the methods used to attracted subjects (what are called *ascertainment biases*). First, there are *concordance-dependence biases* that have to do with the chances that a disproportionate number of target subjects will be similar to their siblings in terms of the trait under consideration (in this case, that there will be some effect on the number of twins who have the same sexual orientation). Second, there are *zygosity-and-concordance-dependence biases* that have to do with the chances that a disproportionate number of target subjects who have siblings of a certain sort will be similar to their siblings in the trait under consideration (in this case, for example, that there will be some effect on the number of identical compared to fraternal twins who are concordant with their sibling for sexual orientation).

Bailey and Pillard try to show that their data are significant even in the face of concordance-dependence bias, that is, even if it is the case that gay people who have gay siblings are more likely to respond to ads like the ones they ran.[1] The idea is that even if, for example, lesbians with a lesbian twin sister are more likely to volunteer than are lesbians with a heterosexual twin sister, the result that the percentage of identical twins who are both lesbians is greater than the percentage of fraternal twins who are both lesbians will still be significant. Even if there are concordance-dependence biases in the subject pool, Bailey and Pillard argue that their results would still be evidence for the heritability of sexual orientation.

Bailey and Pillard cannot, however, make the same argument with regards to zygosity-and-concordance-dependence biases. If it were the case that a gay man with an identical twin who is also gay would be more likely to respond to such ads than a gay man with a fraternal twin, then this would skew the data to make it look like sexual orientation is highly heritable, even if it were not. This scenario is not implausible. A gay man with a gay identical twin is probably more identified with his brother and hence more likely to feel supported and comfortable with being gay than a gay man with a fraternal twin who is gay and who might be less identified with his brother and hence less affected by his brother's sexual orientation—this would be zygosity-and-concordance-dependence bias. If, for whatever reason, gay men with identical twins who are also gay are more likely to volunteer than gay men with fraternal twins who are also gay, then Bailey and Pillard's results would suggest that male homosexuality is heritable, even if it is not.

There is some recently compiled evidence to suggest that precisely these sorts of ascertainment biases do occur in such studies. In a significant (although not yet published) study, Bailey and two Australian collaborators systematically recruited subjects from a registry of over twenty-five thousand pairs of identical and fraternal twins in Australia (Bailey, Dunne, and Martin n.d.). The researchers wrote to over nine thousand of these twins asking them to complete a questionnaire that included questions about sexual behavior. Fifty-four percent of them completed the questionnaire. Of these, 92 percent identified themselves as exclusively heterosexual. As responses were useful only if both twins in a pair responded, there were only 1,761 pairs of twins that could be used in the study. The concordance rate for nonheterosexuality (that is, for having Kinsey ratings from 2 [bisexual but tending towards heterosexuality] to 6 [exclusively homosexual]) among identical twins—the percentage of identical twins of bisexuals or homosexuals who are also either bisexual or homosexual—was 20 percent for men and 24 percent for women. This is a good bit lower than the results of Bailey's earlier twin studies (as well as other such studies) that use less systematic methods for recruiting subjects (see Table 7-1). Although Bailey and his Australian collaborators held that, in light of their results, sexual orientation runs in families and that genetic effects play some role in the explanation of this, they conclude that the results of earlier studies, including those done by Bailey (Bailey and Pillard 1991b; Bailey, Pillard, and Agyei 1993) and Hamer (Hamer et al. 1993), which recruited

Table 7-1. Results of Australian Twin Registry Study Compared
to Other Twin Studies

| | Concordance Rates | | |
| --- | --- | --- | --- |
| | Identical Twin (%) | Same-Sex Fraternal Twin (%) | Other-Sex Fraternal Twin[†] (%) |
| Male nonheterosexuality (Kinsey 2–6) (Bailey et al. n.d.) | 20 | 0 | 11 |
| Male non*exclusive*-heterosexuality (Kinsey 1–6) (Bailey et al. n.d.) | 38 | 6 | 11 |
| Female nonheterosexuality (Kinsey 2–6) (Bailey et al. n.d.) | 24 | 10 | 18 |
| Female non*exclusive*-heterosexuality (Kinsey 1–6) (Bailey et al. n.d.) | 30 | 30 | 11 |
| Male homosexuality (Kinsey 2–6) (Bailey and Pillard 1991b) | 52 | 22 | n/a |
| Female homosexuality (Kinsey 2–6) (Bailey et al. 1993) | 48 | 16 | n/a |

[†]Concordance rates for other-sex fraternal twins are *pairwise* concordance rather than *probandwise* concordance. Probandwise concordance (also used in the twin studies discussed above) is calculated using the following equation: $2C/(2C + D)$ where $C$ = number of concordant pairs for homosexuality and $D$ = number of discordant pairs for homosexuality). Pairwise concordance is calculated by the following equation: $C/(C + D)$ (McGue and Lykken 1992).

subjects through HIV clinics, lesbian and/or gay organizations, newspapers, and through other nonsystematic methods, must have been inflated by sampling bias. As such, their results undermine twin and family studies that recruit volunteers in a nonsystematic fashion, for example, by running an ad in a gay newspaper or recruiting from within gay organizations.[2]

Worries about sampling biases apply to other studies in the emerging research program besides twin and pedigree studies. In general, there might be various social factors that affect who participates in a study, which in turn skews a study's results. People who identify as gay men, lesbians, or bisexuals and take part in such studies belong to the subset of nonheterosexuals who are conscious of their own sexual desires for people of the same sex-gender and who are willing to describe these desires to researchers. In particular, many studies that are supposed to study gay men and/or lesbians in contrast to heterosexuals are in fact studies of some subset of out-of-the-closet gay men and lesbians. As such, the results of the studies may apply only to a distinct subset of gay men and lesbians.

Even if many studies in the emerging research program involve sampling biases, the results of the studies still require some explanation. Why is it, we might wonder, that gay men with gay identical twins are more likely to respond to newspaper ads for studies on homosexuality than gay men with gay fraternal twins? Insofar as the explanations for these phenomena have anything to do with sexual orientation, they probably fit better with the indirect model as opposed to the direct model of how sexual orientations develop. Recall that according to the direct model, which is at the core of the emerging research program, sexual orientation results from genes, hormones, or other biological factors directly shaping the brain and the psychological mechanisms that it instantiates. In contrast, the indirect model sees biological factors affecting a person's temperament and personality, which affect, in turn, how a person interacts with the environment and, in turn, a person's sexual orientation. The results of Hamer's linkage study could, for example, be explained by the existence of a disproportionate number of risk takers among the target subjects. Suppose, as some have argued (Hamer and Copeland 1998), that willingness to buck the system and express unpopular beliefs are genetically based. People who are open about their homosexuality in societies like ours, which stigmatize same-sex sexual desire and behavior, are more likely to be risk takers than either people who are not open about their homosexuality or typical heterosexuals. Thus, the indirect model explains Hamer's results as well as the direct model, in particular, the version of the direct model that posits the existence of a "gay gene." I shall say more about the evidence for the direct model in the fourth section of this chapter and more about Hamer's study in the section that follows. In general, problems with sampling bias undermine the strength of studies in the emerging research program and their support for the direct model, which is the centerpiece of the research program.

### How Are the Subjects Assigned Sexual Orientations?

Setting aside worries about sampling biases, there remains a concern about how a subject in one of these studies is assigned a sexual orientation. Recall that much of chapter 2 was concerned with what a sexual orientation is. It is crucial for scientific research on sexual orientation to carefully define its object of study in order to divide people into sexual orientations in a reasonable fashion and in ways that do not skew its results. A study of sexual orientation must start with some (at least implicit) definition of sexual orientation: who will count as a homosexual or a heterosexual? Most of the studies that are part of the emerging research program concerning sexual orientation assume a simple picture of sexual orientation. Some studies simply equate a person's sexual orientation with his or her sexual behavior, implicitly adopting the behavioral view of sexual orientation. With respect to the dimensionality of sexual orientation,

most studies assume the binary or the bipolar view of sexual orientation, sometimes without even trying to justify this assumption. My discussion in chapter 2
raised problems for the behavioral view and the binary and bipolar views. A
person's sexual orientation has to do with sexual desires and dispositions, not
simply his or her behavior. With respect to the binary and the bipolar views, the
main problems are, respectively, that studies that accept the binary view ignore
the existence of bisexuals—sometimes by simply counting bisexuals as homosexuals (LeVay 1991), sometimes by simply excluding bisexuals from the study
(Hamer et al. 1993)—while studies that accept the bipolar view assume that
the strength of a person's attraction to men and the strength of a person's attraction to women vary inversely. The two-dimensional view of sexual orientation
constitutes an alternative picture of sexual orientation that avoids these problems. Even this more sophisticated view of sexual orientation is, however,
limited in that it focuses on the aspect of sexual desire that concerns the sex-
gender of the people to whom a person is attracted. These points indicate that
a scientific study of sexual orientation is significantly limited insofar as it
assumes a simplistic—and perhaps mistaken—picture of what a sexual orientation is. That most people in our culture see sexual orientation simplistically
does not provide an argument for using such a simplistic account of sexual
orientation to do science. Scientific studies need to make their definitions of
sexual orientation explicit, and they need to provide a rationale for these definitions. When assessing research in the emerging scientific program, one must
uncover the implicit definition of sexual orientation and ask whether it is
adequate. Since most of the biological studies of sexual orientation do not spell
out their definition of sexual orientation, one way to tease out their definition is
by looking at how they assign sexual orientations to their subjects. In this
section, I focus on how studies assign sexual orientations to subjects, given the
picture of sexual orientation that is assumed. In the next section, I focus on the
picture itself.

Consider LeVay's neuroanatomical study. Recall that LeVay's study
involved forty-one subjects—thirty-five men and six women—twenty-six who
had died from AIDS and fifteen who had died from other causes. LeVay classified his male subjects as either heterosexual or homosexual on the basis of
whether their hospital records indicated they had engaged in sexual activity
with people of the same sex-gender. The primary reason a person's hospital
records would have something to say about sexual orientation or sexual
behavior is if he or she was possibly infected with HIV as the result of sexual
activities. In such cases, there might be an indication in a person's hospital
records of sexual activity with a person of the same sex-gender as the route of

HIV transmission. If a person had died from complications from AIDS, he or she might be included in the study only if his or her hospital records indicated that he or she belonged to at least one risk group for HIV infection (LeVay 1991, 1037, note 9). If a man's hospital records suggested that he had been infected with HIV through sexual activity with a person of the same sex-gender, LeVay counted him as homosexual; if not (or if the subject was a woman), LeVay counted the subject as heterosexual. By this procedure, LeVay counted as homosexual at least one bisexual (although he did not specify on what basis he called this subject a bisexual) and perhaps some heterosexuals (that is, he counted as homosexual those heterosexuals who engaged in any homosexual activity; this would include Kinsey 1s who may have engaged in incidental homosexual behavior). LeVay also would have incorrectly counted some gay men as heterosexual if they did not report sexual activity with people of the same sex-gender as their route of HIV infection. Given the social stigma attached to both homosexuality and AIDS and the connections commonly made between AIDS and male homosexuality, especially at the time LeVay's study was conducted, it seems quite possible that LeVay would have in fact classified some homosexuals as heterosexuals.

Note also that LeVay is implicitly adopting a behavioral rather than a dispositional account of sexual orientation (see chapter 2 for a discussion). He classified people as homosexual or heterosexual on the basis of whether they have engaged in behaviors that are risky in terms of HIV transmission. A man who was an IV drug user and who exclusively had sexual fantasies about men but never engaged in sex with men would have been counted as a heterosexual in LeVay's study even though it is clear that he was gay. Moreover, LeVay's method for classifying people in terms of their sexual orientation is especially problematic because it is filtered through issues surrounding AIDS. A gay man whose concerns about HIV transmission led him to limit his sexual activity to kissing, hugging, and mutual masturbation, if asked about his risk-group status, might reasonably say that he was not at risk of HIV transmission through sexual activity. If so, LeVay would misclassify him as a heterosexual. Simply put, LeVay's operational definition of homosexuality is inappropriate for the use he makes of it; a person's HIV risk-group status is a poor tool for classifying people in terms of sexual orientation.

William Byne (1996, 138) has argued that this does not pose a serious problem for LeVay because even if LeVay did in fact mistakenly include some homosexuals in his heterosexual sample, this alone would not weaken his results. To see Byne's point, consider the following contrived example. Suppose that you are testing the hypothesis that, on average, people born in

New Hampshire weigh less than people born in Vermont. Suppose your test procedure is to weigh subjects and then ask them in what state they were born; using this procedure, you get statistically significant results that confirm your hypothesis. Now suppose someone criticizes your study by claiming to have reasons for thinking that some of the subjects who claimed to be born in Vermont were actually born in New Hampshire. Even if you have no way of proving the veracity of your subjects' reports of their state of origin, you still have a potentially strong reply to your critics: even if some subjects lied, the fact that you have statistically significant results in the face of the possibility of some mistakenly labeled Vermonters reaffirms the strength of your hypothesis.

To make this especially clear, consider the fictional data presented in Table 7-2. Using this data, the average weight of a Vermonter is 176 pounds, while the average weight of a New Hampshirite is 155. This is a significant difference. Now suppose that your critic is right and a few of the subjects in your study were misclassified in terms of their state of birth. The fact that your results are significant in the face of some possible mislabeling shows the strength of your hypothesis. Even if a few subjects lied about being born in

Table 7-2.  Hypothetical Weight Comparison of
Vermonters Versus New Hampshirites

| Subject | State of Birth | Weight (in pounds) |
|---------|----------------|--------------------|
| A | Vermont | 200 |
| B | New Hampshire | 170 |
| C | Vermont | 195 |
| D | Vermont | 160 |
| E | New Hampshire | 180 |
| F | Vermont | 210 |
| G | Vermont | 185 |
| H | Vermont | 160 |
| I | New Hampshire | 210 |
| J | New Hampshire | 160 |
| K | New Hampshire | 150 |
| L | Vermont | 140 |
| M | New Hampshire | 130 |
| N | Vermont | 170 |
| O | New Hampshire | 145 |
| P | New Hampshire | 160 |
| Q | Vermont | 190 |
| R | Vermont | 185 |
| S | New Hampshire | 150 |
| T | New Hampshire | 135 |
| U | New Hampshire | 160 |
| V | Vermont | 175 |
| W | New Hampshire | 130 |
| X | Vermont | 180 |
| Y | Vermont | 135 |
| Z | New Hampshire | 135 |

Vermont, this is not enough to significantly bring down the average weight of subjects born in Vermont. Suppose, for example, that subjects G, L, V, and X lied about their state of origin, that is, they claimed to be Vermonters, but were actually born in New Hampshire. Correctly classifying them as New Hampshirites does not change the average weights of the two states very much at all (Vermont's average weight increases by 2 pounds to 178 pounds while New Hampshire's average weight increases by 4 pounds to 159 pounds). You thereby have answered your critic: your hypothesis stands even in the face of some misclassified subjects.

The critic of your study does, however, have a possible further reply. If the people whose state of origin has been misidentified were for some reason *nonrandomly* distributed in terms of their weights, then there could well be a problem with the statistical significance of your results. Suppose, for example, that the people who were actually born in Vermont but said they were born in New Hampshire as a group tended to weigh more than most subjects in your study. Perhaps this was because the really heavy Vermonters felt more welcome in New Hampshire and, hence, felt the need to more closely identify with New Hampshire. Whatever the reason, if there are people who are labeled Vermonters, but who are in fact New Hampshirites, and if as a group they are also atypical of New Hampshirites in terms of weight (or some factor that correlates with it), then your results could be skewed. To see this, note that if these misclassified subjects were moved out of the Vermont group where they were originally classified and into the New Hampshire group where they genuinely belong, the statistically significant difference between the two groups would evaporate. To give a specific example, if subjects A, C, F, and R—who were originally labeled as Vermonters—turn out to actually be from New Hampshire, then the average weight of subjects in each state would change significantly. Without A, C, F, and R, the average weight of Vermonters would be 166 pounds; including A, C, F, and R as New Hampshirites produces an average weight of 165 pounds. This 1 pound difference is not statistically significant. This shows that *systematic* misclassification of subjects can lead to an unrepresentative subject pool.

Returning to LeVay's study, Byne's point in defense of LeVay is that the significance of LeVay's results are not undermined by the possibility that some of his subjects might have been counted as heterosexuals when they are in fact homosexuals (and vice versa). This line of defense is plausible so long as the homosexual men who were mislabeled as heterosexual men (and the heterosexual men who were mislabeled as homosexual, if any) were mislabeled due to factors not in any way correlated with the size of INAH-3. If, however, there is some correlation between INAH-3 size and being the sort of homosexual who is likely, for whatever reason, to be counted as heterosexual by LeVay, then LeVay's subject pool would be unrepresentative, and it would be inappropriate for him to use those results to draw conclusions about the biological bases of sexual orientation. Because LeVay uses such a peculiar method for determining sexual orientation and because we know very little about INAH-3 size and with what it might be correlated, it is possible that he systematically misclassifies his subjects in terms of sexual orientation. In light of this possibility, LeVay's results do not provide evidence for any neuroanatomical determinants of sexual orientation.

Relatedly, LeVay cites Kinsey's male volume (Kinsey, Pomeroy, and Martin 1948) as justification for his assumption that *all* of his male subjects of undetermined sexual orientation are heterosexual even though only two of them denied homosexual sexual activity (LeVay 1991, 1036, note 7). The Kinsey population seems to be the wrong comparison class in this context. For those men who died from AIDS and who had not indicated that they were homosexual, it is more appropriate to look at the statistics for men who died of AIDS to see what percentage of them were identified as homosexual. In partic-ular, given the fact that early in the AIDS pandemic in the United States most of the men who died of AIDS were gay or bisexual, LeVay should not have assumed that all men who died from AIDS whose sexual orientation he could not determine were heterosexual.[3] In fact, it seems almost certain that some of the men who died from AIDS whom LeVay classified as heterosexual were in fact homosexual. Combining this observation with the fact that there is a stigma attached to being gay as well as to having AIDS, it is almost certain that several of the sixteen men LeVay counted as heterosexual were in fact homosexual. If these misclassifications are in some way correlated with INAH-3 size, then LeVay's results would be undermined. This sort of correlation could happen by chance or, more likely, it might be that INAH-3 size is correlated with some other factor, for example, willingness to admit membership in a stigmatized group, having lots of sex, or regular drug use (including the use of alcohol and nicotine). For example, at least six of LeVay's sixteen presumed heterosexual subjects used IV drugs (LeVay 1991, 1037), two had a history of chronic alcohol use (1037), and two died from lung cancer (1036); in other words, ten of the sixteen presumed heterosexuals seemed to have been drug users.

To see the effects of such possible misclassifications on LeVay's results, imagine a scenario in which three of the presumed heterosexuals who died of AIDS and three of the presumed heterosexuals who did not die of AIDS were actually homosexual. If it turns out that these six men have large INAH-3, then recalculating LeVay's numbers would produce results that are not statistically significant. Specifically, the average volume of the INAH-3 of those men LeVay counted as heterosexual was .12 mm$^3$ compared to .051 mm$^3$ for those LeVay counted as homosexual (1035). Recalculating the data assuming that six of

LeVay's subjects were misclassified as heterosexual men, I get .098 mm$^3$ for the "actual" heterosexual men and .076 mm$^3$ for the "actual" homosexual men, not a statistically significant difference.[4] I am not claiming that these recalculated results are more reliable or accurate than LeVay's; I am, however, claiming that it is quite likely that LeVay misclassified some of his subjects in terms of sexual orientation and that this possibility casts doubts on the validity of his results.

Looking at LeVay's data in another way, note that all the subjects that LeVay classified as homosexual died from complications due to AIDS. This is especially relevant in light of two factors. At the time of death, virtually all men with AIDS have decreased testosterone levels as a side effect of particular treatments for AIDS, as the result of AIDS, or one of the opportunistic infections commonly associated with it, or for other reasons not well understood (Croxson et al. 1989). Decreased testosterone levels might in some way be correlated with the size of particular brain regions. This suggests that people with AIDS may be poor subjects for neuroanatomical studies of the general population. In some laboratory animals, the size of sexually dimorphic brain structures (that is, the size of brain structures that differ between males and females) varies with the animal's testosterone level (Commins and Yahr 1984). It is thus possible that the effects on the size of the INAH-3, which LeVay attributed to sexual orientation, were actually due to the hormonal abnormalities associated with AIDS. The inclusion of a few brains from heterosexual men with AIDS does not—contra LeVay (1991, 1036)—constitute an adequate control to rule out this possibility (Byne and Parsons 1993, 245). Neither does LeVay's subsequent examination of the brain of one homosexual man who did not die from AIDS (LeVay and Hamer 1994, 46).

To summarize, LeVay's study assigned subjects to particular sexual orientations in a problematic fashion. LeVay adopted, without argument, a simplistic view of sexual orientation, namely the binary view. Also, LeVay at least implicitly defines sexual orientation behaviorally rather than dispositionally. Further, LeVay classifies people as heterosexuals and homosexuals on the basis of information that, for various reasons, is a bad indicator of whether his subjects have engaged in sexual behavior with people of the same sex-gender.

## What Picture of Sexual Orientation Is Assumed?

There is another cluster of problems associated with assigning sexual orientations to subjects. In order to assign subjects to a sexual orientation, researchers in the emerging research program must make assumptions about what categories of sexual orientation to use. Typically, for example, they accept the binary or bipolar view of sexual orientation and use the associated categories to assign their subjects to sexual orientations. The binary and bipolar views seem, at least roughly, to fit with our cultural assumptions about how sexual desires are organized. Researchers working in the emerging research program are at least implicitly hoping to provide an account of how sexual orientations develop according to which sexual orientations are natural human kinds. This hope follows from their desire to uncover scientific laws that involve human sexual orientations. For this to be the case, the categories and the methods that they use must have the potential to apply to people in other cultures. Many of the studies in the emerging research paradigm fail to do this.

In this section, I consider some of the ways that studies in the emerging research program make unjustified assumptions about sexual orientations. I begin this section by focusing on two assumptions: the assumption that sexual orientation is a sexually dimorphic trait—that is, a trait with two forms, one typically associated with men and the other typically associated with women (the *inversion assumption*)—and the assumption that sexual orientations are natural human kinds (*essentialism*). I then consider a specific example of how assumptions about what sexual orientations are infiltrate the emerging research program; this example involves problems with estimating the rate of homosexuality in the general population.

### The Inversion Assumption

Much of the biological research on sexual orientation is premised on the assumption—dating back at least to the nineteenth century and the work of Ulrichs—that homosexuals are gender inverts. Researchers who accept the inversion assumption expect particular aspects of an individual's brain or physiology to conform to one of two distinct types, one associated with each of two forms, namely, a male form that causes sexual attraction to women (shared by heterosexual men and lesbians), and a female form that causes sexual attraction to men (shared by heterosexual women and gay men). This picture entails seeing homosexuality as a type of hermaphroditism, namely, it sees homosexuals as having both male and female traits. For example, on this view, while a lesbian has XX chromosomes, a vagina, fallopian tubes, and the like (all female-typical traits), she also has sexual desire for women (a male-typical trait) and male-typical characteristics that undergird such a sexual desire (be they genetic, hormonal, neuroanatomical, or some combination of these). According to the inversion assumption, homosexuality results from a sex-reversed or incompletely sexually differentiated anatomy or physiology.[5] This assumption is

present, explicitly or implicitly, throughout almost all of the scientific literature
from Ulrichs to the present. LeVay, for example, accepts the inversion assumption without argument. This is evident in his expectation, for which he has no
evidence, that lesbians will have roughly the same-sized INAH-3 as heterosexual men. Other instances include the equation of homosexual behavior in
men with effeminacy and the search for masculinized cognitive, hormonal, and
neuroanatomical profiles in lesbians, as, for example, in the study of the
acoustic emissions of the inner ear (McFadden and Pasanen 1998). The inversion assumption is present to a greater or lesser degree in most biological
research on sexual orientation from the late nineteenth century to the present.
Even studies that do not explicitly embrace the inversion assumption implicitly
draw on this assumption when they cite studies, like LeVay's, that accept it.

There are, however, alternatives to the inversion assumption. One such
alternative is that, from the neurological point of view, gay men and lesbians
should be grouped together and heterosexual men and women should be
grouped together. This would be the case if the anatomy or physiology of
lesbians and gay men dispose them to be sexually attracted to people of the
same sex-gender, while that of heterosexual women and men dispose them to
be sexually attracted to people not of the same sex-gender. The point here is
connected to my chapter 2 discussion of the difference between the homo-
hetero version and the male-female version of the two-dimensional view of
sexual orientation. Recall that the two-dimensional view of sexual orientation,
in contrast to the binary and bipolar view, does not see attraction to men and
attraction to women as varying inversely. A view of sexual orientation can be
decoupled from attraction to men and attraction to women in two ways.
According to the homo-hetero version of the view, a person's sexual orientation
is classified in terms of his or her degree of attraction to people of the same sex-
gender and the degree of attraction to people not of the same sex-gender. On
this view, for example, gay men and lesbians are grouped together because both
are strongly attracted to people of the same sex-gender and weakly attracted to
others. According to the male-female version of the two-dimensional view, a
person's sexual orientation is classified in terms of his or her degree of attraction to males and to females, respectively. On this view, for example, lesbians
and heterosexual men get grouped together because both are strongly attracted
to women and weakly attracted to men (recall the comparison from chapter 2
of Figures 2-3 and 2-4; this comparison visually depicts the difference between
the hetero-homo version and the male-female version of the two-dimensional
picture of sexual orientation). If the inversion assumption is combined with the
two-dimensional view of sexual orientation, the male-female version of the two-
dimensional view follows. According to this view, lesbians have male-typical

sexual desires, that is, they are attracted to women. To give an account of lesbians' sexual desires, we need to look for neurological structures or other biological factors that lesbians and heterosexual men have in common. One alternative to this picture would combine the two-dimensional view with the hetero-homo view of sexual orientation. For all we know, scientists interested in examining the origins of sexual orientation should look for biological factors in common between lesbians and gay men on the one hand and heterosexual men and homosexual women on the other.

An even more plausible alternative to the inversion assumption is that there might be no interesting generalizable differences in anatomy or physiology that correlate with these categories of sexual orientation. Just as people come to have similar tastes in music from a multitude of different environmental and biological causes, the underlying causes of different sexual attractions could vary even among individuals of the same sex-gender and the same sexual orientation. Various combinations of genetic, hormonal, neurological, and psychological properties could interact with a myriad of experiences (and subjective interpretations of them) to lead different individuals to the same relative degree of sexual attraction to men, women, or both. Sexual attraction to women or to people of the same sex-gender, for example, could be driven by various different psychological and/or neurological factors. There is no reason to expect that, for example, all individuals attracted to women share any particular brain structure that distinguishes them from all individuals attracted to men. When reviewing evidence obtained on the basis of the inversion assumption, it is important to remember that there are scientifically plausible alternatives to it. In particular, it may be a mistake to think that there is a single explanation of how all (or most) people of the same sexual orientation develop their sexual orientation (see my discussion in chapter 8).

Pointing out that there are alternatives to the inversion assumption does not deny that the inversion assumption is intuitively plausible to many people in our culture. This assumption is intrinsically more plausible than its rivals because of a cultural bias in favor of thinking that gay men are feminine and lesbians are masculine. This cultural view is hardly universal. According to Aristophanes' speech in *The Symposium*, men who are attracted to men are "bold and brave and masculine" (Plato 1935b, 192A), while the men who are attracted to women are seen as feminine in virtue of their interest in women. This aspect of Aristophanes' view was shared by his fellow party-goers. In some other cultures, male homosexuality was associated with warrior status (Boswell 1980, 25), while in others, receptive male homosexual activity up to a certain age was universally practiced and believed to be essential for the attainment of virility (Herdt 1984b). Even today in North America, the inversion assumption is not universally accepted. The inversion assumption does not, for example, fit with the lives of many women, for example, those who accept in theory and practice the feminist concepts of the "lesbian continuum" and the "woman-identified woman," which see lesbians as typical and/or paradigmatic women (Rich 1980). The inversion assumption also does not fit with the concept of the macho Latino man who identifies as straight despite the fact that he plays the penetrative role in anal sex with other men (Almaguer 1993).

That the inversion assumption is not universally accepted does not show that it is false. Given, however, the lack of scientific evidence to support it, that the inversion assumption is not culturally universal suggests that it is based as much on our cultural biases as on anything else. The inversion assumption seems plausible to many of us, and most researchers in the emerging research program either explicitly or implicitly accept it without argument. This assumption is plausible, however, primarily because of cultural biases, not because there is significant empirical support for it.

### Essentialism Assumed

Most studies in the emerging research program assume essentialism about sexual orientations. Recall that essentialism is the view that sexual orientations are natural human kinds, namely, that heterosexuality and homosexuality (or some similar groupings, for example, the Kinsey classifications) play a role in scientific laws that explain human sexual desires. In chapter 4, I explained that whether essentialism is true or false is an empirical matter to which scientific studies concerning sexual orientation are relevant. However, in order to establish essentialism, a study cannot unquestionably assume essentialism. If a study is to have a chance of providing support for an empirical thesis, it has to be possible that the study can produce results that count against the thesis.

Consider the following example. Suppose I were trying to conduct a scientific study of swans and their plumage color. Suppose that my hypothesis is that all swans are white. My experimental method is to go out into the world in search of swans. Upon identifying a swan, I note its color. If all the swans turn out to be white, and if I examine a reasonable cross section of swans, then I would provide some support for the hypothesis that all swans are white. This seems like a reasonable, albeit simplistic, scientific project. If, however, built into my procedure for identifying a swan, I assume (perhaps implicitly) that all swans are white—for example, if in order to count a creature as a swan in the first place I require that it be white—then I am assuming, as part of my experimental method, the conclusion that all swans are white. If this were my experimental method, then my study could not possibly fail to show that all swans are white. If the emerging research program assumes essentialism about sexual orientation, then it cannot possibly provide evidence to support essentialism. Some practitioners and advocates of the emerging research program claim that the studies in the research program do provide support for essentialism. If, however, a study in the emerging research program implicitly assumes from the start that sexual orientations are natural human kinds, it cannot provide support for this claim.

Consider again LeVay's neuroanatomical study (LeVay 1991). LeVay concludes that his study shows that "sexual orientation in humans is amenable to study at the biological level . . . and opens the door to" (1036) neuroanatomical studies of sexual orientation. However, LeVay *starts* from the assumption that people can be sorted into heterosexuals and homosexuals, so his study cannot establish essentialism about sexual orientation. I am not claiming that it is impossible to do a neuroanatomical study that would provide support to essentialism about sexual orientation. For this to happen, evidence for the existence of natural human kinds must emerge from the empirical results. (In the next to last section of this chapter, I describe the type of studies that might produce these sorts of results.) Further, I am not claiming that LeVay's study is devoid of any empirical content. Setting my concerns about LeVay's study aside, it is possible that LeVay might have found no correlation between INAH-3 and the sexual-orientation assignments he gave his subjects. (In fact, LeVay found no correlation between sexual-orientation assignment and INAH-1, INAH-2, or INAH-4 size.) Taking his results at face value, if LeVay had found no correlation between sexual orientation and any neuroanatomical structure, this would not have shown that sexual orientations are not natural human kinds, but it would have suggested that his particular account of the scientific laws involving sexual orientations is false.

### Problems with the Base Rate of Homosexuality

In order to show how studies in the emerging research program make unjustified assumptions about sexual orientation, I offer one specific example that exhibits both the inversion assumption and the essentialism assumption made by most studies in the emerging research program. Many of the studies in the emerging research program require assumptions about the *base rate* of homosexuality in the population, that is, the percentage of lesbians and gay men in the general population. There are, however, serious problems involved in calculating this rate and making use of it in a particular study. There are widely divergent estimates about this percentage. Kinsey's pathbreaking studies of human sexual behavior found, for example, that "at least thirty-seven percent of the male population has some homosexual experiences between the beginning of adolescence to old age" (Kinsey, Pomeroy, and Martin 1948, 623), while in the University of Chicago's recent study, less than 3 percent of men reported "some level of homosexual (or bisexual) identity" (Laumann et al. 1994, 293). The divergent estimates may to some extent be due to whether a survey is focusing on sexual experience or sexual identity and the sort of survey that is being used to determine the base rate. There are questions about the accuracy of these sorts of surveys and whether studies should focus on the percentage of homosexuals, however measured, around the world both in the past and present or whether they should focus on, for example, the percentage in the United States at the present.

Any attempt to survey the population, especially in a culture like ours, with the aim of developing an estimate of the number of lesbian and gay men faces various obstacles that relate to what picture of sexual orientation is assumed: here, I focus on one epistemological problem and one metaphysical problem. Recall that epistemology has to do with what we can know about the world, while metaphysics has to do with the nature of the world. The epistemological question takes certain categories of sexual orientation for granted, assumes that people in fact fit into these categories, and then examines whether we can accurately determine which people in fact fit into each of these categories. The metaphysical question is concerned with whether these assumptions are right: are these categories natural human kinds, in other words, are there scientific laws that explain how people are sorted into these categories?

*Epistemological Issues*

Taking the epistemological issue first, it is often said that 10 percent of the adult population (sometimes just the adult *male* population) is homosexual. Harry Hay, one of the founders of the Mattachine Society (the first political group for gay men and lesbians in the United States), made use of this statistic in the 1950s (Timmons 1990, 136). Bruce Voeller, former chair of the National Gay and Lesbian Task Force (then known as the National Gay Task Force), claims that he popularized this estimate in the 1970s (Voeller 1990). The 10 percent figure seems to have come from Kinsey's result that 10 percent of adult white men are "more or less exclusively homosexual for at least three years" (Kinsey, Pomeroy, and Martin 1948, 651). Kinsey, however, also gives quite a few statistics about sexual behavior and desires for people of the same sex-gender, for example, that 25 percent of adult white men have "more than incidental homosexual experience or reactions" (650) and that 4 percent are "exclusively homosexual throughout their lives" from adolescence on (650). Various studies in the emerging research program make different assumptions about the base rate. Hamer, for example, says that 2 percent of the adult male population (lower than all three figures from Kinsey) are gay (Hamer et al. 1993, 322), while LeVay (1991, 1036, note 7) cites Kinsey, Pomeroy, and Martin (1948) to justify assuming that *all* of the men in his study who died of AIDS and who did not identify themselves as gay were heterosexual.

Surveys from which the estimates of base rate of homosexuality are derived assume everyone is conscious of his or her true sexual desires (or is at least a very reliable reporter of such desires), is comfortable admitting them, and is able to fit himself or herself into our commonsense categories of sexual orientation. Further, most studies rely on subjects' reports of their own sexual orientations. Should we trust self-reports of sexual orientation? People often repress their sexual orientations and their sexual desires and hide them from others. Even those who do not suffer from deep repression are likely to find it difficult to speak frankly about their sexual behaviors and fantasies. In fact, given societal homophobia, almost all gay men and lesbians will have at some time identified as having at least one other sexual orientation. The survey conducted by researchers primarily affiliated with the University of Chicago claimed to take special care to get people to speak openly about sex but in fact interviewed 21 percent of their respondents in the presence of a sex partner or family member, hardly a context that would engender honesty, especially about such socially stigmatized activities as sexual activity with people of the same sex-gender (Laumann et al. 1994, 568). In contrast, the researchers involved with the two original Kinsey studies took special care to create contexts in which subjects would feel comfortable sharing their sexual histories.[6]

The epistemological problems that exist with respect to surveying the general population to determine the base rate of homosexuality and heterosexuality may not be intractable. A survey could use the sophisticated population sampling techniques used in a large study of sexual behavior in France (Spira, Bajos, and ACSF 1993) and originally planned for the University of Chicago survey (Laumann et al. 1994),[7] at the same time using interviewing techniques designed to draw people out and make them comfortable talking about sexual desire and activity involving people of the same sex-gender as well as other stigmatized behaviors and desires. Kinsey's discussion of how to establish a rapport and conduct an interview (Kinsey, Pomeroy, and Martin 1948, 36–62) would be a good starting point. Such a survey could also be *longitudinal,* that is, subjects could be interviewed a few times over several years, in order to track changes in their behaviors, desires, and identity, as well as to test the reliability of their responses (neither the Chicago nor the Kinsey studies did this). Further, such a survey, appropriately done, could be less dependent on subjects' self-reports of their sexual orientation; instead, it could make use of subjects' longitudinal reports of their fantasies, desires, and sexual activities. The epistemological problems are in principle solvable; whether the political will and the financial backing exist to enable such a survey to be conducted remains to be seen.

Although the epistemological problems involved in determining the base rate of homosexuality in certain cultural and subcultural groups may be solvable (such as those in North America and Western Europe), more difficult problems emerge when surveys are conducted on people in cultures where sexual desires are organized differently. How can we determine the percentage of homosexuals and heterosexuals in another culture if people in such a culture do not use these categories to think about sexual desires (in themselves or in others)? In an interview with Richard Pillard, Michael Bailey's collaborator on the twin studies, I raised this concern. Pillard answered:

> We ought to be able to interrogate people in such a way as to inquire about their fantasies and be able to get some reasonable anchor points. If, for example, the person said, "Well, I have a lot of sex with men but it's only because the Great Spirit of the Plains tells me I must do this," we'd be puzzled. We could interview people in societies where being gay is more or less recognized or identified. I suppose there are societies in which people don't call themselves gay, but *they certainly do stuff we would call gay.* [Simply put,] I don't agree with the assertion that "gay" isn't a strong category simply because some tribes in New Guinea or the American plains don't have it. Those are small cultural isolates and they might not recognize as many categories as we do just because they lack a large enough data base. What ought to impress is that almost everywhere one looks, "gay" people do so categorize themselves. (Stein 1993, 101, emphasis added)

Pillard seems to be suggesting that the same sort of solutions that might solve the epistemological problems for people in certain cultures in North America could also be used to address the epistemological problems involved with people from other cultures. I think this underestimates the cross-cultural epistemological difficulties. There are genuine problems determining out how to classify *berdache* found in some Native American cultures (Whitehead 1993) or the men who engage in ritualized homosexuality in New Guinea (Herdt 1984a). Further, there is a general problem with transcultural generalizations about sexual desire that goes far beyond a few "small cultural isolates."

Consider, for example, the "sexual geography" of Chicano and northern Mexican cultures (Almaguer 1993; Alonso and Koreck 1993). In certain cultures and subcultural groups in the Western Hemisphere, men who have sex with men divide up into two main types: *machos* (also *machistas* or *activos*) and *jotos* (also *putos* or *pasivos*). *Jotos* are primarily anally *penetrated* by their sexual partners, while *machos* primarily anally *penetrate* their male sexual partners and also may have sex with women (involving vaginal and/or anal penetration). If you asked a *macho* whether he was gay (or homosexual), he would almost surely answer in the negative (to him, that term would probably be seen as applying exclusively to *jotos*). Similarly, it seems unlikely that he would consider himself bisexual; rather, he would say that he is a "normal" and "masculine" man. Pillard would admit this—"there are societies in which people don't call themselves gay" (Stein 1993, 101)—but it seems that he thinks we can determine who the gay men are by looking at behavior—"they certainly do stuff we would call gay" (101). Pillard seems to revert to the *behavioral* view of sexual orientation. A sexually active *macho* would "do stuff we would call gay" in terms of his sexual behavior. The problem is that so might a heterosexual man in prison who has sex with men but almost exclusively fantasizes about sex with women. Also a problem would be a man in a country with a large commercial sex business who frequently gets paid to have sex with other men but primarily has sexual fantasies about women and regularly has sex with his girlfriend. According to the *dispositional* view of sexual orientation, the heterosexual prisoner who has sex with men and the male sex worker should not count as a homosexual. If we want to count the *machos* as homosexual, we have to focus on *more* than actual sexual behavior; the "stuff we would call gay" has to include desires, fantasies, and dispositions. To get at the actual sexual orientation of a *macho* or of the male sex worker, a survey would have to ask them not just about their sexual behavior, but about whom they like to have sex with, whom they fantasize about, and what their ideal sexual activities are. Such a detailed longitudinal survey should allow the *macho,* for example, to be assigned a number on the Kinsey scale. In particular, a *macho* who penetrates both men and women would turn out to be a bisexual (somewhere between a 2 and a 4 on the Kinsey scale). It is, however, far from obvious that this is the right way to categorize the sexual desires of a *macho.*

To review, I am considering a specific problem: even if the technical problems of assigning every *macho* a number on the Kinsey scale could be overcome, it is not clear whether the result of this process actually breaks through the cultural barriers and finds an appropriate classification for each *macho* in terms of his sexual desires. The worry is that self-reports of desires and dispositions cannot be disentangled from the cultural overlay involved in an individual's sexual desires, and that even the sort of sophisticated survey I have described cannot disentangle underlying desires from their cultural influences. A *macho* presumably does not see his desire to anally penetrate men as an atypical desire for a man to have; he does not see it as conceptually distinct from his desire to vaginally or anally penetrate women; he does not see his desire as indicative of the love of men or of a strong emotional attachment to them; he does not see his desire as an inversion of his masculinity; and he may see his sexual desires as quite different from those of *jotos.*

In contrast, the "typical" bisexual man in Anglo cultures of the United States may see his desire for men and his desire for women as distinct from each other (usually they see one as more basic and intrinsic than the other), he may see his desire for men as involving love and emotional attachment, and he may see himself as similar to gay men (that is, he may see himself as having both a gay side and a straight side) (Weinberg, Williams, and Pryor 1994). These differences are almost certain to affect the results of surveys that attempt to place both Chicano and Anglo men onto the same scale for categorizing sexual orientation (for example, the Kinsey scale). Cultural factors are almost certain to affect a person's placement on the Kinsey scale.

In general, it is far from clear, contra Pillard, even assuming the categories of sexual orientation are natural human kinds, that it will be in practice possible to fit people in other cultures into our categories. This epistemological problem is not unique to *machos* and *jotos;* the same problem exists for people in Attic Greece (Halperin 1990), the *hidras* in India (Nanda 1993), the *berdache* of Native American cultures (Whitehead 1993), and innumerable others from various cultures and historical periods (Greenberg 1988). Combining the dispositional view of sexual orientation with the limitations of experimentation on human subjects, it follows that scientists must trust their subjects to report their own sexual orientations or the desires and behaviors that will be used to assess their sexual orientations. Many people across the world and throughout history do not see themselves in terms of the commonsense categories of sexual orientation and do not experience their desires in a manner such that they can be placed into these categories. For example, they may not see same-sex sexual desire as gender inversion. Classifying people using our categories of sexual orientation involves a serious epistemological problem with developing a reasonable estimate of the base rate of homosexuality in the general human population. Yet, it is just this sort of estimate that most biological studies of human sexual orientation require (Bailey and Pillard 1991b, 1093; Bailey, Pillard, and Agyei 1993, 200; Hamer et al. 1993, 322; LeVay 1991, 1036, note 7).

*Metaphysical Issues*

The metaphysical problems involved in determining the base rate of homosexuality are even more serious than these epistemological problems. The search for the base rate of homosexuality in the general human population and in the context of biological research on sexual orientation only makes sense if sexual orientations are natural human kinds, that is, only if essentialism about sexual orientation is true. It would make no sense, for example, to say that 10 percent (or any percent) of all adult men in every culture across the world are yuppies or Democrats; these categories do not apply to other cultures. There simply cannot be yuppies or Democrats in a hunter-gatherer society. If sexual orientations are not natural human kinds, then it will not make sense to apply these categories to other cultures where the social structures surrounding sexual desire are quite different. It would be anachronistic to say, for example, that 10 percent of the population in Attic Greece was homosexual. Even if we had perfect information about the sexual activity, desires, and fantasies of a person in Attic Greece, it would be a mistake to ask whether this person was a heterosexual, a homosexual, or a bisexual.

Suppose, for example, we discovered the lost diaries of Socrates that contained the complete details of his sexual behavior and sexual fantasies (including his masturbatory fantasies). Imagine that it turned out that Socrates regularly had sex with his wife but more frequently had sex with various young men who were his students. Suppose that Socrates' sexual fantasies were primarily directed towards sex with young men but that he also had fantasies about having sex with women of approximately his age. Even if we were sure of all this, would we have grounds for counting Socrates as a bisexual? A homosexual? A heterosexual and a situational homosexual? A pederast? A Kinsey 4? For reasons I discussed in chapter 4, it is not clear that we are justified in believing any of these claims. This is an example of the metaphysical problem involved in determining the base rate for sexual orientations.

Note the difference between this metaphysical problem and the epistemological problem I previously discussed. For the epistemological problem to arise, the metaphysical problem must be in principle resolvable; the epistemological problem assumes that sexual orientations are natural human kinds. Granting that every human has a sexual orientation, the epistemological problem concerns determining the sexual orientation of a particular person (for example, was Socrates gay, straight, or bisexual?). The metaphysical problem arises when these assumptions are questioned (that is, does it make sense to ask whether Socrates was heterosexual, homosexual, or bisexual?). In chapter 4, I developed several reasons for questioning these assumptions. In the present chapter, questions about whether sexual orientations are natural human kinds lead to serious doubts about whether it makes sense to ask what the base rate of homosexuality in the general population is.

In the first published volume of their results, Kinsey and his collaborators said it is obvious that "any question as to the number of persons in the world who are homosexual and the number who are heterosexual is *unanswerable*" (Kinsey, Pomeroy, and Martin 1948, 650, emphasis added). More recently, Laumann and his collaborators on the Chicago survey concurred: "estimating a single number for the prevalence of homosexuality is a *futile exercise* because it presupposes assumptions that are patently false: that homosexuality is a uniform attribute across individuals, that it is stable over time, and that it can be uniformly measured" (Laumann et al. 1994, 283, emphasis added). Even Dean Hamer does not "think there is such a thing as the rate of homosexuality in the population at large." (Hamer and Copeland 1994, 102). Biological studies of sexual orientation that unquestioningly make use of estimates of the base rate of homosexuality fail to acknowledge the serious metaphysical and epistemological problems inherent in such estimates. Even a researcher like Hamer, who seems to acknowledge the problem, does little to address it.

### Summary

In this section, I have discussed various assumptions about sexual orientation that are typically made by studies in the emerging research program. No scientific study (or research program) can do everything; every scientific study must make many assumptions that it does not test (for example, scientists typically make assumptions about the accuracy and appropriateness of their instruments). Nonetheless, the sort of assumptions that I have discussed in this section are central to the claims of the emerging research program. A scientific inquiry into human sexual desire should not, for example, unquestioningly accept essentialism or the inversion assumption or the binary view of sexual orientation. These assumptions are culturally salient, but that does not show that they should be taken for granted by scientific studies. In fact, my arguments have shown that these assumptions are problematic. In the next two sections, I set aside these methodological objections and focus on problems with interpreting the results of such studies.

## Do the Studies Prove Causation?

In his classic work on epistemology, David Hume (1977) discusses how we can determine whether one event causes another. Frequently we witness events similar to the following two occur in close proximity to each other, the first event followed by the second:

1. a moving ball—call it A—hits a stationary ball—call it B
2. B, which was previously stationary, begins rolling

Despite repeated observations of this sort, we never witness events like
(1) *causing* events like (2); we have merely witnessed a series of *correlations* of
such events. Hume's point is that nothing about the correlations that we
observe allows us to make inferences about causes. Note that, in general, two
events can be *correlated* without it being the case that one causes the other.
Suppose that whenever you see me carrying an umbrella in the morning, it
rains in the afternoon. From your point of view, there is a *correlation* between
my having an umbrella and the afternoon rain. This correlation does not,
however, justify the inference that my carrying of the umbrella *causes* the rain.
No matter how many times you notice a correlation between me carrying that
umbrella and the rain, you would be mistaken to infer causation from this.

Hume's conclusion is a radically skeptical one: *we can never be justified in
inferring causation.* In practice, however, no one is as skeptical as Hume (not
even Hume was in the way he lived his life); in everyday life, we make such
inferences all the time. We do not, however, *always* infer causation from correlation. We infer that the rolling ball *causes* the stationary ball to move, but we
do not infer that instances of umbrellas being carried cause rain. My aim here
is not to solve Hume's problem by justifying our practice of inferring causation.
Instead, I want to focus on the commonsense distinction between cases in
which we are justified in inferring causation from correlation and cases in
which we are not. Our attributions of causation have to do with the background
of scientific (and other) theories about the realm we are considering. There are
plausible physical theories that connect contact between balls and the transfer
of energy between them. There are no plausible theories that connect in the
appropriate way instances of umbrellas being carried to subsequent rainstorms.
In fact, there is a commonsense explanation for the correlation of umbrella
sightings and rain, namely, both events are caused by some third event, for
example, the buildup of evaporated water in clouds. Noticing the buildup of
water leads weather forecasters to predict rain, which in turn leads me to carry
my umbrella. The same buildup of water leads to rain. My carrying an
umbrella and the afternoon rain are both caused by some third event; this third
event plays a role in explaining their correlation.

Returning now to research on sexual orientation, scientists doing this
research often infer causation from correlation. For example, those who interpret LeVay's neuroanatomical study as showing that homosexuality is *caused* by
small INAH-3 are inferring causation on the basis of mere correlation. Just as
inferences from correlation to causation are plausible in everyday reasoning if

there is a supporting set of background theories, they are also plausible in the context of scientific reasoning if there is a supporting set of background scientific theories. The question then is whether the appropriate set of background theories exists that support inferring causation in the case of INAH-3 and homosexuality in men or whether the correlation is more plausibly explained in some other way. The general point is that we need to be suspicious about inferences based on correlation when there are no well-supported background theories against which to explain the causation.

Related to whether the data in a particular study are strong enough to allow causation to be inferred is whether the data support the direct model rather than the indirect model. In chapter 5, I distinguished among three ways that biological factors can play a role in the development of sexual orientation. Biological factors can influence the neurological structures that enable experience to shape a person's sexual orientation (the permissive model), biological factors can code for personality factors that shape a person's sexual orientation (the indirect model), or biological factors can directly influence the neurological structures that create a person's sexual orientation (the direct model). Many of the scientific studies of sexual orientation that are supposed to support some particular version of the direct model of sexual orientation are in fact compatible with the indirect model (and, in some cases, even with the permissive model).

Setting aside my previous objections (for example, objections relating to sample size, the assignment of sexual orientations, and the assumption of essentialism), LeVay has at best shown that there is a *correlation* between INAH-3 and sexual orientation; he has not, as he admits when he is careful (LeVay 1991), shown any causation. Further, and relatedly, he has no evidence that biological factors directly affect sexual orientation. Even if he could prove that INAH-3 size and sexual orientation are perfectly correlated in his sample population (and I have argued that he fails to do so), this would not establish any direct causal account of homosexuality. It would remain equally plausible that INAH-3 size leads to certain personality attributes that in certain contexts leads to homosexuality in men. Nothing LeVay says lends support to the direct model as compared to the indirect model. Given these two points, LeVay's conclusion that "sexual orientation in humans is amenable to study at the biological level" (1036) is seriously undercut, as are bolder versions of this statement that he made in the mainstream press (for example, Perlman 1991).

The same general problem applies to Bailey and Pillard's twin studies (Bailey and Pillard 1991b; Bailey, Pillard, and Agyei 1993). Recall my chapter 5 discussion of heritability. The heritability of a trait is the ratio of genetically caused variation (with respect to that trait) to total variation. Heritability represents the extent to which a trait is caused by genetic factors. That a trait has high heritability is not the same as a trait being genetically determined. The heritability of a trait is context-sensitive and highly contingent. In the United States, having ten fingers is not very heritable because most variation in number of fingers is due to environmental factors (for example, bagel-related accidents). One could, however, easily imagine environments in which having ten fingers is highly heritable (for example, a culture in which everyone with blue eyes gets a finger chopped off).

That twin studies have been done almost exclusively in one sort of culture and that the subjects have primarily been selected from a specific socioeconomic and ethnic subgroup within this culture exacerbates the problems with applying Bailey's results to the development of human sexual orientation in general. Twin studies have no bearing on whether sexual orientation is directly or indirectly heritable, that is, whether sexual orientation is caused directly by genes or whether it is caused indirectly, in the context of particular environmental factors, by the effects of some other trait, itself genetically caused. (It may be useful to recall the Brickland example from chapter 5.) Although one of Bailey's twin study articles has the word "genetic" in the title (Bailey and Pillard 1991b), he is more careful in the subsection entitled "Implications for the Genetics of Sexual Orientation." He admits that "heritability is not informative regarding the development of sexual orientation . . . [, t]hat is, given any heritability estimate, there are a variety of possible developmental mechanisms" (1095). In other words, sexual orientation could be the result of indirect effects. Nothing in Bailey's studies establishes that sexual orientation is genetically determined or that it is the direct result of genetic factors. Bailey realizes that his studies do not prove that genes directly cause sexual orientation, but many who cite his studies do not. Generally, although perhaps the central claim of the emerging research program is that it establishes the direct model, none of the studies within this program provide evidence for this claim.

## A Closer Look at Hamer's Genetic Study

As a way of exemplifying and reviewing the objections to the emerging research program that I have discussed thus far, I turn now to a detailed discussion of one of the studies within this program, namely Hamer's genetic study (Hamer et al. 1993). I have chosen to discuss Hamer's study in greater depth because it is the most complex of the three studies and, in a sense, it combines features of LeVay's study and Bailey and Pillard's studies. Recall that Hamer's study has two parts. He began with pedigree analyses to see if he could discover any patterns of the distribution of sexual orientations in families. This part is like Bailey and Pillard's twin studies in that both are looking for evidence that sexual orientations run in families. Having isolated what he took to be a pattern of maternal-linked inheritance in the families of gay men, Hamer did a genetic linkage study to determine where on the X chromosome the gene that was responsible for this pattern is located. This part of Hamer's study is like LeVay's in that he is looking for an account of sexual orientation in the body. I examine the two parts of Hamer's study in turn.

### The Pedigree Studies

Recall that Hamer began his study by looking at the families of gay men. Some of Hamer's target subjects (that is, the gay men whose families he studied) were recruited for "a study of human sexual development" through two Washington, D.C.-area AIDS clinics, an organization of gay Christian Scientists, and a private center for lesbians and gay men dealing with addiction to alcohol and drugs. Other subjects were recruited from ads in D.C. and Baltimore area gay newspapers under the heading "Gay Men—Do You Have a Gay Brother?" (Hamer and Copeland 1994, 48). Further, in order to increase the chances of isolating a maternally linked gene for homosexuality, Hamer's second pedigree study only included target subjects whose fathers were not gay, who had no gay sons, and who had no more than one lesbian relative (see chapter 5). The results of this study were that gay men had significantly more gay male relatives on their mother's side of the family. However, Hamer's pedigree analyses share the same sort of sampling bias problems to which the twin studies are subject, namely, it is not at all clear that his subjects are typical gay men (see the first section of this chapter).

There are further problems with Hamer's pedigree studies. The most significant result of these studies was the increased rate of homosexuality on the maternal side of the gay men's families. Several commentators have expressed concerns about this result and its significance. Some have said that the different rate of homosexuality among maternal and paternal relatives is not statistically significant (Bailey and Pillard 1995; McGuire 1995, 133–134; Risch, Squires-Wheeler, and Keats 1993). Partly this is because Hamer's conclusions are based on seeing the base rate of homosexuality as 2 percent. If the base rate is actually 4 percent or higher, then Hamer's results are not statistically significant (Allen 1997, 257, citing Evan Balaban). In light of the concerns about estimates of the base rate of homosexuality and their use in studies in the emerging research program (see the third section of this chapter), it seems to be a serious problem that a small adjustment in the base rate would completely undermine the significance of the results of Hamer's pedigree study.

Another potential problem with Hamer's pedigree studies concerns the possibility that gay men might be closer to their mother's side of the family, and thereby know more about their families and be in a better position to identify cases of homosexuality on their mother's side. Hamer (Hamer and Copeland 1994, 103–104) makes two points to answer this objection. First, if subjects know more about their mother's families, then subjects should also report more lesbians on their mother's side of the family than on their father's side. Second, if subjects know more about their mother's side of the family, lesbians should also report a higher rate of gay men on their mother's side of the family but not on their father's side. Both of these answers are supported, says Hamer, by a study of sexual orientation in women done in his lab (Pattatucci and Hamer 1995). Hamer's two points begin to defend his results against the objection that they can be explained by the fact that people are simply closer to their mothers.

There remain, however, three possibilities that could undercut Hamer's responses. First, Hamer's responses would not work if mothers of openly gay men are more likely to tell their sons about other gay men in the family than they are to tell them about lesbian relatives. Second, Hamer's responses would not work if mothers of openly gay men are more likely than fathers of gay men to tell their sons about their gay male relatives. Third, Hamer's responses would not work if mothers of openly gay men are more likely than mothers of lesbians to tell their homosexual offspring about gay men in their family. For various social reasons, these three possibilities are not implausible. No doubt, mothers and fathers have different relationships with their sons as compared to their daughters, with their gay sons as compared to their heterosexual sons, and their lesbian daughters as compared to their gay sons. Some of these social differences will be due to sex-gender asymmetries and asymmetries between heterosexuals and nonheterosexuals within our culture. Hamer, in his response to some of his critics, glosses over the existence of significant social differences. In fact, these alternative social hypotheses for the patterns of familial distribution of gay men seem plausible; Hamer's results are thus open to a nongenetic (that is, social) explanation. Unless Hamer can rule out social factors as the source of the results of his pedigree analysis, his initial support for his genetic hypothesis will be undermined.

Others, such as Neil Risch, have suggested that the increased rate of homosexuality on the maternal side of gay men's families could be due to the fertility patterns of gay men. To see this point, suppose that there is a gene that in environments like those commonly found in this culture tends to cause (either directly or indirectly) men to be gay and suppose that it is *not* carried on the X chromosomes (that is, it is not maternally linked). Even so, people in this culture would be less likely to inherit such a gene from their fathers because the gene, by hypothesis, tends to cause men to be gay, and gay men (at least openly gay men) are less likely to have children than other men. The point is that a gene linked to male homosexuality would look like it is maternally linked even if it is not carried on the X chromosome. This is yet another reason for skepticism about Hamer's pedigree analyses. Further, at least two independent research teams have failed to replicate Hamer's studies (Bailey et al. forthcoming; Rice et al. 1999). The only replication of Hamer's initial results is a second study also by Hamer's group (Hu et al. 1995).*

Even if the results from the pedigree analysis studies are replicated, setting aside my concerns about Hamer's methodology, the pedigree studies would not establish a genetic basis for sexual orientation or for homosexuality in particular. As I have discussed in the context of Bailey and Pillard's twin studies, that a trait runs in families does not show that it is the result of direct genetic effects. It is consistent with Hamer's pedigree data that social factors play a primary role in the development of sexual orientation. Hamer himself seems to agree that the pedigree analysis does not establish a genetic cause. However, in some contexts he does use the phrase "gay genes" and other locutions that suggest he thinks he has established a direct cause of homosexuality (Hamer and Copeland 1994; LeVay and Hamer 1994). When he is at his most careful, he says that his results are *suggestive* enough to make the linkage study promising. However, the worries I mentioned above show that the pedigree analyses are not especially suggestive. If the linkage study produces significant results in the form of identifying a stretch of genetic material that seems to code for homosexuality, the suggestiveness of the pedigree analyses would be immaterial. With this in mind, I now turn to Hamer's linkage study.

### The Linkage Analysis

The linkage part of Hamer's study is more technologically innovative than the pedigree studies. The technologies for family studies have been around for a long time, but genetic marker studies have only recently been developed.

---

*Lack of replication is common among studies in the emerging research, perhaps due to the fact that the research program is *emerging*. LeVay's study (LeVay 1991) has not been replicated. Further, LeVay's data have not been shared with other researchers, and similar neuroanatomical studies of nearby hypothalamic regions—as well as other brain regions—have, over time, been *disconfirmed* (Byne 1995). For example, LeVay (1991) disconfirmed Laura Allen's conclusion that INAH-2 was larger in men than women (Allen, Hines, and Shryne 1989), and both LeVay and Allen's studies disconfirmed the conclusion of another laboratory that INAH-1 was larger in men than women (Swaab and Fliers 1985).

Linkage analysis is best suited for discovering the genetic basis of traits that are controlled in a genetically simple manner rather than traits that are controlled by several genes working in concert (*polygenic* traits). On more than one occasion and for more than one trait, linkage analysis has mistakenly indicated that a specific genetic sequence plays a role in the development of a particular trait (Bailey 1995b). Such mistakes are especially likely in the case of genetically complex (that is, polygenic) traits or traits that are strongly affected by environmental factors. Specifically, linkage analysis has not been a fruitful method of study for behavioral traits (Risch and Merikangas 1993).[8] Sexual orientation is of course a behavioral trait, and further, it is a cognitively mediated one. For these general reasons, linkage analysis does not seem an especially promising technique with which to study sexual orientation.

Hamer's linkage analysis is subject to problems similar to those of his pedigree studies (Hamer et al. 1993).[9] In particular, the gay target subjects in the linkage study had to be open about their sexual orientation and to allow researchers to contact and interview their family members. These people, to a considerable extent, had to be risk takers. Suppose, as some have argued (Hamer and Copeland 1998), that willingness to buck the system and express unpopular beliefs are genetically based. Given the subject pool for Hamer's linkage analysis, it seems possible that any genetic linkage that this study discovers is as likely to be associated with risk taking as it is with homosexuality. This point also indicates that the linkage study does not provide evidence for the direct model as opposed to the indirect model of the origins of sexual orientations.

There are more specific problems with Hamer's particular application of linkage analysis to the study of homosexuality. In his original study, Hamer did not examine the q28 regions of the X chromosomes of his gay subjects' heterosexual brothers to see how many shared the same sequence. Hamer suggests that inclusion of heterosexual siblings would have confounded his analysis because the gene associated with homosexuality might be carried by heterosexual men but not expressed by them. In other words, inclusion of heterosexual brothers might have revealed that something other than (or in addition to) genes is responsible for sexual orientation. Despite this concern, in a subsequent study Hamer's group did find that heterosexual brothers of gay men tended not to share genetic markers for Xq28 with their gay siblings (only 22 percent of discordant sibling pairs shared the relevant markers compared to 67 percent of the concordant sibling pairs).

As with the pedigree study, the linkage portion of Hamer's study, while replicated by Hamer's group (although the results of the replication were less strong than the original linkage study) (Hu et al. 1995), have not been independently replicated. Both attempts at independent replication of the linkage analysis aspect of Hamer's study failed to find any evidence of X-linked transmission (Bailey et al. forthcoming; Rice et al. 1999).

Setting aside objections to the linkage study, Hamer's study does not justify talk about the existence of "genes for homosexuality," even though the subtitle of Hamer's book is "The Search for the Gay Gene" (Hamer and Copeland 1994). Genes in themselves cannot directly specify any behavior or psychological phenomenon. Instead, genes direct a particular pattern of RNA synthesis, which in turn specifies the production of a particular protein, which in turn may influence the development of psychological dispositions and the expression of behaviors. There are necessarily many intervening pathways between a gene and a disposition or a behavior, and even more intervening variables between a gene and a pattern that involves both thinking and behaving. The terms "gay gene" and "homosexual gene" are, therefore, without meaning, unless one proposes that a particular gene, perhaps through a hormonal mechanism, organizes the brain specifically to support the desire to have sex with people of the same sex-gender. No one has, however, presented evidence in support of such a simple and direct link between genes and sexual orientation (Allen 1997).

Taken as a whole, Hamer's study faces various methodological problems, its results are open to various interpretations (several of which are more plausible than the existence of a gay gene), and it has not been replicated. Hamer's study, which has been taken by many to be the centerpiece of the emerging research program, actually exemplifies many of its problems.

## Designing Better Research:
## A Paradigm for Future Studies

So far, this chapter has been critical. I have examined the assumptions of the emerging research program and the evidence that is supposed to support them. In particular, I have argued that the evidence for the claim that sexual orientations are inborn or determined at an early age by biological factor is rather weak. Similarly, the evidence does not support the direct model of the development of sexual orientations as compared to the indirect model. The emerging research program makes several bold hypotheses about sexual orientation, but the evidence it has produced for these hypotheses is quite weak. Whether or not the central claim of the emerging research program is plausible, it is surely subject to experimental tests. Testability, as the philosopher Karl Popper has emphasized, is the hallmark of empirical claims (Popper 1959, 1962). The right sort of experiments ought to be able to test the central claims of the emerging research program even if the studies that have been done fail to do so. In this section, I describe the features of studies that would, in various ways, be improvements on those studies that have been done so far. Studies that have these features will actually test the claims of the emerging research program.

Studies of sexual orientation should take all possible steps to avoid sampling biases. The best sort of studies would select subjects using sophisticated statistical sampling methods (Laumann et al. 1994). This is not a trivial procedure. Failing that, it is better to recruit subjects in a way that might encourage "closeted" lesbians and gay men to participate. Lesbian and gay volunteers gleaned from announcements that ask for gay men and lesbians with gay or lesbian siblings or from advertisements in lesbian and gay publications will skew the sample in favor of openly gay people, who may be in some ways atypical. Bailey's Australian twin study, for example, is a good model for a study that avoids much of the likely sampling bias without using statistical sampling methods (Bailey, Dunne, and Martin n.d.).

Also, future studies should involve subjects from various cultures, especially those where sexual desire is conceptualized differently than it is in our culture. Very few studies that are part of the emerging research program involve cross-cultural comparisons. The inclusion of subjects from various cultures is, for several reasons, especially useful. Such studies would potentially do a better job of disentangling social factors and biological factors. Recall my alternative explanation of Hamer's results (Hamer et al. 1993). I suggested that a gene in the q28 region of the X chromosome might have more to do with willingness to buck the system than male homosexuality. Together, the negative attitudes towards homosexuality in this culture and the existence of a genetic basis to bucking the system might be able to explain Hamer's linkage data and his pedigree data. This hypothesis, and others that appeal to social factors like attitudes towards lesbians and gay men, could be tested by cross-cultural data because in other cultures attitudes towards people who have sexual desires for or who engage in behaviors with people of the same sex-gender take different forms. Similarly, in some other cultures homosexuality is not viewed as a kind of gender inversion, and sexual orientations are not viewed as natural human kinds. Including subjects from such cultures in a study would help determine if sexual orientations have these characteristics in virtue of biological influences or cultural influences.

Not just any cross-cultural study will suffice. The few cross-cultural studies that have been done internalize Western cultural assumptions about sexual orientations. Simply asking a *macho* or a *berdache* whether he is gay or to place rate himself on the Kinsey scale will not suffice as a way of doing a cross-cultural study. Simply counting anyone who engages in sexual activity with people of the same sex-gender as a lesbian or a gay man will not suffice either. As an example of cross-cultural data that seems to assume that our ways of thinking about sexual orientation extend to other cultures, consider Fred Whitam's study of homosexuals in the United States, Guatemala, Brazil, and the Philippines (Whitam 1983). One of Whitam's (tentative) conclusions is that "homosexuality . . . is universal, appearing in all societies" (209). Among the evidence that he cites for this conclusion is that guidebooks intended for gay male tourists list meeting places for sexual encounters with other men in almost every country in the world (210–213). This evidence fails to provide any genuine support for his conclusion. Few would deny that all over the world people have sex with people of the same sex-gender; the question is whether the people in other cultures have anything else in common besides the sorts of acts they commit, for example, whether they have the same desires, the same psychological mechanisms, or the same neuroanatomical structures behind their sexual activity with people of the same sex-gender. A guidebook produced in Europe or the United States and intended to speak to men in these countries traveling to other places typically assumes the categories of sexual orientation that the readers of such books would apply to themselves. Such books may make for pleasurable vacations, but they do not make for good science. The inclusion of subjects from various cultures and subcultures would be a significant advance in studies of sexual orientation, but not just any cross-cultural study will do.

Additionally, better studies would be more careful in how they assign subjects to a sexual orientation. Recall that LeVay looked at the deceased subjects' hospital records to try to assess their sexual orientation. In other studies, subjects were placed on the Kinsey scale in virtue of their answer to one question (or something close to it): "What is your current sexual orientation?" Contrast this method and LeVay's method to the method used by Kinsey (Kinsey, Pomeroy, and Martin 1948; Kinsey et al. 1953). In the Kinsey studies, the subjects were interviewed about their sexual behaviors, desires, and self-identification. The Kinsey researchers spent several hours with each subject taking detailed sexual histories. These sexual histories included many open-ended questions, including questions about their (past and present) sexual desires, fantasies, identities, and behaviors.

I have discussed at length the problems with LeVay's method of assigning subjects a sexual orientation. There are also some potential problems with any method that focuses on a subject's self-assessment in assigning sexual orientations. Each subject may have a somewhat different interpretation of sexual orientation and the Kinsey scale. Further, subjects may have internalized the cultural assumption that sexual attraction to men varies inversely to sexual attraction to women. As I argued in chapter 2, this assumption is probably mistaken. Relying on subjects' self-assessment involves the risk of implicitly accepting their culturally infused presumptions about sexual orientations; that is, the binary or bipolar view of sexual orientation, the inversion assumption, and essentialism. Simply put, self-assessment may be a problematic way of assessing sexual orientation.

In contrast, Kinsey's method of sexual-orientation classification has interviewers classify subjects on the basis of their reported sexual histories and sexual fantasies. The researchers take this information and make a determination about a subject's sexual orientation. This "objective" method has the advantage of insuring that roughly the same definitions of the various sexual orientations are being applied to all subjects. This method is far from perfect since not all subjects are going to describe their sexual desires and behaviors honestly. This method, however, is probably more accurate than the method of just asking subjects their sexual orientation. Additionally, a longitudinal study—one that follows the same subjects over several years—would be better for assessing a person's sexual desires in a way that does not make a variety of assumptions about sexual orientations that may be unjustified.

In general, researchers designing sophisticated studies of sexual orientation need to be careful about how they assign subjects to sexual orientations and the sorts of assumptions they make about what a sexual orientation is. For example, if researchers adopted a Kinsey-style procedure for assessing a person's sexual desires, they should not assume that homosexuality is, in any scientifically interesting sense, a form of gender inversion or that sexual orientations are one-dimensional (that is, that the binary or bipolar view of sexual orientation is right).

Relatedly, studies need to be careful about the assumptions they make about the base rate of homosexuality. A cross-cultural study, in particular, should not use a base rate that comes from a survey of people in one culture. In general, it is important to remember that there can be a wide disparity in the percentage of people who experience some sexual desire for people of the same sex-gender, who identify openly as having a particular sexual orientation, and who engage in sexual behavior that typically is associated with that sexual orientation. Of Kinsey's male subjects, 4 percent were "exclusively homosexual" for most of their life, while 25 percent of adult white men engaged in "more than incidental" sexual activity with people of the same sex-gender (Kinsey, Pomeroy, and Martin 1948, 650). To whatever extent possible, a study should make use of a base-rate figure only if it uses the same sort of method to assess a person's sexual orientation as did the survey that generated the base rate. Failing this, a study should use various estimates of the base rate in evaluating its results. Bailey and Pillard, for example, use estimates of 4 and 10 percent for the base rate of male homosexuality in their male twin study (Bailey and Pillard 1991b).

Finally, in analyzing the results of scientific studies of sexual orientations and sexual desires, one needs to be careful not to see a direct causal link where the data do not support it. Various explanations need to be considered before embracing a particular account of the development of sexual desires. In particular, theories that fit the indirect model of sexual orientation need to be seriously considered before theories that fit the direct model are embraced.

To review, studies in the emerging research program would do a significantly better job of providing evidence relevant to the assessment of its primary theses if they:

- used statistical sampling methods (or just better sampling methods);
- drew subjects from various cultures and subcultural groups;
- evaluated subjects' sexual orientations through detailed, ideally longitudinal, sexual histories;
- took greater care not to allow cultural assumptions about sexual desires and how they are organized to influence the classification of subjects and the interpretation of the results of studies;
- considered indirect in addition to direct theories in deciding how to interpret the data.

Studies that make use of all of these design features would probably not be easy to execute. They would be expensive and would take many years to run. It might be difficult to find an adequate number of subjects who would be willing to provide the data needed without introducing some sort of sampling bias. More sophisticated studies are, however, required to genuinely test the central claims of the emerging research program. Whether it is worthwhile to do these more sophisticated studies is a further question. I consider the value of scientific research on sexual orientation in chapter 12.

## Conclusion

At the beginning of chapter 5, I offered several reasons for giving careful consideration to the emerging scientific research program for the study of sexual orientation. These reasons were as follows:

1. looking back over the centuries, science has been very successful in explaining things about humans and the world we inhabit;
2. several studies within the emerging research program have been published in respectable journals and are widely cited;
3. the research fits with many people's intuitions about sexual orientation;
4. animal models of sexual orientation suggest that human sexual orientation will be amenable to scientific research;
5. the emerging research program fits nicely with evolutionary explanations of human sexual orientation;
6. the emerging research program has important ethical implications;
7. scientific studies that are part of the emerging research program have garnered a great deal of public attention;
8. the emerging research program can help resolve the debate between essentialists and constructionists about sexual orientation.

The mere fact, however, that there are reasons to consider the emerging research program does not show that its central claims are true or that the results of studies in the program are valid.

In chapter 6, I showed that the emerging research program rests, in various ways, on an analogy between animal and human sexual behaviors and desires. In that chapter, I raised objections to animal models of human sexual orientation. We have no strong reason for thinking that any particular animal provides an adequate model of human sexual orientation. Also in chapter 6, I indicated how the emerging research program is related to evolutionary theory. I also argued that there is no particular reason to believe any of the evolutionary stories concerning human sexual desires.

In the present chapter, I discussed the experimental evidence that is supposed to support the emerging research program. Although the main studies in this program are well-placed, widely cited, and their conclusions are even more widely believed, I argued that there are serious methodological and interpretive problems facing each of them. Studies in the emerging scientific program embrace—explicitly or implicitly—a problematic account of what a sexual orientation is; have problems finding an appropriate subject pool to study; accept unjustified assumptions about the base rate of homosexuality; and make a variety of implicit, widely varied, and unjustified assumptions about homosexuality. No study in the emerging research program avoids all of these problems, and many of them have additional problems (for example, few of them have been replicated). I do not claim to have addressed every biological theory that has been articulated. So many different theories have been floated and are taken seriously by some scientists that I cannot begin to address them all. I have, for example, said little about the specific problems with studies that concern the fingerprints of gay men (Hall and Kimura 1994) and the inner ears of lesbians (McFadden and Pasanen 1998). Many of the problems I have raised in this chapter are indicative of the central problems facing the emerging research program and can be applied to almost any biological theory of sexual orientation.

The arguments I have made in chapter 6 and the present chapter to some extent undermine six of the reasons that I discussed in chapter 5 in favor of taking the emerging research program seriously (1–5 and 7 from the list above). In subsequent chapters, I discuss the remaining reasons. At the end of chapter 9, I discuss the relevance of the emerging research program to the debate between essentialists and constructionists (8). In chapter 10, I consider the general ethical implications of scientific research on sexual orientation; in chapter 11, I consider some specific ethical implications (6).

Nothing I have said constitutes a conclusive argument against the emerging research program or its central claims. It is possible, for example, that there is a gene somewhere in the q28 region of the X chromosome that codes for a certain pattern of protein synthesis, which in turn leads to certain patterns of prenatal hormonal secretions and/or to certain kinds of reactions to certain hormones, which in turn lead to the development of certain psychological mechanisms, based in specific regions of the hypothalamus, that dispose men to desire sexual activity with other men (LeVay and Hamer 1994). This theory *may* be true, but for reasons developed in this and the preceding chapters, I do not think that it or any other specific theory that is part of the emerging scientific research program is particularly *plausible*. In fact, it is at least as plausible that sexual orientations as we conceive of them are not natural human kinds and do not play an explanatory role in scientific explanations. This is not to say that human sexual desires are not biologically based. As I have noted more than once, everything psychological is in a sense biologically based and sexual orientations are psychological. Sexual orientations may, however, be among those psychological properties that emerge in certain cultures and during certain time periods (more similar to being a yuppie or a Democrat than to having blue eyes or blood type AB). If this is true, it would still be the case that people in other times and places have sexual desires, but it would not be the case that these desires are appropriately classified as sexual orientations. I discuss this possibility more towards the end of chapter 8.

The emerging scientific research program has the character of a not-yet-established research paradigm. Thomas Kuhn, in his classic work, *The*

*Structure of Scientific Revolutions* (Kuhn 1970), distinguishes between periods of *normal science* and *scientific revolutions*. During periods of normal science, the basic theoretical and metaphysical assumptions of a scientific field are accepted and held constant. Practitioners of such a field conduct experiments inside a well-established framework. In contrast, during revolutionary periods, significant portions of a field's paradigm are up for grabs. The scientific study of human sexual desire is, at best, going through a period of revolution. Practitioners in the field have not yet established a paradigm in which normal science can proceed. In fact, it is not obvious, especially in light of my arguments in chapter 6 and the present chapter, that they are close to establishing such a scientific paradigm. A decade or so from now, the emerging research program might turn out to have been a false start in the search for an account of how human sexual desires develop. Our categories of sexual orientation might prove to be empty human kinds in much the same way that phlogiston turned out to be an empty kind and thus a false start on the path towards developing a sophisticated theory of combustion (recall my discussion of empty kinds and empty human kinds in chapter 3).

In order to establish a sophisticated scientific paradigm, researchers must pay attention to the sorts of theoretical and metaphysical worries I have raised in this and previous chapters. Even if essentialism is true, much work remains before practitioners engaged in the scientific study of sexual orientation will be able to practice normal science. On the other hand, if essentialism about sexual orientation is false and the categories of sexual orientation are not natural human kinds, then much of the current research program is mistaken. Partly because this is a possibility, in the next chapter, I consider some alternatives to the emerging research program. In particular, I consider theories that see experience playing a primary role in the development of sexual orientation. Regardless of the conclusions that I reach in my discussion (in chapter 8) of experiential theories of sexual orientation, for reasons developed in this and the previous chapter, we need to adopt a position of cautious skepticism towards scientific research on sexual orientation.

# CHAPTER 8

# Experiential Theories of Sexual Orientation

**A**lthough today the most widely believed theories of the development of sexual orientations see biological factors playing the primary role, *experiential* theories once held the greatest sway. For much of the twentieth century, most people believed that the effects of a person's experience on his or her psychological makeup would explain how he or she develops sexual orientations. While such theories are biological in some sense—only through its effects on bodies and brains can experience affect a person's psychological makeup—more often than not, these theories see people (or, depending on the theory, men or women) as starting from roughly the same place in terms of developing one sexual orientation rather than another. According to such theories, at birth (or perhaps before puberty) we all have roughly the same potential with respect to our sexual orientations and sexual desires; our different experiences and environments account for our differences in terms of sexual orientation. In fact, many people today still believe—sometimes only implicitly—that experiences, especially childhood and adolescent ones, play a greater role than biology in accounting for differences in people's sexual orientations. On the face of it, theories that emphasize the experiential causes of sexual desires seem plausible especially because we think that many other differences among humans in terms of our preferences—for example, musical preferences, tastes for food, and preferences for friends—are mostly to be explained by the differences among people in terms of experience rather than genetic makeup or other aspects of our biological makeup not primarily shaped by experience. Further, given my critique thus far of the emerging scientific research program and its emphasis on the contributions of inborn and early biological differences between individuals to explain differences in sexual orientation, it makes sense to consider theories that explain differences in sexual orientation through differences in experiences.

In the last couple of decades, the number of people who think that experience plays a role in the development of sexual orientations seems to have decreased dramatically, more than the evidence seems to warrant. I suspect that changes in social and political attitudes concerning homosexuality and the increasing popularity of biological theories of sexual orientation have a lot to do with the declining popularity of experiential theories of sexual orientation.

Around the same time as the decline in the popularity of experiential theories of sexual orientation, attitudes towards homosexuality have changed. Whereas most people used to think of homosexuality as a disease or mental illness, of sexual acts among people of the same sex-gender as immoral or criminal, and of intimate relationships between people of the same sex-gender as fleeting and merely sexual, many of these perceptions have changed, in some cases dramatically. This is not to say that most people now look favorably on homosexuality, but some of the reasons why many people look at same sex-gender sexual behavior and desire in an unfavorable fashion have changed. Perhaps this shift is due to the apparent success of biological theories of sexual orientation. Maybe people are thinking that homosexuality cannot be a mental illness if one's genes code for it or that homosexuality cannot be a moral failing if one's sexual orientation is not a choice but is caused by biological factors (I discuss these ideas in chapter 10). Although some individuals' attitudes about homosexuality may have been changed by the claims of biological researchers (LeVay 1996, 4), I doubt this is the correct explanation for the general shift in attitudes. Many of the social changes actually predate the scientific ones. Further, as I will argue in chapter 10, the biological evidence does not entail (logically or even pragmatically) the shift in ethical views. In fact, it is more plausible that changes in attitudes about homosexuality have made biological theories seem more palatable and made psychological theories seem less so: a person who is favorably inclined towards lesbians and gay men may be more willing to accept biological theories than psychological ones; a person who is not so inclined might have the reverse dispositions (Bem 1996b). While these social facts might explain why fewer people now accept psychological theories of the development of sexual orientation, such social facts do not count as evidence against these psychological theories.

The lack of popularity of psychological theories is connected to the dramatic attention that biological research on sexual orientation has received. This attention has lead many people to conclude that there is overwhelming evidence for a biological (rather than a psychological) explanation of how people develop sexual orientations. As I have argued in chapters 6 and 7, the evidence in favor of the emerging scientific research program on sexual orientation is not as strong as many people perceive. Moreover, some of the theories in the emerging research program require psychological and experiential theories to provide a full account of the development of human sexual orientation. For example, differences in experience seem required to explain the differences among identical twins discordant for sexual orientation (see chapter 7).

A remaining reason why the popularity of psychological theories of sexual orientation has declined is that people think that the fact that most well-articulated psychological theories of sexual orientation are not well supported lends support to the conclusion that sexual orientations cannot be explained experientially. It is, however, a mistake to think that all psychological theories are false just because the few that have been articulated do not seem true. Further, it seems plausible that there are multiple pathways to the various sexual orientations. A myriad of experiences (and subjective interpretations of them) could lead different individuals to the same degree of attraction to men, women, or both. Even if no particular psychological theory of sexual orientation stands out, psychology may be the right place to look for a theory of sexual orientation. Even if the evidence against specific psychological theories is significant, this evidence does not show that psychological theory in general is a dead end.

In this chapter, I examine several theories of how sexual orientations develop that give a primary role to experience. I discuss methodological and evidentiary problems with these theories. Towards the end of this chapter, I offer an alternative theory of the origins of sexual orientation that suggests there are multiple origins for human sexual orientations and sexual desires.

## Three Experiential Theories

As I have already argued, any viable account of the development of sexual orientations (or almost any other human trait) will give some role to genetic and other biological factors but will also give some role to experiential factors. At a minimum, genetic and biological factors make it the case that humans, but not rocks or amebas, have sexual orientations. However, even advocates of the emerging research program have to admit that experiential factors play a role in shaping sexual orientation: it is due to nongenetic, nonbiological factors that a significant percentage of identical twins are discordant for sexual orientation (Bailey, Dunne, and Martin n.d.; Bailey and Pillard 1991b; Bailey, Pillard, and Agyei 1993). Whereas the theories that are part of the emerging research program see biological factors, in particular genetic and neuroanatomical ones, as playing the primary role in the development of sexual orientations, the main rivals to these biological theories attribute a primary role to experience. Three types of experience have been offered as especially relevant to the development of a person's sexual orientation: a person's first sexual experiences; his or her familial environment, especially his or her relationship with parents and their personality types; and his or her childhood gender-related behaviors.[1] I discuss each of these theories and say why they might be plausible. I then turn to a critical evaluation of them.

### Early Sexual Experience

In the middle part of this century, perhaps the most popular theories of sexual orientation were those that saw early sexual experiences as crucial to the shaping of a person's sexual orientation (Churchill 1967). If a person had pleasurable sex with another person of a particular sex-gender, then the thought was that this person would want to have sex with people of that sex-gender in the future. On the other hand, if a person had *un*pleasurable sex with another person of a particular sex-gender, then this person would not be interested in sex with people of that sex-gender in the future. The idea behind early-sexual-experience theories parallels *operant-conditioning theory,* according to which behaviors followed by positive reinforcement tend to be repeated and behaviors followed by negative reinforcement tend not to be repeated.

There are various versions of what might be called *early-experience theories* that have been and continue to be held, some explicitly, some implicitly. One indication of the continuing hold that such theories have is the commonly accepted notion that a person, especially a sexually inexperienced one, can be "seduced" or "recruited" into becoming a lesbian or gay man by the sexual advances of a person of the same sex-gender. The *seduction theory* implicitly accepts that people will "naturally" develop into heterosexuals unless seduced into homosexuality by a "predatory" homosexual. A structurally similar but more innocuous early-experience theory is the *first-encounter theory,* according to which one's sexual orientation is fixed by one's first pleasurable sexual experience (McGuire, Carlisle, and Young 1965).

Part of the appeal of early experience theories is that such theories seem to provide the right account for explaining some human preferences. For example, people's restaurant preferences seem to be shaped by their experiences of particular restaurants. Some people, if they have a bad experience at a restaurant, will avoid eating there in the future; a good experience, on the other hand, will lead them to eat there again. A certain range of preferences are explicable in terms of positive and negative experiential reinforcement. Early-experience theories of sexual orientation fit into this explanatory framework.

### Family Dynamics

Another cluster of experiential theories of the development of sexual orientation sees one's relationships with one's parents as crucial in determining his or her sexual orientation. The classic version of such theories, which stems from Freud's Oedipal theory (Freud 1975), sees male homosexuality as the result of having a strong mother and a distant father, while male heterosexuality is the result of having a strong identification with one's father and relinquishing to him one's mother as a love object, replacing her with other women (Bieber et al. 1962). Freud and more recent psychoanalysts, as well as other psychodynamically oriented psychologists, have articulated various versions of family-dynamic theories of sexual orientation that deal (in complex and contradictory ways) with sexual orientation in women and that flesh out (also in varied and contradictory ways) the development of gay and lesbian sexuality (Chodorow 1994; Lewes 1988). Insofar as these theories have some general core claims in common, they say that there should be some ascertainable causal differences between heterosexuals and homosexuals in terms of family dynamics.

Some sociobiologists have also articulated a particular kind of family-dynamics theory, sometimes called *parental-manipulation* theories. Such theories have been developed in the context of trying to explain how genes that code for homosexuality remain in the gene pool, given that homosexuality seems to be selectively disadvantageous. According to parental-manipulation theories, parents subconsciously determine that it would be better for them, in terms of getting a larger number of copies of their genes into subsequent generations, if their family focused its reproductive and survival resources on the offspring of certain of their children but not others. Having made this determination, parents behave towards certain of their children in such ways that these children become homosexual (Trivers 1974). Michael Ruse offers the following example: "[S]uppose that a parent has four children, each potentially having two children. But if one of the children is turned towards a homosexual helper role, the other three children will each have three children. Biological features aimed at achieving such an end would be favored by selection" (Ruse 1988,

136). This theory provides an experiential explanation of the development of homosexuality that involves the behaviors of an individual's parents. Although sociobiologists developed this theory in the context of trying to provide an account of how homosexuality can be selectively advantageous, this psychological theory could be true even if evolutionary theory does not, as I suggested in chapter 6, necessarily provide support for the emerging research program.

### Childhood Gender Roles

One of the most widely believed commonsense theories of how sexual orientations develop focuses on the role of childhood behaviors, in particular the extent to which a child's behaviors are gender-typical or gender-atypical. Every known culture associates at least somewhat different behavioral stereotypes with men and women, respectively. A gender-typical child conforms to the behavioral stereotypes associated with his or her sex-gender in his or her culture. Childhood gender-conformity theories claim that gender-typical children will develop into heterosexual adults, while gender-atypical children will develop into homosexual adults. Specifically, in much of the United States and many other Western cultures, boys who play sports involving physical contact and pretend to be soldiers will become heterosexual men, while boys who play with dolls and pretend to cook and clean ("sissies") will become gay men. This theory is summarized by a slogan of Richard Green's: "Barbie dolls at five, sex with men at twenty-five (Green 1995, 6). Similarly, girls who play with dolls and pretend to cook and clean will become heterosexuals, while those who play sports involving physical contact and pretend to be soldiers ("tomboys") will become lesbians. According to some versions of this theory, something about the experience of engaging in gender-atypical behaviors as children shapes a person's sexual desires as an adult. Belief in this theory is reflected in the reactions that many parents and some clinicians have to childhood gender-atypical behavior: they try, using whatever means necessary, to get the child to stop engaging in gender-atypical behavior in order to prevent the development of adult homosexuality (Burke 1996; Feder 1997; Rekers 1982; Wyden and Wyden 1968).

## The Evidence

Experiential theories of sexual orientation can be evaluated in two general ways. One is *retrospectively:* you can survey people and ask them what their sexual orientation is and what their childhood experiences were (in particular, what their early sexual experiences were, what their relationships with their parents were, and whether their childhood gender-role behaviors were typical or not). On the other hand, they can be evaluated *prospectively:* you can find children and follow them from childhood—ascertaining their sexual experiences, family dynamics, and gender-conformity—and ultimately, when they mature, you can assess their sexual orientations. Retrospective studies are relatively easy to do, but because subjects are asked to look back on their childhood from the perspective of adults, the subjects in these studies may experience *memory bias.* Prospective studies, on the other hand, are difficult to do: they are longitudinal studies and thus require a minimum of several years to run (one needs to start with subjects who are quite young and follow them until they are old enough to give a reliable assessment of their sexual orientation). Furthermore, prospective studies may also suffer from bias in the selection of subjects. I consider both sorts of studies in turn.

### Retrospective Studies

One of the most detailed and frequently cited retrospective studies relating to sexual orientation was done in 1970 by researchers affiliated with the Alfred Kinsey Institute for Sex Research (Bell, Weinberg, and Hammersmith 1981). In this study, 686 gay men, 293 lesbians, 337 heterosexual men and 140 heterosexual women living in San Francisco were surveyed. Lesbian and gay volunteers were obtained by recruiting through advertisements in gay gathering places and by word of mouth. Heterosexual subjects were obtained using random sampling techniques. In the tradition of the original Kinsey studies, subjects were interviewed in their own homes for three to five hours. They were asked about two hundred questions, some of them open-ended, some specifying a limited number of possible answers. While this study has been criticized on various grounds—including that all of its subjects were living in San Francisco (arguably, not a typical place with respect to sexual orientation)—its conclusions with respect to experiential theories seem to have been confirmed and accepted.

The San Francisco study suggests that early sexual experience does not play a significant role in the development of sexual orientation. The data showed that sexual orientation

> is likely to be established quite early in life and that childhood and adolescent sexual expression by and large *reflect* rather than *determine* a person's underlying sexual [orientation]. . . . Sexual experiences with members of the same sex were common among both the homosexual and the heterosexual respondents; so were experiences with members of the opposite sex. What differs markedly between the homosexual and heterosexual respondents, and what appears to be more important in signaling eventual sexual [orientation] . . . , is the way respondents felt sexually, not what they did. (113)

According to this study, early sexual experience may play some secondary role in the development of sexual orientations, but it does not seem to play the primary role that early-experience theories give it. These results have been widely accepted.

Retrospective studies do not provide positive support for family-dynamics theories either. The San Francisco study found that "a boy's mother seems to have only a limited influence on his sexual orientation in adulthood" (50). In particular, there was no difference between heterosexual men and gay men in the strength of attachment to their mothers. With regards to fathers, the study reported that "[u]nfavorable relationships with fathers do seem to be connected with gender nonconformity and early homosexual experience . . . [but] the connection to adult sexual [orientation] . . . is not a strong one" (62). For women, the study found roughly the same results as for men: "parental relationships, traits, . . . [and] identification should not be construed as critical factors in the development of female homosexuality" (134). The data do not support parental manipulation theory either. This theory would predict that children with no siblings would almost never be lesbian or gay and that children with a large number of siblings would be more likely to be so. The San Francisco study found no differences between homosexuals and heterosexuals in terms of family size for either men (72) or women (143). Some later studies, however, suggest that gay men, on average, have more siblings than heterosexual men do (Blanchard et al. 1995), but these studies may be subject to sampling errors of the sort discussed in chapter 7.

In contrast to the other two experiential theories, childhood gender-conformity theories were supported by the San Francisco study. With respect to males, the researchers found that

> prehomosexual boys . . . [are] less stereotypically "masculine" than preheterosexual boys, at least in their self-images. Fewer of the homosexual men . . . remembered themselves as having been very masculine while growing up, and more homosexual than heterosexual respondents recalled dislike for typical boys' activities and enjoyment of those they thought were "for girls" . . . . [T]hese kinds of gender nonconformity are directly related to experiencing both homosexual activities and homosexual arousal before age 19, a sense of an explicitly sexual . . . difference from other boys, and a delay of feelings of sexual attraction to girls, as well as . . . adult homosexual[ity]. (81)

Similarly, with respect to females, "[c]hildhood [g]ender [n]onconformity does appear to have been related to homosexual feelings and behaviors, both while . . . growing up and in adulthood" (151).

Partly because of these results, many other retrospective studies have been conducted to look at childhood gender-conformity. A recent review of forty-eight such studies in which adults were asked to recall their childhood behaviors found that homosexuals recall "substantially more" gender-atypical behavior in childhood than heterosexuals (Bailey and Zucker 1995, 49). According to this review, a boy who exhibits significant gender-atypical behavior has about a 50 percent chance of becoming a homosexual; a gender-atypical girl has about a 6 percent chance. These numbers are based on estimates of 4 percent and 1.5 percent for the rate of homosexuality among men and women, respectively, in the general population (Gebhard 1972); the numbers thereby reflect a twelvefold increase among men who were gender-atypical as boys and a fourfold increase in the rate of homosexuality among women who were gender-atypical as girls.

### Prospective Studies

Comparatively few prospective studies have been conducted. The largest and most frequently cited prospective study was done by Richard Green (1987). His sample consisted of fifty-six boys who were controls and sixty-six boys whose "extreme cross-gendered behavior," which usually included discomfort with being male and the desire to become female, caused their parent(s) to seek clinical assistance. Green was able to follow two-thirds of his subjects to adolescence or beyond, long enough, he thought, to assess their sexual orientation. Green's study seems to have the potential to provide retrospective data relevant to experiential theories. Although Green does not provide systematic data on his subjects' early sexual activities, he does provide some data on the other two experiential theories I have been discussing, and he pays special attention to gender nonconformity. With respect to family dynamics, Green reports two findings:

> A very weak trend emerged for fathers of "feminine" boys to report having spent less time with their sons in the first year compared to fathers of "masculine" boys. There was a significant difference in reported father-son shared time in the second year, and the difference became greater in years three to five. (70)
>
> Whether [his] mother or father was preferred by the boy was highly correlated with the extent of his "femininity," with more feminine boys preferring [their] mother. (77)

This evidence is subject to a very plausible alternative explanation. It may be that the time spent with the father does not explain the development of gender nonconformity and homosexuality. Rather, the causation may go in the other direction: fathers may spend less time with gender-atypical sons.

With respect to gender nonconformity, Green found that, depending on the measure used, between 75 and 80 percent of the extremely gender-atypical boys, compared to only 0 to 4 percent of controls, were rated between 2 and 6 on the Kinsey scale, that is, they were judged to be homosexual, bisexual, or heterosexual with more than incidental homosexual desires. This is a very significant result; it seems to provide strong evidence that, for men, childhood gender nonconformity and adult homosexuality are correlated. However, compared to other similar studies, Green's results seem somewhat exaggerated. A survey of six similar prospective studies found that 51 percent of gender-atypical boys were homosexual as adults, 36 percent were heterosexual, and 14 percent were transsexual (Zucker 1990). These results are still rather dramatic.

Together, the retrospective and prospective studies suggest that the experiences associated with being a gender nonconforming child are significantly correlated with homosexuality, that various features of parental family dynamics are somewhat correlated with adult sexual orientation, and that one's early childhood sexual experiences have no particular connection to adult sexual orientation. This is not to say that, for some particular individuals, the quality and kind of early sexual experiences one has are unrelated to one's sexual orientation. The same is true with respect to one's relationship to one's parents and one's parents' personality traits. There does not, however, seem to be a clear pattern across individuals of how these factors affect sexual orientation. In a way, this should not come as a big surprise. We do not have good theories, for example, about how individuals develop most complex psychological personality traits. For example, what factors lead people to pursue certain careers? Clearly, biological factors in some way shape the possible careers one might pursue and the career interests one might develop. Cultural factors do so as well. Individual experiences of a wide variety also play a role, but different factors are crucial for different people. Family dynamics and the personalities, careers, and values of one's parents also play an important role, but one's teachers, other adult role models, and one's peers also shape career preferences. Sexual orientation might well be shaped in similarly varied and complex ways.

## Problems for Experiential Theories

Although the evidence suggests that gender nonconformity is connected to adult sexual orientation and that other experiential theories fare less well, various worries can be raised concerning the evidence that is supposed to bear on experiential theories of sexual orientation. I now turn to consideration of these worries.

### Preexperiential Sexual Orientations

Setting aside the evidence against theories that link early sexual experience to sexual orientation, such theories seem to have a problem accounting for the fact that many people seem to have sexual orientations and particular sexual desires *before* they have ever had any sexual experiences (Bell, Weinberg, and Hammersmith 1981, 99–104 and 164–180). Early-sexual-experience theories have no internal resources for explaining sexual orientations and desires that are present before one's first sexual experience. A defender of such theories could respond by saying that for some reason, perhaps biological, people have some *preexperiential sexual orientation* that is either changed or reinforced by early sexual experience. The problem with this response is that, for most people, preexperiential sexual orientation and ultimate sexual orientation are usually the same: in particular, people who think they are gay or lesbian before they become sexually active usually turn out to be gay or lesbian once they have become sexually active.

A defender of early-experience theories might respond by saying that a person's preexperiential sexual orientation leads one to engage in sexual activity that fits with that preexperiential orientation, thereby reinforcing the preexperiential orientation. The reason why a person might seek out sexual activities with people of the same sex-gender is because he or she has some disposition to develop into a lesbian or a gay man that exists before a person has a sexual orientation. This account of the development of sexual orientations would not, however, give a primary role to experience. A person's preexperiential dispositions to develop one sexual orientation rather than another is, by stipulation, not due to experience. On this theory, the early sexual experience that was supposed to play a deep explanatory role in determining a person's sexual orientation would not do so. Instead, one's preexperiential sexual desires would do the explanatory work. These preexperiential sexual desires would themselves need to be explained. Early sexual experiences could not explain these preexperiential dispositions to develop sexual desires.

### Problems with Retrospective Studies

The main problem with retrospective studies is that they seem likely to involve some sort of memory bias. If I asked you to describe your behaviors as a child, it seems quite likely that your description and assessment of your childhood behaviors will be influenced by your present and past self-assessment and self-identity in terms of gender, sexual orientation, and the like. In particular, as M. W. Ross (1980) suggested, lesbians and gay men may remember being gender-atypical children partly because they have internalized the stereotype that gay men are feminine and lesbians are masculine. Similarly, heterosexuals will forget or reinterpret childhood gender-atypical behaviors as gender-typical. Or perhaps homosexuals will overreport and heterosexuals underreport gender-atypical behavior (Bailey and Zucker 1995, 45). There is no unambiguous empirical evidence for this claim, but it is rather plausible. Most people see homosexuality as a sort of sex-gender inversion, that is, they see homosexuals as having some physiological or psychological features not typically associated with their sex-gender (see chapter 7 for a detailed discussion of the inversion assumption). Because of this, lesbians and gay men might see themselves as having been gender-atypical children, and in constructing a self-image, they may have enhanced these memories. Further, the inversion assumption combined with the stigma attached to homosexuality make it plausible that many heterosexuals repress or forget gender-atypical behaviors. Similarly, given the increasing tendency in our culture to self-analyze using pop psychology and quasi-Freudian ideas, it seems quite possible that adults will see their childhood relationships with their parents through the lenses of their adult sexual identity and of family-dynamics theory. The thought is that if an adult homosexual has internalized the idea that certain aspects of one's relationship with one's parents are relevant to adult sexual orientation, then this person is likely to selectively recall aspects of his or her family dynamics that conform to some theory about the psychodynamic causes of homosexuality. The same internalization process may well happen to a heterosexual.

It is well established that self-perception can be profoundly affected by experience, especially the feedback one gets from others. Consider the following psychological experiment on empathic abilities (Ross, Lepper, and Hubbard 1975). Subjects were given several suicide notes and asked to distinguish the authentic suicide notes from the novel ones. Then, regardless of their actual performances, subjects were given continuous false feedback in that they were told they were either doing an excellent or a poor job at distinguishing authentic from fake suicide notes. After several trials, subjects were debriefed and informed that the assessments of their empathic abilities were assigned at random. Although the actual experimental design was thoroughly explained to subjects, the assessment they received still significantly affected their own judgments about their ability to understand others, to empathize, and the like. In other words, subjects who had been told they were doing a good job distinguishing authentic from fake suicide notes rated themselves much higher on various abilities than did subjects who had been told they had been doing a poor job. This sort of effect has been shown to last at least two months (Harman 1986, 29–42; Ross and Anderson 1982).

Given the strength and duration of the effects of the feedback from this brief experiment, it would not be at all surprising if some of the cultural stereotypes associated with gender nonconformity and homosexuality were internalized by lesbians and gay men. Specifically, memory bias problems seem likely to occur in retrospective studies of sexual orientation given the charged nature of sexual orientation in our society, the central role that we feel our sexual orientations have to our characters, and for lesbians and gay men, the sense of needing to explain homosexuality to oneself and to others. That almost all of the retrospective studies have been done in English-speaking, Western countries (Bailey and Zucker 1995, 50) suggests that cultural biases may be infiltrating the retrospective studies. In light of these worries, retrospective studies seem to say little of interest concerning the origins of sexual orientation.

### Problems with Prospective Studies

There are several problems with prospective studies. Since the most striking prospective results are those that relate to childhood gender nonconformity, I focus on these. First, the sissies whom researchers lose track of—they account for one-third of Green's subjects (Green 1987, 26) and about one-fourth of the subjects in other studies (Zucker 1990)—might be less likely to be homosexual than those whom researchers are able to follow until their studies are completed. If this is true, then the results of the prospective studies are undermined. If a significant percentage of those sissies whom researchers lose track of turn out to be heterosexuals as adults, then the correlation between childhood gender nonconformity and adult homosexuality is much weaker than researchers claim. Since Green's sissy subjects were brought to him because of concerns about their gender nonconformity and their future sexual orientation, it is possible to infer that the boys who did not develop into gay men were likely to drop out of the study. For example, boys who, for whatever reasons, began to behave in ways that were less gender-atypical or whose parents perceived them to be doing so might have been removed from Green's study by their parents. If the sissies whom Green lost track of were, as a group, less likely to be homosexual, he would have probably overestimated the correlation between childhood gender roles and adult sexual orientation.

Second, sissies might identify as homosexuals earlier than nonsissies (Bem 1996a, 327), or given their childhood gender nonconformity, they might be more willing to act on and admit their same sex-gender sexual desire compared to gender-conformists, who probably repress or ignore such desires. If this is true, a higher percentage of Green's controls (the nonsissies) than was reported might turn out to have been gay, and the apparent correla-

tion between gender nonconformity and adult homosexuality would be somewhat undercut.

Third, almost all of the gender-atypical subjects were children whose
parents brought them to gender-identity disorder clinics for treatment. In order
to be willing to subject themselves and their children to the frequent questioning and extensive monitoring of their personal lives involved in Green's and
similar studies, the parents must have had very serious worries about the well-
being of their children. This suggests that the subjects are extreme cases of
gender-atypical boys. Also, the unusual (and sometimes cruel) clinical treatments to which the boys were subjected (Burke 1996; Feder 1997) might well
have affected their future gender identity and sexual orientation. For these
reasons, sissies are probably an unrepresentative pool to use for the study of the
origins of sexual orientation in general. Even Bailey and Zucker (1995, 44),
who in general accept the connection between childhood gender conformity
and adult sexual orientation, admit this.

Note also that even advocates of the connection between childhood gender
conformity and adult sexual orientation admit that only between a quarter to a
third of all gender-atypical children become homosexual. Further, not all homosexuals report gender-atypical behavior as children, and some heterosexuals
report gender-atypical behavior. Childhood gender roles cannot, then, stand
alone as an explanation of sexual orientation in adults. Other explanations will
be required for the majority of lesbians and gay men. Finally, even setting aside
these worries, there are no prospective studies on gender-atypical girls; it is a
mistake to draw conclusions about all gender-atypical children based only on
boys. A recent review of the relevant literature concludes that

> [a]lthough it is logically possible that the prospective findings [that seem to
> suggest that childhood gender-nonconformity is associated with homosexu-
> ality] were due to an extremely unrepresentative group of boys and the retro-
> spective findings [that are similarly suggestive were due] to memory bias, a
> more parsimonious interpretation is that both kinds of findings reflect a
> rather strong association between childhood . . . [gender-atypical] behavior
> and sexual orientation. (Bailey and Zucker 1995, 50)

This conclusion is not compelling. It is equally plausible that a child's experience of gender-atypicality makes him or her more likely to be nonconformist in
general and hence more willing to embrace same sex-gender sexual desires and
homosexual or bisexual identities. Alternatively, the child's *general* nonconformity might be the source of *both* his or her gender nonconformity and his or her
nonheterosexuality. Or, gender-typical children might later experience an equal

amount of same sex-gender sexual desire, but they might repress it, hide it, and/or be less willing to admit it to researchers. This explanation fits quite nicely with the claim that social acceptance of the inversion assumption might bias adult memories of childhood gender-role behaviors.

Although I have raised various worries about the evidence that exists in favor of some experiential theories of sexual orientation, I have not shown that these theories are false or unlikely. Rather, I have shown that they are, at present, either unsupported or weakly supported. I have said nothing against the general idea that experiences, in particular childhood and adolescent ones, can influence sexual orientation. The effects of experience are, in general, still a plausible factor involved in the development of sexual desires.

## Exotic-Becomes-Erotic Theory

### The Theory

Daryl Bem has recently articulated a psychological theory of how people develop sexual orientations (Bem 1996a). Although Bem is in some ways impressed with the strength of the biological evidence related to sexual orientation, he offers an alternative explanation of this evidence. Theories developed within the emerging research program suffer from what he calls an explanatory gap: they fail to give an account of how biological factors (genetic, hormonal, and neuroanatomical) actually lead to adult sexual orientations. Bem proposes to fill this explanatory gap by offering an "experience-based developmental" (321) theory of sexual orientation that gives a crucial role to childhood gender nonconformity. Recall the tripartite distinction of various models of the role that biological factors might play in the development of sexual orientations, that is, the direct model, the indirect model, and the permissive model. The experiential theories I have discussed in this chapter fit the permissive model, according to which biological factors shape the brain structures on which experiences inscribe sexual orientations. In contrast, indirect models see biological factors as shaping temperament and/or personality, which shape how one interacts with one's environment, which in turn shapes the development of sexual orientation. Bem's theory is a paradigmatic indirect theory.

Unlike most biological and experiential theories of how people develop sexual orientations, Bem's theory, called *exotic-becomes-erotic theory*, describes somewhat explicitly the roles played by both biological factors and experiential factors. According to this theory, biological factors code for childhood personality types and temperaments such as aggressiveness and willingness to engage in physical contact. In gender-polarized societies like ours where there are significantly different gender roles typically associated with males and females, these different personality and temperament types get molded into gender roles. In such societies, children are socialized into feminine gender roles (for example, playing with dolls) or masculine gender roles (for example, engaging in rough-and-tumble play). Once a child has developed a gender role, children with different gender roles are seen as exotic and "other." In children, being in the presence of people who are seen as exotic produces general physical and psychological arousal. As children develop sexually, this general arousal develops into a more specific erotic arousal (Bem 1996a, 325–237). As a child develops, those "others" that a child once found exotic become sexually attractive to a maturing child. According to this theory, lesbians develop from girls who fit masculine gender roles while heterosexual women develop from girls who fit feminine gender roles. See Figure 8-1 for a schematic diagram of Bem's theory.

To work through a specific example of how exotic-becomes-erotic theory might combine the biological and the experiential, consider once again Dean Hamer's genetic study. A Bem-Hamer synthesis might be as follows: some genetic sequence in the q28 region of the X chromosome leads in boys to the development of either an interest in or an aversion to rough-and-tumble physical contact. In gender-polarizing societies, boys with an aversion to this sort of physical contact develop to fit feminine gender roles, that is, they develop into sissies. Sissies, in turn, find boys who fit masculine gender roles exotic; in the presence of masculine children, sissies become generally aroused. As they mature, this general arousal in the presence of masculine children develops into a sexual attraction to masculine children; as adults, this erotic attraction

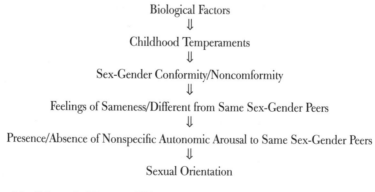

Biological Factors
⇓
Childhood Temperaments
⇓
Sex-Gender Conformity/Noncomformity
⇓
Feelings of Sameness/Different from Same Sex-Gender Peers
⇓
Presence/Absence of Nonspecific Autonomic Arousal to Same Sex-Gender Peers
⇓
Sexual Orientation

Figure 8-1. Schematic Diagram of "Exotic-Becomes-Erotic" Theory. Chart is adapted from Bem (1996, 321).

develops into homosexuality. This account fits the indirect model because it sees biological factors (genes) leading to temperamental traits (for example, aversion to rough-and-tumble play), which under certain environmental conditions (gender-polarizing societies) leads to the development of sexual orientations. This account fits with Hamer's genetic data as well as the psychological data that homosexuality and childhood gender nonconformity are correlated. I am not saying that either Bem or Hamer (or anyone else, myself included) endorses this particular theory. I offer it to give a concrete example of the theory that Bem is advocating.

### Who Will the Gender-Atypical Children Find Attractive?

I now turn to an assessment of Bem's theory. I begin by looking at whom a child finds exotic. Bem claims that whether a child is gender-typical plays a major role in affecting how he or she feels towards children of the same sex-gender and those of a different sex-gender. Boys who are gender-atypical will find most other boys exotic, while boys who are gender-typical will find most other girls exotic. If a person's gender role is crucial to determining which sex-gender a child finds exotic, and if exotic becomes erotic, then a rather unexpected set of predictions follows: gender-atypical children should find not only gender-typical children of the same sex-gender exotic and ultimately erotic, they should *also* find gender-atypical children who are not of the same sex-gender exotic and ultimately erotic. For example, gender-atypical boys should find both gender-typical boys and gender-atypical girls exotic and ultimately erotic; hence, gay men should be attracted to most other men but also to masculine women. There are, however, no data to support these results. In general, neither gay men nor heterosexual women are even moderately attracted to masculine women, and neither lesbians nor heterosexual men are attracted to feminine men.

Bem might reply that in a gender-polarized society, social pressures push children who are developing a sexual identity and a sexual orientation to fix on either men or women as their primary sexual object.[2] This pressure pushes gender-atypical boys (who according to Bem's theory are developing an attraction to masculine people) to fix on either gender-typical boys or gender-atypical girls (both of whom are masculine). To defend his theory against my above criticism, Bem might note that the social pressures of a gender-polarizing society push boys faced with these two possibilities to become gay men. Although this possible reply seems to fit with Bem's theory, I do not think it is plausible. First, it would suggest that there will not be many or any bisexuals.

Various studies suggest that many people are, in fact, sexually attracted to both men and women (Kinsey, Pomeroy, and Martin 1948; Kinsey et al. 1953; Klein and Wolf 1985; Weinberg, Williams, and Pryor 1994). Second, this explication of exotic becomes erotic seems not to fit with the strong pressures against being a lesbian or a gay man in our society. Among the various pressures present in many gender-polarizing societies is the pressure to be heterosexual. This is among the pressures included under Adrienne Rich's useful concept of "compulsory heterosexuality" (Rich 1980). In a society that has very negative attitudes towards lesbians and gay men (see chapter 10 for a discussion of the climate for lesbians and gay men), the pressure to be heterosexual is so strong that a boy faced with developing attraction towards either masculine men or masculine women would likely be pushed towards developing attraction to masculine women. That this does not seem to happen suggests that children are neither consciously nor unconsciously faced with these options. This is a problem for Bem's theory because it entails that sissies will (at least initially) be attracted to both masculine men and masculine women, but it does not seem that they are.

### Bisexuality

A related point has to do more explicitly with bisexuality. Bem accepts the two-dimensional rather than a binary or bipolar view (see chapter 2 for discussion of these views) of gender roles, according to which a person's masculinity and femininity are independent variables, that is, a person can be very masculine and very feminine (*androgynous*) or not very masculine and not very feminine (*undifferentiated*) (Bem 1996a, 323). Although the two-dimensional view has much to be said for it, it leads to a problem for Bem. If exotic becomes erotic, then an undifferentiated child should ultimately develop into a bisexual (since such a child would find both masculine and feminine children to be exotic) and an androgynous child should develop into an asexual (since such a child would find neither masculine nor feminine children exotic). Bem's theory, when combined with the two-dimensional view of gender roles, predicts that there will be a significant number of bisexuals whose attraction to both sexes emerges at the same time because, as undifferentiated children, they found both masculine and feminine children exotic. There is no evidence to support either of these predictions. In fact, most bisexuals report that their attraction to one sex-gender was established first and their attraction to the other sex-gender was added later (Bem 1996a, 331; Weinberg, Williams, and Pryor 1994). More generally, the fact that there are relatively few bisexuals and asexuals, at least among men, compared to the number of androgynous and undifferentiated children causes trouble for Bem's theory.

### Other Kinds of Exoticness

There is a further related problem. Gender is not the only characteristic that causes feelings of dissimilarity towards others. As Bem (1998, 396) acknowledges, differences in race, class, and religion, for example, are also significant sources of the feeling that someone is different and exotic. If exotic becomes erotic, one would suspect that, just as most people are attracted to people not of the same sex-gender, most people would be sexually attracted to people not of the same race, class, level of intelligence, and so on. This does not, however, seem to be the case. One bit of relevant evidence is that most married couples are very similar with respect to these sorts of traits (race, class, and so on) (Bem 1996a, 323). This suggests that exotic does not always become erotic. Bem says that "an erotic or romantic preference for partners of a different sex, race, or ethnicity is relatively common" (325), but this covers up an important statistical difference between sex-gender preferences and other preferences. Most people are primarily attracted to people of the opposite sex, while fewer seem primarily attracted to people of a different race, ethnicity, and so on (Bem 1996a, 323; Feingold 1988). Bem needs to give an account of why gender-role differences are important to sexual desire but most other differences are not. Saying that we live in a gender-polarized society does not provide such an account since we also live in a race- and class-polarized society (Peplau et al. 1998).

### Does Bem's Theory Fit Men and Women Equally Well?

One of the advertised virtues of Bem's theory is that it provides a single theory of sexual orientation that applies to heterosexuals as well as homosexuals and men as well as women (Bem 1996a, 320). While, all else being equal, it may be a good thing to have a single theory to explain all sexual orientations, a unified theory is only useful if it is true. The evidence from prospective studies provides weaker support for Bem's theory applied to women than applied men (Peplau et al. 1998); there are only five prospective case studies of gender-atypical women (that is, only five gender-atypical girls have been studied from childhood through adolescence) (Zucker and Bradley 1995, 294–295). On the other hand, the retrospective studies of women have the odd result that more than half of the women surveyed said that they had been gender-atypical (that is, tomboys) as children (Hyde, Rosenberg, and Behrman 1977), suggesting

that it is gender-typical to be gender-atypical. More generally, for reasons
discussed in chapter 5 and by Anne Peplau and her colleagues in their critique
of Bem (Peplau et al. 1998), it is quite likely that women and men, at least in
cultures like ours, develop sexual orientations and desires in ways that are
significantly different.

### Further Comments

In general, Bem's notion of "exotic" leads to a class of erroneous predictions
about the development of sexual desires and orientations. There are further
problems with the evidence Bem offers for his theory. On the one hand, Bem
cites evidence from prospective studies like Green's that is supposed to show
that gender conformity in childhood is part of the cause of sexual orientation in
adulthood. On the other hand, he appeals to biological evidence that is
supposed to cause children to have certain personality and temperament types,
which in cultures like ours, leads to the development of either masculine or
feminine gender roles. Earlier in this chapter, I suggested that the evidence
from prospective studies like Green's is in fact far from conclusive in establishing the connection between childhood gender nonconformity and adult
sexual orientation. In chapters 6 and 7, I raised a series of objections to the
biological evidence that relates to sexual orientation. Most of these objections
would still apply even if the theories are, as interpreted by Bem, about childhood personality types rather than about sexual orientations. Consider, for
example, Hamer's study of Xq28. If, as I suggested in chapter 7, there are
methodological or technical problems with Hamer's genetic study, then the
same problems would emerge when his results are interpreted as providing
evidence for the genetic basis of childhood personality and/or temperament.
With regards to the evidence for exotic-becomes-erotic theory, one does not
produce a new theory with significant evidential support by combining two
theories, each with weak evidential support. Thus, when objections are raised
to theories in the emerging research program and to theories that link childhood gender nonconformity with adult sexual orientation, these two sets of
objections undercut much of Bem's evidential support. Bem's theory may be
true, but presently it has no particular evidential support.

Still, exotic becomes erotic might be true for a subset of men (and
perhaps women), at least in cultures similar to ours. This is, however, consistent with the truth of many other psychological explanations of how people
develop sexual orientations. Recall that fewer than half of lesbians and gay men
remember being gender nonconforming children. Some other theory must
explain their sexual orientation. More generally, it is highly improbable that

a single pathway can lead to the development of a particular sexual orientation in everyone who has that sexual orientation. While it may be "politically, scientifically, and aesthetically satisfying" to explain everyone's sexual orientations with a single simple theory (Bem 1996a, 320), most likely, there are multiple pathways towards becoming heterosexual, homosexual, bisexual, and asexual, as well as being attracted to blondes, tall people, people with a sharp wit, and so on (Byne and Parsons 1993, 237; Stein 1990, 338). Just as it seems quite plausible that there are multiple pathways towards becoming a yuppie, a coffee drinker, or a person who usually sleeps on his or her stomach rather than his or her back, the same should be true with the development of sexual orientations and desires.

Despite its shortcomings, exotic-become-erotic theory does have an important advantage over the biological theories of sexual orientation discussed in chapters 5 through 7. As Bem (1996a, 327–330) notes, the various theories that are part of the emerging research program suffer from an explanatory gap: none of them constitute a complete theory of how people develop sexual orientations. In particular, these theories fail to offer an account of how the various proposed biological factors lead to a complex psychological property such as a sexual orientation. Bem's theory attempts to provide a more comprehensive account of how biological factors might lead to sexual orientations: biological factors affect childhood personality and temperament, which in turn affect childhood gender conformity, which in turn affects sexual orientation. Consequently, his theory is more detailed than those of his biological rivals; neither LeVay nor Hamer, respectively, gives an account of how the INAH-3 region of the hypothalamus or some unidentified genetic sequence in the q28 region of the X chromosome causes people to have the kinds of sexual desires that they do. And most psychological rivals to Bem's theory do not offer any account of the biological underpinnings of the experiential determinates of sexual orientation (a common problem with theories that fit the permissive model of the role played by biological factors in the development of sexual orientation); the first-encounter theory, for example, does not provide any hint of why the biological constitution of humans would enable early sexual experience to determine sexual orientation. Bem's theory gives us a hint of the biological story behind exotic becomes erotic. Compared to his rivals, then, Bem's theory has the virtue of being more complete; exotic becomes erotic is at least a serious and complete theory of how people develop sexual orientations. Nonetheless, it does not mean that this theory is correct in explaining how people develop sexual orientations. In fact, because of problems with the evidence for the emerging biological paradigm for the scientific study of sexual orientation and with the evidence for the correlation between childhood gender behaviors and adult sexual orientation,

I do not think Bem has a very strong case for his theory. Bem's theory, to use a slogan, is "in the right church but the wrong pew."

## Multiple Origins

### *To Zomnia and Back Again*

Recall from chapter 3 my example of Zomnia, the country where people are grouped into backers and fronters in virtue of their behaviors and dispositions related to sleep positions. I return to sleep positions in this section for two purposes: as an example of behaviors and characteristics that seem likely to have multiple explanations, and as a prelude to considering the empirical questions associated with whether sexual orientations are natural human kinds. Presumably, no one would contest that humans differ with respect to their sleep patterns and behaviors. Included among the differences in how people sleep and what dispositions underlie these differences are differences relating to the *positions* in which people sleep. Zomnians happen to make more of these differences than most other people do, but that could be a cultural difference of little importance.

In earlier discussions relating to sleep positions, I argued that Zomnian scientific theories that explain the development of "sleep orientations" were probably mistaken. In making this argument, I emphasized that such theories implicitly assume that sleep orientations are natural human kinds. There is a further reason for thinking that no single specific theory of sleep orientations will be right. Prima facie, it seems that people develop their particular sleep-position preferences for a panoply of reasons. For example, some gross physical features such as stomach size and spine shape probably affect what sleep positions a person finds comfortable and what one's sleep preferences are. Other bodily factors like sensitivity to light and noise probably play a role as well. These physical features are no doubt significantly affected by genetic and other biological factors, but developmental and environmental factors will also play a role in shaping these bodily characteristics and, hence, in shaping sleep preferences that are affected by these bodily characteristics. Childhood experiences, such as the sort of conditions under which one slept as a child, might also play a role in shaping the dispositions a person has with regards to sleep position. Conscious decisions might affect these dispositions as well. And cultural forces, such as the negative attitudes to which backers are subject in Zomnia, might play a role in shaping sleep preferences. I must confess that I have no special expertise concerning the origins of sleep orientations and that I have done no extensive research on the topic. I discuss sleep positions and the dispositions that underlie them as a contrast to the way many people think about sexual orientations. Short of evidence to the contrary, we have no particular reason to think that there will be a single theory that explains the development of human sleep orientations. The same is true, I will suggest, with respect to the development of human sexual orientations, namely, it is likely that there are *multiple origins* to human sexual orientations and sexual desires.

In chapters 6 and 7, I raised many objections against various theories in the emerging research program. Earlier in this chapter, I argued that the evidence for the various experiential theories of the origins of sexual orientation was also rather weak. In the previous section, I argued that, although exotic-becomes-erotic theory is the right sort of theory to explain human sexual desires, there is no strong evidence to support this theory either. I do not, however, have an alternative concrete and explanatory theory to offer in place of these theories. This is partly because we simply do not have enough evidence on the origins of human sexual orientation. Moreover, it is unlikely that there is going to be a single theory that explains what causes differences among humans with respect to our sexual desires or our sexual orientations. No one has successfully argued that there is a theory that will correctly explain everyone's sexual orientation. In the absence of such an argument, it seems more likely that there are multiple pathways to the various sexual orientations. Consider, for example, how people probably develop a preference for classical music, a taste for certain sorts of food, an interest in pursuing a particular kind of career, or the disposition to sleep in a certain position. It is highly unlikely that all or most people who have developed one of these preferences, tastes, interests, or dispositions will have done so through the same developmental path. Rather, we should expect that there are a multiplicity of accounts about how different people develop such cognitively mediated dispositions.

Even according to most theories of how sexual orientations develop, multiple theories will be required to explain everyone's sexual orientations. This is because most theories of how sexual orientations develop fail to explain even most people's sexual orientations. Most notably, there are even fewer plausible theories concerning how women develop sexual orientations. In fact, researchers and theorists inside and outside of the emerging research program have described women as having fluid sexual orientations and as having sexual orientations that are hard to pin down (for example, Bohan 1996, 84–88; Hamer and Copeland 1998, 184–189; Hu et al. 1995; Stein 1993). In interviews and surveys, many women, though not all, see social factors and personal choices as playing a role in their sexual orientation (Golden, 1987, 1994; Kitzinger and Wilkinson 1995; Whisman 1996). (I discuss whether sexual orientations are chosen in chapter 9.) In addition to this social scientific research, scientific and theoretical research suggests that, at least for women, social factors (such as the effects of sexism and the influences of feminism) play a significant role in shaping sexual desires and sexual orientations. If women's sexual desires were put at the center of our theorizing about the origins of sexual orientation, the case for multiple origins would be readily apparent.

Even focusing on men, the most widely cited theories are, in various ways, incomplete. Hamer, for example, admits that, at best, his results apply to "one *subtype* of male homosexuality" (Hamer et al. 1993, 321, emphasis added), but he does nothing to describe what subtype of gay man he is talking about. Further, theories in the emerging research program suffer from an explanatory gap (Bem 1996a, 321), namely, they fail to explain how it is that biological factors lead to sexual desires. Outside the emerging research program, experiential theories that claim childhood gender nonconformity leads to adult homosexuality can, at best, account for the sexual orientation of the approximately 50 percent of gay men who exhibited gender nonconforming behavior as children (Bailey and Zucker 1995, 49). Moreover, we have little reason to believe that any particular theory of sexual orientation that I have discussed applies to people in cultures where sexual desires are conceptualized and experienced differently because few if any of these theories are supported by any cross-cultural evidence. As I will argue below, the existence of multiple developmental pathways for sexual orientations fits better with the cultural variation with respect to how sexual orientations and desires are organized, conceptualized, and experienced.

### The Indirect Model

Recall the distinction (first discussed in chapter 5) among the three different ways that biological factors might affect the development of sexual orientations, namely, the permissive model (biological factors influence neurological structures or other biological structures that make it possible for experience to shape sexual orientation), the indirect model (biological factors code for personality traits and psychological dispositions that shape sexual orientation), and the direct model (biological factors influence neurological factors that create sexual orientation). One of my criticisms of the emerging scientific research program in chapter 7 was that the research program claims to provide evidence for the direct model but fails to do so. In fact, I have noted that the evidence offered by scientific researchers working in that program is consistent with both the indirect model and the direct model.

There are, however, some general reasons to prefer the indirect model (Byne 1995; Byne and Parsons 1993, 236–237). The indirect model allows that psychology plays an important role in the development of our sexual orientations. This fits with various commonsense theories of human nature and some intuitions about sexual orientation (Bem 1996a). The indirect model sees personality traits as playing a crucial role in the development of sexual orientation, thereby incorporating the fact that there are interesting cultural variations with regards to sexual orientations. It is easier to see how cultural differences might interact with personality traits to lead to variations in sexual desires and experiences and the cultural organizations and conceptualizations of them than it is to see how cultural differences might interact with neurological factors that lead to cultural variation in sexual desires and the cultural categorizations of them. Part of the reason why the Ancient Greeks seem to have experienced sexual desire differently than we do is that their culture shaped their psychological profiles in ways that are significantly different from the ways that our culture shapes our psychological profiles. Theories that fit the indirect model are better suited to explain this fit than the direct model. The indirect model also meshes with the results of twin studies of homosexuality that at least half of identical twins raised together (Bailey and Pillard 1991b; Bailey, Pillard, and Agyei 1993)—and probably more than two-thirds of them (Bailey, Dunne, and Martin n.d.)—are discordant for sexual orientation. Further, theories that fit the indirect model, unlike those that fit the direct model, do not suffer from the existence of an explanatory gap between the proposed neurological or biological factors and the psychological properties that they are supposed to cause (Bem 1996a). Indirect theories have the potential to explain how biological factors influence psychological characteristics such as temperament, personality, and the like, and how these psychological characteristics, in various contexts and given certain environmental inputs, affect sexual orientations and desires.

Finally, the indirect model fits nicely with the idea that there are multiple origins of sexual orientation. Some theories that fit the indirect model of the role biological factors play in shaping sexual orientations might posit a single psychological characteristic that leads to the development of sexual orientations. The more plausible indirect models will most likely involve multiple psychological characteristics that potentially play a role in the development of sexual orientations and desires, especially across different cultures. If the indirect model is right and biological factors are going to explain how various sexual orientations emerge in different cultures or environments, different biological factors will probably come into play. Consider Bem's exotic-becomes-erotic theory. Recall that this theory is limited to gender-polarized cultures. Although Bem does not develop this point, some cultures are more gender-polarized than others. It seems plausible that different biological factors will shape sexual orientations and desires in a culture that is only slightly gender-polarized than those biological factors that will do so in a highly gender-polarized culture. Even two cultures that are equally gender-polarized might associate different characteristics with various genders and, hence, different biological factors might be involved. For example, in some cultures, farming is associated with men, while in others it is associated with women, and in others it is not linked to gender at all. If there are biologically based personality and other psychological factors associated with being interested in or especially good at farming, then these factors could lead a child to be gender-typical in one culture, gender atypical in another, and play no role in gender-typicality in yet another.

There are reasons to prefer the indirect model and the multiple-origins theory. This is different, however, from saying that these theories are true. I made this same point with respect to the emerging research program. The reasons I gave at the beginning of chapter 5 for why we should be interested in biological theories of the development of sexual orientation did not preclude me from raising objections to the emerging research program in chapters 6 and 7. The claims that human sexual orientations have multiple origins and that the indirect model correctly describes the roles that biological factors have in the development of sexual orientation are both complex and hard to prove. As William Byne has noted, "[I]t is the difficulty of conducting research that adequately addresses the possibility of multiple and interactive pathways to sexual orientation that fosters nearly exclusive reliance on the direct model" (Byne 1996, 143). I have not presented convincing arguments or strong evidence for the claim that sexual orientations have multiple origins or the claim that biological factors play indirect roles in these multiple pathways to sexual orientations. Instead, I have introduced these theories because they seem more plausible and more complete than most theories of how sexual orientations develop.

### Natural Human Kinds and Multiple Origins

Suppose that there are in fact multiple origins to the development of sexual orientations in humans and that the indirect model is the best way to understand the role of biological factors in these multiple developmental pathways. What are the implications of this for whether sexual orientations are natural human kinds? Since I have not embraced any specific account of what the multiple origins of sexual orientations are, a simple answer is not possible. Instead, I describe two possible scenarios based on the view that sexual orientations have multiple origins: that sexual orientations are natural human kinds and that sexual orientations are not natural human kinds.

### Sophisticated Essentialism

First, consider a position that I call *sophisticated essentialism* (Stein 1990, 338). According to this view, sexual orientations are natural human kinds, but our commonsense categories of sexual orientations may not be. This would be the case if there are multiple origins to sexual orientations and thereby various natural human kinds associated with sexual orientations that play distinct roles in multiple scientific laws that concern sexual desires. Consider the following extended example of sophisticated essentialism. Suppose that in highly gender-polarized cultures (but not all cultures), some men develop their sexual orientations through a process like the Bem-Hamer synthesis I mentioned in the previous section, namely that some genetic sequence in the q28 region of the X chromosome leads in boys to the development of either an interest in or an aversion to rough-and-tumble physical contact, which in turn leads to adult sexual orientations. For other men in such cultures, their sexual orientations are better understood in terms of the two-dimensional model of sexual orientations described in chapter 2. For them, suppose that sexual orientation is the result of sexual experiences in the two years following puberty combined with the adult role models to which they were exposed: if they had pleasurable sexual experiences with other boys or men and positive homosexual or negative heterosexual role models, then they will be sexually attracted to men as adults; if they had pleasurable sexual experiences with girls or women and positive heterosexual and negative homosexual role models, then they will be sexually attracted to women as adults; if they had pleasurable sexual experiences with both men and women and positive heterosexual and homosexual adult role models, then they will be sexually attracted to both men and women as adults. Finally, for men whose sexual orientations did not develop through either of these processes, their sexual orientations developed through a complex process involving experiences and indirect choices. Correspondingly, suppose that women in gender-polarized societies develop their sexual orientations through two or three distinct pathways (different from the pathways that men develop theirs) and that both women and men in *less* gender-polarized societies develop their sexual orientations in roughly the same way as each other, but in ways that are different from how either men or women develop sexual orientations in *highly* gender-polarized cultures.

This account of how humans develop sexual orientations is more complex than any of the theories that I have discussed so far (it is, for example, more complex than Bem or Hamer's theory since it incorporates both of them). I do not claim this account is true, but I think it is much closer to being the right sort of theory of how sexual orientations develop than its less sophisticated rivals. Note that according to this complex account of how sexual orientations develop, sexual orientations are natural human kinds. Whether or not a man or a woman grew up in a gender-polarized society, this theory says that he or she will have a sexual orientation, a complex set of psychological dispositions related to sexual attraction to people in virtue of their sex-gender. The existence of several distinct pathways that lead to development of these psychological characteristics is consistent with these psychological states playing an explanatory role in scientific laws. Just as there might be more than one way to become a biological mother (at least since the advent of artificial insemination and surrogacy technologies) but being a biological mother is a natural kind, and just as there might be various subtypes of people who are right-handed (perhaps because of different patterns of brain lateralization) but the categories of handedness are natural human kinds, sexual orientations might still be natural human kinds if there are multiple pathways to the development of sexual orientations.

### Sophisticated Constructionism

There might, however, be multiple pathways to the development of sexual orientations despite the fact that sexual orientations are *not* natural human kinds. Sexual orientations might develop in this culture and some other cultures that are similar in relevant ways, but in other cultures, sexual desires might be organized in quite distinct ways. In these other cultures, people would of course still have sexual desires and some people might be more attracted to men than women, but in such cultures, the psychological structures that underlie sexual desires would not constitute sexual orientations. In these other cultures, it would be a mistake to say that there are heterosexuals, homosexuals, and bisexuals, just as it might be a mistake to say that there are yuppies in some other cultures or backers and fronters in our culture. (Refer to chapters 3 and 4 for more details on constructionism.) The existence of multiple pathways for the development of sexual orientations in some cultures leaves open the possibility that in other cultures, sexual desires could be organized in different ways; while there might be multiple pathways that lead to the development of these sexual desires, these would not be pathways to sexual orientations. If this were the right account, then essentialism would be false and constructionism—what might be called *sophisticated constructionism*—would be true since sexual orientation would not be a natural human kind.

## Conclusion

At the beginning of this chapter I considered several reasons why experiential theories of the development of sexual orientation are not as widely believed as they once were. Although I have not attempted to defend a particular experiential theory of sexual orientation, I have tried to show that there remain various reasons to be interested in experiential and psychological factors in the development of sexual orientation. Although there is little evidence for any specific experiential or psychological theory, experiences and environmental factors seem likely to be relevant in some ways to explaining the development of the complex psychological dispositions that we call sexual orientations. My arguments that experiential and psychological theories are relevant to understanding human sexual orientation should not, however, be construed as counting against the existence of various biological factors that underlie sexual orientation. Biology underlies every plausible theory of the development of sexual orientation. Even theories that fit the permissive model require that biology plays some role. Given this, even if the development of sexual orientations in humans is to be explained by several distinct psychological mechanisms, underlying all of these mechanisms will be genes and neurons. Biology necessarily plays a role in explaining the development of sexual desires, even if its role is complex and indirect.

Toward the end of this chapter, I sketched a model of the development of human sexual orientations that involves multiple developmental pathways. I argued that there is no convincing reason for thinking that a single theory will explain the origins of everyone's sexual orientation and, further, that multiple-origins theory has several virtues. I also speculated on the theoretical implications of multiple-origins theory on the debate between essentialism and constructionism. Multiple-origins theory fits with either sophisticated essentialism or sophisticated constructionism. If either of these theories is true, then scientific research on sexual orientation and sexual desires is going to be much more complex than current work in the emerging research program suggests.

# CHAPTER 9

# *Sexual Orientation and Choice*

I began chapter 5 by enumerating various reasons why scientific research concerning sexual orientation warrants careful consideration. Among the reasons I gave was that many people think that sexual orientations are determined, namely, they think that a person does not have a choice as to what his or her sexual orientation is. Perhaps the most straightforward explanation of why people believe sexual orientations are determined is because it is true: people think that biological factors determine sexual orientations because the direct model of the role of biological factors in sexual orientation is true. However, in chapters 6 and 7, I raised various objections to the emerging research program, which provides the main source of support for the direct model. I argued that the evidence for the emerging research program is weak and many of its theoretical assumptions are unsupported. It is not clear, in light of these criticisms, what to say about the role that choice plays in the development of sexual orientations.

In this chapter, I focus on two positions about sexual orientation and choice: *voluntarism* about sexual orientation, the view that people choose their sexual orientations, and *determinism* about sexual orientation, the view that people do not choose their sexual orientations (this view is not to be confused with determinism, a traditional metaphysical view that says all events are determined; I will have more to say about this traditional metaphysical view later in this chapter). There are various reasons why many people favor determinism about sexual orientation over voluntarism about sexual orientation. I consider some of these reasons in the following section. Many people's intuitions against voluntarism are so strong that they might lead them to reject the multiple-origins theory that I sketched at the end of chapter 8 on the grounds that it seems to leave room for voluntarism. In the next two sections, after I discuss some traditional philosophical questions relating to free will, I show that the issues between voluntarism and determinism about sexual orientation cannot be settled by appeal to the debate between essentialism and constructionism about sexual orientation. Then in the fourth section, I introduce the distinction between a direct choice and an indirect choice. I argue that the reasons some people have for rejecting voluntarism are undercut by the distinction between direct and indirect choices. In the following section, I consider and reject another argument against voluntarism about sexual orientation. In the final section, I develop a third position about sexual orientation and choice, what I call nondeterminism about sexual orientation.

## The Case Against Voluntarism about Sexual Orientation

I begin with the various reasons for believing that people do not choose their sexual orientations. Most significantly, there is introspective evidence that sexual orientations are not chosen. Think about your own sexual orientation. Insofar as you are clear as to what your sexual orientation is, do you recall having chosen it? You have probably made lots of decisions that relate (in various ways) to your sexual orientation—such as whether to engage in certain sexual behaviors and whether and in what contexts to identify yourself as having a particular sexual orientation—but these decisions are different from *choosing* your sexual orientation. Consider the following observation. On a particular occasion, you might decide to have sex with a person of the same sex-gender. Doing so does not in itself constitute deciding to become a homo-sexual. You might do it because you are horny and there is no one else around. You might do it for money. You might do so as a favor to the other person involved. These three cases involve deciding to have sex with someone of the same sex-gender, but they do not involve choosing to be a homosexual. Similarly, you might decide to *say* that you are a heterosexual. Doing so does not, however, constitute deciding to *become* a heterosexual. You might say you are a heterosexual because you do not want to lose your job. You might do so because you think you are a heterosexual, when in fact you are not. These cases involve choosing to *identify* as heterosexual, but they do not involve choosing to *become* a heterosexual. To have a sexual orientation, roughly, is to find certain sorts of people sexually attractive in virtue of, to some extent, their sex-gender and to be disposed, all else being equal, to want to have sex with such people. The introspective evidence against voluntarism about sexual orientation is the feeling, shared by most men and some women in this culture, that one did not choose one's sexual orientation or one's sexual desires and dispositions. In some Western countries, however, many women and some men feel their sexual orientations are fluid and that some conscious choice is involved in the development of sexual orientation (Card 1995, 47–57; Golden 1987; Whisman 1996); I discuss this alternative intuition later.

There is also observational evidence that suggests that sexual orientations are not chosen, that is, scientific, clinical, psychological, and testimonial evidence that a person cannot change his or her sexual orientation (Haldeman 1991, 1994; Murphy 1992; Silverstein 1991). Countless numbers of gay men and lesbians have attempted to change their sexual orientation through one or another kind of treatment. Attempted treatments have included lengthy psychoanalysis, prayer, hormonal injections, and electric shock treatment to name just a few. All such treatments have been dramatic failures. That most people who have tried to change their sexual orientations have failed seems to count against voluntarism about sexual orientation. Further, in places where there are no positive representations of lesbians and gay men, where homosexuals are violently repressed and severely punished, and in which social pressures push an individual to be heterosexual, there are still people who are sexually attracted to people of the same sex-gender. It seems that at least some of these people living under such conditions would choose to be heterosexuals if they could. Since they are not in fact heterosexuals, this suggests that they do not have a choice in the matter.

There is additional introspective evidence that coheres with this observational evidence. Imagine trying to change your own sexual orientation. In doing so, I am not asking you to imagine trying to have sex with a person of a sex-gender other than the one to which you are primarily attracted or to imagine trying to identify as having a sexual orientation different from the one you have. Instead, I am asking whether you could change your underlying desires with respect to the sex-gender to which you are sexually attracted and whether you could make yourself disposed to have sex with people with whom you are not disposed to have sex. If you think it would be basically impossible to do this, then this seems to provide evidence for the view that voluntarism about sexual orientation is false.

There is another reason why voluntarism about sexual orientation is implausible. Both nativist and experiential theories of sexual orientation and both primarily biological and primarily psychological theories of sexual orientation seem to argue against voluntarism. The thought is that whichever sort of theory is true, or if there are multiple origins to sexual orientations, a person does not choose his or her sexual orientation—either genetic makeup determines sexual orientation or environmental conditions do. However a person's sexual orientation develops, choice is not involved. I consider this argument against voluntarism later in this chapter.

To summarize, voluntarism about sexual orientation seems implausible because most people do not feel like they chose their sexual orientation, most people's sexual orientations do not seem changeable, and the most plausible theories of how human sexual orientations develop seem to entail that choice does not play a role in its development. Even granting that voluntarism about sexual orientation is implausible, should we care whether it is true or false? We should. There are reasons for pursuing the debate between voluntarism and determinism and for seeing whether the reasons why voluntarism seems implausible withstand scrutiny. Insofar as there are good scientific reasons to be interested in how sexual orientations develop, there are good scientific reasons to be interested in the role choice plays in the development of sexual orientations. This is true even if all my arguments in chapters 6 and 7 concerning the emerging research program are successful. Despite our ignorance of how people develop sexual orientations, we may still be able to ascertain whether there is any element of individual choice in the development of sexual orientations. Perhaps sexual orientation is like eye color: even if we did not know what gene causes eye color or the mechanisms by which eye color develops, we would still have strong evidence that eye color is not a choice. Second, for many people, especially many gay men and some lesbians, the fact that their sexual orientation is not a choice is important for their sense of self (Whisman 1996). Finally, many people have suggested that whether or not sexual orientations are chosen is relevant to various ethical and political questions related to lesbian and gay rights. In particular, the idea is that if a person did not choose his or her sexual orientation, then he or she should not in any way be punished because of it. In this chapter, I assess voluntarism as an empirical thesis. In chapter 10, I examine the legal and ethical relevance of voluntarism about sexual orientation.

## The Traditional Problem of Free Will

To begin, I need to bracket a traditional philosophical problem, the problem of *free will*. The traditional problem of free will concerns whether any person ever freely chooses to do anything. Most people feel that they make choices. Consider the case of Helena, who is trying to decide whether to have a chocolate eclair or an orange for dessert. Helena is on a diet, which counts in favor of choosing the low-calorie orange over the high-calorie eclair. Still, Helena prefers the taste of the eclair and has not eaten any sweets for several days. After a few moments of hesitation, Helena opts for the eclair. If you ask her, Helena would say she had a genuine choice: she could have chosen the eclair or the orange, but she chose the eclair. She might regret her choice later that day, but her regret seems to confirm the fact that she made a choice. Most people share Helena's intuition and feel that on a regular basis they make choices about what to do.

One problem for the general view that humans have free will—and the particular view that Helena in fact had a choice with regard to eating the eclair—is that free will seems in tension with *physicalism* (or *materialism*), the view that all facts are material facts, that every entity that exists is a physical entity, and that every force that has impact on such entities is a physical force. Physical things are governed by physical laws. If you know the relevant physical laws, you can (bracketing issues about quantum physics and indeterminacy) predict the outcome of any physical process. If, for example, I knew the exact state of every neuron in Helena's brain at some time before she eats dessert and if I knew the physical laws governing the operation of her brain and body, I could predict with certainty Helena's dessert selection, what she would say about it, whether she would finish it, and whether her dieting will ever prove successful. But if I could predict this well in advance of her selecting the eclair or even in advance of her decision to do so, it seems that Helena does not in fact have a choice, even if she thinks she does. If our actions, beliefs, and desires are the result of the straightforward operation of physical laws on physical entities, then it seems that people do not have free will. For many people, physicalism is quite a plausible theory, but for some, that physicalism is incompatible with free will is a fatal objection to physicalism. Most of us believe that we have genuine choices and that we control our own actions. If physicalism is incompatible with this, so much the worse for physicalism.

Various philosophers since Hume have, however, tried to argue that physicalism is compatible with free will; they have tried to explain how it is possible for physicalism to be true and yet people can still make choices (their position is called *compatibilism*). If compatibilism is true, we can consistently accept physicalism while also believing that we have choices (Dennett 1984; van Inwagen 1993, 184–199; Watson 1982). If physicalism is true and compatibilism is false, then we do not have free will—the operation of physical laws determines our thoughts and actions. If physicalism is false and there are nonphysical facts (for example, spiritual or supernatural facts), then we might

Table 9-1. Relations Among Physicalism, Compatibilism, and Free Will

|  | Every entity and every force that exists is physical (physicalism is true) | There are nonphysical entities and forces (physicalism is false) |
| --- | --- | --- |
| Compatibilism is true | we might have free will | we might have free will |
| Compatibilism is false | we cannot have free will | we might have free will |

have free will, although it is still possible that we do not. Finally, if physicalism is true and compatibilism is true, then it is possible for us to have free will, although we might not. (Table 9-1 lays out the relevance of physicalism and compatibilism to whether we have free will.)

The problem of free will is a serious philosophical problem that I will not attempt to solve here (Dennett 1984; van Inwagen 1993, 184–199; Watson 1982). Instead, since this book concerns sexual orientation and desire, I focus on the question of whether sexual orientation is chosen. For this to be an interesting question, it must be the case either that physicalism is false or that some version of compatibilism is true. If we do not have free will, then voluntarism about sexual orientation would be false, but sexual orientation would not be any different from anything else; it would be the case that people do not chose their sexual orientations in just the same way that it would be the case that Helena did not choose to eat the eclair and, in general, that people do not make any choices. For the question of whether sexual orientation is a choice to be interesting, it needs to be the case that *some* things are chosen (perhaps things like Helena's choice of the eclair). For the purposes of considering this question, I assume that we make some genuine choices.*

## Why Voluntarism Versus Determinism Does Not Reduce to Essentialism Versus Constructionism

Various thinkers have tried to connect the question of whether a person's sexual orientation is a choice to the debate between essentialists and constructionists about sexual orientation. Many people (among them, constructionists and essentialists) think that constructionists must be voluntarists and that essentialists must be determinists (Epstein 1992; Padgug 1992). While it may turn out

*Because I have bracketed the traditional philosophical questions involving free will and compatibilism, I can define determinism about sexual orientation as the view that people do not choose their sexual orientations without opening up a complex set of metaphysical issues. If compatibilism is true, then determinism (in general, not about sexual orientations) is compatible with the view that people make choices.

that many constructionists are voluntarists and many essentialists are determinists, the pairings are neither universal nor necessary. Constructionism is compatible with determinism (Halperin 1990, 41–53). Consider the category of being a peasant or being a member of royalty. These are surely paradigmatic examples of *social* human kinds, but it might very well not be a choice whether someone has and continues to have one of these properties. Just as one might not be able to choose to be a member of any social or economic class even though membership in such a class constitutes a social human kind, so too it might be that sexual orientation is not chosen even if sexual orientation is a social human kind.

Similarly, essentialism is compatible with voluntarism; it is possible that sexual orientations are natural human kinds and that choice plays a role in the development of sexual orientations. Consider the example of being a biological mother (previously discussed in chapter 4). There are scientific laws that apply to people who have given birth, for example, all people who have given birth have two X chromosomes. (There may be some borderline cases about what counts as giving birth, for example, stillbirths and in vitro fertilization, but these issues need not detain us.) In virtue of these and other scientific laws, whether a person has given birth is a natural human kind. Essentialism about biological mothers is thus true. It is, however, possible to choose to be a mother, or at least to choose not to be (by refraining from intercourse, by using contraceptives, by having one's Fallopian tubes blocked, and so on).

Just as someone could choose to be or not to be a biological mother even though being a biological mother is a natural human kind, it might be possible to choose to be a homosexual or a heterosexual even if essentialism about sexual orientation is true, that is, even if sexual orientations are natural human kinds. An example of a theory of the origins of sexual orientations that is essentialist and voluntarist is the first-encounter theory (see chapter 8 for discussion). According to one version of this theory, one's sexual orientation is fixed by one's first sexual experience. On such a view, being a heterosexual or homosexual is a natural human kind (because there would be scientific laws associated with the sex-gender of the person one first had sex with), but one can have a choice in what his or her sexual orientation is by appropriately choosing the first person with whom he or she has sex. Although the first-encounter theory is almost surely false (for reasons I discussed in chapter 8), it provides an example of a theory of sexual orientation that is both essentialist and voluntarist. Most theories that see biological factors playing an indirect role in the development of sexual orientation allow that experiences and decisions in the face of these experiences play a role in the development of sexual orientation. As I explained at the end of chapter 8, some of the psychological theories that fit the indirect model are essentialist theories (albeit sophisticated ones). Given that essentialism and voluntarism are compatible and that constructionism and determinism are compatible, it is a mistake to collapse the distinction between constructionism and essentialism into the distinction between determinism and voluntarism, or vice versa. We cannot determine whether sexual orientation is a choice by turning to the question of whether sexual orientations are natural human kinds.

## Problems with Determinism about Sexual Orientation

My discussion thus far has been overly simple. I have glossed over two different ways of understanding what a choice is. Consider the distinction between what I call a *direct* choice and an *indirect* choice. I make a direct choice to X if I do something with the conscious intention of doing X. When Helena chose to eat the eclair, she made a direct choice because she consciously intended to do so. A person makes an *indirect* choice to X if she does something *without* the conscious intention of doing X. Suppose the eclair that Helena was eyeing belonged to Fred, who planned to eat it for dessert. If Helena eats the eclair without knowing Fred's plans for it, she made an *in*direct choice to eat Fred's dessert. Even though she made a direct choice to eat the eclair, she did not make a direct choice to eat *Fred's* eclair; her direct choice to eat the eclair did, however, result in an indirect choice to eat Fred's eclair.

With the distinction between a direct and an indirect choice in mind, consider preferences for different foods. Some people like spicy foods, some do not; some people have a sweet tooth, others do not. Clearly, a person's food preferences are going to be partially based on one's biological constitution—for example, a person who is allergic to oranges typically will not like to eat oranges and a person with a sensitive stomach will not typically like spicy food. One's food preferences are also going to be shaped by one's environment: a person who has been brought up in India will have more experience eating foods flavored with cumin than a person who has never been out of rural France. These different experiences have an impact on a person's food preferences, although two people can have quite similar experiences without ending up having similar food preferences. Consider Bob's food preferences. Bob, let us suppose, likes carrots and does not like cucumbers. What might we say about whether Bob's preferences are the result of choice? If we ask Bob, he would say that he does not remember ever having made a decision to like carrots and dislike cucumbers. Also, we might note that Bob's preference is hard to change, perhaps even impossible—he might *try* to like cucumbers, but they might remain totally unappealing to him. These two observations are compatible with it being the case that a choice Bob made at some time affected his current food preferences. For example, deciding to move to India might have had the unforeseen consequence of affecting Bob's preferences with respect to certain vegetables, just as it might have affected his preferences with respect to spicy foods. In terms of the distinction between direct and indirect choices, we might say that Bob made a direct choice to move to India and, as a result, indirectly chose to change his tastes with respect to spicy foods.

Returning to sexual orientation, recall the reasons I sketched for thinking that voluntarism about sexual orientation is false. First, there is introspective evidence: most people would say that they do not recall ever choosing a sexual orientation. The same may, however, be true about food preferences: Bob may not recall ever having decided to like carrots but not cucumbers. Even though he might not recall having chosen to like carrots, he might have made an *indirect* choice to do so. Thus, it is compatible with introspective evidence that one made an *indirect* choice that resulted in having the sexual orientation one does. For all we know, one's sexual orientation might be the result of a decision to play basketball more often than chess, to play with soldiers more often than with dolls, to eat spinach more often than Jell-O, or some combination of these and other (direct) choices that one might have made. Even a genetic theory of sexual orientation has to allow that for at least a significant number of people, sexual orientation is caused by environmental factors that differ even among identical twins raised together (see chapters 5 and 7). Choices that individuals make, whether direct or indirect, might explain why so many identical twins are discordant for sexual orientation. That you made an indirect choice to have the sexual orientation that you do is compatible with your sense of not having (directly) chosen to have the sexual orientation that you do.

The second reason for thinking that sexual orientations are not chosen was the observational evidence that people's sexual orientations seem irreversible or incorrigible. There are, however, lots of *choices* (direct and indirect) that have results that are irreversible or incorrigible. Our food preferences might be incorrigible. It might be that, after a certain age, one's food preferences become fixed. Or, to give another example, having an abortion is irreversible, yet a person can make a choice to have one (assuming the person is a pregnant woman). The fact that I cannot change my sexual orientation is compatible with my sexual orientation being the result of a choice (either direct or indirect) (Card 1995, 48). The evidence that those people who are unhappy (at least initially) about their sexual orientation (or sexual desires) find it impossible to change (Haldeman 1991, 1994; Murphy 1992; Silverstein 1991) is compatible with the fact that their sexual orientations are the result of choices (direct or, more plausibly, indirect) made much earlier in life.

My argument about sexual orientation and choice thus far is rather weak. I have claimed that voluntarism is compatible with the sense that some people have that they did not choose their particular sexual orientation. I have also claimed that voluntarism is compatible with the evidence that it is very difficult to change a person's sexual orientation. Something can, of course, be compatible with the facts and still be false. In the remainder of this section, I offer some reasons for thinking that determinism about sexual orientation is less plausible than it initially seemed.

How each of us develops the whole range of desires we have (for specific kinds of food, recreational activities, sex, and so on) is rather mysterious. Certainly, our genetic makeup plays a role and so does our environment. However, one significant conclusion from chapters 5 through 8 is that we do not have a clear picture of how these factors produce any sort of desires in us. We are not, for example, surprised to find identical twins raised in the same environment who have different desires and preferences in various realms, ranging from food and music to friends and careers. There must be factors other than genes and aspects of the environment that identical twins share that shape how people develop desires, tastes, and dispositions. We do not have a good theory of what are the experiential factors that identical twins do not share and how these factors affect people's traits. This relates to the fact that the equal environments assumption discussed in chapter 5, which says that a pair of identical twins and a pair of fraternal twins share the same amount of environment factors, is, at best, unsupported. There are various reasons for thinking that identical twins share more environmental factors than fraternal twins. Given that we know so little about how human desires and preferences develop in general, why should we be so confident that sexual orientations are not chosen?

Focusing more specifically on sexual desires in general, few people think that a person's sexual desire for people of a certain sex-gender is chosen, while many think that other features of a person's sexual interests—for example, how often he or she likes to have sex; what kind of sex he or she likes to have; the hair color, race, and size of the people he or she likes to have sex with—are chosen.[1] Further, most people will agree that people can learn to enjoy and desire sexual activities that they once did not enjoy or desire. Think about whether the following description fits your mature attitude towards some particular sexual activity: at first, the very idea of it disgusted you; when you first tried it, it was not particularly pleasurable, perhaps it was even painful; over time, however, you came to enjoy it and desire it; eventually, in certain contexts, the desire to do it may become almost overwhelming. The phenomenon of acquiring a taste seems to apply to various sexual activities and other things such as the desire for certain foods, but not, most people think, to sexual orientation. (The comedian Jackie Mason [1991] raised a related issue when he asked why it is that people have to acquire a taste for brie, but nobody needs to acquire a taste for potato chips.) Many people, while they believe that sexual orientations are prewired or that they develop at such an early age that they cannot possibly have been chosen, also believe that other desires, including other sexual desires, develop later. What, if anything, justifies the intuition that there is a difference between sexual orientation and other aspects of sexual desires? If nothing justifies it, what explains it?

Historians of sexuality and other scholars doing work in lesbian and gay studies and working in the paradigm of constructionism have argued for a thesis that helps explain why most people think their sexual orientation, but *not* most other aspects of their desires, are determined. According to a popular version of constructionism, people only became focused on sexual orientation as *the* important feature of the whole range of sexual desires and interests just over one hundred years ago (Foucault 1978). Before that time, the sex-gender of the person one wants to have sex with was not taken to provide any more insight into the type of person one was or the nature of one's character than we think the hair color of the person one wants to have sex with provides. Late in the nineteenth century, a conceptual change took place: the sex-gender of the people a person wanted to have sex with emerged as *the* crucial feature of his or her sexual desire and a particularly important feature of his or her character. In the oft-quoted words of Michel Foucault,

> As defined by the ancient civil or canonical codes, sodomy was a category of forbidden acts; their perpetrator was nothing more than the juridical subject of them. The nineteenth-century homosexual became a personage, a past, a case history, and a childhood, in addition to being a type of life, a life form, and a morphology, with an indiscreet anatomy and possibly a mysterious physiology. Nothing that went into his total composition was unaffected by his sexuality. It was everywhere present in him: at the root of all his actions because it was their insidious and indefinitely active principle; written immodestly on his face and body because it was a secret that always gave itself away. It was consubstantial with him, less as a habitual sin than as a singular nature. (43)

I am not particularly concerned with the details of this hypothesis (for example, whether our categories of sexual orientation are one hundred, two hundred, or two thousand years old). The salient point is that our fascination with sexual orientation, as opposed to other features of human sexual desire more generally (Sedgwick 1990, 22–27), seems the result of historical and cultural factors, not biological or genetic ones. This historical hypothesis should weaken the intuition that there is a clear distinction between sexual orientation, which is not chosen, and other features of our sexual desires, which may or may not be chosen. This observation—together with the facts that neither introspective evidence nor observational evidence that sexual orientation is incorrigible entails determinism about sexual orientation—suggests that some of the arguments against voluntarism about sexual orientation, canvassed at the beginning of this chapter, are not as strong as they first seemed.

Note that one does not have to be a constructionist to accept this observation about choice and sexual orientation as compared to choice and other aspects of sexual desire. Whether or not sexual orientations are natural human kinds is independent of whether or not people believe that a person's sexual orientation is a deep and important fact about him or her. Take handedness for example. At certain times in history, many people thought that which hand one favored revealed something deep and important about that person. It was quite common to think that left-handed people were possessed by the devil. We now believe that handedness has to do with the pattern of lateralization in certain regions of the brain. We thus accept that there are natural human kinds associated with handedness, but we do not think that there are especially deep and significant things about a person that result from this (Murphy 1997, 50–51 and 64). Most of us, at least most people in Western cultures, are essentialists about handedness, even though we acknowledge that handedness came to be seen as an important property of a person at a particular time and that it ceased to be seen this way at a later time. Similarly, an essentialist about sexual orientations can accept the claim, typically (but mistakenly) seen as part of constructionism, that sexual orientation came to be seen as a deep and essential property of humans at a specific historical moment.

I have been suggesting that some of the reasons for embracing determinism are not as strong as they might have initially seemed. This does not mean that I think voluntarism is plausible. Given all of the societal pressures, especially in certain cultural contexts, pushing people to become heterosexual, it seems unlikely that people would choose to be homosexual. And yet even in the most repressive and homophobic environments, there are still gay men and lesbians. Clearly, some of these people (if they had a chance) would have chosen to be heterosexual. As neither voluntarism nor determinism are particularly plausible, it is fortunate that there is a third position about sexual orientation and choice. Recall the distinction between a direct and an indirect choice. Suppose that some choices that I made affected my sexual orientation.

This would not necessarily entail that voluntarism is true. If the choices that I made that affected my sexual orientation were only *indirect* choices with respect to my sexual orientation, then this would not support voluntarism about sexual orientation, which involves a conscious choice about sexual orientation. I call the view that sexual orientations are the result of *in*direct choices *nondeterminism*. According to this view, sexual orientations are the result of choice, but not the result of direct choices concerning sexual orientation. In the penultimate section of the present chapter, I argue that nondeterminism about sexual orientation is more plausible than either voluntarism or determinism.

## The Disjunctive Argument Against Voluntarism

In an earlier section, I considered three arguments that seemed to count against voluntarism about sexual orientation. In the previous section, I argued that two of these arguments do not in fact count against voluntarism. In this section, I turn to the remaining argument that voluntarism is implausible. The thought is that whichever theory of the origins of sexual orientation is true, sexual orientations are not chosen, but rather are the result of one's genetic makeup or one's environment. This argument can be spelled out as follows (where [1], [2], and [3] are premises in the argument and [4] is the conclusion):

(1) Either sexual orientation is the result of a person's genetic makeup or it is the result of a person's environment.
(2) If sexual orientation is due to genes, then sexual orientation is not a choice.
(3) If sexual orientation is due to the environment, then sexual orientation is not a choice.
(4) Therefore, sexual orientation is not a choice.[2]

This argument seems plausible, and it has the seeming virtue of settling the issue about whether sexual orientations are chosen independent of knowing what causes a person's sexual orientation.

The first problem with this argument has to do with (1). As I argued in chapters 4 and 5, the issue between nature and nurture theories, as typically discussed, is based on a false dichotomy. No human trait is strictly the result of genetic or other biological factors or strictly the result of environmental factors. All human traits are the result of both. There are genetic factors that affect even the most seemingly environmental traits—for example, what a person's major will be in college. On the other hand, environmental factors contribute to the development of even the most seemingly genetic traits—for example, eye color (if I did not have enough of the right sorts of vitamins and minerals at crucial times, my eyes might have been yellow rather than hazel). Further, as I argued in chapter 8, sexual orientations might be the result of multiple factors. This suggests the following revision to the argument that sexual orientation is not a choice:

(1') Sexual orientation is the result of both genetic (or other biological) factors and environmental factors.

(2') To the extent that sexual orientation is due to genetic (or other biological) factors, it is not a choice.

(3') To the extent that sexual orientation is due to environmental factors, it is not a choice.

(4') Therefore, sexual orientation is not a choice.

This argument avoids a false dichotomy, but there is another problem with it.

Consider (3'), the claim that, to the extent that a person's sexual orientation is due to environmental factors, one's sexual orientation is not a choice. This mistakenly assumes that one cannot have any effect on one's environment, but if one's choices can affect one's environment, it is possible that one's choices could effect one's sexual orientation. Recall the earlier example of food preferences. Bob's decision to move to India would likely have some effect on his future food preferences, perhaps with respect to spicy foods. His indirect choices, then, do affect his food preferences. In the same way, unless we think I can have no effect on the parts of my environment that affect my sexual orientation, (3') would be false. Suppose, for example, that my childhood decision to play basketball more often than chess or to eat spinach more often than Jell-O in some way affects my sexual orientation as an adult. According to both of these hypotheses, sexual orientation is due to environmental factors, but according to both of these hypotheses, sexual orientation is at least partly due to choices, although they are due to *indirect* choices. Claim (3') is thus false because some theories that see sexual orientation as due to environmental factors allow that sexual orientation is the result of some choices a person makes. If this is the case, then the argument fails.

There are two ways one might try to save this argument for determinism about sexual orientation. First, one might argue that denying that I have an effect on my environment because I am entirely determined by my genetic makeup and my environment would involve denying that I have free will. I have already explained why this is too strong a position to take in order to make a claim just about sexual orientation. Second, one might argue that sexual orientation is primarily the result of genetic factors and that the contribution of the environment is minimal. Every human trait is affected by genetic and environmental factors, but as I noted in chapter 5, there are some traits that seem strongly genetic and others that seem less so—my blood type is more tightly constrained by genetic factors than my taste in music. The proposed argument that sexual orientation is not a choice involves embracing a nativist theory of sexual orientation. The idea is to accept that (3') is false but to save the argument that sexual orientation is not a choice by relying on evidence for the antecedent of (2'), namely for the claim that sexual orientation is primarily due to genetic factors. However, as I have argued in chapters 6 and 7, this claim is far from decisive. In fact, it was because this claim is unsupported that this chapter addresses arguments and evidence concerning sexual orientation and choice that do not rely on a specific scientific theory of how human sexual orientations develop. Relying on the truth of a nativist theory of sexual orientation to establish determinism would not satisfy the attempt to argue for determinism without relying on a specific scientific theory; rather, it would be making a circular argument. If there were strong evidence for the view that sexual orientations are biologically based, then this might be strong reason to believe that sexual orientations are not chosen. However, the evidence for such biologically based theories is not especially strong.

## Nondeterminism about Sexual Orientation

I have argued that the intuition that people do not choose their own sexual orientations and the evidence that attempts to change sexual orientations have failed do not establish determinism about sexual orientation. I do not, however, think that most people actually develop their underlying sexual desires simply by deciding what their sexual orientation is in much the way one might decide what candidate to vote for in an election or what dessert to order in a restaurant. Even a woman who decides for political reasons to identify as a lesbian does not, thereby, change her underlying sexual desires. As the philosophers Joyce Trebilcot (1984) and Sandra Lee Bartky (1990) have shown in two especially engaging essays, wanting to be a lesbian for political or philosophical reasons does not necessarily lead to a change in one's sexual attractions—a woman might still be sexually attracted to men and not sexually attracted to women even if she wants to become a lesbian. The considerations discussed so far point to the plausibility of nondeterminism about sexual orientation. Nondeterminism is the view that a person does not consciously choose his or her sexual orientation, but that indirect choices do play a role in the development of sexual orientations. Even though a person cannot choose his or her sexual orientation, a person's choices can affect his or her sexual orientations; we just do not know which choices play a role—for example, if at a certain age certain people cannot do anything to change their sexual orientations, even though some choices they made as, say, a child did play a role. While I do not have any completely compelling arguments or evidence for nondeterminism, there are some further considerations that count in its favor.

Some of the evidence offered by researchers working in the emerging research program is compatible with nondeterminism. Recall the results of Bailey's twin studies (Bailey, Dunne, and Martin n.d.; Bailey and Pillard 1991b; Bailey, Pillard, and Agyei 1993). At least 50 (and perhaps 70) percent of identical twins—one of whom is gay—who were raised in the same environment had different sexual orientations. Since their genes are identical, there must be something in their experiences that explains their different sexual orientations. But if they were raised together, had similar relationships with their family members and peers, and had the same patterns of early sexual experiences, one plausible source of a difference in their experience is their choices. I am not suggesting that one of the twins just decided to be gay or lesbian while the other decided to be heterosexual. Rather, I am suggesting that one of them made some choices that had the unintended effect of influencing the shape of his or her future sexual desires. The experiential factors that explain identical twins who are discordant for sexual orientation, whatever they are, could be the result of choices, in particular, *indirect* choices with respect to sexual orientation. If this is the case, then nondeterminism about sexual orientation would be true.

Nondeterminism about sexual orientation fits nicely with theories that fall into the indirect model as discussed at the end of the previous chapter. Recall that the indirect model sees biological factors as coding for personality traits or other psychological factors that shape sexual orientation. One example of a theory that fits this model is Daryl Bem's exotic-becomes-erotic theory. According to this theory, biological factors code for childhood personality characteristics, that in certain social environments lead to certain gender-related behaviors, which in turn may lead to the development of certain sexual desires. According to this theory, determinism about sexual orientation is false. However, neither is it the case that a child chooses his or her sexual orientations; if exotic becomes erotic were the right account of how people develop sexual orientations, then nondeterminism about sexual orientation would be true. For similar reasons, nondeterminism would be true if any theory that fits the indirect model of how people develop sexual orientation, including the multiple-origins theory discussed at the end of chapter 5, is true.

## Conclusion

In this chapter, I have tried to weaken the intuition that many people have about the role of choice (or lack thereof) in the development of sexual orientations. I have not, however, tried to argue that people choose their sexual orientations in a way that is similar to the way they choose what clothes to wear or what to eat for dinner. Further, I have not tried to argue that an adult's sexual orientation can be easily changed or even changed at all. Instead, I have tried to weaken the intuitions in favor of determinism by showing that much of the evidence for this view is weak and by developing an alternative position on the issue of the extent to which people choose their sexual orientations, namely, nondeterminism. I do not claim to have established that nondeterminism is true and both determinism and voluntarism are false. I only claim to have undercut determinism and articulated a promising alternative to it. This alternative fits nicely with the multiple-origins theory that I discussed at the end of chapter 8.

# PART III
## Ethics

# CHAPTER 10

## Lesbian and Gay Rights
## and the Science
## of Sexual Orientation

**M**any of the scientists working in the emerging research program for the study of sexual orientation (and some researchers doing work outside of it) say that part of their motivation for their research is its ethical and political implications. In the past, many scientists hoped they could cure homosexuality and rid society of the vices of sexual activity and sexual desire among people of the same sex-gender. In contrast, today some scientists (but not all) hope to improve the legal and social situation for lesbians and gay men by showing that sexual orientation is primarily genetic and rooted in biology. Various thinkers sympathetic to lesbian and gay rights accept some version of what I call the *biological argument for lesbian and gay rights*. Arguments of this form hold that some claims of the emerging research program are relevant to making the case for lesbian and gay rights. Perhaps the most plausible version of this argument tries to use scientific research on sexual orientation to show that sexual orientations are not chosen, and then use this result to show that lesbians and gay men should not be punished for their sexual orientation.

In chapters 6 and 7, I argued that scientific research on sexual orientation is far from conclusive. In this chapter, I set aside these previous arguments in order to examine the relevance of scientific research on sexual orientation to ethical and political issues relating to sexual orientation. I do not here try to provide general arguments for lesbian and gay rights or to argue that sexual activity among people of the same sex-gender can be as fulfilling, fun, and frustrating as sexual activity among people not of the same sex-gender. Others have provided various arguments for these and related claims, and although I do not necessarily agree with all of these arguments, I do agree with most of their conclusions (Blasius 1994; Calhoun 1995; Eskridge 1999; Kaplan 1997; Koppelman 1988; Mohr 1990; Phelan 1995; Posner 1992; Richards 1982, 1998; Rubin 1984; Sullivan 1995). I begin my discussion of biological arguments for lesbian and gay rights with a survey of the current legal, political, and social situation with respect to homosexuality and of the various legal and political claims that lesbians, gay men, and bisexuals make.

## The Current Situation

At various times and in various places, people have had different attitudes towards sexual activities between people of the same sex-gender and the desire to engage in such activities. Focusing on men, in Attic Greece, adult men who were sexually attracted to young men were widely accepted—in fact, homo-erotic desire was taken as a sign of virility and intelligence. However, a man who wanted to be anally penetrated (or worse, who acted on this desire) was highly stigmatized (see discussion in chapter 4); the attitude in some contemporary Latin American cultures is somewhat similar (see discussion in chapter 7). In some Native American cultures, *berdache,* transgendered males who have sex with men, were held in great respect and were among the most powerful and influential people of their tribes (see chapter 1 for a brief discussion). English men were imprisoned for sexual activity with other men at the turn of the century (Sinfield 1994; Weeks 1977). In Nazi Germany, gay men were put to death (Heger 1980; Plant 1986). Women who desire to have sex with other women have also been subject to a wide range of attitudes, although same sex-gender sexual desire in women has been ignored (legally and socially) more often than among men.

I do not have the space to survey the wide varieties of attitudes, past and present, towards having sex with or sexual desires for people of the same sex-gender. In order to evaluate the ethical and political relevance of scientific research on sexual orientation, I focus instead on the present global context in which this scientific research is currently received and is likely to be received in the future. I begin this analysis by looking at the situation in the United States. I begin here for several reasons (besides the fact that I live in the United States and know more about it than I do other countries). First, a considerable percentage of the research on sexual orientation is done by researchers in the United States. Second, lawyers in the United States have explicitly attempted to make a connection between scientific research on sexual orientation and the legal status of lesbians and gay men (Green 1988; Halley 1993; Keen and Goldberg 1998). Various others in the United States, including gay activists, conservative commentators, and some scientists, have made similar arguments (Bawer 1993; LeVay 1996; Sullivan 1995). Third, the United States is an interesting case study with respect to attitudes toward homosexuality. On the one hand, there is a strong and visible community of lesbians, gay men, bisexuals, and transgendered people in the United States, and some would argue the contemporary lesbian and gay rights movement got its start here. On the other hand, the United States is home to a strong antigay movement, much of it affiliated with conservative religious groups, and attitudes towards gay people, while improving, are still generally negative.

### The Example of the United States

#### Legal Status

One way to assess the situation of people who desire to have sex with people of the same sex-gender and who act on this desire is to look at a country's laws. In the United States, depending on how one counts, between five and eighteen states as well as the District of Columbia have laws that criminalize many forms of same sex-gender sexual activity (Posner and Silbaugh 1996; Robeson 1992, 47–59; Rubinstein 1997, 145–282). Further, the U.S. Supreme Court has ruled that the Constitution allows states to prohibit consensual homosexual activity (even though it does not seem to allow states to prohibit comparable forms of heterosexual activity) (*Bowers v. Hardwick* 1986). Although no state regularly enforces these laws (often called sodomy laws or laws regarding unnatural sex acts), they are selectively enforced by some states. Even in states where such laws are not generally enforced, laws against sexual activity between people of the same sex-gender are used to support and justify other laws and social practices relating to homosexuality. For example, to justify the ban on lesbians and gay men serving in the armed forces, some people have noted that same sex-gender sexual activity is illegal in many states. They then compare banning lesbians and gay men from military service to barring criminals and probable criminals from military service. This is just one example of how laws criminalizing same-sex sex carry weight even if they are not enforced. The criminal prohibitions relating to sexual activity between people of the same sex-gender restrict people's sexual behaviors and embody as well as enforce negative attitudes that exist towards lesbians and gay men.

Not only is sex between people of the same sex-gender criminalized, lesbians, gay men, and bisexuals are also subject to a multitude of discriminatory practices (Eskridge and Hunter 1997; Rubinstein 1997). For example, it is legal in forty states to discriminate in terms of hiring and housing against a person in virtue of one's sexual orientation. In other words, a gay man or lesbian—even if he or she can prove that sexual orientation was used as a reason not to hire him or her for a job—has no legal recourse in most states. Even those states that have antidiscrimination laws relating to sexual orientation allow for various exemptions, for example, religious organizations and small organizations are often allowed to discriminate on the basis of sexual orientation.

The legal situation in the United States with respect to discrimination on the basis of sexual orientation is in contrast to the situation with respect to various other groups of people that have historically been subject to discrimination. The Supreme Court has interpreted the Constitution as requiring a higher standard of review of laws that selectively apply to people who have historically suffered unjustified discrimination and disenfranchisement. Laws that make classifications based on race require the state to demonstrate an exceedingly strong state interest for crafting a law that makes use of racial categories (other classifications that trigger the invocation of special judicial scrutiny include religious affiliation, ethnicity, country of origin, and gender). As an example, consider a law that makes it easier for the spouse of a male government employee to receive benefits than it does for the spouse of a female government employee. This law makes use of a sex-gender classification. As such, it requires heightened scrutiny; a court should require that the state demonstrate a strong interest in using this classification (*Frontiero v. Richardson* 1972). Despite the discrimination and disenfranchisement that lesbians and gay men face, the courts do not require that the state demonstrate an exceedingly strong state interest in a law that makes use of sexual-orientation classifications (Eskridge and Hunter 1997, xlv–il and 73–123).

Further, no state provides lesbian and gay relationships with legal recognition that comes even close to the sort of recognition it provides heterosexual relationships. A heterosexual couple can legally formalize their relationship by getting married, and there are many rights and privileges associated with marriage. They include:

- the right to receive, or the obligation to provide, spousal support and, in the event of separation or divorce, alimony and an equitable distribution of property
- preference in being appointed the personal representative of the spouse if he or she dies without a will

- priority in being appointed guardian of or person in charge of making health-care decisions for an incapacitated spouse
- various rights associated with the involuntary hospitalization of the spouse
- the right to bring a lawsuit for the wrongful death of a spouse and for the intentional infliction of emotional distress through harm to one's spouse
- the right to spousal benefits including disability payments and health and life insurance
- the right to invoke special state protection against domestic violence and other intrafamily offenses
- the right to visit one's spouse on furlough while incarcerated in prison
- the right to claim an evidentiary privilege for marital communications
- a presumption of joint ownership of real estate as a tenancy in common
- a right of priority in claiming human remains and to make anatomical donations on behalf of the deceased spouse
- various inheritance rights
- the right for one's spouse to receive preferential immigration treatment and to become an American citizen
- the right to receive additional Social Security benefits based on spouse's contribution
- survivor's benefits on the death of a veteran spouse
- various rights and privileges associated with adopting and obtaining custody of children (Eskridge 1996, 66–67; Kaplan 1997, 207–238)

These and various other rights and privileges associated with marriage (the details vary depending on the jurisdiction) are readily and cheaply available to heterosexual couples that meet certain basic requirements (for example, they cannot be related in certain ways and must be of a certain age or have parental permission). Couples of the same sex-gender can obtain only some of the these rights and privileges, and those that are obtainable are only available with a great deal of time, effort, and (often) expense.

Further, the legal disparities that exist between heterosexual couples and lesbian and gay couples are vigilantly guarded by many U.S. citizens. A court case that might result in making Hawaii the first state to recognize lesbian and gay marriages (*Baehr v. Lewin* 1993) sparked a nationwide movement to ensure that jurisdictions outside of Hawaii do not have to recognize same-sex marriages that might take place in Hawaii. Dozens of states and the U.S. federal government have passed laws to this effect; the most notable of these is the federal Defense of Marriage Act (1996).

The legal asymmetries surrounding sexual orientation do not stop with the rights and privileges withheld from gay and lesbian individuals. They affect lesbian and gay institutions and lesbian and gay community structures. For example, lesbian and gay government employees and lesbian and gay students in government-funded schools are often denied funding for their organizations. Such treatment is even more likely among nongovernmental organizations (that is, private corporations and schools). Such asymmetries also appear with respect to various manifestations of what might be called lesbian and gay culture. For example, plays, photographs, and other forms of artistic expression have been banned from receiving government support. In fact, representation of and by lesbians and gay men have played a central role in debates over government funding of the arts and public standards of "decency."

## Social Conditions and Attitudes

Although the law provides unique insight into a society's attitudes, it is not the only place to find them. Some frequently occurring practices that are illegal are ignored (for example, software piracy), while some practices that are legal are subject to considerable social condemnation (for example, interracial marriage, although constitutionally protected since 1967 [*Loving v. Virginia* 1967], remains a social taboo in most parts of the United States). The social conditions for lesbians and gay men are not especially good even in the most liberal communities. Many people in our society have strong feelings against lesbians, gay men, and bisexuals. For example, a 1997 Gallup poll found that 59 percent of American adults believe "homosexual behavior is morally wrong" (Gallup 1998, 221). These antigay sentiments are manifested in diverse ways. Especially noteworthy is the violence committed against lesbians and gay men in the United States: more bias-related hate crimes are committed against people because of their sexual orientation than for any other reason (Comstock 1991).

Society's hatred of them also manifests itself in how lesbians and gay men, especially impressionable ones, feel about themselves. Perhaps among the most striking evidence of this is that lesbian and gay teenagers are three times more likely to attempt to commit suicide than their heterosexual counterparts (Gibson 1997). Further, most people have strong preferences for heterosexual children: a 1993 poll found that *80* percent of adult Americans said that they would be "upset" or "very upset" if a college-aged child of theirs said he or she was gay or lesbian (Schmalz 1993). Presumably, the number is so high because it includes people who hate lesbians and gay men as well as those who are more sympathetic to homosexuals but do not want their children to be homosexual because they realize that lesbians and gay men live in harsh circumstances. The evidence is overwhelming that the United States is a society where there is a strong fear and a deep hatred of lesbians and gay men. This hatred and fear are manifested in discriminatory and oppressive laws and social practices.

### The Closet

There is, however, a further feature of lesbian and gay existence in the United States that warrants discussion: lesbians, gay men, and bisexuals are, in a variety of ways—some subtle, some not—encouraged to keep their sexual orientations secret, that is, "in the closet." The closet is a distinctive, pervasive, and, some have argued, singular feature of lesbian and gay existence (Sedgwick 1990). Its effects are easily underestimated. Some of the most powerful and influential men and women in the United States are lesbians and gay men who are afraid to make their sexual orientations public. People remain in the closet who are financially and professionally secure enough to survive any negative ramifications that may follow the disclosure of their homosexuality and despite the energy and emotional stress involved in hiding a big part of their lives from family, friends, and coworkers (Gross 1993). Even open lesbians and gay men must worry about the closet. On the one hand, since in many contexts people are presumed to be heterosexual, the question of who to tell about one's homosexuality or bisexuality continually arises. If, for example, you are a lesbian and your mail carrier asks you how your sister is, when in fact the woman he is referring to is your lover, should you come out to him? Similarly, lesbians and gay men may find themselves having to worry about protecting the secrets of other lesbians and gay men: you may know that someone is a lesbian, but you do not know who else knows and who she wants to know. Some have argued that being forced (or obliged, perhaps by unwritten rules of the lesbian and gay community) to keep someone else's homosexuality secret is an assault on one's dignity as a gay man or lesbian (Mohr 1992a).

Relatedly, there are parts of the United States, primarily certain neighborhoods in large cities, where lesbians and gay men constitute a significant percentage of the population. In these communities, the quality of life for lesbians and gay men may be considerably better than those in other parts of the country. Even in such neighborhoods, sometimes called *gay ghettos* or *enclaves,* the situation is still not problem free. For example, police in these neighborhoods may selectively enforce laws against lesbian and gay-owned businesses or lesbian and gay home owners; queer bashers may travel to these neighborhoods in order to harass or assault residents. Further, the very fact that lesbians and gay men continue to feel pressured to live in such neighborhoods speaks to the nature of conditions of lesbians and gay men in the United States.

### The Situation in Other Countries

The situation for lesbians and gay men in other countries varies, although, compared to the United States, few countries are dramatically better and some are quite a lot worse (Hendriks, Tielman, and van der Veen 1993; West and Green 1997). I do not have the space here to systematically compare the situation in other countries with that in the United States; I limit myself instead to a couple of comparisons. In Singapore, for example, sex acts between people of the same sex-gender are a criminal offense punishable by sentences ranging from two years to life imprisonment, and people are charged and imprisoned under this law. Few people there are openly gay, and there are only a few places where gay men and lesbians can openly congregate. Discrimination is widely practiced, and there are no visible support groups for lesbians and gay men (Hendriks, Tielman, and Veen 1993, 323–324; West and Green 1997, 127–144). They are not only subject to arrest, imprisonment, and state-sanctioned harassment; they are subject to various forms of attempts to "convert" them to heterosexuality or at least celibacy (Lim 1995).

On the other hand, the new constitution of South Africa specifically mentions sexual orientation as a "protected category," formally declaring equal rights and liberty for people of all sexual orientations just as it declares them for people of all races (West and Green 1997, 5–42). And in the Netherlands, the percentage of people who think that "homosexuals should be left as free as possible to lead their own lives" is 97 percent, while 93 percent think that "homosexual couples should have the same rights as ordinary married couples to inherit from each other" (300). The social and legal situation for lesbians, gay men, and bisexuals is also better in various ways in the Netherlands than in the United States, although there are still inequities in the Dutch law (299–321).

## What Are Lesbian and Gay Rights?

Having sketched the current situation for lesbians, gay men, and bisexuals in the United States and, briefly, in other countries, I now turn to what kinds of legal and social rights and privileges lesbians, gay men, and bisexuals might claim. I do not attempt to make arguments for these claims. Rather, I articulate these claims so that I am in a better position to assess the biological argument for lesbian and gay rights, which appeals to scientific research on sexual orientation.

### Decriminalization

First, sexual activity between people of the same sex-gender could be decriminalized. So long as a sexual act involves two consenting adults and no physical harm takes place, the state has no good grounds for interfering. The philosopher Jeremy Bentham (1984) made this point in an essay written in the early 1800s but not published until the latter part of the twentieth century. He said that as distasteful and unnatural as one may find homosexuality, there are no grounds for the state to interfere with homosexual activity (no one is harmed, and no state interest is adversely affected). Further, he said that antipathy to homosexuality is grounded only in prejudice. This was quite a radical thesis for Bentham's times (and given that Bentham seems to have had no special stake in the status of homosexuality, it is not surprising that it was not published until well after his death). In the United States, the right to have sex with any consenting adult seems as though it should be included under "the right to be left alone" (Olmstead 1928), but the Supreme Court's ruling in *Bowers v. Hardwick* (1986) suggests otherwise. In particular, in the United States, lesbian and gay activists and their allies are trying to repeal sodomy laws in various states as well as other laws that regulate consensual same sex-gender sexual activity.

### Antidiscrimination

Second, lesbians and gay men could be protected against discrimination on the basis of sexual orientation. Richard Mohr (1990, 137–187) has persuasively argued that the state should play the role of a "civil shield" against practices that discriminate against lesbians and gay men (see also Kaplan 1997, 13–47). The underlying rationale of the antidiscrimination provisions of civil rights legislation in the United States is the recognition that if pervasive social inequalities exist, formal legal equality is inadequate to provide for full citizenship. In certain contexts, states may need to protect unpopular minorities against retaliation for the exercise of their basic rights of citizenship. In the United States, for example, African Americans were oppressed under Jim Crow laws not only by state laws mandating segregation, but also by the deployment of white supremacist social and economic power to punish any citizen, black or white, who attempted to change the status quo through political means. It is precisely the intensity and extent of the prejudice against homosexuality that justifies the claims of lesbians and gay men for protection against discrimination. In other countries, the underlying rationale for protecting unpopular minorities applies as well. Lesbians and gay men are entitled to protection against discrimination to ensure basic rights of citizenship and political participation. Protections against discrimination attempt to guarantee basic and fundamental rights that all citizens are supposed to enjoy, but that some unpopular minorities have to struggle to obtain. This explains why some conservative opponents of lesbian and gay rights are wrong to characterize protections against discrimination on the basis of sexual orientation as "special rights" (*Romer v. Evans* 1996). Antidiscrimination law protects the basic rights of citizens; it does not grant them special rights.

### Positive Rights

Morris Kaplan (1997, 13–46 and 207–238) has explained how claims for lesbian and gay rights should include not only the decriminalization of same sex-gender sexual activity and the prohibition of discrimination against lesbians, gay men, and bisexuals, but, further, the recognition of lesbian and gay relationships and institutions. Such recognition includes, among other things (many of which I enumerated earlier):

- being able to marry or establish a domestic partnership with a person of the same sex;
- for lesbian mothers and gay fathers, being able to gain custody of their children;
- being able to become foster and adoptive parents;
- being able to visit one's same-sex partner in the hospital;
- being able to get bereavement leave when one's partner dies;
- being able to file joint income tax returns with one's same-sex partner;
- for lesbian and gay organizations, being able to get official status in schools, universities, and professional associations.

This broader picture of lesbian and gay rights sees the state functioning as a "positive agency for actualizing the aspirations of queer citizens" (16). This third group of claims for lesbians and gay rights goes beyond decriminalization and antidiscrimination and is crucial to obtaining full-fledged equal rights of citizens and equal recognition for their relationships, families, and well-being. I refer to these claims as involving *positive rights*.

## The Biological Argument for Lesbian and Gay Rights

Having reviewed both the current legal and social situation of lesbians and gay men and articulated some of the central legal, social, and ethical questions of particular concern to lesbians and gay men, I turn to an evaluation of various ways scientific research on sexual orientation might be relevant to lesbian and gay rights. In this section, I consider a set of arguments made by some advocates of lesbian and gay rights and by some scientists working in the emerging research program. Arguments of this form begin with the claim that homosexuality is primarily biologically based, for example, that it has a genetic, neuroanatomical, or hormonal basis. From the claim of a biological basis to homosexuality follows the second claim that people do not choose their sexual orientations. This second claim is in turn linked to an ethical claim related to lesbian and gay ethical concerns. In its schematic form, the argument can be laid out as follows (where X is a variable for the second claim):

(1) Homosexuality is primarily biologically based.
(2x) If homosexuality is primarily biologically based, then X.
(3x) If X, then lesbians and gay men deserve rights, protection against discrimination, etc.
(4) Therefore, lesbians and gay men deserve rights, protection against discrimination, etc.

The different versions of this argument result from different ways of replacing X in the above argument scheme. Collectively, I call arguments of this form *biological arguments for lesbian and gay rights.* A particular example of this argument, which I call *the determinist version* of the biological argument for lesbian and gay rights, substitutes a claim about determinism for X as follows:

(1) Homosexuality is primarily biologically based.
(2d) If homosexuality is primarily biologically based, then people do not choose to be lesbians or gay men.
(3d) If people do not choose to be lesbians or gay men, then lesbians and gay men deserve rights, protection against discrimination, etc.
(4) Therefore, lesbians and gay men deserve rights, protection against discrimination, etc.

In this section, I consider the biological argument for lesbian and gay rights, beginning with the determinist version.

### Choice

Recall from chapter 9 that one of the reasons for being interested in whether people choose their sexual orientations is the relevance to lesbian and gay rights of voluntarism and determinism about sexual orientation (respectively, the view that people choose their sexual orientations and the view that they do not). The intuitive plausibility of the determinist argument seems based on the general principle that people should not be punished or discriminated against on grounds over which they have no control. If homosexuality has a biological basis, then sexual orientation is not a choice, in which case people should not be punished or discriminated against because they are gay men or lesbians. The determinist argument has many adherents (Bawer 1993; LeVay 1996, 231–254; Sullivan 1995). Under careful scrutiny, however, this argument proves weak.

Consider (1), the first premise of the biological argument for lesbian and gay rights, the claim that homosexuality is biologically based. In chapter 5, I explained how every psychological trait is biologically based in some sense of the term. Even a preference for classical music and a decision to eat an eclair must be biologically based in that they are based in the brain. Premise (1) must make a stronger claim, namely that a person's sexual orientation is either inborn or develops at a very early age on the basis of nonenvironmental effects (the sort of claim typically made by researchers working in the emerging research program). For reasons discussed in chapters 6 and 7, the evidence for this claim is rather weak. For purposes of this chapter, however, I want to set aside concerns about the evidence in favor of the central claims of the emerging research program and consider the ethical import of such claims if they were true. For most of the remainder of this chapter, I will assume that (1) is true. I shall argue that even granting this empirical premise, the biological argument for lesbian and gay rights is impotent.

Consider (2d), the second premise of the determinist version of the biological argument, which says that if homosexuality is primarily biologically based, then people do not choose to be lesbians or gay men. In chapter 9, I argued that the evidence and arguments for determinism about sexual orientation are not especially strong either. I suggested that nondeterminism, the view that people make indirect choices that affect their sexual orientation, was more plausible. For the sake of argument, I also want to grant the truth of (2d), that is, I assume, given the truth of the first premise, that the truth of determinism about sexual orientation follows. Even granting both the first and the second premise, I shall show that the biological argument for lesbian and gay rights is not successful.

The main problem with the determinist version of the biological argument is that its ethical implications are very limited. Even if one's sexual orientation is primarily biological and not a choice, much of what is ethically relevant about being a lesbian or a gay man is not biologically based and is not determined. These nonbiological aspects of a person's sexual orientation would not be protected by the determinist version of the biological argument. For example, even if homosexuality were genetic, engaging in sexual acts with a person of the same sex-gender, identifying as a lesbian or a gay men, and deciding to establish a household with a person of the same sex-gender are *choices*, choices that each lesbian or gay man might well not have made (for example, he or she could have decided to be celibate, closeted, and companion-less). Someone who was convinced that lesbians and gay men deserve rights only because homosexuality is biologically based and not the result of choices would allow that people can be treated differently on the basis of their choices relating to sexual desires. If, for example, I was convinced by the determinist version of the biological argument, I would think that people who had sexual desires for people of the same sex-gender should not be discriminated against *only on the basis of having these desires*. This is perfectly compatible, however, with my thinking that people who engage in sexual acts with people of the same sex-gender *are* appropriate targets of discrimination, criminal penalties, and the like. At best, then, the determinist version of the biological argument for lesbian and gay rights protects a person from being discriminated against on the basis of having a desire to have sex with people of the same sex-gender, but this is quite limited; in fact, few if any people are discriminated against simply on the basis of their underlying dispositions.

Consider, for example, the attitudes of some religious conservatives towards homosexuality. Such people claim that *being homosexual*—namely, having the desire to have sex with people of the same sex-gender—is not a sin, is not immoral, and does not warrant prejudice or discrimination. But *expressing* this desire by engaging in sex with someone of the same sex-gender, having a romantic relationship with such a person, or advocating homosexuality (perhaps by being open about one's own sexual orientation) are, on this view, morally problematic. This view about homosexuality—which is surely incompatible with any robust version of lesbian and gay rights—is compatible with the determinist argument for lesbian and gay rights.

As an analogy, consider alcoholism.[1] Suppose that a predisposition for alcoholism is primarily genetic and hence not chosen. This might establish that it is morally unacceptable to discriminate against someone with the disposition to be an alcoholic. This, however, would *not* make it morally unacceptable to discriminate against someone who is an "active" alcoholic, that is, who gets drunk on a regular basis. Regardless of the biological basis of alcoholism and the truth of determinism about alcoholism, it is morally *acceptable* to decide not to share an apartment with someone, not to hire her as a pilot, and the like because she is frequently under the influence of alcohol. The point of the analogy is that even if the *disposition* to engage in a behavior is not a choice, actually engaging in that behavior may be a choice, and thus, discrimination on the basis of whether one actually engages in such a behavior might be acceptable. Further, even if (contrary to fact) being an active alcoholic were biologically determined, it would *still* be acceptable to discriminate on the basis of being an active alcoholic. If this were the case, it would be wrong to *blame* someone for being an active alcoholic (since nothing one could do would, by stipulation, prevent one from drinking to excess), but this does not make it wrong to discriminate on that basis. Just because I cannot be blamed for a behavior does not mean that I should obtain any rights in virtue of my behavior or that it is morally wrong to discriminate against me in virtue of it. Even if an active alcoholic is not to be blamed for his condition, he does not deserve rights or protection on the mere basis of his status as an alcoholic.

The analogy to alcoholism shows two things. First, it makes clear that the absence of choice with respect to fitting into a certain category does not guarantee that people who are members of a category deserve rights and/or protection against discrimination merely on the basis of their membership in that category. This objection counts against (3d), the third premise of the determinist version of the biological argument for lesbian and gay rights. Second, the analogy makes clear why (3d) seems appealing at first glance. If one has no choice whether or not one falls into a particular human kind, then one should not be blamed for fitting that kind. Freedom from blame might entail pity and perhaps freedom from prosecution on the mere basis of membership in a kind, but it does not necessarily entail freedom from discrimination or the receipt of rights. Friends of the determinist argument for lesbian and gay rights seem to miss this point. Premise (3d) seems plausible only if one thinks that the absence of blame entails rights beyond the right not to be punished. The absence of blame does not have this implication.

The objection to the determinist version of the biological argument for lesbian and gay rights is that the lack of choice about one's sexual orientation does not in itself provide grounds for lesbian and gay rights—in other words, (3d) is false. It is false because the lack of choice about one's sexual desires fails to include much of what should be protected under the rubric of lesbian and gay rights. So, for example, even if my desire to have sex with other men was determined biologically, my decision to actually engage in sexual acts with other men would *not* be determined biologically; it would be a choice and thus would *not* be the basis for lesbian and gay rights or protection against discrimination. Further, even if, contrary to fact, all facets of being a lesbian or a gay man, such as identifying as a lesbian or gay man and engaging in sexual acts with a person of the same sex-gender, were biologically determined, this would only show that one should not be blamed for one's sexual orientation and all its facets, but this would not entail lesbian and gay rights since the lack of blame is not in itself grounds for rights. In summary, even granting its empirical premises, the determinist version of the biological argument for lesbian and gay rights fails because it does not entail lesbian and gay rights that are robust enough to be valuable; they deliver lesbian and gay rights in name alone.

### Immutability

In chapter 9, I noted that some choices are irrevocable, that is, some things that are the result of choices eventually become fixed. Even if a person's sexual orientation is the result of a direct or indirect choice, once such a choice has been made, a person's sexual orientation might be unchangeable. In fact, as I have already mentioned, regardless of whether sexual orientations result from choices, sexual orientations are basically impossible to change (Haldeman 1991, 1994; Murphy 1992; Silverstein 1991). Sexual orientations are *immutable,* that is, beyond a certain point in a person's development, a person's sexual orientation cannot be changed. Immutability is a distinct claim from determinism. Some people have suggested the immutability of sexual orientations might be relevant to ethical arguments concerning lesbians and gay men.

(1) Homosexuality is primarily biologically based.
(2i) If homosexuality is primarily biologically based, then homosexuality is immutable.
(3i) If homosexuality is immutable, then lesbian and gay men deserve rights, protection against discrimination, etc.
(4) Therefore, lesbians and gay men deserve rights, protection against discrimination, etc.

Note that the claims necessary for this argument to succeed are easier to establish (and more likely to be true) than those necessary for the determinist version of the biological argument to succeed. For the immutability version of the argument to succeed, it would be sufficient for homosexuality to be immutable and various theories *outside* the emerging research program are committed to this claim (for example, even according to early experience theories, sexual orientations are immutable; see chapters 8 and 9). Given this, the following immutability argument for lesbian and gay rights works as well as the immutability version of the biological argument:

(2i') Homosexuality is immutable.
(3i) If homosexuality is immutable, then lesbian and gay men deserve rights, protection against discrimination, etc.

(4) Therefore, lesbians and gay men deserve rights, protection against discrimination, etc.

This is not, strictly speaking, a version of the biological argument for lesbian and gay rights as I have defined it, but it is similar in structure. In fact, I shall argue that the immutability version suffers from some of the same problems as the determinist version of the biological argument for lesbian and gay rights.

Consider (3i). What is supposed to support the link between the immutability of sexual orientation and lesbian and gay rights? Presumably, the thought is roughly the same as the one behind the crucial premise of the determinist version of the biological argument: if people cannot change their sexual orientation, then it is wrong to punish them for continuing to have this sexual orientation. The problem with this, as with the determinist version of the biological argument, is that the ethical conclusions that follow from immutability are quite limited. Having sexual desires for people of the same sex-gender can plausibly be claimed to be immutable. Being sexually active with people of the same sex-gender, being in a relationship with a person of the same sex-gender, or identifying as a lesbian, gay man, or bisexual are states of affairs that are subject to change—a person can stop having certain kinds of sex, end a relationship, and go into the closet. Since these states of affairs are subject to change (that is, they are not in any way determined), they would not be protected by the immutability argument for lesbian and gay rights. In other words, it is consistent with the immutability argument for a person to be punished for having sex with people of the same sex-gender, for identifying as a lesbian or gay man, and the like.

There is an additional problem with the immutability argument for lesbian and gay rights. If someone has an immutable trait in virtue of a choice he or she made, it might still be appropriate to discriminate against or punish him or her for having that trait. It might be impossible for someone addicted to heroin to decide to stop taking it, but we might still blame that person for the decision to start using heroin in the first place. If a choice is behind someone having an immutable trait, then it might be permissible to discriminate against such a person, to punish him or her, and not to grant him or her various rights. Immutability alone does not deliver what the immutability argument for lesbian and gay rights promises; the immutability argument for lesbian and gay rights does not provide what is necessary for lesbian and gay rights worth having.

### Conclusion

Many people have claimed that scientific evidence for a genetic, hormonal, or biological basis for sexual orientation would be good news for lesbian and gay rights. Above, I have considered possible ways of connecting this biological thesis to ethical claims relating to lesbians and gay men. Even granting these empirical claims and allowing that there is a way to connect some empirical claims about homosexuality to ethical claims relating to the rights of lesbian and gay men, the sorts of ethical claims that the biological argument could support are quite weak. The biological argument for lesbian and gay rights can protect lesbians and gay men only with respect to those aspects of being lesbian or gay that are biologically determined. In other words, at best, this argument will only protect lesbians and gay men from being discriminated against in virtue of their sexual desires for people of the same sex-gender. Such protections are so minimal as to be virtually worthless.

## Immutability in Legal and United States Constitutional Arguments

Some advocates of lesbian and gay rights have articulated a version of the immutability argument in the context of the United States Constitution (Green 1988; Halley 1994; Yoshino 1996, 1998) and in international contexts (Wintemute 1995). Although this legal argument involves claims about immutability, it differs from the ethical arguments discussed in the previous section. In general, there are significant differences between legal and ethical arguments. For example, there is nothing inherently unethical about driving on the left side of the road in the United States, but it is illegal. Some things that are legally permissible are morally problematic: no law requires me to keep promises I make to my mother, but all else being equal, I should keep them. The point is that even if, as I have argued, the ethical arguments for lesbian and gay rights that involve immutability fail, the legal arguments involving immutability might succeed.

In the United States, perhaps the most promising legal argument for lesbian and gay rights involves equal protection claims. The Equal Protection Clause of the Fourteenth Amendment to the U.S. Constitution says that no state shall "deny to any person within its jurisdiction the equal protection of the laws." This passage has been interpreted to require states to articulate a rational basis to distinctions that the law makes between people. Some classifications, however, require more than mere rational justification. Classifications that are *suspect* demand heightened scrutiny, which means that a stronger justification must be given for their use. Equal protection arguments have succeeded in protecting the rights of various minority and underprivileged groups. The Supreme Court has ruled that classifications involving race, sex, gender, religious affiliation, age, disability, nationality, and ethnic status demand especially careful judicial review to determine whether there is a strong governmental interest in making use of these classifications. If the Court ruled that sexual orientation was a suspect classification, then lesbians and gay men would have a much stronger claim for positive rights and for protections against discrimination.*

The Supreme Court has not, however, ruled on whether sexual-orientation classifications are suspect (Eskridge and Hunter 1997, xlv–il, 92–132).† The Court has, however, articulated some factors that should be considered in assessing when more than a rational basis is required to evaluate the constitutionality of a statute that invokes a classification. These factors include whether the classification has historically been used to intentionally discriminate against a particular group (*Frontiero v. Richardson* 1972); whether the use of this classification bears any "relation to ability to perform or contribute to society" (686); whether any groups demarcated by this classification lack the political power to combat the discrimination (*Cleburne v. Cleburne Living Center* 1985, 441); and whether groups demarcated by this classification exhibit obvious, immutable, or distinguishing characteristics that define them as a discrete and insular group (*Bowen v. Gilliard* 1987, 602). The importance of immutability in determining whether a classification is suspect is unclear (Yoshino 1998). The Supreme Court has, on some occasions, discussed heightened scrutiny without mentioning immutability (*Cleburne v. Cleburne Living Center* 1985, 440–441; *Massachusetts Board of Retirement v. Murgia* 1976, 313; *Plyler v. Doe* 1982, 218–223).

Interestingly, in its most recent decision relating directly to lesbian and gay rights, the Supreme Court overturned an amendment to Colorado's constitution that restricted the rights of lesbians, gay men, and bisexuals (*Romer v. Evans* 1996). The Court held that the Colorado amendment violated the Equal Protection Clause, but it reached its conclusion *without* employing heightened scrutiny, at least not in a technical sense. The amendment at issue precluded state and local legislative, executive, and judicial action protecting homosexual and/or bisexual orientation, conduct, practices, and relationships. The Court found that this amendment violated the Equal Protection Clause

---

*For simplicity, I am here glossing over the distinction between strict scrutiny (which the Court applies, for example, to racial classifications) and intermediate scrutiny (which the Court applies, for example, to gender classifications) (Eskridge and Hunter 1997, xlvii–xlviii and 73–92).

†At least one federal appeals court has held that sexual orientation plausibly satisfies all of these criteria (*Watkins v. United States Army* 1988), but one court has also refused to grant heightened scrutiny on the grounds that sexual orientation is not immutable (*High Tech Gays v. Defense Industrial Security Clearance Office* 1990).

because it failed to bear any rational relation to a legitimate state interest (631–636). The Court did not address the question of whether sexual-orientation classifications warrant heightened scrutiny because it found the amendment failed to pass constitutional muster even on the more lenient standard of rational review. For my purposes, it is interesting to note that in *Romer* the immutability of sexual orientations had nothing to do with the court's decision about the rights of lesbians and gay men.

Some people have argued that establishing a genetic or neurological basis for homosexuality would prove that sexual orientations are immutable and thereby entail that sexual orientations should be a suspect classification and deserving of heightened scrutiny (for example, LeVay 1996, 231–254). However, the scientific evidence is, as I argued in earlier chapters, far from conclusive. The evidence that sexual orientations are immutable is stronger, especially since it is possible to show that a trait is immutable without showing that it has a genetic, neuroanatomical, or hormonal basis; psychological studies might be all that is needed (Haldeman 1991, 1994; Silverstein 1991). Generally speaking, however, even assuming that sexual orientations are immutable, lesbians and gay men deserve protection against discrimination and positive rights with respect to their *actions* and *decisions* rather than for their mere orientations. It is when they engage in same sex-gender sexual acts, identify as gay men and lesbians, and create lesbian and gay families that they especially need protections for and rights based on choices that build on their underlying (and perhaps immutable) desires (Stein 1994).

This problem with the legal argument based on immutability can be seen in the contentious issue of whether lesbians and gay men can openly serve in the United States Armed Forces. Soon after he was sworn into office, President Bill Clinton announced that he would ask the secretary of defense to draft an executive order that would end the practice of excluding homosexuals from serving in the military "solely on the basis of status," that is, solely on the basis of their sexual orientation. Several months later, after much public and congressional debate, a new law, the *Policy Concerning Homosexuality in the Armed Forces,* dubbed "Don't Ask, Don't Tell, Don't Pursue," became law (1994). Under this law and the Defense Department directive that implements it (Defense Department 1993), a service member may be discharged from the armed forces if he or she states that "he or she is homosexual or bisexual" (H.1.b.[2]), if he or she holds hands or engages in any other bodily contact with a person of the same sex that "demonstrates a propensity or intent to engage in sexual contact" (1994, [f][3][B]), or "attempt[s] to marry a person known to be of the same biological sex" (1994 [b][3]). Even though the policy, as interpreted by some of its defenders, protects lesbians and gay men from being discriminated against in virtue of their sexual desires for people of the same sex-gender, they can be discharged for any public expression of their sexual orientations, any evidence of romantic relationships with people of the same sex-gender, and any form of remotely intimate physical contact with people of the same sex-gender. The Don't Ask, Don't Tell, Don't Pursue law, as it is implemented and enforced, fails to protect lesbians and gay men from discrimination or to give them rights. This exemplifies the sort of laws that we can expect to see implemented in the face of the legal version of the immutability argument for lesbian and gay rights. Such laws protect people for merely having a sexual orientation, but not for any behavior that might result from such desires (Halley 1996, 1999).

The legal argument for lesbian and gay rights that involves immutability claims faces roughly the same problems as the ethical argument for lesbian and gay rights that involves immutability claims. Lesbian and gay rights built on immutability would not provide lesbians and gay men with basic rights and privileges. Further, the argument rests on the unclear question of whether the Supreme Court would hold that immutability is necessary for sexual orientations to count as suspect classifications; an argument for lesbian and gay rights would be stronger if it did not rest on either shaky constitutional theory or weak empirical claims (Halley 1996, 1999).

## Naturalness

Another strategy for using biological research to support ethical conclusions involves trying to show that sexual activities with and sexual desires for people of the same sex-gender are "natural." Many people claim that certain sexual desires or acts are unnatural (or "perverted"). The term "natural" gets used in various and contradictory ways, and which acts and desires are seen as unnatural change over time and in various cultures. Think about it for a moment. What do you think makes a trait, a behavior, or a desire unnatural? What do you think makes a *sexual* behavior or desire unnatural? In general, it is not at all clear if the claim that a sexual behavior is unnatural means anything more than the claim that certain people think that such a behavior is unappealing.[2] Turning to same sex-gender sexual activities and desires, when people say that homosexuality is unnatural, which they still say today, they mean various things. In this section, I focus on attempts to show that homosexuality is *natural* that appeal to scientific theories of how sexual orientations develop.[3]

### *Animal Homosexuality Revisited*

Although Plato's *Symposium* presents sexual desire among people of the same sex-gender in a positive light (see chapter 4), in some of his other dialogues, Plato is less sympathetic. In the *Laws* (Plato 1934, 840d–e), he argues in favor of prohibiting sexual activity among people of the same sex-gender. In the context of discussing such prohibitions, he said that citizens should not "behave worse than birds and many other creatures." Birds, he says, "live in continence and unspotted virginity" until "the age of procreation" whereupon "they pair together, the male with the female and the female with the male . . . and they live thereafter in piety and justice, steadfastly true to their contract of first love." (Obviously Plato had not heard about the lesbian seagulls discussed in chapter 6.) Humans, according to Plato, ought to follow the example of the birds and avoid sexual activity with people of the same sex-gender. Homo-sexual behavior, on this view, is unnatural. The unnaturalness of homosexuality suggests, Plato argued, that there should be laws against sexual activity among people of the same sex-gender. The general idea behind Plato's argument can be laid out as follows:

(P1) Nonhuman animals do not engage in same-sex sexual activity.
(P2) Therefore, such sexual activity is unnatural for humans.
(P3) Therefore, there should be laws against such sexual activity.

This argument is not exclusive to Plato; many subscribe to this sort of argument today. For example, Anita Bryant—orange-juice spokesperson and outspoken opponent of lesbian and gay rights—made roughly this argument in an interview with *Playboy* magazine in the late 1970s: "Homosexuality is a perversion of a very natural thing . . . it is a sin and very unnatural . . . [and] even barnyard animals don't do what homosexuals do" (Kelley 1978, 82).

Scientific research might be relevant to ethical claims regarding sexual orientation insofar as it could show that the argument made by Plato, Bryant, and others fails because there are animals that engage in same-sex sexual activity. Studies show that animals do engage in sexual activities with members of the same sex (see chapter 6). Further, people who want to use scientific research to make the case for lesbian and gay rights might—by turning the general form of the Plato-Bryant argument on its head—use the existence of same-sex sexual activity in animals to try to prove that homosexuality is natural. They might argue as follows:

(N1)  Nonhuman animals engage in same-sex sexual activity.

(N2)  Therefore, such sexual activity is natural for humans.

(N3)  Therefore, such sexual activity should be legal, lesbian and gay rights should be granted, and so on.

Scientific research on sexual orientation might be used to show that homosexuality occurs among animals (and that [P1] is false but [N1] is true). For example, the existence of lesbian seagulls could prove the existence of same-sex sexual activities among animals. This was probably LeVay's motivation when he took his students south in search of lesbian seagulls (see chapter 6).

In chapter 6, I developed a line of reasoning that accepted the existence of same-sex sexual activity among animals, but argued that there is no *homosexuality* among animals because sexual orientations involve a complex array of cognitive functions that nonhuman animals lack. Plato and Bryant might try to make use of this line of reasoning by modifying (P1) as follows:

(P1')  Nonhuman animals do not engage in *homosexual* sexual activity.

The idea is that although nonhuman animals might engage in physical activities such as genital contact between males or females, such activities do not constitute homosexual acts because homosexual acts require certain sorts of psychological dispositions that involve cognitive abilities that nonhuman animals lack.

The problem is that this line of argument shows that *hetero*sexuality does not exist among nonhuman animals either (because they lack the relevant cognitive functions for heterosexuality as well). Using (P1') together with (P2) and (P3) to argue that there should be laws against homosexual behavior proves too much. We have exactly the same reasons for believing that nonhuman animals do not engage in *heterosexual* sexual activity (understood as involving cognitively mediated sexual activity) as we do for believing that they do not engage in homosexual activity (again understood as involving cognitively mediated sexual activity). The Plato-Bryant argument thus fails. Premise (P1), which talks about same-sex sexual activity, is false. If the argument is modified by replacing (P1) with (P1'), which implicitly talks about complex psychological properties, then the argument fails to distinguish homosexuality from heterosexuality, which was the point of the argument in the first place.

The Plato-Bryant argument has much in common with the argument for lesbian and gay rights based on the naturalness of homosexuality. Both arguments try to connect the existence or nonexistence of same-sex sexual activity in animals to the naturalness of such behavior in humans. There are, however, many behaviors that animals engage in that are wrong for humans, and there are many behaviors that animals do not in engage in that humans do. For example, some nonhuman animals eat members of their own species and some kill animals of other species in especially painful and gruesome ways; in general, nonhumans do many things that we think are not natural or morally acceptable for humans. On the other hand, nonhuman animals do not, for example, communicate in complex languages, while humans do, yet we think it is natural for humans to use language. Neither the Plato-Bryant argument nor the biological argument for the naturalness of homosexuality provides any reason for connecting the behaviors of animals with the naturalness of behaviors in humans. Research on the sexual desires and behaviors of animals may be relevant to understanding human sexual orientation (see chapter 6 for discussion), but such research is not relevant to ethical issues concerning human sexual orientations and behaviors.

### Other Biological Arguments about the Naturalness of Homosexuality

People have tried to make other ethical arguments that appeal to scientific claims about humans to show that homosexuality is either natural or unnatural. For example, one might try to argue that if homosexuality is natural, then lesbians and gay men deserve rights, or one might try to argue that the existence of homosexuality in animals shows that humans should *not* engage in homosexuality. Anita Bryant seemed to embrace this sort of argument when her interviewer told her that nonhuman animals do engage in homosexuality; abandoning her own argument made moments earlier, she said that the existence of animal homosexuality "doesn't make it right" (Kelley 1978, 82).

There are several general problems with these sorts of arguments (Mohr 1990, 21–45; Murphy 1997, 165–192; Ruse 1988, 176–202; Stein 1994). Arguments that try to show that homosexuality is unnatural typically prove too much (that is, if such arguments are successful, then some other arguments that have highly counterintuitive conclusions will also be successful) because they apply to a whole range of behaviors that almost everyone finds natural (for example, celibacy, masturbation, contraceptive sex, and skiing). Further, even if there is a sense in which sexual desires for and sexual activities with people of the same sex-gender are unnatural, it is not clear what, if anything, would follow from this ethically or legally. It is not at all clear why unnaturalness entails immorality. Air travel for humans might be unnatural (in some senses of the term), but it does not follow from this that air travel is immoral, unethical, or illegal.

More generally, empirical facts alone cannot entail moral and ethical conclusions. Attempts to derive ethical conclusions from empirical facts are, in general, referred to as committing the *naturalistic fallacy* (Moore 1903). A person commits the naturalistic fallacy if he tries to derive an "ought" claim (a *normative* claim, that is, a claim about how humans ought to act) from an "is" claim (a claim about how things are). It is a mistake to derive ethical principles (which say how we *ought* to act) from empirical claims (which say how the world *is* and how we are constituted). Just because, for example, humans have teeth that were selected for and are capable of ripping flesh does not mean that we should in fact use our teeth to rip flesh. Moral arguments might show that we should not eat meat. The empirical facts about our teeth and their evolutionary function would not count against such arguments. In general, normative concepts (such as it is wrong to cause unnecessary pain and suffering) cannot be the subject of empirical inquiry.[4] In particular, ethical questions concerning sexual orientation will not be settled by empirical facts about sexual orientation.

This is not to say that empirical considerations are never relevant to ethical and political issues. Science has some bearing on certain legal, ethical, political, and philosophical questions. For example, if you have the view that it is wrong to cause wanton pain and suffering to any animal that can feel pain and be conscious of it, then the empirical discovery that pigs feel pain and are conscious of it would be relevant to the issue of whether the factory farming of pigs is morally acceptable. However, the empirical facts do not determine whether, for example, the view that it is wrong to cause unnecessary pain and suffering is correct. In the particular case of the ethical, political, legal, and philosophical questions associated with lesbian and gay rights, the evidence for scientific explanations of why people have the sexual orientations and desires they do is not especially relevant, although empirical evidence may be of interest to some of the political goals of many lesbians, gay men, and their political allies. Showing that sexual orientations are determined at birth, for example, might help to convince people that it is perfectly acceptable for lesbians and gay men to teach elementary school. Or showing that determinism about sexual orientation is true might convince people of the futility of attempting to change queer people's sexual orientations (Pillard 1997). I do not mean to trivialize these possibilities and the extent to which they might be able to help forward parts of a gay-positive political agenda; nevertheless, in chapter 12, I will express some skepticism about the relevance of scientific research on sexual orientation to even these limited political goals. The arguments I have made in this chapter provide good reason to think that there are no empirical arguments for lesbian and gay rights that are both general and strong.

## Why Pragmatic Arguments Are Not Pragmatic

Various opinion polls have shown that people who think that homosexuality is biologically based or that people do not choose their sexual orientations are more likely to favor lesbian and gay rights than those who do not (Aguero, Bloch, and Byrne 1984; Ernulf, Innala, and Whitam 1989; Piskur and Delegman 1992; Whitley 1990). In the previous sections, I have shown that the conceptual connection between scientific research on sexual orientation and ethical/legal claims is, at best, weak. Despite this, some advocates of lesbian and gay rights claim that the biological argument for lesbian and gay rights should still be embraced because it persuades people (LeVay 1996, 1–9). The idea is a *pragmatic* one: whatever their strength, make the arguments that persuade people to support lesbian and gay rights.

Unfortunately, this pragmatic approach is not promising. Linking lesbian and gay rights to biology seems a bad strategy even on pragmatic grounds. To begin, the attempt to link the rights of homosexuals to a presumed biological cause is not new. There is historical evidence for doubting the efficacy of such an argument, which will be considered more fully in chapter 12, when I discuss the history of how scientific research on sexual orientation has been used. In Nazi Germany, for example, Magnus Hirschfeld attempted to gain legal protections for homosexuals on the grounds that they constituted a third sex. Hirschfeld's belief in a strong biological basis for sexual orientation led him to lobby for lesbian and gay rights, but it also led him to refer at least three or four homosexual men for surgery to reduce their "homosexual inclinations" (Herrn 1995). Prior to his death, Hirshfeld conceded that not only had he failed to prove his biological thesis, but that he had unwittingly contributed to the persecution of homosexuals by stigmatizing them as biologically defective. (He presumably had in mind the fact that lesbians, gay men, and other sexual minorities were imprisoned, castrated, mutilated in other ways, and sent to death camps to remove them from the breeding stock.) Note that the Nazis espoused experiential theories about homosexuality at the same time. Thus, homosexuals were imprisoned and sent to death camps to prevent "contamination" of the German youth by exposure to adult homosexuals (Plant 1986). The example of Germany shows that seeing sexual orientation as biologically based in no way guarantees a positive result for lesbians and gay men.

Further, even if belief in a biological basis for homosexuality would persuade people to favor lesbian and gay rights in the short run, it might at the same time spark calls for genetic engineering to prevent homosexuality and for the development of amniocentesis techniques for the detection of homosexuality so as to enable the abortion of fetuses with the strongest potential to develop into homosexuals. (For a detailed discussion of this possibility, see chapter 11.) Many biologically based characteristics (including even being female; chapter 11 also discusses female infanticide and similar practices) are viewed as undesirable, shameful, and so on.

Also, it is a risky strategy to link lesbian and gay rights to the ups and downs of scientific research, especially since, as I have argued in chapters 6 and 7, such research is, at best, in its early stages. Biological research into sexual orientation has a poor track record when it comes to reliability (Byne 1995); what appear to be valid results today could turn out to be mistaken. Making lesbian and gay rights contingent on a particular scientific finding is simply too risky. That people are persuaded by biological arguments for lesbian and gay rights may suggest a public relations strategy that will be successful in the short term, but it does not suggest a strategy suited to grounding a set of rights that are deeply important and that profoundly impact the lives of many people. Biological sophistry is still sophistry.

As an example of the risks of connecting particular scientific and/or empirical theories with lesbian and gay politics, consider the relationship of the lesbian and gay movement in America to psychiatry (Bayer 1987). In the pre-Stonewall stage of the gay rights movement (from World War II to the late 1960s), many lesbian and gay rights activists embraced psychiatry and its language, partly on political grounds. The idea was that psychiatry could help legitimate lesbians and gay men and their organizations (D'Emilio 1983, 116–117). But as the gay movement grew, it began to question psychiatry, ultimately protesting against the American Psychiatric Association's classification of homosexuality as a psychological disorder. This example shows that science and medicine are tricky ethical and political weapons; at best, they are double-edged swords.

This pragmatic argument for lesbian and gay rights is committed to a picture of science that is potentially self-undermining. Advocates of this argument defend a particular scientific theory only because of its political effects. But if it becomes known that this is the justification for favoring one scientific theory over another, the persuasiveness of scientific theories in general—and with it, the persuasiveness of the pragmatic argument itself—will be undermined. In other words, pragmatic arguments that appeal to science depend on the distinction between science and propaganda; but pragmatic arguments, if widespread, would erase this distinction.

Further, it is not clear that the pragmatic argument for lesbian and gay rights will be successful. The genetic basis of skin pigmentation, for example, does not seem to have a mitigating influence on racism. With respect to sexual orientation—as the example of attitudes towards homosexuality in Germany suggests, and as I will discuss further in chapter 12—history suggests that, in the absence of social tolerance, any theory of the origins of sexual orientation may be turned against lesbians and gay men.

In sum, the pragmatic argument for lesbian and gay rights does not fare any better than its nonpragmatic counterparts. Scientific research concerning sexual orientation is for the most part irrelevant to lesbian and gay rights. Attempts to link the science of sexual orientation to the case for lesbian and gay rights are misguided. The question remains why lesbians and gay men should have to appeal to science in the first place. Questions about origins, choice, and immutability are selectively applied to homosexuals and not to other marginalized groups. For example, members of religious minorities are not asked to demonstrate that either their religious affiliation or their religious practices are biologically based, innate, or immutable. Despite the facts that a person's religious affiliation is not genetic and that a person can convert from one religion to another, most modern democracies protect religious liberty.[5] That issues of origins, choice, immutability, and the like are applied selectively to lesbians and gay men suggests that implicit in the immutability argument is the view that homosexuality needs explaining, that the choices of lesbians and gay men are not respected and not valued. I return to these issues in the concluding chapter. The same concerns arise with attempts to link more specific political aims to scientific research. Lesbians and gay men should be able to teach elementary school *even if* sexual orientation is not determined before puberty.

## Implications of Essentialism and Constructionism

Some people have argued that the debate between essentialism and constructionism has ethical and political implications (Epstein 1992; Fuss 1989). Some essentialists have suggested that the gay and lesbian community will be hurt and the case for lesbian and gay rights undermined if the commonsense categories of sexual orientations are not natural human kinds (Boswell 1989). On the other hand, some constructionists have suggested that essentialism has negative ethical implications because, for example, the truth of essentialism, since it undergirds the categories of heterosexuality and homosexuality, is in tension with sexual liberation, which involves getting beyond these categories. If either of these connections follow, and given my conclusion (see chapters 4, 5, and 8) that whether or not sexual orientations are natural human kinds is an empirical question to which scientific research on sexual orientation may make some contribution, then *empirical* issues might still be relevant to *ethical* questions related to sexual orientations. The attempt to connect either essentialism or constructionism to ethical ramifications fails. A group does not have to be a natural human kind to deserve or to be granted rights or to be protected against discrimination. For example, most classifications (such as race, illegitimacy, and national origin) that are given heightened scrutiny under the Supreme Court's understanding of the Fourteenth Amendment are social human kinds, not natural human kinds. As with the other empirical questions relating to sexual orientations that I have discussed previously, the debate between essentialists and constructionists is not relevant to ethical questions related to sexual orientations.

## Conclusion

The political, legal, and social situation for lesbians and gay men around the world, though better than forty years ago, remains problematic. Lesbian and gay men are subject to social disapprobation and, legally, are treated as second-class citizens. Although various people have argued that scientific research on sexual orientation will help to improve this situation, I have shown that scientific evidence has little to contribute to ethical arguments relating to lesbians and gay men. Biological arguments for lesbian and gay rights fail theoretically, legally, and pragmatically. In order to make the case for lesbian and gay rights, strong ethical, legal, and political arguments are needed. The results of scientific research are basically irrelevant to such arguments.

Consider, for example, the sorts of arguments that get made for equal rights for racial or religious minorities. Rather than appealing to any facts about the constitution of these types of people, these arguments appeal to justice, rights, privacy, equality, and liberty. The arguments are ethical and/or political in nature. The same is true of arguments for lesbian and gay rights; for protection for lesbians and gay men against discrimination; for respect for lesbian and gay relationships, organizations, families, and communities. These issues are ethical and political in nature, and arguments for them should be cast in terms of justice, rights, privacy, equality, and liberty. On any plausible theory of how we develop sexual orientations, lesbians, gay men, and bisexuals deserve positive rights, as well as full protection against discrimination.

# CHAPTER **11**

# Selecting and Changing the Sexual Orientation of Children

**A**s the emerging scientific research program concerning sexual orientation has garnered mainstream attention, some commentators have begun to worry (Hamer et al. 1993, 326; Knox 1993; Murphy 1990), and other commentators have begun to hope (Burr 1996b), that prospective parents in the future will be able to determine the sexual orientation of a child by using an amniocentesis or some other genetic screening technique and, further, that they will abort or in some other way prevent the birth of the fetus if the parents believe that the resulting child would not be heterosexual. This seems a live possibility since parents worldwide sometimes choose to abort a fetus (or to kill an infant) if it is not of the sex-gender they desire. Given the widespread hatred of and prejudice and discrimination against lesbians, gay men, and bisexuals (surveyed in chapter 10) and the connections people make between sex-gender and sexual orientation, it seems quite likely that, if technology permits, abortions and other procedures will be used to select the sexual orientation of children. In this chapter, I explore ethical and legal questions surrounding such selection procedures. I also consider the ethical and legal questions surrounding postnatal techniques for ensuring heterosexuality.

Ethical concerns aside, it is unlikely, especially in light of the considerations developed in chapter 7, that *successful* techniques for selecting the sexual orientation of children—what I call *orientation-selection* procedures—will be developed. Whether or not this is true, there are interesting and important ethical questions surrounding such procedures because people might make use of them even if they did not work. This is partly because, for various reasons, it will be difficult for people who are considering making use of orientation-selection procedures to determine whether such procedures work. Let me explain why.

Many children turn out to be heterosexual even without the use of such procedures. Because of this, many parents who attempt orientation selection will believe that the procedure has worked on their child, even though the procedure did nothing since their child would have been heterosexual in any event. Further, most people take a while to come to grips with their own sexual orientation. Parents who make use of an orientation-selection procedure might think that it had been successful, but only because their child had not yet figured out his or her sexual orientation. Also, because many lesbians, gay men, and bisexuals hide their sexual orientation once they figure it out, many parents will think that their attempt at orientation selection has worked when it has not. If a lesbian, gay man, or bisexual knows that his or her parents used an orientation-selection procedure to ensure that he or she would be a heterosexual, this would just increase the likelihood that a person would hide his or her sexual orientation from them. For these reasons, even if available orientation-selection procedures fail to work, such procedures are likely to *appear* to work.

Orientation-selection procedures are more likely to appear to work to people who believe that homosexuality is genetic. If the particular genetic configuration or set of configurations that they believe to be responsible for homosexuality is identifiable (or at least is claimed to be) in fetuses, sperm, or eggs, the chances that homosexuality will appear genetic will increase further. Given current trends in social attitudes about these questions—the percentage of people who think that sexual orientation is something a person is born with has more than doubled between 1977 and 1998 (Berke 1998)—and trends in scientific research as described in chapter 5, it seems likely that many people will believe that some set of genes directly determines sexual orientation and that scientists will be able to determine whether a fetus has the genes that are believed to be responsible for sexual orientation. This is perfectly compatible with the scientific studies of sexual orientation being deeply flawed in any number of ways. Gay men and lesbians have been and continue to be subject to various forms of medical and psychological interventions for which no evidence of effectiveness exists (Haldeman 1991, 1994; Irvine 1990; Katz 1976; Murphy 1992; Silverstein 1991; Somerville 1994). For example, gay men were injected with testosterone with the aim of turning them into heterosexuals despite studies showing no correlation between sexual orientation and testosterone levels (Meyer-Bahlburg 1984). The general point is that although doubts about the scientific research, such as those discussed in chapters 6 and 7, are well-founded, there is every reason to believe that people will believe such studies anyway. The result could well be the widespread selection (using techniques that may or may not involve abortion) against fetuses thought to be carrying genes for homosexuality or bisexuality. This shows that ethical questions about orientation-selection procedures remain even if such procedures fail to work; in such a case, people are still likely to make use of them.

Similar sorts of ethical problems arise if it is possible—or if people think that it is possible—to use psychological procedures to change the sexual orientation of a child after he or she is born. In fact, many parents currently attempt to use psychological treatments, religious counseling, and other procedures to change the sexual orientation of children they believe might not be heterosexual. Towards the end of this chapter, I discuss the ethical implications of these postnatal techniques, sometimes called *conversion therapies,* to change the sexual orientation of children.

There have been extensive philosophical, legal, and popular discussions of the morality of abortion (for example, Kamm 1992; Steinbock 1992; Tooley 1983) and genetic engineering (British Medical Association 1995; Fenwick 1998; Kaplan and Tong 1994; Purdy 1996) and less extensive discussions concerning ethical issues surrounding techniques to select the sex of children (Asch and Geller 1996; Overall 1987; Warren 1985; Wertz and Fletcher 1992). I do not attempt to deal with these issues in general, although I touch on them in what follows. Given the possibility of developing orientation-selection procedures that do *not* involve abortion, I can discuss the ethical issues surrounding orientation selection without taking a stand on the general morality of abortion (I make this case later in this chapter). With respect to genetic engineering, I will assume that it is morally acceptable for parents to try to control *some* genetic traits of their offspring. This assumption seems justified given the possibility of controlling the genetic traits of offspring without abortions or the direct altering of human genes. I discuss *sex*-selection procedures (that is, techniques to select the sex of children) primarily as an analogy for orientation selection.

## Genetic Screening and Fetal Selection

There are various ways that a pregnant woman can get information about the fetus she is carrying. An amniocentesis is a diagnostic medical procedure whereby a needle is inserted into the uterus of a pregnant woman to obtain some of the fluid that surrounds a fetus in the uterus. This fluid contains some cells that can be grown in a culture in a laboratory to detect various chromo-somal or metabolic abnormalities in the fetus, including Tay-Sachs disease and Down's syndrome, two particularly serious conditions. An amniocentesis also enables the determination of the chromosomal sex of the fetus, usually either XX (female) or XY (male). Currently, because performing an amniocentesis involves a small risk to the mother and the fetus, the procedure is typically performed only when there is a particular risk of chromosomal abnormality, either because of a family history of genetic diseases or because the mother is over the age of thirty-five. Because an amniocentesis must be performed when the woman is at least fourteen weeks pregnant and because it takes a while for the relevant cells to develop in the lab, an abortion that follows an amniocentesis must occur during the second trimester of pregnancy, when abortions are more difficult and riskier than those performed during the first trimester. Other diagnostic medical procedures such as chorionic villus sampling (CVS) and maternal serum alpha-fetoprotein testing (MSAFP) make it possible to gather information about the genetic makeup of a fetus (Kurjack and Chervenak 1994).

At present, the primary means for selecting a fetus on the basis of its traits is abortion; if a fetus has a trait that a mother finds undesirable, then she can choose to abort it. For example, when a screening procedure indicates that her child will be born with a serious genetic disorder, most mothers opt for an abortion.[1] There are, however, other ways to select for a fetus. One possibility is to extract several eggs from the potential mother, fertilize each egg with sperm in a laboratory, examine the genetic composition of each fertilized egg, and implant in the woman's uterus a fertilized egg with the potential to produce a child with the desired traits (Robertson 1995, 154–156). Another possibility is to filter out sperm that carry certain undesired genes. One technique is to sepa-rate sperm carrying X chromosomes (a fetus that results from an egg fertilized by such sperm will be female) from sperm carrying Y chromosomes (such a fetus will be male), artificially inseminate an egg with the sperm of the desired type, and then implant the fertilized egg into a uterus (Corea 1985, 198–201; Kolata 1998; Raymond 1993, 21–22). Another technique with similar effects, which is at present science fiction, would involve a diaphragm-like filter that would block out certain types of sperm: if the parents desired a son rather than a daughter, they might use a "blue diaphragm" that allows only sperm carrying Y chromosomes a chance to fertilize the egg (Warren 1985, 11–12). Tech-niques might be developed to screen out sperm carrying genes that code for other undesired traits. A final possibility, also unrealized at present despite recent technological advances, involves cloning: one could control the genetic makeup of an offspring that is an exact genetic copy of a person (Nussbaum and Sunstein 1998).

Orientation-selection techniques could potentially be developed using any one of these techniques for selecting a fetus. To be successful, all of them would require the discovery of a genetic basis for homosexuality or at least of a gene sequence that is likely to lead to homosexuality. As I argued in chapters 6 and 7, there is no convincing evidence for a genetic basis to homosexuality. But even if there were, it is not clear that genetic-engineering techniques would be successful in allowing people to insure heterosexuality. Take cloning as an example. Of the possible reproductive techniques for ensuring heterosexuality, cloning a heterosexual seems the most promising. If any reproductive procedure could guarantee success, it seems this one could because a person and his or her clone are genetically identical. Cloning does not, however, guarantee that a person and his or her clone will share all the same psychological traits or even the same physical traits. As I have mentioned several times in previous chapters, any plausible view of human nature, even one that is committed to genetic determinism, must acknowledge that a person's physical and psychological characteristics are not simply read off of one's genes. Genes in themselves cannot directly specify any behavior or psychological phenomenon. Instead, genes direct patterns of RNA synthesis, which in turn specify the production of proteins, which in turn may influence the development of psychological characteristics, which in turn undergird behaviors. At every step of this process between genes and psychological properties or behaviors, nongenetic factors play a role. A person's development is significantly affected by a wide range of nongenetic factors, for example, prenatal hormone levels and diet during puberty. Due to the panoply of developmental factors, it is possible for genetically identical individuals to have different sexual orientations.

Concrete evidence of this can be found by looking at twin studies of sexual orientation. As I have repeatedly observed, the most interesting and consistent finding of recent twin studies is that at least half of the pairs of identical twins in the studies are discordant for sexual orientation. This is the case even though the identical twins in these studies shared *all* of their genes and *most* environmental factors. As I discussed in chapters 5 and 7, it is not clear how to use twin studies to disentangle the genetic and environmental influences that operate on the sexual orientation of identical twins. Genetic factors no doubt play *some* role in shaping a person's sexual orientation (as I mentioned many times before, the role that they play is similar to the role that genetic factors play in shaping a person's dietary and religious preferences), but how much of a role they play and how the role is mediated are far from clear. The consequence for cloning and other genetic technologies that might hope to guarantee heterosexual children is that no such technique can ensure success. Despite this, for reasons I have already articulated, some people are still very likely to make use of orientation-selection techniques, even if they do not in fact work.

## Possible Arguments in Favor
## of Orientation Selection

There are various reasons for thinking that it is morally acceptable to use orientation-selection procedures and that such procedures should be legal. People who think that homosexuality is unnatural, a disease, or immoral are likely, all else being equal, to look favorably on orientation-selection procedures. One does not, however, have to accept any of these views in order to think that orientation-selection procedures are morally permissible and/or should be legal. For example, one might believe that, regardless of their effects, orientation-selection procedures, like most other reproductive technologies, are morally permissible and should be legal. Further, having a negative view of homosexuality does not entail a positive view of orientation-selection procedures (although, all else being equal, people who think that homosexuality is a disease or a moral failing are likely to think that it is acceptable to use orientation-selection procedures to avoid having lesbian or gay offspring). A particular view of homosexuality is neither a necessary nor a sufficient condition for thinking that orientation-selection procedures are moral and should be legal.

The most general arguments that screening and selecting a fetus of a particular sexual orientation is morally acceptable and should be legal has to do with reproductive liberty and the right of a woman to have control over her body and its procreative capacities; simply put, a woman should be able to decide whether or not to have children. The U.S. Supreme Court (*Roe v. Wade* 1973) ruled that, regardless of the reason she has for wanting to terminate her pregnancy, the government cannot prevent a woman from having an abortion during the first trimester of her pregnancy and that, although states may in various ways regulate licensing and related medical procedures involved in second-trimester abortions, a women's motives for an abortion are not relevant to these regulations. Most people who favor a woman's right to choose whether or not to get pregnant and whether or not to terminate her pregnancy would agree that the state should not be involved in evaluating the reasons a woman has for terminating a pregnancy. If one accepts that women have a legal right to choose whether or not to terminate a pregnancy, then it seems to follow that it should be legal to terminate a pregnancy because of the sexual orientation of the fetus. Similarly, given that it is legal for a woman to use contraceptive devices, then it should be legal to use filtering devices to select for sperm with genes that code for a particular sexual orientation. The legal permissibility of orientation selection seems to follow directly from the view that women have reproductive liberty.

Not every act that is legal is morally permissible and/or morally praiseworthy. Even if orientation-selection procedures should be legal, it does not follow that people should make use of them. For example, while it might be legal for a woman to terminate a first-trimester pregnancy simply because she believes that being pregnant will interfere with a planned trip to the beach, this might be a poor reason to terminate a pregnancy. Arguing that orientation-selection abortion is morally acceptable requires more than the argument that it should be legal for women to make use of such a procedure.

One argument for the moral acceptability of orientation-selection procedures stems from the view that reproductive liberty entails the right to ensure that one's offspring will have desirable traits. It is both reasonable and permissible to want a healthy baby (Robertson 1995). It follows that it is morally permissible for a woman to choose to terminate a pregnancy if the fetus has a serious genetic disorder. Perhaps because of moral concerns about abortion, many of those who do not think this is permissible will allow that *preimplantation* procedures (genetic screening procedures that take place *before* a fertilized egg is implanted in the womb)[2] to prevent the birth of such a baby are permissible. Behind this is the view that parents can engage in "quality control" (10) with respect to their (potential) offspring. If it is permissible to engage in some selection procedures to ensure that an offspring has certain desirable traits, then it follows that it is permissible to engage in some selection procedures to ensure that an offspring does not have certain undesirable traits. This view is particularly plausible if one were to focus on *pre*implantation selection procedures.

Even those who think that all or most abortions are immoral and/or should be illegal will allow that women have *some* reproductive liberty; they just think that the rights entailed by reproductive liberty are trumped by the rights of the fetus. The relevant question is whether the arguments against orientation-selection abortion are strong enough to trump reproductive liberty with respect to the quality control of one's offspring. With respect to preimplantation orientation-selection procedures, the question is whether there are any factors about these procedures that suggest women's reproductive liberties ought to be trumped. To answer these questions, I turn now to arguments against orientation selection; first, I look at arguments against orientation-selection abortion specifically, and then, I look at arguments against orientation-selection procedures in general.

## Arguments Against Orientation-Selection Abortion

Perhaps the most obvious arguments against orientation selection focus on orientation-selection abortion and appeal to the wrongness of abortion, either in general or in cases where the decision to abort is based on "trivial" reasons. Arguments against orientation-selection abortion that turn on the supposed wrongness of abortion in general focus on the wrong to the fetus, namely, wrongfully killing it. These arguments do not typically count against orientation selection in general; in particular, they would not count against preimplantation selection procedures.[3]

Few foes of abortion are, however, unequivocally opposed to the practice; many allow for abortions in the case of rape, incest, serious health risks to the mother, or severe fetal defects. Given that they are willing to allow some abortions, such foes of abortion need to distinguish between *permissible* and *impermissible* reasons for abortions. This seems to be the rationale behind the portion of a 1989 amendment to the Pennsylvania abortion law that says "no abortion which is sought solely because of the sex of the unborn child shall be deemed a necessary abortion."[4] The Pennsylvania law thus prohibits physicians from performing sex-selection abortions since such abortions are "unnecessary" and the law only allows physicians to perform only those abortions that are "necessary." The general idea behind positions that, like the one embodied in Pennsylvania abortion law, allow for some abortions but not others is to distinguish *trivial* from *nontrivial* reasons for an abortion. Abortion for purposes such as saving a mother's life, preventing the birth of a child with a serious congenital disease, or terminating a pregnancy that is the result of rape would count as nontrivial reasons for terminating a pregnancy; abortion to avoid disrupting one's vacation plans, to select for a child of a particular sex, or to select for a child of a particular sexual orientation would count as trivial reasons.

Even accepting this distinction, it is difficult to determine, for example, whether an abortion is done for trivial or nontrivial reasons. Consider sex-selection abortion in a very sexist culture in which some women will almost certainly face a life of extreme poverty if they give birth to daughters—poverty so extreme that these daughters are likely to teeter on the edge of malnutrition for many years—in contrast, if they give birth to sons, the sons' prospects in both the short and long term would almost surely be much brighter. This is not, unfortunately, such an unrealistic scenario considering the situation of women in certain economic and social classes in various countries, notably India (Bumiller 1990; Kussum 1993; Miller 1981). Under such conditions, it is not at all clear that a woman's reasons for aborting a female fetus would be trivial. A daughter born in this situation might suffer as much as a child born with a serious genetic disorder. If such a disorder provides grounds for an abortion, why is the sex of a fetus not also grounds for an abortion, at least given certain circumstances? Similarly, given the amount of suffering that might be involved in being a lesbian or gay man in a very homophobic society, might the future sexual orientation of a fetus also be grounds for an abortion? The point is that distinguishing between trivial and nontrivial reasons for abortion in general and orientation-selection abortion in particular seems quite difficult.

The arguments against orientation-selection abortion do not count as arguments against orientation-selection procedures that do not involve abortion. With orientation-selection abortion, there is the possibility that the rights of the fetus might trump the mother's reproductive liberty; in the case of preimplantation orientation selection, there is no fetus and hence no rights that might conflict with the rights of the mother. A woman who uses a diaphragm-like filter to screen out sperm carrying genes for a serious genetic disorder does not seem to violate any plausible general moral principle; a woman who uses a diaphragm-like filter to screen out sperm carrying genes that cause a certain sexual orientation does not seem to be doing anything morally different. Even if arguments about the morality of abortion establish that orientation-selection abortion is wrong, other forms of orientation selection could be permissible.

To see this point in a different way, note that even people who think all abortions are immoral and that all abortions should be illegal can allow that women have some reproductive liberty. Such anti-abortionists can accept that preimplantation orientation-selection procedures may be permissible and perhaps should be legal. For such people, the status of such procedures should turn on an evaluation of these procedures, not on the morality of abortion. But people who think that some instances of abortion are moral and some instances of abortion should be legal also need to look at orientation-selection abortion in particular to determine whether it is among the permissible sorts of abortion. Whatever one's views on abortion, the legitimacy of orientation-selection procedures requires an examination of these procedures in particular. It is to such an examination that I now turn.

## General Arguments Against Orientation Selection

### The Social Context

Recall my discussion in chapter 10 about the conditions of lesbians and gay men in the United States. Most people in the world live in a society that has a deep hatred of lesbians and gay men, a society that discriminates against and oppresses them. In particular, recall the poll that found that 80 percent of adult Americans said that they would be "upset" or "very upset" if a college-aged child of theirs said he or she was gay or lesbian (Schmalz 1993). This suggests that parents would go to great lengths to prevent their children from becoming lesbian, gay, or bisexual. Even many supportive parents of lesbians, gay men, and bisexuals admit that they would have tried to ensure that their children would be heterosexual. For example, Louise Coburn, one-time program director of Parents and Friends of Lesbians and Gays, a group active in supporting parents of lesbians, gay men, and bisexuals, as well as working for lesbian and gay rights, suggested that, given the homophobia and heterosexism of our society, no one would want his or her kid to be gay, saying, "No parent would choose to have a child born with any factor that would make life difficult for him or her" (Gelman 1992). Judge Richard Posner, in a book sympathetic to some claims relating to lesbian and gay rights, confidently asserts that if there was a procedure that would ensure that a child would not be a homosexual, "you can be sure that the child's parents would administer it to him, believing, probably correctly, that he would be better off" (Posner 1992, 308). The point is that most people, particularly most heterosexuals, have a strong preference for having heterosexual children. Even some lesbians and gay men themselves are concerned about the possibility that their children might turn out to be gay or lesbian (Kirby 1998). One might wonder whether the preference for heterosexual children is strong enough to bring people to make use of orientation-selection procedures. To help settle this question, consider the analogy with sex selection.

Most prospective parents throughout the world have preferences with respect to the sex of their future children, and many of them often have preferences for sons over daughters. This preference for sons can take various forms, including preferring to have one's firstborn child be a son, preferring to having more sons than daughters, preferring to have only sons, or preferring to have only one child and for that child to be a boy. Son preference is stronger in some cultures than others; in particular, son preference is especially strong in India, China, and most nations of Africa and Latin America. Even in countries such as the United States where the most common preference is for having two children, one boy and one girl, there is still a preference for sons that appears in the form of a preference for having a son first (Kolker and Burke 1994, 142–150; Raymond 1993, 21–25; Warren 1985, 12–19).

Given that most people's preference for having a heterosexual child is stronger than their preference for having a son and given that some women are willing to have an abortion to avoid having a daughter, it seems that some women would be willing to have an abortion to avoid having a nonheterosexual child. If preimplantation orientation-selection procedures were available, it seems that even more people would opt for such procedures to ensure that they will have heterosexual children. Further evidence for this claim is that parents of nonheterosexual children or of children who they fear are likely to develop into homosexuals (in many cases because their children display gender-atypical behavior, that is, because they consider their children to be sissies or tomboys) frequently seek professional help to ensure that their children will eventually become heterosexuals (Burke 1996; Feder 1997; Green 1987). Even assuming that some lesbians and gay men—by making use of artificial insemination techniques, surrogate mothers, group parenting arrangements, cloning, gene splicing, or some as yet undeveloped reproductive technologies (Eskridge and Hunter 1997, 774–778 and 849–853; Eskridge and Stein 1998; Hollandsworth 1995)—would decide to reproduce genetically and to make use of orientation-selection procedures to have gay or lesbian children, it seems very likely that most people who decide to make use of orientation-selection procedures will choose to have heterosexual children.[5]

### The Likely Impact of Orientation Selection

Consider why there is a strong preference for heterosexual children versus homosexual and bisexual ones. Perhaps the most charitable explanation for the preference for heterosexual children is that parents, while not themselves against homosexuality, do not want their children to experience the intolerance, discrimination, and violence faced by lesbians and gay men. One problem with this charitable interpretation is that in many cases it does not ring true. A significant number of people find homosexuality immoral, unnatural, and/or disgusting. These people are likely to make use of orientation-selection procedures, if they are available, because they dislike homosexuality and not simply to protect their children from social disapprobation. The claim that a parent is simply trying to protect a child from the wrath of society's prejudice often is a rationalization for homophobia and heterosexism; it is similar to a parent who reacts to a son or daughter who is dating (or marrying) a person of a different race by saying, "What will the neighbors think?" and "Just imagine how much trouble this will cause you (and your future children)!" The relevant point is that behind many of the preferences for heterosexual children is a negative attitude towards homosexuality. An ethical assessment of orientation selection needs to take this into consideration.

Even if parents desire heterosexual children because they do not want their children to face the manifestations of homophobia and heterosexism, what matters are the *effects* of making use of orientation-selection procedures. Whether or not orientation-selection procedures work, their availability, the acceptability of their use, and the knowledge that they are used will affect attitudes—of heterosexuals and nonheterosexuals alike—towards lesbians, gay men, and bisexuals. The emergence of orientation-selection procedures in cultures with negative attitudes towards homosexuals will reinforce the preference for heterosexual over homosexual children and will likely encourage the view that homosexuals and bisexuals are diseased.

In the United States, until quite recently, most people viewed homosexuality as a disease. Although some people, among them some doctors and psychiatrists, still see homosexuality as a mental illness, there has been a shift away from such a view. One indication of this shift was the American Psychiatric Association's 1973 decision to declassify homosexuality as a mental disorder (Bayer 1987). The effects of such a shift from seeing homosexuality as a disease have been significant: some of the stigma associated with homosexuality has lifted and more lesbians and gay men have become comfortable and open about their sexual orientation. The availability and use of orientation-selection procedures would suggest that screening for homosexuality is a reasonable and sanctioned medical procedure; this could potentially tip the scales of public and professional opinion back towards seeing homosexuality as a physical/mental disorder. Further, the availability and use of orientation-selection procedures would increase the pressure to hide one's homosexuality and decrease the collective power of lesbians and gay men. By strengthening the disease view of homosexuality and increasing pressure to keep one's homosexuality secret, the use of orientation-selection procedures to select against nonheterosexuals would engender and perpetuate attitudes that lesbians and gay men are undesirable and not valuable, policies that discriminate against lesbians and gay men, violence against lesbians and gay men, and the very conditions that give rise to the preference for heterosexuals rather than nonheterosexuals (Suppe 1984, 401–414). These are serious results that demand careful ethical consideration. All else being equal, these results should be prevented.

Consider, as an analogy, the impact of the availability of sex-selection procedures in India, where the conditions of women, particularly in certain regions, are quite poor (Bumiller 1990; Miller 1981). In India, the economic status of women compared to men is low, and in general, their job opportunities are severely limited. In many Indian families, the birth of a daughter is sometimes mourned, while the birth of a son is usually celebrated. Women receive significantly worse health care, less nourishment, and have a lower life expectancy than men, and the death rate for female infants is substantially higher than for male infants. Since sex-selection procedures have become available in India, they have been widely used, and the number of men has increased compared to the number of women (Kussum 1993). Some women in India admit that they might prefer to have a daughter if the conditions for women in their society were different, but given the abuse and oppression that women experience, they prefer to have sons. Several commentators have observed that the availability and use of sex-selection procedures, especially in places like India, is likely to lower the status of women, increase sexism, and lead to a worsening of the conditions of women (Asch and Geller 1996; Holmes 1984; Overall 1987; Patel 1989; Wertz and Fletcher 1992). Not surprisingly, an overwhelming majority of actual cases of sex selection in India involve selection against females because women are valued less than men. The availability and use of sex-selection techniques both legitimizes and strengthens this profound sexism and also implicitly endorses associated gender stereotypes. More generally, given this context, sex selection is in tension with principles of equality. Further, although it is difficult to establish with any precision the causes of changes in the conditions of women in India, the widespread use of such sex-selection practices seems to contribute to both negative attitudes towards women and to the perpetuation of their poor conditions.

The availability of orientation-selection procedures will likely have a similar impact on the condition of lesbians, gay men, and bisexuals. This is not to say that lesbians and gay men are oppressed in the same way that women are (in India or in general). Although the oppression of lesbians, gay men, and bisexuals in this society is *connected* to the oppression of women (Koppelman 1988, 1994; Law 1988), the two forms of oppression are still quite different (Calhoun 1994, 1995; Rubin 1984; Sedgwick 1990, 27–35). The availability of orientation-selection procedures poses a serious threat to lesbians, gay men, and bisexuals in a society that is both overwhelmingly unfriendly to lesbians and gay men and in which most people have a strong preference for heterosexual children. The stronger the oppression of lesbians and gay men, the greater the moral pressure to regulate orientation-selection procedures. Given this, what should be said and done legally, morally, and otherwise about such selection procedures? I turn to these questions in the next section.

## Should Orientation-Selection
## Procedures Be Prohibited?

In the previous section, I discussed the negative impact that orientation-selection procedures would likely have on lesbians, gay men, and bisexuals given existing attitudes towards them. Concern for women's reproductive liberty and the rights of parents counts against restrictions on orientation selection. Given such societal conditions, there is a tension between protecting lesbians, gay men, and bisexuals, on the one hand, and protecting parental rights and women's reproductive liberty, on the other. Many feminist commentators on sex selection have recognized a parallel tension with regards to sex selection (Overall 1987, 34; Warren 1985). If the conditions of lesbians and gay men relative to heterosexuals in a society are poor and if the preference for hetero-sexual children is quite strong, legal recourse seems necessary to protect lesbians, gay men, and bisexuals, although women's reproductive liberty and parental freedom should be respected as much as possible.

It is useful to contrast two laws that relate to the practice of sex-selection abortion: the portion of the Pennsylvania abortion law that prohibits abortions based solely on the sex of the fetus and the Regulation of Prenatal Diagnostic Techniques Act, a law passed in the Indian state of Maharashtra. The Maha-rashtra law, which was passed in the late 1980s in response to the widespread use of sex-selection procedures, bans prenatal tests to determine the sex of the fetus (although it allows for prenatal tests for genetic diseases). While the law has many loopholes and there are various problems with its enforcement, it seems to have led to a decrease in the use of prenatal screening procedures to determine the sex of the fetus, and it seems to have fostered a negative attitude towards the use of sex-selection procedures (Patel 1989). The Maharashtra law, unlike the Pennsylvania law, does not regulate abortions or attempt to assess the reasons a woman has for terminating a pregnancy. Given the complexity of a woman's decision to terminate a pregnancy, it would be difficult to determine whether a particular decision involves a preference for a child of a particular sex-gender. Barbara Rothman (1986, 142–143) convincingly argued that in a situation in which a woman is ambivalent about terminating a pregnancy, knowledge of fetal sex is bound to have some effect on her decision. In fact, the Pennsylvania law, which prohibits abortions performed solely based on the sex of the fetus, may fail to prohibit any abortions since no abortions are performed *solely* because of the sex of the fetus—such a decision is usually so complex that other factors are sure to play a role.

Besides being easier to enforce, one might claim that the Maharashtra law does not directly interfere with a woman's reproductive liberty in the way that the Pennsylvania law does. This difference may be only apparent. Some have argued that a woman's reproductive liberty includes access to all information relevant to whether or not she will want to continue her pregnancy (Robertson 1995, 158); if a woman is prohibited from gaining access to information concerning the sex of a fetus, her reproductive liberty is thereby curtailed. Even if this is the case, limiting access to information about the sex of a fetus, as in the Maharashtra law, is preferable to banning all prenatal tests or prohibiting abortions. Under a Maharashtra-like law, a woman may decide whether to terminate a pregnancy, but she is not allowed to know the sex of her fetus and hence cannot include this information in her decision-making process. This may be a restriction on reproductive liberty, but it is a relatively weak restriction. Perhaps, then, the best way to resolve the tension between women's reproductive liberty and the conditions of lesbians, gay men, and bisexuals is to restrict access to genetic information concerning the future sexual orientation of the fetus.

One might point out that, short of legal intervention, there are things the state can do, if it is so inclined, to attempt to block the potential effects of the availability of orientation-selection procedures. The state can attempt to educate people, especially potential parents, about sexuality, homophobia, and the potential impact of orientation-selection procedures. Doctors and genetic counselors are particularly well-placed to inform people of these facts.[6] Most importantly, the state could work in various ways to undercut the oppression of lesbians and gay men and in general to improve the conditions of lesbians, gay men, and bisexuals in this society. This is not, however, a trivial or straightforward thing to do. The state can attempt to initiate social change, but deeply entrenched social attitudes typically can be changed only when the state wields its legal powers. Given existing attitudes towards homosexuality in most countries, it is unlikely that the governments of most countries will act to encourage such social change.

There is, however, a deeper problem for a Maharashtra-like law concerning orientation-selection procedures: such a law would not deal with preimplantation selection procedures that could have the same effects as postimplantation procedures. It is, for example, legal under the Maharashtra law for a woman who wants to have a son to be artificially inseminated with sperm that has been processed to eliminate X chromosomes. If this technique were accurate and widely available (Kolata 1998), it could have similar results that the widespread use of sex-selection abortion has on women in India. The parallel point holds with respect to orientation selection: the availability of preimplantation orientation-selection procedures would lead to the same sort of effects on lesbians and gay men as postimplantation orientation-selection procedures. In fact, the availability of preimplantation orientation-selection procedures would pose an even more dramatic threat to lesbians, gay men, and bisexuals than postimplantation procedures because preimplantation procedures, if available, provide an alternative that avoids abortion and would be cheaper and easier to use. Given that preimplantation procedures could pose a serious threat to the well-being of lesbians, gay men, and bisexuals, there would be moral pressure against the use of such procedures.

Consideration of preimplantation selection procedures reveals a serious tension between reproductive liberty and protecting lesbians, gay men, and bisexuals. Among the ways of addressing this tension are especially strong restrictions on a woman's reproductive liberty, since restrictions on the use of preimplantation orientation-selection procedures involve saying, hypothetically, that a woman cannot use a diaphragm that keeps out sperm containing genes thought to code for homosexuality. This tension between protecting reproductive liberty and protecting lesbians, gay men, and bisexuals could be avoided if the development of techniques that screen for sexual orientation could be discouraged or prevented. This could be achieved only by restricting certain technological and scientific research. This sort of restriction might be tantamount to prohibiting research to develop a gun that would elude metal detectors: the restriction would be justified because it would prevent especially negative effects of some technology. The problem is that the technology for orientation selection might be an unintended result of research into the origins of sexual orientation. For now, I will set that problem aside and will consider, in chapter 12, the general question of whether scientific research on sexual orientation ought to be restricted or prohibited.

Given the possible effects of the use and availability of orientation-selection techniques, it follows that individuals in a society have the responsibility to consider the larger social impact of using orientation-selection procedures.[7] A person who decides to make use of such a procedure is morally responsible for the impact of doing so. A person who makes use of such a procedure to ensure that a child is heterosexual perpetuates the negative conditions of lesbians, gay men, and bisexuals in this society. This implies that making use of orientation-selection procedures is morally problematic; all else being equal, given the impact of such procedures, a person ought not to make use of them. Relatedly, all else being equal, medical personnel and medical facilities should not perform or encourage such procedures and insurance companies should not pay for them. Further, people are also responsible for examining the source of their own preferences with respect to the sexual orientation of their children and to see if the reasons behind their preferences are justified. There is, in addition, cultural inertia: in societies where nonheterosexuals are oppressed, the structure of society maintains these conditions and thereby ensures the popularity of orientation-selection procedures (Warren 1985, 105; Weiss 1995). In such a society, any individual who acts to preserve conditions that oppress lesbians, gay men, and bisexuals when it is possible to do otherwise bears moral responsibility for his or her actions.

People familiar with ethical theory should note that my argument is neutral with respect to the moral theory that underlies it, namely, my argument is compatible with either *consequentialism* (the view that the consequences of

an act determine its morality) or *nonconsequentialism* (the view that consequences are not relevant to the morality of an act). Consequentialists can interpret my talk about the impact of orientation-selection procedures in terms of
the consequences of their use and availability. Nonconsequentialists can understand me as arguing that the use and availability of orientation-selection procedures, under current societal conditions, would entail violating moral principles; for example, the dignity and respect due to all persons would be denied
to lesbians, gay men, and bisexuals if such procedures were available and used.
The fact that my argument does not depend on either consequentialism or
nonconsequentialism does not mean that I have no opinion on these two positions. Rather, I remain neutral on these issues because taking and defending a
stand on them is beyond the scope of the present project.

## Is the Argument
## Against Orientation Selection Too Strong?

One might wonder whether my overall argument against the use of orientation-
selection procedures proves too much. The worry is that an argument isomor-
phic to the one I have developed above concerning the legality and morality of
orientation-selection procedures might also apply to the legality and morality of
procedures to select against fetuses with serious genetic disorders. Such an argument would focus on the negative impact such selection practices would have on
people who have these conditions. One example of such an argument would be
as follows: using selection procedures to prevent the birth of children with spina
bifida, a serious congenital condition affecting the vertebral column, might have
a negative impact on children born with this condition; this counts against this
use of selection procedures to prevent the birth of children with this condition.
This is supposed to show that the argument of the previous section is too strong
because techniques to select against fetuses with serious genetic disorders are in
fact morally and legally permissible, that is, it is morally and legally permissible
for a parent to prevent the birth of a child with a serious disease like spina bifida.
The concern is that there is a tension between the argument of the previous
section that suggests that selecting against homosexuality is impermissible and
the claim that selecting against spina bifida is permissible.

    I do not have the space here to fully articulate a response to this worry, but
I can sketch one. There is a disanalogy between my argument about orientation-selection procedures and the proposed argument about the permissibility
of using genetic technology to prevent the birth of babies with serious medical
conditions. Such conditions may dramatically decrease life expectancy, cause

great suffering, and intrinsically undermine a person's quality of life; further, a person with such a condition would say that she wishes that she did not have this condition. Homosexuality and bisexuality are not like this; in particular, the primary negative features of being a lesbian, gay man, or bisexual have to do with societal attitudes towards these sexual orientations, not with intrinsic features of them. This is not to deny that there may be tricky ethical and legal questions about using selection procedures to prevent the birth of children with medical conditions less serious than spina bifida (for example, epilepsy, asthma, and deafness). For my purposes, I can bypass these tricky questions because homosexuality is not this sort of condition (Bayer 1987; LeVay 1996, 211–230; Ruse 1988, 203–235).

Conversely, some people have made a general argument against reproductive technologies. They argue that the use of procedures to select for or against a particular trait leads us down a slippery slope: once any sort of genetic (or psychological) engineering becomes common, we are irreversibly heading towards the day when parents choose children and their traits the way a consumer decides what kind of car to buy and what features it should have. I have not made this type of argument. My concern has been whether there are special considerations that should be brought to bear on using reproductive technologies or psychological techniques to choose the sexual orientation of children. I have not argued that there is something intrinsically special about sexual orientation that entails such techniques should not be used to control it. Instead, I have argued that the conditions for lesbians, gay men, and bisexuals today warrant paying legal, ethical, and social attention to attempts to choose the sexual orientations of children.

## Postnatal Procedures to Change the Sexual Orientation of Children

Suppose that sexual orientation is *not* primarily genetic but is instead primarily, or at least significantly, the result of some environmental factors. More particularly, suppose, as discussed in chapter 8, that some theory that fits the indirect model of the role of biological factors in the development of sexual orientations is true. If the environmental factors that affect sexual orientation are well understood or even if people just have strong (though perhaps mistaken) beliefs about how such factors affect sexual orientation, it seems that many parents would try to control these environmental factors to shape the sexual orientation of their children. The concern here is with *postnatal* procedures to affect a child's sexual orientation rather than prenatal or even preimplantation ones.

Such procedures might include genetic alteration (Burr 1996b), neurosurgery, hormonal injections, or psychological interventions. Some of these procedures have been used in the past (see chapter 12), and today many parents try to control the sexual orientation of their children in various ways based on commonsense theories about how sexual orientations develop. For example, some parents, thinking that homosexuality is somehow contagious, try to keep their children away from lesbians or gay men—especially those in role-model positions like school teachers or sports coaches[8]—and from other children who seem to them likely to develop into lesbians or gay men (perhaps because they are gender-atypical children or because their parents are lesbians or gay men). Also, parents try to get their children to avoid gender-atypical activities, thinking the act of playing in a gender-atypical manner increases the likelihood that the child will be a homosexual as an adult (Burke 1996; Feder 1997). Lawrence Crocker (1979), in a provocative but problematic article, considered the implications of the possibility that a special diet consisting of Brussels sprouts, given to children at an early age, could guarantee heterosexuality in adulthood.

If the arguments made earlier in this chapter concerning prenatal, postimplantation procedures for choosing the sexual orientation of children are strong, then the same kind of argument ought to count against using postnatal techniques to choose the sexual orientation of children. The availability of conversion programs, hormonal therapy, dietary supplements, or other techniques for changing sexual orientations would encourage the view that lesbians, gay men, and bisexuals are diseased; increase pressure to keep one's homosexuality secret; engender and perpetuate attitudes that lesbians and gay men are worthless; encourage policies that discriminate against lesbians and gay men; and increase violence towards them. In particular, the availability of techniques for ensuring heterosexuality in children encourages and lends legitimacy to attempts to convert homosexuals.

Although the state should do all it can to discourage such negative effects on lesbians and gay men, the state and its laws should be highly deferential to parents' decisions about their children's upbringing. Unless a child is being physically or psychologically harmed, a parent's decisions about a child should be respected both as a moral and a practical matter. Parents are allowed and encouraged to make decisions about their children's education, religious upbringing, and sexual morality within certain broad constraints (for example, the state requires children to receive a basic education). There is a risk to this strategy: adopting this attitude towards parents and how they want to raise their children does not mean that the decisions parents make will always be the right ones morally or otherwise. For example, parents are allowed to teach their children racist attitudes, religious intolerance, sexism and homophobia. On the other hand, just because parents are allowed to raise their children in certain ways does not mean that the state or other individuals must collaborate in raising children in ways that are problematic. For example, school teachers should not reinforce racist attitudes, religious intolerance, or homophobic sentiments. Further, the state can and should intervene in extreme cases of parental negligence or abuse, for example, if parents refuse to provide their child with adequate health care or physically or psychologically abuse their children.

With regards to sexual orientation in particular, as both a practical and an ethical matter, the law should not dictate what parents teach their children about lesbians and gay men, various sexual activities, and sexual desires. Moreover, it should be legal for parents to try to influence the sexual orientation of their children. The state can, however, intervene if a parent takes extreme measures to try to influence a child's sexual orientation. For example, the state might stop a parent from using electric-shock therapy to try to make a child heterosexual or intervene if a parent's actions towards a child's sexual desires or activities leads, as they do all too often, to a child's attempt to commit suicide (Gibson 1997).

That parents may legally try to insure that their children develop into heterosexuals does not, however, mean that the state and others must collaborate with them in these practices. Doctors, psychologists, and others who might be in a position to help parents try to change their children's sexual orientation should resist these attempts. Health-care providers should inform parents that lesbians and gay men are not diseased, do not (in virtue of their sexual orientations) suffer from mental illness, and that lesbians and gay men can and do lead full, productive, and happy lives.

My proposal (earlier in this chapter) with regards to postimplantation (and prenatal) orientation-selection procedures, modeled on the Maharashtra law concerning prenatal screening for sex, attempted to walk the line between interfering with parental rights and protecting lesbians and gay men. The same strategy should be adopted here with regards to postnatal procedures that are supposed to change a child's sexual orientation. On the one hand, we want to protect the rights of parents to raise their children how they wish; on the other hand, we want to protect lesbians and gay men against violence, discrimination, and the views that they are diseased and not valuable.

Frederick Suppe's discussion of psychological procedures to convert homosexuals to heterosexuality points in the right direction (Suppe 1984). Suppe argues that the existence of programs to convert people to heterosexuality strengthens prejudice and discrimination and that, partly for this reason, there are moral problems with attempting to cure homosexuality. In particular, therapists and other mental health and medical practitioners should not attempt to change the sexual orientation of even a willing lesbian or gay man. Above, I argued that the availability of orientation-selection techniques would have serious negative effects on lesbians and gay men. Similarly, Suppe argued that the availability of psychological conversion programs have these effects whether or not they are "successful." If Suppe's argument is right, parents should not try to change their children's sexual orientation. The argument is not that trying to change (postnatally) the sexual orientation of one's child should be illegal, but rather that it is unethical. Given the negative attitudes that exist towards lesbians and gay men, conversion therapy would have profound negative effects on lesbians and gay men. It is not *illegal* for parents to teach their children that all Jews are deceitful and miserly, but given that it is both false and dangerous to teach children these views, it is unethical to do so.

There are, however, differences between a parent attempting postnatal changes to the sexual orientation of a child and a parent opting to make use of orientation-selection procedures. In contrast to prenatal orientation-selection procedures (both preimplantation and postimplantation ones), with postnatal orientation-selection procedures, the rights and wishes of the child are clearly relevant: the child may not want to undergo conversion therapy or at least may have a right to decide whether or not to do so. Perhaps parents should not decide for their children what their sexual orientation will be; instead, this decision should be put off until the child is able to decide for him or herself.

As an example, consider surgery to alter ambiguous genitalia (Kessler 1998). As I mentioned in chapter 1, some intersexuals are born with ambiguous genitalia. Presently, standard medical practice is to perform surgery on children with this condition as early as possible with the goal of producing external genitalia that are close to "normal" for either males or females. Some surgeons admit that such surgery, while not medically necessary, is *psychosexually* necessary. They claim that a child with ambiguous genitalia will face social ridicule, will have a sense of not fitting in, and will experience confusion and discomfort with his or her gender identity. This sort of social experience will so adversely affect the life of a child that surgery to "correct" a child's genitalia is warranted. Critics of this practice argue that such surgery is usually not necessary, that in fact significant psychological harm can result from this surgery, and that the resulting genitalia can be significantly less sensitive and less able to produce sexual pleasure. Unless genital surgery is *medically* necessary—for example, if it is necessary to reduce the risk of infection or to allow for urination without pain—these critics argue that parents should not decide to have such surgery performed on a child. Doctors should advise parents of the dangers of such surgery and make clear to them that it is not medically necessary to have such surgery. Rather, such surgery should be put off until a person can decide for him or herself what, if anything, to do (Kessler 1998).

The same sorts of arguments apply to trying to change a child's sexual orientation. Advocates of conversion therapy argue that, given the negative attitudes that exist towards homosexuality, it would be to a child's psychological benefit to try to ensure heterosexuality, especially if there is evidence (whatever that might be) of a disposition for homosexuality (Rosen, Rekers, and Bentler 1978). Homosexuals, the argument goes, are lonely, less happy, more likely to commit suicide, and so on. According to this argument, parents have the right to decide to postnatally change the sexual orientation of their children and may even have an obligation to do so. Given that gay men and lesbians are more likely than heterosexuals to commit suicide, the thought is that taking measures to ensure that a child is heterosexual is a form of suicide prevention; surely parents ought to reduce their children's risk of suicide.

There are various problems with this line of argument (Morin and Schultz 1978). Most notably, conversion therapy does not work (Haldeman 1991, 1994; Silverstein 1991). Further, the risks of conversion therapy are significant. In fact, it would not be surprising if a majority of the gay men and lesbians who attempted suicide did so because their parents tried to convert them to heterosexuality or in some other way expressed disapproval of their homosexuality. Additionally, the negative aspects of being a lesbian or gay man are due to society; they are not medical problems or intrinsic psychological problems. Conversion therapy is no more an appropriate response to social conditions facing lesbians and gay men than bleaching the skin of nonwhites is an appropriate response to racial injustice. Under no circumstance is a procedure to change a child's sexual orientation medically necessary. Given the effects of the existence and use of conversion therapy, medical and psychological interventions to postnatally change a child's sexual orientation are morally problematic. They are subject to the same sort of ethical concerns as orientation-selection procedures. But conversion therapies, like surgery to alter ambiguous genitalia, may conflict with the rights and wishes of children. In general, we all have a moral obligation to create a just society in which individuals have liberty and are treated fairly. Rather than trying to change a person's sexual orientation to avoid social disapprobation, people should instead try to change society.

To summarize, conversion therapies to ensure that children will be heterosexual, even if they will be unsuccessful, are very likely to have negative effects on lesbians, gay men, and bisexuals. Because of these likely effects, it is unethical to try to change a child's sexual orientation. Health-care professionals should not offer such conversion therapies, and they should advise against them. The government should educate the public about the ineffectiveness of such procedures and their negative social effects. Finally, although parents should be allowed to raise their children as they want, the state should intervene when a parent attempts to change the sexual orientations of a child using methods that are—as many attempts to change the sexual orientation of children are—life threatening, abusive, or cruel.

## Conclusion

In societies in which lesbians and gay men face discrimination, prejudice, and hatred, procedures that enable parents to attempt to select or change the sexual orientation of their children raise serious ethical questions. Even if such procedures are not likely to work, their mere availability or claimed efficacy will perpetuate and perhaps amplify the negative conditions faced by lesbians, gay men, and bisexuals. Determining precisely how to prevent these effects is difficult, particularly because simply prohibiting these procedures potentially conflicts with women's reproductive liberties and the rights of parents. In this chapter, I sketched a proposal (modeled on an Indian provincial law that addresses sex-selection procedures) that tries to protect lesbians, gay men, and bisexuals from the effects of orientation selection without infringing on women's reproductive liberties. This proposal does not, however, address potential preimplantation and postnatal procedures designed to ensure heterosexuality or the effects that such procedures might have on lesbians, gay men, and bisexuals. Although the ethical issues raised by such procedures are similar to those involving postimplantation, prenatal selection, the public-policy issues are more complex. A full discussion of the relevant public-policy questions is a matter for more detailed examination than I can provide here. My general conclusion is that the availability and use of procedures to select or change a child's sexual orientation will likely have a serious negative impact on lesbians, gay men, and bisexuals; as a result, such procedures are morally problematic and warrant careful public-policy solutions.

# CHAPTER 12

## Should Scientific Research on Sexual Orientation Be Done?

In the previous chapter, I provided an extended example of how advances in scientific research on sexual orientation have the potential to harm lesbians and gay men. If people think that they can use genetic, reproductive, and other technologies to select the sexual orientation of their children, then it seems likely that they will attempt to do so. The availability and use of such techniques could worsen the conditions of lesbians, gay men, and bisexuals. This should be of concern not just to lesbians and gay men but to everyone concerned with liberty and justice. Considerations like the possible impact of orientation-selection technologies and conversion therapies, whether or not they would work, have led people to warn of the potential abuse of scientific research on sexual orientation; some have gone so far as to call for a moratorium on such research (Schmidt 1984; Schüklenk and Ristow 1996). This call has been strongest in Germany, where under the Nazis research of this very sort took place with horrific results (Heger 1980; Plant 1986).

In this chapter, I survey some ethical arguments for and against scientific research on sexual orientation. In chapter 10, I argued that scientific research does not have the direct and positive connections to lesbian and gay rights that some have claimed it does. Even if my argument is right, it does not necessarily follow that such scientific research has negative ethical implications or that such scientific research should be curtailed. Some people think that scientific research, at least most of it, has no intrinsic positive or negative ethical implications. In fact, scientific research on sexual orientation could also be ethically neutral. Whether it is will be the subject of the present chapter.

## Ethical Arguments Against Scientific Research on Sexual Orientation

Critics of scientific research on sexual orientation argue that scientific research concerning sexual orientation faces serious ethical problems, especially given the social conditions for lesbians and gay men—particularly in places such as Singapore (see chapter 10). History suggests that such research will be used to try to "cure" lesbians and gay men of their homosexuality and that it will perpetuate the hatred of and discrimination against lesbians and gay men. It is important to remember that these effects are more likely to occur when the research being done makes implicit homophobic assumptions.

### Historical Evidence

Scientific research on sexual orientation has a gruesome history of being used to harm lesbians, gay men, and other sexual minorities (Bullough 1994; Katz 1976, 197–316; Murphy 1992). Historically, almost every investigation into the causes of homosexuality has aimed at its elimination, that is, such research was directed at discovering "treatments" for homosexuality. The results of such research have been used to force many lesbians and gay men to undergo various procedures to change their sexual orientation, even when there was little reason to think such procedures would have any effect. For example, Alan Turing, a brilliant British mathematician and the father of theoretical computer science, after being convicted of "an offense against morals" (namely, he was convicted for engaging in homosexual sex), was sentenced to either a prison sentence or an extended period of hormone treatment. During his subsequent treatment with estrogen, he committed suicide (Hodges 1983). Other gay men and lesbians, who were either unhappy with their sexual desires or with the social conditions that went along with them, chose to undergo conversion therapies. Such therapies included electroshock treatment, genital mutilation, brain surgery, and lengthy and wrenching psychoanalysis. Some of these procedures were widely used in Western countries until surprisingly recently, and many continue to be used around the world today. For example, as recently as 1974, the *Journal of the American Medical Association* reviewed the results of using brain surgery to "cure" gay and bisexual men of their sexual desires for men (the idea was to remove their "female mating center"). Without any moral commentary, the review glibly concluded that brain surgery is more effective than chemical castration as a treatment for homosexuality ("Stereotaxic Surgery Results" 1974). In general, scientifically questionable therapeutic approaches have all too often destroyed the lives of perfectly healthy people.

Even today, psychological techniques are available to convert lesbians and gay men to heterosexuality. "Conversion therapy" and "reparative therapy" are the terms used by practitioners of psychoanalytic, "twelve-step," religious, and other techniques designed to convert to heterosexuality lesbians and gay men who are unhappy with their sexual orientation. Although there is no serious evidence that such techniques work (Haldeman 1991, 1994; Silverstein 1991), parents continue to force their children to undergo such treatment, and some self-identified lesbians and gay men who wish to become heterosexual willingly participate in such programs. In fact, the American Psychological Association recently debated whether to prohibit its members from offering reparative therapy to clients who request it (Sleek 1997). Ultimately, the organization did not pass this prohibition. In chapter 11, I argued that there are ethical concerns that arise from the availability of orientation-selection procedures and postnatal procedures to change the sexual orientation of children. Here the question is whether the fact that scientific research on sexual orientation potentially undergirds procedures to select for or change sexual orientations entails that this research ought not be done. Some people have argued that, given its history, scientific research on sexual orientation brings with it significant risks of doing further harm to lesbians and gay men; they claim that this counts against doing such research (Halperin 1990, 49–51; Schmidt 1984; Schüklenk 1993; Schüklenk and Ristow 1996; Suppe 1994).

### Homophobic Assumptions

Merely pointing out that scientific research on sexual orientation has a bad history does not, on its own, constitute strong criticism of it. In medieval times, barbers tried to heal people using an assortment of gruesome and unsubstantiated techniques such as bloodletting and the application of leeches, which caused a great deal of pain and suffering; despite this, we do not boycott barbers or call for the government to shut down hair salons. This is because, over time, barbers have gotten rid of their negative historical baggage. There seems no connection between medieval barbers and contemporary hair stylists. Those who make ethical arguments against scientific research on sexual orientation think that such research has not yet shed its problematic past. In particular, some critics say that much contemporary scientific research maintains—sometimes implicitly, sometimes not—the antigay and antilesbian assumptions that characterized such research in the recent past.

One way to see this implicit homophobia is in the *framing* of this research. Many studies past and present assume, often implicitly, that all they need to do to give an account of human sexual orientation is to explain why some people are lesbians or gay men; the assumption is that heterosexuality is not in need of any explanation. (I discussed an example of this in chapter 6 with respect to sociobiologists who feel they need to give an evolutionary explanation for homosexuality, while thinking that heterosexuality does not require one.) Given the different positions of power that lesbians and gay men, as opposed to heterosexuals, have in most cultures, there exists an asymmetry in how the origins of sexual orientation are explored and a recurring pattern of who asks such questions and in what contexts these questions are asked. Lesbians and gay men often ask themselves why they are not heterosexual; parents often wonder what they did to "make" their children homosexual; and scientists, psychiatrists, and others study the causes of homosexuality. In contrast, few heterosexuals worry about why they are not homosexual; few parents worry about what they did to "make" their children heterosexual; and few scientists, psychiatrists, and others study the causes of heterosexuality. From the point of view of science properly done, it is no less a mystery how people become heterosexual than it is how people become homosexual. Simply saying that heterosexuality is the norm does not explain how people become heterosexual. Why some people are attracted to people of a different sex-gender is as much a mystery as why other people are attracted to people of the same sex-gender. A robust science of sexual orientation needs to explain both phenomena, and it needs to do so as part of an explanation of sexual desire more generally. Despite the fact that all sexual orientations are equally in need of scientific explanation, even "gay-friendly" researchers often assume that homosexuality needs more of an explanation than heterosexuality does. This assumption, whether implicit or not, biases much scientific research.

Additionally, the homophobic assumptions of contemporary scientific research can be seen by looking at the terminology contemporary researchers use. Gunter Dörner (1989, emphasis added), for example, describes homosexuality as a "disease," a "dysfunction," as resulting from "*abnormal* brain development," as due to abnormal hormone levels, as a deficiency, and as a "gene-controlled *disarrangement* of psychosexual maturation patterns." Researchers also talk, often implicitly, of making changes in the factors that they think underlie homosexuality. As long as homosexuality is seen as a dysfunction, prevention and treatment therapies are more likely to be pursued. In fact, treatment continues to be discussed, often in terms like "optimizing natural conditions" or "correcting abnormal concentrations" (Dörner 1989). Traits perceived as undesirable and of biological origin are often assumed, sometimes incorrectly, to be amenable to medical remedy or prevention. The persistent use of such language reflects entrenched homophobia, regardless of whether or not individuals admit or even realize they have these biases. This worry has been elegantly stated by Eve Sedgwick, who notes that

> the presentation, often in ostensibly or authentically gay-affirming contexts, of biologically-based "explanations" for deviant behavior . . . are absolutely invariably couched in terms of "excess," "deficiency," or "imbalance"— whether in hormones, in the genetic material, or . . . in the fetal endocrine environment. If I had ever, in any medium, seen any researcher or popularizer refer even once to any supposed gay-producing circumstance as the *proper* hormone balance, or the conducive endocrine environment, for gay generation, I would be less chilled by the breezes of all this technological confidence. (Sedgwick 1990, 43)

Sedgwick's point can be taken even further. It is not only "biologically-based 'explanations'" that involve this sort of homophobia. The same phenomenon is apparent in psychological research as well. Consider, for example, research on children with gender-identity disorder, the term officially approved by most psychiatric associations to refer to children who behave in a gender nonconforming fashion. Because such children are assumed to be at risk of becoming homosexuals, they are often subject to extreme forms of psychiatric, emotional, and medical interventions. Such treatment assumes that adult homosexuality is a condition worth avoiding at great costs to children (Burke 1996; Feder 1997).

Scientific research on sexual orientation may use terminology that treats homosexuality as a pathology or assumes that homosexuality—but not heterosexuality—needs to be explained. Sometimes the research is based on the implicit homophobia of researchers, although not all researchers interested in the origins of sexual orientation are homophobic. If, however, they have a picture (even an implicit one) of homosexuality as a pathology or an unexplained aberration, their very own terminology may contribute to the stigmatization of homosexuality and the perpetuation of homophobia, and it may thereby bias their research.

Some defenders of scientific research on sexual orientation have replied that some of the recent studies in the emerging scientific research program do not make homophobic assumptions and do not use stigmatizing language

(LeVay 1996, 255–295; Murphy 1997, 49–73). In fact, they argue, scientific research can undermine these very assumptions. Other critics have argued that the very project of trying to understand this origin of sexual orientation is implicitly homophobic (Bersani 1995, 1–7; Halperin 1990, 49–51).

Commentators can be overly optimistic about the absence of implicit homophobic assumptions in much of the current scientific research. The fact that a researcher is a lesbian or gay man or that his or her intentions towards lesbians and gay men are benevolent does not immunize his or her research from accepting implicit biased assumptions about lesbians and gay men. For example, in chapter 7, I argued that most research in the emerging research program accepts, at least implicitly, the inversion assumption, namely, that lesbians and gay men are gender inverts. This assumption is so entrenched in scientific research that many scientists, even those who are sympathetic to lesbians and gay men, accept it without question. On the other hand, critics of scientific research are wrong to assume that simply because much of the scientific research up to now has made problematic assumptions, all current and future research will make such assumptions. In considering the merits of a particular research project, it is appropriate to look at the assumptions and terminology of that research, but it is a mistake to condemn all scientific research on sexual orientation because of its troubling history.

### Effects of Contemporary Research

The main ethical argument against scientific research on sexual orientation is that lesbians and gay men will be harmed and treated unjustly as a result of this research. The history of the abuse of scientific research on sexual orientation is suggestive, as is the frequency with which such research makes homophobic assumptions, but it is open to defenders of scientific research to say that times have changed. Given the condition of lesbians and gay men throughout the world, however, there seems good reason to expect that this research could have the effect of hurting lesbians and gay men—either physically (by leading to techniques to cure them or by buttressing attitudes that lead to violence against them) or socially (for example, by perpetuating negative stereotypes that lead to discrimination and criminalization). In the words of Gunter Schmidt (1984, 139), a German sexologist, "As long as society has not made peace with the homosexuals, research into the possible causes [of homosexuality is] . . . potentially a public danger."

To appreciate this point, consider a discussion of similar ethical issues in a different realm. In various contexts over the last couple of decades, Richard Herrnstein and other researchers have argued for the existence of a genetic component to intelligence that is responsible for the differential performance by blacks and whites on IQ tests (Herrnstein 1971; Herrnstein and Murray 1994). In response, Noam Chomsky (1976) (among others) has argued that the results of such an investigation—whatever they turn out to be—as well as *the very undertaking* of such an inquiry, would reinforce racism and other despicable attitudes. That such experiments are being performed will, he claims, perpetuate the assumption that black people are less intelligent than white people and, further, the results of the studies will be used by racists to justify their favored public policies, such as the elimination of head-start programs, which are programs designed to help minority children better prepare for elementary school. He offers the analogy of "a psychologist in Hitler's Germany who thought he could show that Jews had a genetically determined tendency toward usury (like squirrels bred to collect too many nuts)" (294). Chomsky notes that

> there is the likelihood that even opening this question and regarding it as a subject for scientific inquiry would provide ammunition for Goebbels and Rosenberg and their henchmen. Were this hypothetical psychologist to disregard the likely social consequences of his research (or even his undertaking of research under existing social conditions), he would fully deserve the contempt of decent people. (295)

Chomsky thinks that the same attitude is appropriate with respect to research on race and intelligence. I read critics of scientific research on sexual orientation as making a similar claim with respect to such research: a scientist who disregards the likely consequences of his research on sexual orientation is *morally* suspect. Others who support such research are open to the same charge.

Chomsky claims that scientists should weigh the social implications of their work. In light of the history of the abuse of scientific research on sexual orientation as well as the social conditions of lesbians and gay men, it seems that there is an obvious and significant potential for this research to be used in morally problematic ways (for example, to justify hormone treatments to cure homosexuality and to support the development of orientation-selection techniques). As Timothy Murphy says, "It is unclear that sexual orientation research, under social arrangements such as these [that is, those that exist today], could serve as anything more than a prop to stigmatizing effects" (Murphy 1997, 69). That scientific research on sexual orientation will likely lead to these results is a serious ethical objection to it.

In the previous chapter, I argued that the availability of orientation-selection procedures would almost certainly perpetuate negative conditions for lesbians and gay men and, as a result, is ethically problematic. The argument under consideration here is similar but more general. In the context of the hatred of lesbians and gay men and societal prejudice against them, scientific research on sexual orientation—particularly when it makes implicit homophobic assumptions, but even when it does not—perpetuates the negative conditions that exist for lesbians and gay men.

### Other Kinds of Research on Sexual Orientation

It is important to point out that some of the same sorts of ethical concerns that can be raised with respect to scientific research about sexual orientation can also be raised with respect to research in the humanities and the social sciences, for example, with respect to historical, sociological, anthropological, philosophical, and literary research. Just as scientific research can be based on homophobic assumptions and can be used against lesbians and gay men, so can humanistic and social scientific (broadly construed) research. Just as scientific research can perpetuate unsubstantiated assumptions about lesbians and gay men that lead to morally problematic social policies, so can social scientific research. Insofar as there are general worries about scientific research on sexual orientation, there are parallel worries about any sort of research on this topic. One might, for example, raise ethical concerns about this book. Some critiques of the emerging research program have been used by opponents of lesbian and gay rights. For example, William Byne's critical discussions of the emerging research program (Byne 1994; Byne and Parsons 1993) have, to his dismay, been quoted and circulated by members of opponents of lesbian and gay rights (Burr 1996a, 79–88; Jefferson 1993). Arguments made in this book—against determinism, against the emerging research program, and so on—might be used in this unintended way as well. This is not to say that science, social science, and the humanities each has the same effect and thus the same potential for harming lesbians and gay men. Rather, my point is that social scientists and humanists as well as scientists need to worry about the effects of their research. Regardless of the discipline, *well-intentioned* research does not entail *good* research in either the ethical or the scientific sense. Social scientists and humanists who point to the ethical problems with scientific research about sexual orientations should turn the same critical eye towards their own disciplines and their own inquiries concerning sexual orientations and sexual desires more generally.

### Sexual Orientation Research in the Future

Note that the ethical argument against research on sexual orientation is based on existing conditions for lesbians and gay men. The claim is that the social effects of this research are morally problematic at this time and place, not that such research is bad in *all* times and places. For example, research on the cause of right- versus left-handedness did, at one time, have bad social effects since left-handed people were thought to be diseased and cursed (Suppe 1994, 260). In various explicit and subtle ways, left-handed people were demonized, discriminated against, and forced to convert to being right-handed. At present, research on handedness is ethically neutral and may be of some scientific interest (perhaps because it can be used in exploring differences between the two hemispheres of the brain).[1] The point is that in some future society—where, for example, prejudice, discrimination, and legal asymmetries on the basis of sexual orientation have disappeared—research on the origins of sexual orientation and desire would not have the negative social effects it has had in the past or is likely to have in the present, at least in some contexts. If in the (perhaps all-too-distant) future such a nonprejudicial society were to emerge, scientific research on sexual orientations and desires could be free of its present ethical problems.

Critics of scientific research concerning sexual orientations might respond, however, that the only motivation for such research in the first place is fear, hatred, and ignorance of lesbian and gay men (Bersani 1995; Halperin 1990, 49–51; Schüklenk 1993; Suppe 1994); in an enlightened society such as the one I described, why people have the sexual orientations that they do will be uninteresting and irrelevant or the differences in people's sexual orientations that currently exist will disappear and be replaced with a polymorphous sexuality. In such a society, the social interest and importance of differences in people's sexual orientations and desires will change compared to our present society.

For reasons that I sketched in various places previously, I do not think that our interest in understanding human sexual desires would or should disappear completely. Why people have the sexual desires they do involves the intersection of two deeply interesting and important questions about humans: how do people develop such widely divergent preferences, tastes, and desires? and how should sex be understood as part of the human condition? Both of these questions span many disciplines—from biology to history, from cognitive science to sociology—and cut to the heart of our understanding of human nature. It is unlikely that changes in attitudes towards lesbians and gay men will result in either the resolution of these questions or in the dissolution of our interest in them.

## In Defense of Such Research

The arguments I have considered in chapter 11 and thus far in the present chapter make a prima facie case for restricting scientific research on sexual orientation when such research is likely to have negative effects on lesbians and gay men and when it is based on even implicit homophobic assumptions. In this section, I consider arguments in defense of scientific research on sexual orientation.

## Positive Implications

Defenders of scientific research on sexual orientation have argued that such research has positive ethical and legal implications, in particular for lesbian and gay rights. Even if there are potential negative effects of this scientific research, perhaps its positive implications cancel out these negative effects. However, I argued in chapter 10 that scientific research does not have the positive ethical, legal, and political ramifications that many have claimed it does. Showing that sexual orientation is biologically based or that it is determined does not make the case for lesbian and gay rights (not legally, ethically, or pragmatically). Generally, empirical facts do not entail moral and ethical conclusions.

Although in chapter 10 I argued against the relevance of scientific research to ethical questions concerning sexual orientation, I did allow that scientific evidence may have some impact (at least in the short term) on some aspects of how homosexuality is viewed, for example, on how the mental health profession views homosexuality. Some defenders of scientific research have argued that evidence of a biological basis for homosexuality will discourage psychiatrists, psychologists, and therapists from trying to cure homosexuality (Pillard 1997). The strength of this impact is, however, easily overemphasized. Even if the results of the emerging research program convince a therapist that a patient cannot change his or her sexual orientation, the therapist might encourage the patient to change his or her behaviors, sexual relationships, and public sexual identity. Even if a therapist does not try to *cure* a patient's homosexuality, he or she might still view homosexuality as less desirable than heterosexuality and continue to accept a variety of mistaken and potentially harmful stereotypes about lesbians and gay men. This could adversely affect the therapeutic goals set for lesbian and gay patients (Byne and Stein 1997). Additionally, therapists (and others) who think homosexuality is undesirable will, in the face of such research, simply switch their support away from conversion therapy to medical or genetic therapies (see chapter 11). More significantly, arguments against conversion therapy can be made *independent* of any biological evidence. One can show that there is no good reason to convert homosexuals by arguing that there is nothing morally wrong with homosexuality. As I discussed towards the end of chapter 11, there are also some ethical considerations that count against trying to change the sexual orientation of even an individual with the strong desire to do so. The availability of conversion therapies may have the effect of labeling homosexuality as an inferior condition, thereby increasing prejudice and discrimination towards lesbians and gay men. In general, scientific research on sexual orientation does not have the positive ethical implications that many have claimed it does.

### The Value of the Truth

To defend research on sexual orientation in the face of ethical concerns, some people have appealed to the value of the truth. For example, Michael Ruse says that it is best "to try to do good through knowledge" (Ruse 1988, 20). The idea is that the truth will set us free. It is the case that, all else being equal, it is better to believe things that are *true* rather than things that are false: truth has a certain stability to it and arguments based on truths fare better than those based on uncertainty or falsehoods. Scientific research does, however, have its costs, and not every research program is of equal importance. Even granting that, in general, knowledge is better than ignorance, not all risks for the sake of knowledge are worth taking. In fact, there are an infinite number of truths about the world. Scientists cannot possibly try to determine all of the truths that exist. Instead, in the face of limited resources, scientists and funders of scientific research must select which topics are the most appropriate for scientific inquiry. The ethical implications of a research program are relevant to deciding whether the program is worth pursuing. If, for example, a research program offers the potential for saving lives, then it is worth the risk of negative ethical results. There is, however, no suggestion that scientific research on sexual orientation holds any such promise. As I argued in chapter 10 and above, the positive implications of scientific research on sexual orientation are minimal at best; as I argued in chapter 11 and above, the negative ethical implications of this research are, in contrast, quite serious. In light of this, the pursuit of truth alone is not a strong enough reason for conducting such research.

### Scientific Freedom

In response to arguments against scientific research on sexual orientation, some people have suggested that any restrictions on such research would be incompatible with intellectual and academic freedom. Scientists, they say, should be free to undertake whatever kind of research they deem scientifically appropriate. But what if the scientifically appropriate research is ethically problematic? In general, scientific research is in various ways balanced against ethical considerations. Many research laboratories and universities have ethical oversight committees to weigh the potential benefits of research, for example, in terms of how it will advance knowledge and help people, and the likely costs of such research in terms of its effects on experimental subjects (both human and animal) and its social consequences. Given this, the general response that scientific research should not face any restrictions fails.

Instead, defenders of such research might argue that the mere possibility of negative effects of the research is not enough to warrant a general restriction. If, however, the potential harms of such research on balance outweighed its benefits, it would be unethical to proceed. For example, one might argue that permitting sexual-orientation researchers to continue their work could lead to attempts to select or change sexual orientations and, thus, engender the sort of harmful effects discussed in chapter 11. Such effects could, then, outweigh the benefits of developing such a technology in the first place. The implications of not funding or restricting specific research programs need to be considered on a case-by-case basis. The appeal to scientific freedom is powerful, but it is not strong enough to trump every particular argument against specific scientific projects, for example, it is not necessarily strong enough to trump the arguments from the previous section of this chapter. The German constitution provides an interesting example of how to deal with ethical issues relating to scientific research (Schüklenk and Ristow 1996). It links the freedom of academic inquiry to the responsible behavior of those conducting the research. If researchers act unethically, the constitution allows for intervention.

### The Risk of Ignorance

Finally, some defenders of scientific research have argued that the risk of ignorance is too great to not continue studying the origins of human sexual desires. They claim that, given how important human sexual orientation is in many cultures and given that scientific research on sexual orientation already plays a role in ethical and public policy discussion, it would be a mistake to simply bring such research to a halt (Hamer and Copeland 1994, 219–221; Money 1988, 152–154; Murphy 1997, 49–73). At present, the emerging research program, as I outlined in chapter 5, is the leading paradigm for thinking about sexual orientation. Cessation of research on sexual orientation would leave the emerging research program with the upper hand in discussions of how sexual desires develop. Given the arguments I have made so far, the ethical and scientific risks of doing that should be apparent.

## Conclusion

Building on the central argument of chapter 11, I considered various ethical concerns about research on sexual orientation in the first section of this chapter. In the next section, I considered some attempts to rebut these ethical concerns. Some people, in evaluating these sorts of issues, have concluded that there should be a moratorium on scientific research on sexual orientation, especially because of the negative impact such research is almost sure to have in countries where the situation for lesbians and gay men is the most precarious. Although I am tempted by such arguments (Stein, Kerin, and Schüklenk 1998), I here embrace a less broad conclusion. In deciding whether to engage in research on sexual orientation, people have a moral responsibility to consider the impact of such research—locally and globally. For example, they need to consider whether such research is likely to produce a genetic screening test that would make orientation-selection procedures possible. Research institutions, universities, governments, and other bodies that support research should weigh the likely negative effects of the research and its potential benefits. The effects of such research need to be considered against the background of homophobia and heterosexism. Further, if such research is to be done, it should be done with an eye towards its use and effects and in the context of respect for the rights, liberties, and social conditions of lesbians, gay men, and bisexuals. This is not necessarily an ethical argument against scientific research on sexual orientation, but it is consistent with such arguments.

As a possible example of how the ethical implications of scientific research might influence whether such research should be conducted, consider the work of Dean Hamer. The first article on his Xq28 study ended with the following paragraph:

> Our work represents an early application of molecular linkage methods to a normal variation in human behavior. As the Human Genome Project proceeds, it is likely that many such correlations will be discovered. We believe that it would be fundamentally unethical to use such information to try to assess or alter a person's current or future sexual orientation, either heterosexual or homosexual. . . . Rather, scientists, educators, policy makers, and the public should work together to ensure that such research is used to benefit all members of society. (Hamer et al. 1993, 326)

While this statement is well-intentioned, it is not clear that Hamer's approach is sufficiently proactive. Instead, before conducting such research, scientists should ask whether the study is likely to do more harm than good. For example, is there any use of Hamer's results that will "benefit all [or even most] members of society"? How does this compare to the risks of such research? Hamer seems to be aware of the potential harms, but he is rather naive about preventing them (Hamer and Copeland 1994, 214–219).

To illustrate a more carefully considered approach to the ethical implications of research on sexual orientation, let me be so bold as to offer my own book as an example. As I discussed above, research on sexual orientation in the humanities and social sciences, like scientific research, has the potential to have negative effects on lesbians and gay men. For example, my critique of the emerging research program, of determinism, and of biological arguments for lesbian and gay rights might be used by opponents of lesbian and gay rights. In the face of that possibility, I have explicitly discussed a variety of ethical issues relating to sexual orientation, and I explicitly developed my own views and in some instances gave reasoned arguments for them. In my discussion of ethical issues, I adopt, contra Hamer, a proactive approach to lesbian and gay rights. That I have proactively addressed the effects of my research does not guarantee that my arguments will have no bad effects; one can never be certain that one's work will be used only as one intends it to be.

Scientific research on sexual orientation has had and will continue to have various negative effects on lesbians, gay men, and bisexuals. Such effects should be taken seriously by scientists considering doing such research, by governments and organizations considering funding such research, and by subjects considering participating in it.

# CONCLUSION

In his speech in *The Symposium,* Aristophanes divides humans into four groups according to their sex-gender and to the three types of globular humans (male, female, and hermaphrodites) from whom they descended. These four groups are men who descended from globular males and who thereby desire other men, women who descended from globular females and who thereby desire other women, men who descended from globular hermaphrodites and who thereby desire women, and women who descended from globular hermaphrodites and who thereby desire men. A natural interpretation of this speech—one that I discussed extensively in chapter 4—is that Aristophanes was talking about gay men, lesbians, heterosexual men, and heterosexual women, respectively.

Compare Aristophanes' speech to one that might have been made in a Zomnian dialogue that discusses the significance of sleep, how we sleep, why we sleep, and other issues relating to sleep. Suppose that a character in this imaginary dialog, call her Dormitima, offers a myth of the origins of backers and fronters which proposes to explain their different sleep orientations by saying that they were separately created. While Zomnians might not see this myth as providing an accurate account of the origins of preferences for different sleep positions, the myth might capture the flavor and the spirit of how they think about people's sleep preferences.

How do these two mythological stories compare? While many people in most contemporary cultures do not accept the *details* of Aristophanes' myth, certain central aspects of this myth will probably ring true to them. On one straightforward reading of his speech, Aristophanes is suggesting that men and women can be either homosexual or heterosexual and that this difference in sexual orientation is both inborn and important. Further, Aristophanes' myth fits nicely with the view that sexual orientations are natural human kinds. Similarly, for Zomnians, Dormitima's myth would ring true insofar as it suggests that people should be divided into backers and fronters and that differences in sleep orientations are important and either innate or determined at an early age.

342

For those of us who are not Zomnians, Dormitima's myth seems odd, especially because we do not think that backers and fronters play any significant role in scientific laws or scientific explanation, that is, we do not think they are natural human kinds. Similarly, people in some other cultures (for example, New Guinea, some Native American cultures, and on some accounts, Attic Greece) do not accept the view that homosexuals and heterosexuals are natural kinds; from their perspective, sexual orientations seem like social human kinds.

In the introduction of this book, I quoted Bertrand Russell's observation that one of the central purposes of philosophy is to free us from the "tyranny of custom." One of the central aims of this book is to free us from custom's tyranny with respect to sexual orientation and sexual desire. It has become the custom in many cultures to think of all humans as having sexual orientations and to see these orientations as revealing something significant and important about a person's overall personality and character. Along with this custom has emerged a related custom of a curiosity about the origins of some but not all sexual orientations. In particular, science, medicine, and psychiatry have been and continue to be interested in why people become homosexuals. An interest in the nature and origins of sexual desires and sexual orientation, especially same sex-gender sexual attraction, seems only natural to many people, but it is a live question whether this peculiar fascination is scientifically and metaphysically justified.

I began to address this question in chapters 1 and 2 by analyzing the notion of sexual orientation. At first pass, a person's sexual orientation has to do with the sex or gender of the people to whom he or she is attracted. In chapter 1, I discussed sex-gender and its relationship to sexual orientation. Then in chapter 2, I discussed various answers to the question, what is a sexual orientation? I argued that a sexual orientation is best understood as a multidimensional dispositional and psychological property that is one feature of a person's general sexual desires. With this conceptual analysis as background, I introduced the notions of natural kinds and natural human kinds in chapter 3, and I applied these notions to sexual orientation in chapter 4, where I began to discuss essentialism and constructionism about sexual orientation. In various places throughout the book, I have discussed the conceptual and empirical relationships among essentialism, constructionism, and other claims about sexual orientation. In chapter 4, I argued that the debate between essentialism and constructionism does not reduce to the debate between nativism and environmentalism about sexual orientation. And, in chapter 8, I argued that the debate between essentialism and constructionism does not reduce to the debate between voluntarism and determinism about sexual orientation.

In chapter 4, I also argued that the theoretical justifications for thinking that sexual orientations are natural human kinds are weak. The fact that we have cultural, political, and legal practices built around sexual orientations does not prove sexual orientations are natural human kinds anymore than the fact that Zomnians have cultural, political, and legal practices built around sleep orientations proves sleep orientations are natural kinds. Whether or not sexual orientations or sleep orientations are natural human kinds is an empirical question to which scientific research on sexual orientations may be relevant.

Partly because of its relevance to whether sexual orientations are natural human kinds, but also because such research is so central to how many contemporary cultures conceptualize sexual orientations ethically, politically, and socially and because such research has received so much attention in the media and has shaped public consciousness, in chapters 5 through 8, I considered in detail contemporary scientific research on sexual orientations. After discussing some of the central contemporary research in chapter 5—focusing on attempts to locate the origins of sexual orientation in the body (especially the brain), in family trees, and in genes—in chapters 6 and 7, I argued that such research has serious methodological problems and rests on various undefended assumptions. In contrast to the dramatic claims that advocates of the emerging scientific research program make, I argue that we are very far from understanding human sexual orientation and human sexual desires more generally. Such research is partly hindered by various problems with respect to its subject pool. Most of its nonheterosexual subjects come from a particular subset of nonheterosexuals, for example, people who are to some extent open about their sexual orientation. Also, most of the studies are done on men rather than women and on people in Western countries. Further, many of the scientific studies depend crucially on problematic animal models of human sexual orientation (chapter 6) as well as on undefended assumptions about human sexual orientation (chapter 7), for example, that lesbians are biologically more like men than they are like heterosexual women (the inversion assumption). Scientific research on sexual orientation has also failed to produce strong evidence that homosexuals, heterosexuals, and bisexuals are natural human kinds. In fact, most of the studies that are part of the emerging scientific research program concerning sexual orientation assume implicitly that sexual orientations are natural human kinds and thus do not provide support for essentialism.

Towards the end of chapter 8, I described some features of possible scientific studies that would avoid certain problems facing scientific research on sexual orientation. Studies with such features would help settle whether or not sexual orientations are natural human kinds. Such studies would, for example, involve people from a broad range of cultures and would take special care not to assume that certain culturally salient ways of organizing sexual desires apply to all humans. Further, such studies should be open to the possibility that human sexual orientations (and human sexual desires more generally) will not be adequately explained by a single theory or mechanism, but rather, will have multiple origins. Additionally, such studies should take seriously the possibility that biology plays an indirect role (rather than a direct role) in the development of sexual orientations and desires, namely, that biological factors play a role in personality and temperamental characteristics that under some (but not all) environmental conditions affect the development of sexual orientations (the indirect model), rather than such factors actually shaping a person's sexual orientation in the way that biological factors shape eye color (the direct model). Chapter 5 discusses the distinction among the direct, indirect, and permissive models of the role of biological factors in the development of sexual orientations.

Compared to sexual orientations, there is even less evidence about whether or not sleep orientations are natural human kinds. This is not so surprising since only in an imaginary culture do people think that sleep orientations are natural human kinds. Most of us are quite confident that sleep orientations are *social* kinds, *not* natural kinds. Similarly, most of us are confident that the role of biological factors in the development of sleep orientations is limited to their influence on neuroanatomical structures that experience molds into the mechanisms underlying the preference for a particular sleep position (in other words, that the permissive model applied to the development of sleep orientations is true).

Why are we inclined to think that sexual orientations are natural human kinds and disinclined to think that sleep orientations are natural human kinds? Similarly, why are we inclined to think that the direct model correctly characterizes the role of biological factors on sexual orientations, while the permissive model correctly characterizes the role of biological factors on sleep orientation? The answers should be obvious when put in the context of the arguments in this book. Most of us have been brought up with the view that something deep and important about a person is uncovered by learning about his or her sexual desires, in particular, that the sex-gender of the people he or she is sexually attracted to reveals something especially significant about him or her. It is, however, a truism that not everything we are brought up to believe is true. The very reasons I gave in the introduction of this book for being interested in sexual orientations and desires in general, and in chapter 5 for being interested in scientific research concerning sexual orientation in particular, are applicable to whether a person's sexual orientation reveals something deep about his or her true nature. Does a person's sexual orientation reveal more about him or her than, for example, the position in which he or she sleeps? After all, most of us spend more of our lives sleeping than we do having sex. This is a nontrivial empirical question. One of the central claims of this book is that *we do not have strong evidence to support the commonly held belief that sexual orientations are natural human kinds.*

If in a hundred years a sophisticated science of human sexual desire is developed, it might establish that some aspects of a person's sexual desires— *perhaps* a person's sexual orientation—reveal a great deal about human nature (that is, about deep features of human biology and psychology). Perhaps the sorts of experiments I described at the end of chapter 8 might provide support for this sort of claim. I suspect, however, that sexual orientations, as we understand them, will *not* play a central role in an advanced science of human sexual desires. Throughout this book, in various places, I have observed that human sexual desires vary widely, that various cultures attach different values to various sexual desires, and that sexual orientation is one small slice of sexual desire more generally. From a historical and anthropological perspective and in light of my discussions in chapter 3 (about natural kinds and natural human kinds generally) and in chapter 4 (about how these concepts apply to sexual orientation), we can see that our way of organizing human sexual desires and our prioritization of sexual orientation over other aspects of human sexual desires is far from universal. Given this, and given my arguments in chapters 6 and 7 against the emerging research program, there is no especially strong reason for thinking that sexual orientations will turn out to be the most important part of human sexual desires from a scientific point of view. It is *cultural chauvinism*— a form of what Stephen Stich (1990, chapters 4 and 5) calls *epistemic chauvinism*—to think, in the absence of either strong scientific evidence or strong theoretical arguments, that our conceptual framework, which gives sexual orientation such a central role, is going to be confirmed by an advanced science of human sexual desire.

Some people think that if it turns out that sexual orientations are not what I call natural human kinds, then their importance is somehow undermined. For reasons I developed in chapter 10, *even if sexual orientations are merely social human kinds, sexual orientations might still play a very important role in law, politics, and ethics.* Social kinds, especially social human kinds, can have legal, ethical, and political significance. Membership in a political party, a neighborhood community, or a religious group are social human kinds, but they can still be important legally, ethically, and politically.

In chapter 10, I also emphasized some complementary claims. Even if sexual orientations were natural human kinds or if determinism about sexual orientation were true or if one particular theory of human sexual orientations among the various theories within the emerging scientific research program were true, there would be few ethical, legal, and political implications that follow. My argument focuses on the centrality of *choices* that lesbians and gay men make in light of their sexual desires, the culture that they live in, and their life experiences. It is the choices they make about how to live their lives, not the origins of their sexual desires, that are most important for lesbian and gay rights. Regardless of whether sexual orientations are directly chosen, indirectly chosen, or not chosen at all (as I discussed these issues in chapter 9), people choose with whom they have sex, people choose whether to be open about their sexual orientations, people choose whether or not to enter romantic relationships, and whether or not to build families. In chapter 10, I emphasized that such choices should be the centerpiece of lesbian and gay rights. Arguments that appeal to the supposed biological basis of sexual orientation focus on the lack of choice (or related claims) and, as such, are unable to undergird a robust version of lesbian and gay rights. Understanding the role, if any, that choice plays in the development of sexual orientation should form an important part of our scientific understanding of sexual orientation. It is a distinct scientific question from whether sexual orientations are natural human kinds or social human kinds. Neither question is, however, relevant to settling ethical, political, and legal questions about sexual orientations.

I have argued that the truth of metaphysical claims (claims about what things there are and the form their existence takes) and scientific claims (claims about the details of the entities that exist and the laws that operate on them) about sexual orientations are not important to ethical, legal, and political claims related to sexual orientation. However, nothing I have said should suggest that people's *opinions* regarding scientific and metaphysical issues relating to sexual orientations do not affect their ethical, legal, and political opinions. As I mentioned in chapter 10, opinion polls indicate that people who believe sexual orientations are biologically based are more likely to support lesbian and gay rights than people who do not. Also, public policy is influenced by people's scientific and metaphysical beliefs about sexual orientations. How else can we understand the logic of the U.S. military's policy concerning homosexuality (see discussion in chapter 10)? This policy was shaped, to a considerable extent, by views about the nature and origins of human sexual orientation and sexual desires more generally. Public opinion and public policy are related to beliefs about the nature and origins of sexual orientation, but such connections are tenuous and hard to predict over time and across different places. In chapter 10, I showed that attempts to make pragmatic ethical, political, and legal arguments that appeal to metaphysical and scientific arguments are risky and unlikely to be successful in the long term.

Chapters 11 and 12 discussed some aspects of the complicated relationship between scientific research on sexual orientation and social, political, legal, and ethical questions related to lesbians and gay men. In social contexts in which lesbians and gay men face discrimination and disapprobation, scientific research is a potential minefield. This is not to say that ignorance about things sexual is better than knowledge. Rather, my claim is that we need to temper our desire for knowledge with a strong concern about the effects of such research and how it is framed.

Why are we interested in understanding human sexual orientations and desires? Attempting to understand human sexual orientations is a legitimate part of the quest to understand human nature (that is, to understand universal features of human biology and psychology). However, social factors have a significant effect on what questions get the most attention and how research gets framed. Most notably, scientists doing research on sexual orientation are almost always concerned with how and why people become homosexual, not how and why people become heterosexual. It is important to weed out cultural presumptions about sexual orientation, especially those that infiltrate scientific research and its metaphysical foundations. Once we have done so, the character and shape of scientific research (as well as social scientific and humanistic research) and our general thinking about sexual orientation will be dramatically changed for the better.

In the introduction to this book, I described queer theory as the project of dredging up the heterosexist and homophobic assumptions deeply embedded in various disciplines. By exploring sexual orientation in metaphysics, science, and ethics, I have tried to break free of the tyranny of custom in thinking about sexual orientation using philosophy and queer theory. One might say I have queered the metaphysical, scientific, and ethical approaches to sexual orientation.

If intelligent creatures visited us from another planet and asked us about the ways that we think and behave scientifically and socially in relation to sexual orientations, what would we be able to say in defense of our practices? How would our replies compare to what the Zomnians could say in defense of their thoughts and behaviors with respect to sleep orientations? Much of the argument of this book suggests that we are not better off in terms of justifying our metaphysical and scientific views about sexual orientation and sexual desires than the Zomnians are in justifying their views about sleep positions and the dispositions that underlie them. Our confidence that we have advanced a great deal in our understanding of sexual orientation compared to Aristophanes and his fellow celebrants in *The Symposium* is premature.

# NOTES

## Chapter 2

1. This view is implicit in lots of thinking about sexual orientation. Janet Halley (1993) shows how the behavioral view (as well as something like the dispositional view discussed below) is implicit in the Supreme Court's ruling in *Bowers v. Hardwick* (1986), in which the majority of the justices ruled that it is constitutional for states to pass laws that make homosexual sodomy illegal. The behavioral view is also implicit in the writings of therapists who think that they can "cure" people's homosexuality. I consider issues relating to whether sexual orientations can be cured in chapters 9 and 12.

2. For defenses of behaviorism, see John Watson (1913) and B. F. Skinner (1965). For a classic critique of behaviorism, see Noam Chomsky (1980).

3. For an elementary discussion of counterfactuals, see Samuel Guttenplan (1986, chapter 16). For a technical discussion, see David Lewis (1973).

4. Because we live in a society in which, for the most part, people are presumed to be heterosexual, it takes lesbians and gay men a longer time to figure out and come to grips with their sexual orientation than it does for heterosexuals to figure out theirs. See chapter 10 for a further sketch of the social situation for lesbians and gay men.

5. Among the most detailed rating systems for sexual orientation is one developed by Fritz Klein, Barry Sepekoff, and Timothy Wolf (1985), which makes use of a *twenty-one*-point rating system. Klein's system rates people on a scale of zero to six, and in terms of past, present, and ideal, on seven criteria: sexual attraction, sexual behavior, sexual fantasies, emotional preference, social preference, self-identification, and lifestyle (heterosexual or gay/lesbian). Klein's twenty-one-point view of sexual orientation, by adopting the bipolar view (namely, by rating people on a scale of 0 to 6), seems to inherit the problems of that view (twenty-one times over). B. R. Berky, T. Perelmanhall, and L. A. Kurdek (1990) offer a more sophisticated version of Klein's view that does not inherit these problems. It is interesting to note that one research team claims to be able to reduce the twenty-one factors to just three (Weinrich et al. 1993).

6. This account of the distinction between the sexual and nonsexual draws to a limited extent on Thomas Nagel (1979).

## Chapter 3

1. Among those who think that scientific research is relevant to lesbian and gay rights are Simon LeVay (1996), Andrew Sullivan (1995), Bruce Bawer (1993), and

Richard Green (1988). For criticism of this view, see articles by Janet Halley (1994), me (Byne and Stein 1997; Stein 1994), and chapter 10.

2. Many commentators on scientific research on sexual orientation seem not to understand constructionism. For example, Dean Hamer, a scientist, and Peter Copeland, a journalist, discuss such an extreme version of constructionism that the position is barely recognizable (Hamer and Copeland 1994, 176–77). Michael Ruse, a philosopher, thinks he has refuted constructionism in three pages of rather superficial discussion of it (1988, especially 15–18). James Weinrich, a biologist, starts out with a fairly good discussion of the issues, but his proposed compromise position—"interactionism"—is not really a compromise at all; his interactionism contains no concession to anything but the most trivial constructionism (1987b, chapter 5). Somewhat less confused, but still problematic in their discussions of constructionism are Simon LeVay (1996), a scientist, and an essay by Richard Mohr (1992b), a philosopher. LeVay simply writes off "strong social constructi[on]ism"; he just says that "little interaction" between constructionism and biology is possible (LeVay 1996, 55–58); at the end of his chapter 2, LeVay seems to allow that at least a "weak" version of constructionism *might* be true, although he says that it is appropriate to assume that it is not (65). Some discussions of scientific research on sexual orientation ignore constructionism where it seems relevant, for example, LeVay's first book (1993) and a book by Chandler Burr (1996a). Burr's unsophisticated book should at least *consider* constructionism in chapter 3—which discusses arguments for the view that homosexuality is not biological—but fails to do so.

3. I first developed the example of Zomnia as an analogy for constructionism about sexual orientation in an essay I wrote in 1990 (Stein 1990). A few years later, I discovered that the Kinsey report also discussed sleep as analogy to sexual orientation.

> [I]t must not be forgotten that the basic phenomenon to be explained is an individual's preference for a partner of one sex, or for a partner of the other sex, or his acceptance of a partner of either sex. This problem is after all part of the broader problem of choices in general: the choice of the road that one takes, of the clothes that one wears, of the food that one eats, of *the place in which one sleeps,* and of the endless other things that one is constantly choosing. A choice of a partner in a sexual relation becomes more significant only because society demands that there be a particular choice in this matter, and does not so often dictate one's choice of food or of clothing. (Kinsey, Pomeroy, and Martin 1948, 661, emphasis added)

4. I say "typically" because of groups like (k), the group of groups that are not members of themselves. Consider whether (k) is a member of itself (as, for example, [d]—the group of all groups than can be described in less than twenty words—is a member of itself). It seems certain that *either* (k) is a member of itself or (k) is not a member of itself. Suppose the first possibility is true. Then, since (k) is a member of itself, (k) would not be a member of (k) because (k) is the group of groups that are not members of themselves. This is a contradiction: it says (k) is both a member of itself and not a member of itself. Suppose, then, the second possibility is true. If (k) is not a member of itself, then (k) is a member of the group of groups that are not members of itself. This is also a contradiction: it says (k) is both not a member of itself and yet is a member of itself. The general problem (this is just one version of it) is known as *Russell's paradox* (after Bertrand Russell, who discovered it). Logicians deal with this

paradox by saying that for some entities, it is not the case that they either are or are not members of a specific group. It is for this reason that I need to say "typically" a thing is either a member of a group or not; because of Russell's paradox, some things are neither members or nonmembers of particular groups.

5. "Let us carve them according to their natural divisions as we would carve a sacrificial victim" (Plato 1952, 287c), as quoted in Ian Hacking (1991, 124).

6. I here sidestep the debate about whether species are natural kinds or individuals (Ghilsen 1974; Hull 1976; Hull and Ruse 1998, 295–368; Wilson 1999). Although I am somewhat persuaded by the arguments that species are individuals, this argument need not be discussed here.

7. I have made things seem simpler than they actually are. It is in practice hard to distinguish between an empty kind and a bona fide natural kind that has been mischaracterized. Consider the following example: for centuries, people thought that the earth was the center of the universe and that the heavenly bodies (including the planets, the sun, and the stars) revolved around the earth. Copernicus argued that the sun is the center of the solar system and that the earth and planets revolve around it. In the shift from the Ptolemaic world view to the Copernican world view, it is not clear whether the group of "heavenly bodies" was determined to be an empty kind or whether we learned that it is a natural kind but that it includes the earth. See Thomas Kuhn (1957, 1970).

8. Frank Keil (1989, 47) notes that "an anthill is a natural kind rather than an artifact[ual kind] . . . because the ant has no conscious intention to construct such a hill and because its behaviors are presumably describable in terms of biological laws having to do with survival in various ecological niches." As we move towards humans from creatures of greater cognitive complexity than ants, the line between a natural kind and an artifactual kind may blur. The issues here are interesting, but not particularly relevant to my project. On a somewhat related point, see my discussion of whether animals have sexual orientations in chapter 6.

9. Among the various nominalists in the history of philosophy are Thomas Hobbes, John Locke (to a certain extent), and, more recently, Nelson Goodman (1978). David Armstrong (1989, chapter 1) gives a taxonomy of some types of nominalism; much of the rest of Armstrong's book is an evaluation of these different flavors of nominalism. For further discussion, see Ian Hacking (1991).

10. It is perfectly respectable for a scientific law to make claims involving "typical" outcomes. The technical term for this feature of scientific laws is that they involve *ceteris paribus*—all else being equal—clauses. For a discussion of the inelim- inability of *ceteris paribus* clauses, see Nancy Cartwright (1983). For a useful introduc- tion to *ceteris paribus* clauses in the social sciences, see Alexander Rosenberg (1988, chapter 2).

11. In an essay I wrote several years ago (Stein 1990), I tried to capture this feature of natural kinds under the rubric "transcultural." Some people misinterpreted this term (for example, Mohr 1992b, 237). My discussion of natural kinds here should preempt such misunderstanding.

12. I have slightly simplified matters here. There are various senses of the word "could." Does the category "person taller than nine feet" refer to an empty kind? There is a sense in which there could be a person who is taller than nine feet even though there

has never been such a person. Even in this sense of "could," there could not be any witches.

## Chapter 4

1. In a footnote, Boswell (1989, 25) does admit that there are "some complex aspects" to Aristophanes' speech. As it turns out, these aspects are the linchpins of the argument for an alternative reading of this speech.

2. David Greenberg (1988, 26–40) distinguishes among *transgenerational* (the two same-sex sexual partners are of significantly different ages), *transgenderal* (the two same-sex sexual partners have different genders—typically, one of the two partners is in some way transgendered while the other is not), *transclass* (the two same-sex sexual partners are of significantly different classes), and *egalitarian* forms of homosexuality (the two same-sex sexual partners are of approximately the same age, class, and of the same gender; this is also called *androphilic* homosexuality).

3. The date Halperin (1990) gives is of the publication of Kertbeny's anonymous pamphlet arguing against (what we would call) antigay portions of Prussian law. The first recorded use of the word "homosexual" as well as the word "heterosexual" is, however, in a private letter to Karl Ulrichs in 1868. In 1869, instead of "heterosexual," Kertbeny used the German word *"normalsexual"* as a contrast to "homosexual" (Herzer 1985). Jonathan Ned Katz (1995, 19–21 and 207), attributes to James Kiernan (1892) the first *published* use of the English word "heterosexual."

4. Other noteworthy early constructionists are Michel Foucault (1978), John Gagnon and William Simon (1973), Jeffrey Weeks (1977), Kenneth Plummer (1975), many of the contributors to the anthology *Sexual Meanings* (Ortner and Whitehead 1981), and some of the contributors to *Forms of Desire* (Stein 1990).

5. Many constructionists deny that their view is empirically falsifiable in this fashion. David Halperin (1990, 49) is one constructionist who admits that it is.

6. As an example of the vagueness in Ruse's and Mohr's definitions, consider whether they mean to count a person as homosexual if he or she only *rarely* has the desire to have sex with people of the same sex or whether they would disqualify someone as being a homosexual if he or she ever has the desire to have sex with people of a different sex. I set this worry aside for now.

7. Simon LeVay (1996, 56) also offers a wide definition of "homosexual" that he seems to think makes the case for essentialism. Much of his book assumes essentialism, but in one place (65) he seems to admit that he has not really provided an argument for essentialism. For a discussion of LeVay, see my review (Stein 1998).

8. The argument I make here dates back to Plato (1935a, especially 170–171). For discussion, see Peter van Inwagen (1993, chapter 4).

9. For a discussion of Sullivan, see the review I wrote with Morris Kaplan (Kaplan and Stein 1996).

## Chapter 5

1. Of the people surveyed in 1970, 44 percent said none or hardly any "homosexuals were born that way," 18 percent said less than half were born that way, 14

percent said it is more than half, and 17 percent said all or almost all were born that way (Klassen, Williams, and Levitt 1989).

2. Michael Bailey (1995a, 104) admits that there are some not very "meaningful and interesting construals of the question" whether homosexuality is "biological" (he cites the same passage from Money just before he says this); oddly though, Bailey goes on to say: "To encourage more responsible usage, I recommend referring to 'biological' causes, influences, theories, or explanations (i.e., with quotation marks). This draws attention to the problematic term that has numerous connotations and an uninformative literal meaning" (104–105). He then continues to use "biological" in scare quotes throughout. While this does serve the purpose of signaling the ambiguities, it hardly helps to get rid of the confusion. Instead, he might have tried to spell out what sense of "biological" he thinks is appropriately applied to the sources of sexual orientation.

3. For a discussion of the social conditions for lesbians and gay men in New York City around the time of this study, see George Chauncey (1994).

4. My friend, psychologist Paul Bloom, first pointed out to me the possible analogy between language and sexual orientation under the guise of developing a "Chomskyian" theory of sexual orientation. (This was not surprising since he seemed to believe in a Chomskyian theory of just about everything.) John Money (1988, 11) also offers an analogy between sexual orientation and language.

5. Besides Simon LeVay's study of the hypothalamus, discussed below and in chapter 6, two other neuroanatomical studies that relate to sexual orientation are worth mentioning. Laura Allen and Roger Gorski (1992) studied the anterior commisure, and Dick Swaab and M. Hoffman (1990) studied the suprachiasmatic nucleus. Neither of these studies has been replicated, and it is hard to know what to make of them (Byne 1996; Byne and Parsons 1993). As I will discuss later, LeVay's results have not been replicated either.

6. This is a bit of a simplification because it leaves out ascertainment bias; see chapter 6 for further discussion.

7. While Kallman (1952b) does not give the data, which, he says, is incomplete, he does say that the concordance rates for fraternal twins and nontwin brothers of the target cases "do not seem to differ significantly" (142).

8. This may be a bit of a simplification because it is possible that parents (whether consciously or not) treat biologically related children differently than they do adopted children. In this case, the environmental factors would be different.

9. This too may be a bit of a simplification because people may adopt children who are more genetically similar to them than a child chosen at random; for example, some states in the United States have a strong bias in favor of allowing people to adopt only children of the same race.

## Chapter 6

1. There are other sociobiological accounts of homosexuality including, for example, that homosexuality is an evolutionary adaptation to deal with overpopulation and that, in cultures with ritualized homosexuality, homosexuality is an adaptive strategy used by older men to keep younger men away from the young women (Barkow 1989). On sociobiology generally, see James Weinrich (1987b, 310–336) and Jim McKnight

(1997). For critiques, see Philip Kitcher (1985), Douglas Futuyma and Stephen Risch (1983–1984), Mildred Dickemann (1995), and Martha McCaughey (1996).

## Chapter 7

1. The statistically gifted reader can consult Michael Bailey and Richard Pillard (1991b, 1094, table 4) for the details.

2. The Australian study does provide some support for the significance of familial factors on male and female homosexuality. It does not, however, provide especially strong evidence to distinguish between genetic and environmental factors (Bailey, Dunne, and Martin n.d.).

3. Around the time of LeVay's study, only *30* percent of the men who had AIDS were thought to be heterosexual. LeVay could have made a somewhat better case for presuming the heterosexuality of the six men involved if he had referred to the fact that these men had become infected through IV drug use and then cited the statistic that about *75* percent of the men with AIDS who become infected with HIV through IV drug use are heterosexual (Center for Disease Control 1992, 8). However, even granting the validity of this observation, there is no justification for assuming the heterosexuality of 100 percent of the subjects about whose sexual orientation he had no particular information.

4. I base my calculations on the data as presented by LeVay in the table I have reprinted as Figure 5-3. I selected the three people from each of the categories of heterosexuals who had the largest INAH-3 size and recalculated LeVay's results assuming that these six people were in fact homosexual. I did this to model the possibility that the homosexuals who were misclassified as heterosexuals were misclassified for reasons correlated with INAH-3 size, a possibility that LeVay has done nothing to rule out. In fact, given LeVay's assumption that all the men with AIDS whose sexual orientation was unknown were heterosexual, I do not think my recalculated results are much (if at all) less plausible than LeVay's.

5. William Byne (1994) calls this the *intersex* expectation.

6. The Kinsey studies have, however, been criticized as unreliable on other grounds, most notably for the makeup of their subject pool (Cochran, Mosteller, and Tukey 1953; Laumann et al. 1994, 43–57).

7. For political reasons, the federal funding required to complete the project as originally planned was not granted; a scaled-back version of the project was funded by other sources.

8. For example, a 1988 study claimed to isolate a gene associated with schizophrenia (Sherrington et al. 1988), but two subsequent studies disconfirmed it (Detera-Wadleigh et al. 1989; McGuffin et al. 1990).

9. It is also worth noting that one of Hamer's collaborators has raised concerns about the methodology of the studies. She is reported to have claimed that some subjects were eliminated from the final data pool in a post hoc fashion, that is, certain pairs of subjects may have been eliminated because they did not fit with the hypothesis that homosexuality is maternally linked. These charges were serious enough that the Office of Research Integrity of the Department of Health and Human Services conducted a confidential investigation of the study (Marshall 1995). Although Hamer

was ultimately cleared of any wrongdoing, some researchers in the field take Hamer's collaborator's charges seriously and remain skeptical about Hamer's methodology.

## Chapter 8

1. Janis Bohan (1996, 75–91) divides experiential theories of sexual orientation into psychodynamic approaches, social-learning approaches, interactionist approaches, and volitional/cognitive approaches and then enumerates various theories that fit into each approach. My discussion is not as fine-grained, but my assessment of these theories is basically the same.

2. In a reply to his critics, Daryl Bem (1998, 395) wrote:

> Most cultures, including our own, polarize the sexes, setting up a sex-based division of labor and power, emphasizing or exaggerating sex differences, and, in general, superimposing the male-female dichotomy on virtually every aspect of communal life. These practices ensure that most boys and girls grow up feeling different from opposite-sex peers and, hence, will come to be erotically attracted to them later in life. This, according to [exotic-becomes-erotic] theory, is why biological sex is the most common criterion for selecting a sexual partner in the first place and why heteroeroticism is the modal preference across time and culture.

## Chapter 9

1. Even some scientists working in the emerging research program allow that other aspects of a person's sexual desires besides sexual orientation are more environmentally determined and more likely to be chosen. For example, Richard Pillard, in my interview with him, predicted that: "[A]side from a very general identity as 'homosexual,' how gender atypical you are, whether you like to suck or fuck, whether you're a top or bottom [that is, what position you prefer to play in penetrative sex], and so on, is probably determined more environmentally" (Stein 1993, 102).

2. The form of this argument is what logicians call a *simple constructive dilemma*. This is a *valid* argument form, that is, if its premises are true, its conclusion necessarily follows. Given its validity, the question is whether the premises of this argument are true.

## Chapter 10

1. This is an especially apt analogy since Senator Trent Lott in an interview compared homosexuality to alcoholism (and kleptomania) (Mitchell 1998). Even a virulent homophobe like Lott could accept the determinist argument for lesbian and gay rights because the ethical claims that this argument supports are extremely limited, as my discussion of alcoholism makes clear.

2. In a classic essay, Thomas Nagel (1979) defends an account of sexual perversion according to which the linchpin of natural sex is a multilayered communication between the people having sex. Nagel's account has at least two virtues. He provides a precise account of what natural sex is, and according to his account, same sex-gender sexual activities and desires are as natural as such activities and desires among people not of the same sex-gender. I am not, however, certain that Nagel's account captures

what most people have in mind when they describe a sexual behavior as unnatural or perverted.

3. I do not discuss other claims that lesbians and gay men are unnatural or have unnatural sex. See, for example, Michael Levin (1984) and John Finnis (1995). For a critical discussion of these arguments, see, respectively, Timothy Murphy (1987), and Stephen Macedo (1995) and Michael Perry (1995).

4. This is a rather dramatic simplification since the line between conceptual and empirical questions is far from clear (Quine 1961; Stein 1996, 20–23).

5. In fact, it has been argued that the basic principles that underlie the U.S. Constitution's protection of religious liberty (namely, freedom of conscience, freedom of association, and the rights to free speech and free assembly) also provide a robust defense of lesbian and gay rights (Richards 1994), providing a much stronger defense than the lack of choice argument possibly could.

## Chapter 11

1. According to Aliza Kolker and Meredith Burke (1994, 126), "[a]bout two percent of all women who have prenatal testing will receive a diagnosis of a serious abnormality. Most, but not all, will choose an abortion." That most women who receive an abnormal diagnosis chose to abort is probably due to the fact that women who would not want to have an abortion if their child is going to have such a disease do not bother with genetic screening.

2. Another distinction that might be important here, but which for simplicity's sake I ignore, is the distinction between prefertilization and postfertilization procedures. I focus instead on the distinction between preimplantation and postimplantation procedures. The main difference between these distinctions concerns in vitro fertilization. Selection that took place after an egg has been fertilized yet before it is implanted would be a *pre*implantation but *post*fertilization procedure.

3. An exception to this is an argument that says abortion is wrong because it involves interfering with nature, playing God, or disturbing the natural process of reproduction. This argument might count against preimplantation selection procedures as well as postimplantation ones. This argument, however, proves too much since it would also count against contraception, most forms of genetic screening, and so on. Arguments against the naturalness of various practices, including homosexuality, masturbation, recreational sex, as well as contraception and abortion, run the risk of proving too much and, even worse, may be incoherent since the sort of notion of naturalness that is required cannot be consistently articulated. See chapter 10 for a discussion concerning the naturalness of homosexuality.

4. When the constitutionality of the Pennsylvania abortion law was challenged in *Planned Parenthood v. Casey* (1992), the portion of the law dealing with sex-selection abortion was not challenged. The American Civil Liberties Union lawyer who argued the case before the Supreme Court said that this portion of the law was not challenged because they could not find a woman who would claim injury from it; see Charlotte Allen (1992).

5. Although some sociobiologists might be concerned about such a decrease in the numbers of nonheterosexuals in the population because they think that the pres-

ence of lesbians and gay men improves the overall fitness of the community (see discussion chapter 6), the crucial issue is not the ethical significance of a decrease in the number of lesbians, gay men, and bisexuals, but rather the general impact of the availability and use of orientation-selection procedures in various societies.

6. For a useful discussion of current practices of genetic counselors with respect to sex-screening and sex-selection procedures, see Kolker and Burke (1994, 141–162) and Barbara Rothman (1986, chapter 5).

7. See Cheshire Calhoun (1989) and Tracy Isaacs (1997) for discussion of questions related to this sort of moral responsibility.

8. A recent poll found that 50 percent of people surveyed would feel uncomfortable if their child's teacher was gay (Thinking about Social Values, 1998).

## Chapter 12

1. The possible exception is research on handedness and sexual orientation (Gladue and Bailey 1995; Hamill 1995; Holtzen 1994; McCormick, Witelson, and Kingstone 1990). Such research has produced conflicting results.

# BIBLIOGRAPHY

Abelove, Henry, Michèle Aina Barale, and David Halperin, eds. 1993. *The Lesbian and Gay Studies Reader.* New York: Routledge.

Adkins-Regan, Elizabeth. 1988. "Sex Hormones and Sexual Orientation in Animals." *Psychobiology* 16:335–347.

Adkins-Regan, Elizabeth, and M. Ascenzi. 1987. "Social and Sexual Behaviour of Male and Female Zebra Finches Treated with Oestradiol During the Nestling Period." *Animal Behaviour* 35:1100–1112.

Aguero, J. E., L. Bloch, and D. Byrne. 1984. "The Relationship Among Beliefs, Attitudes, Experience and Homophobia." *Journal of Homosexuality* 10:95–107.

Allen, Charlotte. 1992. "Boys Only: Pennsylvania's Anti-Abortion Law." *New Republic*, March 9, 16–19.

Allen, Clifford. 1958. *Homosexuality: Its Nature, Causation and Treatment.* London: Staples Press.

Allen, Garland. 1997. "The Double-Edged Sword of Genetic Determinism: Social and Political Agendas in Genetic Studies of Homosexuality, 1940–1994." In *Science and Homosexualities,* edited by Vernon Rosario. New York: Routledge.

Allen, Laura, and Roger Gorski. 1990. "Sex Differences in the Bed Nucleus of the Stria Terminalis of the Human Brain." *Journal of Comparative Neurology* 302:697–706.

———. 1991. "Sexual Dimorphism of the Anterior Commissure and Massa Intermedia of the Human Brain." *Journal of Comparative Neurology* 312:97–104.

———. 1992. "Sexual Orientation and the Size of the Anterior Commissure in the Human Brain." *Proceedings of the National Academy of Sciences* 89:7199–7202.

Allen, Laura, M. Hines, and J. E. Shryne. 1989. "Two Sexual Dimorphic Cell Groups in the Human Brain." *Journal of Neuroscience* 9:497–506.

Allen, Woody. 1971. *Getting Even.* New York: Random House.

Allen, Woody (director). 1972. *Everything You Ever Wanted to Know about Sex (But Were Afraid to Ask).*

Almaguer, Tomás. 1993. "Chicano Men: A Cartography of Homosexual Identity and Behavior." In *The Lesbian and Gay Studies Reader,* edited by H. Abelove, M. A. Barale, and D. Halperin. First published in *differences: A Journal of Feminist Cultural Studies* 3 (1991): 75–100.

Alonso, Ana Maria, and Maria Teresa Koreck. 1993. "Silences: 'Hispanics,' AIDS, and

Sexual Practice." In *The Lesbian and Gay Studies Reader,* edited by H. Abelove, M. A. Barale, and D. Halperin. First published in *differences: A Journal of Feminist Cultural Studies* 1 (1989): 101–124.

Altman, Dennis. 1971. *Homosexual: Oppression and Liberation.* New York: Outerbridge and Dienstfrey.

Arendash, G. W., and Roger Gorski. 1983. "Effects of Discrete Lesions of the Sexually Dimorphic Nucleus of the Preoptic Area or Other Medial Preoptic Regions on the Sexual Behavior of Male Rats." *Brain Research Bulletin* 10:147–154.

Armstrong, David. 1989. *Universals: An Opinionated Introduction.* Boulder: Westview.

Asch, Adrian, and Gail Geller. 1996. "Feminism, Bioethics, and Genetics." In *Feminism and Bioethics: Beyond Reproduction,* edited by Susan Wolf. New York: Oxford University Press.

*Baehr v. Lewin,* 852 P. 44 (Hawaii 1993).

Bailey, J. Michael. 1995a. "Biological Perspectives on Sexual Orientation." In *Lesbian, Gay and Bisexual Identities over the Lifespan,* edited by Anthony D'Augeli and Charlotte Patterson. New York: Oxford University Press.

———. 1995b. "Sexual Orientation Revolution." *Nature Genetics* 11:353–354.

Bailey, J. Michael, and B. A. Benishay. 1993. "Familial Aggregation of Female Sexual Orientation." *American Journal of Psychiatry* 150:272–277.

Bailey, J. Michael, Michael P. Dunne, and Nicholas G. Martin. n.d. The Distribution, Correlates, and Determinants of Sexual Orientation in an Australian Twin Sample. *Journal of Personality and Social Psychology.* Under review.

Bailey, J. Michael, and Richard Pillard. 1991a. "Are Some People Born Gay?" *New York Times,* December 17, A19.

———. 1991b. "A Genetic Study of Male Sexual Orientation." *Archives of General Psychiatry* 48:1089–1096.

———. 1995. "Genetics of Human Sexual Orientation." *Annual Review of Sex Research* 6:126–150.

Bailey, J. Michael, Richard Pillard, and Yvonne Agyei. 1993. "Heritable Factors Influence Sexual Orientation in Woman." *Archives of General Psychiatry* 50:217–223.

Bailey, J. Michael, Richard Pillard, Khytam Dawood, Michael Miller, Lindsay Farrer, Shruti Trivedi, and Robert Murphy. Forthcoming. "A Family History of Male Sexual Orientation Using Three Independent Samples." *Journal of Personality and Social Psychology.*

Bailey, J. Michael, and Kenneth J. Zucker. 1995. "Childhood Sex-Typed Behavior and Sexual Orientation: A Conceptual Analysis and Quantitative Review." *Developmental Psychology* 31:43–55.

Baker, Robert, and Frederick Elliston. 1984. Introduction to *Philosophy and Sex.* Rev. ed., edited by Robert Baker and Frederick Elliston. Buffalo: Prometheus Books.

Bakker, J., T. Brand, J. van Ophemert, and A. K. Slob. 1993. "Hormonal Regulation of Adult Partner Preference Behavior of Male Rats in Neonatally ATD-Treated Male Rats." *Behavioral Neuroscience* 107:480–487.

Banks, Amy, and Nanette Gartrell. 1995. "Hormones and Sexual Orientation: A Questionable Link." *Journal of Homosexuality* 28 (3/4):247–268.

Barinaga, Marcia. 1991. "Is Homosexuality Biological?" *Science* 253:956–957.

———. 1995. "Bisexual Fruit Flies Point to Brain Courtship Centers." *Science* 267:791–792.

Barkow, Jerome. 1989. *Darwin, Sex and Status: Biological Approaches to Mind and Culture.* Toronto: University of Toronto Press.

Barkow, Jerome, Leda Cosmides, and John Tooby, eds. 1992. *The Adapted Mind: Evolutionary Psychology and the Generation of Culture.* New York: Oxford University Press.

Bartky, Sandra Lee. 1990. "Feminine Masochism and the Politics of Personal Transformation." In *Femininity and Domination.* New York: Routledge. First published in *Women's Studies International Forum* 7 (1984): 323–334.

Baum, M. J., M. S. Erskine, E. Kornberg, and C. E. Weaver. 1990. "Prenatal and Neonatal Testosterone Exposure Interact to Affect the Differentiation of Sexual Behavior and Partner Preference in Female Ferrets." *Behavioral Neuroscience* 104:183–198.

Bawer, Bruce. 1993. *A Place at the Table: The Gay Individual in American Society.* New York: Poseidon.

Bayer, Ronald. 1987. *Homosexuality and American Psychiatry.* 2d ed. Princeton: Princeton University Press.

Beach, Frank. 1979. "Animal Models for Human Sexuality." In *Sex Hormones and Behavior,* edited by Ruth Porter and Julie Whelan. Amsterdam: Excerpta Medica.

Bell, Alan, and Martin Weinberg. 1978. *Homosexualities: A Study of Diversity Among Men and Women.* New York: Simon and Schuster.

Bell, Alan, Martin Weinberg, and Susan Hammersmith. 1981. *Sexual Preference: Its Development in Men and Women.* Bloomington: Indiana University Press.

Bem, Daryl. 1996a. "Exotic Becomes Erotic: A Developmental Theory of Sexual Orientation." *Psychological Review* 103:320–335.

———. 1996b. "Exotic Becomes Erotic: A Political Postscript. Unpublished manuscript. Available on the World Wide Web at http://comp9.psych.cornell.edu/dbem/ebe_politics.html.

———. 1998. "Is EBE Theory Supported by the Evidence? Is It Androcentric? A Reply to Peplau et al. (1998)." *Psychological Review* 105:395–398.

Bem, Sandra. 1974. "The Measurement of Psychological Androgyny." *Journal of Consulting and Clinical Psychology* 42:155–62.

———. 1977. "On the Utility of Alternative Procedures for Assessing Psychological Androgyny." *Journal of Consulting and Clinical Psychology* 46:195–205.

Bentham, Jeremy. [1814?] 1984. "An Essay on 'Paederasty.'" Reprinted in *Philosophy and Sex.* Rev. ed., edited by Robert Baker and Frederick Elliston. Buffalo: Prometheus Books.

Berke, Richard. 1998. "Chasing the Polls on Gay Rights." *New York Times,* August 2, Week in Review, 3.

Berky, Branden Robert, T. Perelmanhall, and L. A. Kurdek. 1990. "The Multidimensional Scale of Sexuality." *Journal of Homosexuality* 19 (4):67–87.

Berlant, Lauren, and Michael Warner. 1995. "What Does Queer Theory Teach Us about X?" *PMLA* 110:343–349.

Bersani, Leo. 1995. *Homos.* Cambridge, MA: Harvard University Press.

Bieber, I., H. J. Dain, P. R. Dince, M. G. Drellich, H. G. Grad, R. H. Grundlach,

M. W. Kremer, A. H. Rifkin, C. B. Wilbur, and T. B. Bieber. 1962. *Homosexuality: A Psychoanalytic Study*. New York: Basic Books.

Billings, Paul, Jonathan Beckwith, and Joseph Alper. 1992. "The Genetic Analysis of Human Behavior: A New Era?" *Social Science and Medicine* 35:227–238.

Blanchard, Ray, and A. F. Bogart. 1996. "Homosexuality in Men and Number of Older Brothers." *American Journal of Psychiatry* 153:27–31.

Blanchard, Ray, Kenneth Zucker, Susan Bradley, and Caitlin Hume. 1995. "Birth Order and Sibling Sex Ratio in Homosexual Male Adolescents and Probably Prehomosexual Feminine Boys." *Developmental Psychology* 31 (1):22–30.

Blasius, Mark. 1994. *Gay and Lesbian Politics*. Philadelphia: Temple University Press.

Blasius, Mark, and Shane Phelan, eds. 1997. *We Are Everywhere: A Historical Sourcebook of Gay and Lesbian Politics*. New York: Routledge.

Bleier, Ruth, William Byne, and I. Siggelkow. 1982. "Cytoarchitectonic Sexual Dimorphisms of the Medial Preoptic and Anterior Hypothalamic Areas in Guinea Pig, Rat, Hamster and Mouse." *Journal of Comparative Neurology* 212:118–130.

Block, Ned. 1995. "How Heritability Misleads about Race." *Cognition* 56:99–128.

Block, Ned, and Gerald Dworkin. 1974a. "IQ, Heritability, and Inequality." In *The IQ Controversy*. New York: Pantheon.

———, eds. 1974b. *The IQ Controversy*. New York: Pantheon.

Blumstein, Philip, and Pepper Schwartz. 1983. *American Couples*. New York: William and Morrow.

———. 1990. "Intimate Relationships and the Creation of Sexuality." In *Homosexuality/Heterosexuality: Concepts of Sexual Orientation*, edited by D. P. McWhirter, S. A. Saunders, and J. M. Reinisch. New York: Oxford University Press.

Bogart, A. F., and Ray Blanchard. 1996. "Physical Development and Sexual Orientation in Men: Height, Weight, and Age of Puberty Differences." *Personality and Individual Difference* 21:77–84.

Bohan, Janis. 1996. *Psychology and Sexual Orientation*. New York: Routledge.

Boswell, John. 1980. *Christianity, Social Tolerance and Homosexuality*. Chicago: University of Chicago Press.

———. 1989. "Revolutions, Universals and Sexual Categories." In *Hidden From History: Reclaiming the Gay and Lesbian Past*, edited by Martin Duberman, Martha Vicinus and George Chauncey. New York: New American Library. First published in *Salmagundi* 58–59 (1982–1983): 89–113.

———. 1992. "Concepts, Experience and Sexuality." In *Forms of Desire: Sexual Orientation and the Social Constructionist Controversy*, edited by Edward Stein. New York: Routledge.

Bouchard, Thomas, L. L. Heston, E. Eckert, M. Keyes, and S. Resnick. 1981. "The Minnesota Study of Twins Reared Apart: Project Description and Sample Results in the Developmental Domain." In *Twin Research: Intelligence, Personality and Development*, edited by L. Gedda, P. Parisi, and W. E. Nance. New York: Alan R. Liss.

*Bowen v. Gilliard*, 483 U.S. 587 (1987).

*Bowers v. Hardwick*, 46 U.S. 186 (1986).

Boyd, Richard. 1991. "Realism, Anti-Foundationalism and the Enthusiasm for Natural Kinds." *Philosophical Studies* 61:127–148.

Brand, T., J. Kroonen, J. Mos, and A. K. Slob. 1991. "Adult Partner Preference and Sexual Behavior in Male Rats Affected by Perinatal Endocrine Manipulations." *Hormones and Behavior* 25:323–341.

Brand, T., and A. K. Slob. 1991. "Neonatal Organization of Adult Partner Preference Behavior in Male Rats." *Physiology and Behavior* 49:107–111.

British Medical Association. 1995. *Our Genetic Future: The Science and Ethics of Genetic Technology.* Oxford: Oxford University Press.

Bronski, Michael. 1984. *Culture Clash: The Making of Gay Sensibility.* Boston: South End Press.

Brown, Roger. 1986. *Social Psychology: The Second Edition.* New York: Free Press.

Bullough, Vern. 1994. *Science in the Bedroom: A History of Sex Research.* New York: Basic Books.

Bumiller, Elisabeth. 1990. *May You Be the Mother of a Hundred Sons: A Journey among the Women of India.* New York: Fawcett Columbine.

Burke, Phyllis. 1996. *Gender Shock: Exploding the Myths of Male and Female.* New York: Anchor Books.

Burr, Chandler. 1996a. *A Separate Creation: The Search for the Biological Origins of Sexual Orientation.* New York: Hyperion.

———. 1996b. "Why Conservatives Should Embrace the Gay Gene." *Weekly Standard,* December 16, 22–26.

Buss, David. 1994. *The Evolution of Desire: Strategies of Mating.* New York: Basic Books.

Byne, William. 1994. "The Biological Evidence Challenged." *Scientific American* 270 (May):50–55

———. 1995. "Science and Belief: Psychobiological Research on Sexual Orientation." *Journal of Homosexuality* 28 (3/4):303–344.

———. 1996. "Biology and Sexual Orientation: Implications of Endocronological and Neuroanatomical Research." In *Comprehensive Textbook of Homosexuality,* edited by R. Cabaj and T. Stein. Washington, DC: American Psychiatric Press.

Byne, William, and Bruce Parsons. 1993. "Human Sexual Orientation: The Biologic Theories Reappraised." *Archives of General Psychiatry* 50:228–239.

Byne, William, and Edward Stein. 1997. "The Ethical Implications of Scientific Research on the Causes of Sexual Orientation." *Health Care Analysis* 5:136–148.

Califia, Pat. 1994. "Gay Men, Lesbians and Sex: Doing It Together." In *Public Sex: The Culture of Radical Sex.* Pittsburgh: Cleis Press.

Calhoun, Cheshire. 1989. "Responsibility and Reproach." *Ethics* 99:389–406.

———. 1994. "Separating Lesbian Theory from Feminist Theory." *Ethics* 104:558–581.

———. 1995. "Sexuality Injustice." *Notre Dame Journal of Law, Ethics, and Public Policy* 9:401–434.

Card, Claudia. 1995. *Lesbian Choices.* New York: Columbia University Press.

Cartwright, Nancy. 1983. *How the Laws of Physics Lie.* Oxford: Oxford University Press.

Center for Disease Control. 1992. HIV/AIDS Surveillance Report. Atlanta.

Chauncey, George. 1989. "Christian Brotherhood or Sexual Perversion?: Homosexual Identities and the Construction of Sexual Boundaries in the World War I Era." In

*Hidden from History: Reclaiming the Gay and Lesbian Past,* edited by Martin Duberman, Martha Vicinus, and George Chauncey. New York: New American Library. First published in *Journal of Social History* 19 (1985): 189–212.

———. 1994. *Gay New York: Gender, Urban Culture, and the Making of the Gay Male World, 1890–1940.* New York: Basic Books.

Chodorow, Nancy. 1994. *Femininities, Masculinities, Sexuality: Freud and Beyond.* Lexington, KY: University of Kentucky Press.

Chomsky, Noam. 1976. "The Fallacy of Richard Herrnstein's I.Q." In *The IQ Controversy,* edited by Ned Block and Gerald Dworkin. New York: Random House. First published in *Cognition* 1 (1973): 11–46.

———. 1980. "A Review of B. F. Skinner's *Verbal Behavior.*" In *Readings in Philosophy of Psychology,* edited by Ned Block. Cambridge, MA: Harvard University Press. First published in *Language* 20 (1959): 26–58.

———. 1986. *Knowledge of Language.* New York: Praeger.

Christina, Greta. 1992. "Are We Having Sex Now or What?" In *The Erotic Impulse: Honoring the Sensual Self,* edited by David Steinberg. New York: G. P. Putnam's Sons.

Churchill, Wainwright. 1967. *Homosexual Behavior Among Males: A Cross-Cultural and Cross-Species Investigation.* New York: Hawthorn Books.

*Cleburne v. Cleburne Living Center,* 473 U.S. 432 (1985).

Cochran, W., F. Mosteller, and J. Tukey. 1953. "Statistical Problems of the Kinsey Report." *Journal of the American Statistical Association* 48:673–716.

Commins, D., and P. Yahr. 1984. "Adult Testosterone Levels Influence the Morphology of a Sexually Dimorphic Area in the Mongolian Gerbil Brain." *Journal of Comparative Neurology* 224:132–140.

Comstock, Gary David. 1991. *Violence Against Lesbians and Gay Men.* New York: Columbia University Press.

Conant, James Bryant. 1950. *The Overthrow of Phlogiston Theory: The Chemical Revolution of 1775–1789.* Cambridge, MA: Harvard University Press.

Corea, Gena. 1985. *The Mother Machine: Reproductive Technologies from Artificial Insemination to Artificial Wombs.* New York: Harper and Row.

Cosmides, Leda, and John Tooby. 1987. "From Evolution to Behavior: Evolutionary Psychology as the Missing Link." In *The Latest on the Best: Essays on Evolution and Optimality,* edited by John Dupré. Cambridge, MA: MIT Press.

Crocker, Lawrence. 1979. "Meddling with the Sexual Orientation of Children." In *Having Children: Philosophical Perspectives on Parenting,* edited by Onora O'Neill and William Ruddick. Oxford: Oxford University Press.

Croxson, T. S., W. E. Chapman, L. K. Miller, C. D. Levit, R. Senie, and B. Zumoff. 1989. "Changes in the Hypothamalic-Pituitary-Gonadal Axis in Human Immunodeficiency Virus-Infected Homosexual Men." *Journal of Clinical Endocrinology and Metabolism* 68:317–321.

Darwin, Charles. 1859. *On the Origin of Species.* London: John Murray.

Dawkins, Richard. 1976. *The Selfish Gene.* Oxford: Oxford University Press.

———. 1986. *The Blind Watchmaker.* New York: W. W. Norton.

de Lacoste-Utamsing, M. C., and R. L. Holloway. 1982. "Sexual Dimorphism in the Human Corpus Callosum." *Science* 216:1431–1432.

Defense Department, 1993. *Enlisted Administrative Separations.* Directive #1332.14.
*Defense of Marriage Act,* 1996. U.S. Public Law 104–199.
D'Emilio, John. 1983. *Sexual Politics, Sexual Communities: The Making of a Homosexual Minority in the United States, 1940–1970.* Chicago: University of Chicago Press.
Dennett, Daniel. 1984. *Elbow Room: The Varieties of Free Will Worth Wanting.* Cambridge, MA: MIT Press.
Denniston, R. H. 1980. "Ambisexuality in Animals." In *Homosexual Behavior: A Modern Reappraisal,* edited by Judd Marmor. New York: Basic Books.
Descartes, Rene. [1691] 1960. *Meditations Concerning First Philosophy.* Indianapolis: Bobbs Merrill.
Detera-Wadleigh, Sevilla, Lynn Goldin, Robin Sherrington, Ignacio Encio, Carlos deMiguel, W. Berrettini, H. Gurling, and E. S. Gershon. 1989. "Exclusion of Linkage to 5Q11-13 in Families with Schizophrenia and Other Psychiatric Disorders." *Nature* 340:391–393.
Devor, Holly. 1997. *FTM: Female-to-Male Transsexuals.* Bloomington: Indiana University Press.
Diamond, Jared. 1992. *The Third Chimpanzee: The Evolution and Future of the Human Animal.* New York: Harper.
Dickemann, Mildred. 1995. "Wilson's Panchreston: The Inclusive Fitness Hypothesis of Sociobiology Re-Examined." *Journal of Homosexuality* 28 (3/4):147–183.
Dörner, Gunter. 1989. "Hormone-Dependent Brain Development and Neuroendocrine Prophylaxis." *Experimental and Clinical Endocrinology* 94:4–22.
Dörner, Gunter, W. Rhode, F. Stahl, and H. Halle. 1975. "A Neuroendocrine Predisposition for Homosexuality in Men." *Archives of Sexual Behavior* 4:1–8.
Duberman, Martin. 1993. *Stonewall.* New York: Dutton.
Dupré, John. 1993. *The Disorder of Things: Metaphysical Foundations of the Disunity of Science.* Cambridge, MA: Harvard University Press.
Dynes, Wayne. 1990. *The Encyclopedia of Homosexuality.* New York: Garland.
Eckert, E. D., Thomas Bouchard, J. Bouhlen, and L. L. Hetson. 1986. "Homosexuality in Monozygotic Twins Reared Apart." *British Journal of Psychiatry* 148:421–425.
Ehrhardt, A. A., K. Evers, and John Money. 1968. "Influence of Androgen and Some Aspects of Sexually Dimorphic Behavior in Women with Late-Treated Androgenital Syndrome." *Johns Hopkins Medical Journal* 123:115–122.
Epstein, Steven. 1992. "Gay Politics, Ethnic Identity: The Limits of Social Constructionism." In *Forms of Desire: Sexual Orientation and the Social Constructionist Controversy,* edited by Edward Stein. New York: Routledge. First published in *Socialist Review* 93/94 (1987): 9–54.
Ernulf, Kurt, Sune Innala, and Fredrick Whitam. 1989. "Biological Explanation, Psychological Explanation and Tolerance of Homosexuals: A Cross-National Analysis of Beliefs and Attitudes." *Psychological Reports* 65:1003–1010.
Escoffier, Jeffrey. 1990. "Inside the Ivory Closet: Challenges Facing Lesbian and Gay Studies." *Out/Look* (Fall):40–48.
Eskridge, William, Jr. 1996. *The Case for Same-Sex Marriage: From Sexual Liberty to Civilized Commitment.* New York: Free Press.
———. 1999. *Gaylaw: Challenging the Apartheid of the Closet.* Cambridge, MA: Harvard University Press.

Eskridge, William, Jr., and Nan Hunter, eds. 1997. *Sexuality, Gender and the Law.* Westbury, NY: Foundation Press.

Eskridge, William, Jr., and Edward Stein. 1998. "Queer Clones." In *Clones and Clones: Facts and Fantasies about Human Cloning,* edited by Martha Nussbaum and Cass Sunstein. New York: Norton.

Fausto-Sterling, Anne. 1992. *Myths of Gender: Biological Theories about Men and Women.* Rev. ed. New York: Basic Books.

―――. 1993. "The Five Sexes: Why Male and Female Are Not Enough." *The Sciences* (March/April):20–24.

―――. 1995. "Animal Models for the Development of Human Sexuality: A Critical Evaluation." *Journal of Homosexuality* 28 (3/4):217–236.

Fay, R. E., C. F. Turner, A. D. Klassen, and John Gagnon. 1989. "Prevalence and Patterns of Same-Gender Sexual Contact Among Men." *Science* 243:338–348.

Feder, Ellen. 1997. "Disciplining the Family: The Case of Gender Identity Disorder." *Philosophical Studies* 85:195–211.

Feingold, A. 1988. "Matching for Attractiveness in Romantic Partners and Same-Sex Friends: A Meta-analysis and Theoretical Critique." *Psychological Bulletin* 104:226–235.

Fenwick, Lynda. 1998. *Private Choice, Public Consequences: Reproductive Technology and the New Ethics of Conception, Pregnancy and Family.* New York: Dutton.

Ferveur, Jean-François, Klemens Störtkul, Reinhard Stocker, and Ralph Greenspan. 1995. "Genetic Feminization of Brain Structures and Changed Sexual Orientation in Male Drosophila." *Science* 267:902–905.

Finnis, John. 1995. "Law, Morality and 'Sexual Orientation.'" *Notre Dame Law, Ethics and Public Policy* 9:11–39.

Fodor, Jerry. 1983. *The Modularity of Mind.* Cambridge, MA: MIT Press.

Fortunata, Jacqueline. 1980. "Masturbation and Women's Sexuality." In *Philosophy of Sex,* edited by Alan Soble. Savage, MD: Littlefield.

Foucault, Michel. 1977. *Discipline and Punish: The Birth of the Prison.* Translated by Alan Sheridan. New York: Pantheon.

―――. 1978. *History of Sexuality: An Introduction.* Translated by Robert Hurley. Vol. 1, New York: Random House. Original edition, Paris: Editions Gallimard, 1976.

Freud, Sigmund. [1905] 1975. *Three Essays on the Theory of Sexuality.* Translated by James Strachey. New York: Basic Books.

Freund, Kurt. 1963. *Die Homosexualität beim Mann* [*Homosexuality in Man*]. Leipzig: S. Hirzel.

*Frontiero v. Richardson,* 411 U.S. 677 (1972).

Fry, Michael. 1993. "The Rest of the Story." *The Living Bird Quarterly* 12 (1): 19.

Frye, Marilyn. 1992. "Lesbian 'Sex.'" In *Willful Virgin: Essays in Feminism 1976–1992.* Freedom, CA: Crossing Press. First published in *Sinister Wisdom* 35 (1988): 46–54.

Fuss, Diana. 1989. *Essentially Speaking: Feminism, Nature and Difference.* New York: Routledge.

Futuyma, Douglas, and Stephen Risch. 1983–1984. "Sexual Orientation, Sociobiology and Evolution." *Journal of Homosexuality* 9 (2-3):157–168.

Gagnon, John, and William Simon. 1973. *Sexual Conduct.* Chicago: Aldine.

Gallup, George, Jr. 1998. *The Gallup Poll: Public Opinion 1997.* Wilmington, DE: Scholarly Resources.

Garde, Noel [pseud.]. 1964. *Jonathan to Gide: The Homosexual in History.* New York: Vantage.

Gebhard, Paul. 1972. "Incidence of Overt Homosexuality in the United States and Western Europe." In *National Institute of Mental Health Task Force on Homosexuality: Final Report and Background Papers,* edited by J. M. Livinghood. Washington, DC: U.S. Government Printing Office.

Gelman, David. 1992. "Born or Bred?" *Newsweek,* February 24, 46–53.

Gettier, Edmund. 1963. "Is Justified True Belief Knowledge?" *Analysis* 23:121–123.

Ghilsen, Michael. 1974. "A Radical Solution to the Species Problem." *Systematic Zoology* 23:536–544.

Gibson, Paul. 1997. "Gay and Lesbian Youth Suicide." In *Sexual Orientation and the Law,* edited by William Rubenstein. St. Paul, MN: West. First published in *U.S. Department of Health and Human Services, Youth Suicide Report,* Washington, DC: GPO, 1989.

Gladue, Brian, and J. Michael Bailey. 1995. "Spatial Ability, Handedness, and Human Sexual Orientation." *Psychoneuroendocrinology* 20:487–497.

Gladue, Brian, Richard Green, and R. E. Hellman. 1984. "Neuroendocrine Response to Estrogen and Sexual Orientation." *Science* 225:1496–1499.

Golden, Carla. 1987. "Diversity and Variability in Women's Sexual Identities." In *Lesbian Psychologies: Explorations and Challenges,* edited by Boston Women's Psychologies Collective. Urbana: University of Illinois Press.

———. 1994. "Our Politics, Our Choices: The Feminist Movement and Sexual Orientation." In *Lesbian and Gay Psychology: Theory, Research and Clinical Applications,* edited by B. Greene and G. M. Herek. Thousand Oaks, CA: Sage.

Goldschmidt, Richard. 1916. "Die biologischen Grundlagen der kontraren Sexualitat und des Hermaphroditismus beim Menschen [The Biological Foundation of Sexual Inversion and Hermaphroditism]." *Archiv fur Rassen-und Gesellschafts-Biologie [Archive for Racial and Social Biology]* 12:1–14.

Goodman, Nelson. 1978. *Ways of Worldmaking.* Indianapolis: Hackett.

Gooren, Louis. 1986. "The Neuroendocrine Response of Lutenizing Hormone to Estrogen Administration in the Human Is Not Sex Specific But Dependent on the Hormonal Environment." *Journal of Clinical Endocrinology and Metabolism* 63:589–593.

———. 1995. "Biomedical Concepts of Homosexuality: Folk Belief in a White Coat." *Journal of Homosexuality* 28 (3/4):237–246.

Gould, Stephen Jay. 1991. *The Mismeasure of Man.* New York: Norton.

Goy, Robert, and Bruce McEwen. 1980. *Sexual Differentiation in the Brain.* Cambridge, MA: MIT Press.

Green, Richard. 1987. *The "Sissy Boy" Syndrome and the Development of Homosexuality.* New Haven: Yale University Press.

———. 1988. "The Immutability of (Homo)sexual Orientation: Behavioral Science Implications for a Constitutional (Legal) Analysis." *Journal of Psychiatry and Law* 16:537–575.

———. 1995. "Sugar and Spice: Scientific Study Attempting to Link Child Tomboys to Adult Lesbians." Television interview by Victoria Corderi, April 14. Available from the WESTLAW database, document #1995 WL 6295869.

Greenberg, David. 1988. *The Construction of Homosexuality.* Chicago: University of Chicago Press.

Greenspan, Ralph. 1995. "Understanding the Genetic Construction of Behavior." *Scientific American* 272 (April):72–78.

Gross, Larry. 1993. *Contested Closets: The Politics and Ethics of Outing.* Minneapolis: University of Minnesota Press.

Guttenplan, Samuel. 1986. *The Language of Logic: An Introduction.* New York: Blackwell.

Hacking, Ian. 1984. "Five Parables." In *Philosophy in History: Essays on the Historiography of Philosophy,* edited by Richard Rorty, J. B. Schneewind, and Quentin Skinner. Cambridge: Cambridge University Press.

———. 1986a. "The Invention of Split Personalities." In *Human Nature and Natural Knowledge,* edited by Alan Donagan, Jr., Anthony Perovich, and Michael Wedin. Dordrecht: D. Reidel.

———. 1986b. "Making Up People." In *Reconstructing Individualism: Autonomy, Individuality, and the Self in Western Thought,* edited by Thomas Heller, Morton Sosna, and David Wellbery. Stanford: Stanford University Press.

———. 1990. "Natural Kinds." In *Perspectives on Quine,* edited by Robert Barrett and Roger Gordon. Cambridge: Blackwell.

———. 1991. "A Tradition of Natural Kinds." *Philosophical Studies* 61:109–126.

———. 1992. "World-Making by Kind-Making: Child Abuse for Example." In *How Classification Works: Nelson Goodman Among the Social Sciences,* edited by Mary Douglas and David Hull. Edinburgh: Edinburgh University Press.

———. 1995. *Rewriting the Soul: Multiple Personalities and the Sciences of Memory.* Princeton: Princeton University Press.

Haldeman, D. C. 1991. "Sexual Orientation Conversion Therapy for Gay Men and Lesbians: A Scientific Examination." In *Homosexuality: Research Implications for Public Policy,* edited by J. C. Gonsiorek and James Weinrich. Newbury Park, CA: Sage Publications.

———. 1994. "The Practice and Ethics of Sexual Orientation Conversion Therapy." *Journal of Consulting and Clinical Psychology* 62:221–227.

Hall, Jeff, and Doreen Kimura. 1994. "Dermatoglyphic Asymmetry and Sexual Orientation in Men." *Behavioral Neuroscience* 108:1203–1206.

Hall, Jeffrey. 1994. "The Mating of a Fly." *Science* 264:1702–1714.

Halley, Janet. 1993. "Reasoning about Sodomy: Act and Identity in and After *Bowers v. Hardwick.*" *Virginia Law Review* 79:1721–1781.

———. 1994. "Sexual Orientation and the Politics of Biology: A Critique of the New Argument from Immutability." *Stanford Law Review* 46:503–568.

———. 1996. "The Status/Conduct Distinction in the 1993 Revisions to Military Anti-Gay Policy." *GLQ: A Journal of Lesbian and Gay Studies* 3:159–252.

———. 1999. *Don't: A Reader's Guide to the Military's Anti-Gay Policy.* Durham: Duke University Press.

Halperin, David. 1990. *One Hundred Years of Homosexuality and Other Essays in Greek Love.* New York: Routledge.

Hamer, Dean, and Peter Copeland. 1994. *The Science of Desire: The Search for the Gay Gene and the Biology of Behavior.* New York: Simon and Schuster.

——. 1998. *Living with Our Genes: Why They Matter More Than You Think.* New York: Doubleday.

Hamer, Dean, Stella Hu, Victoria Magnuson, Nan Hu, and Angela Pattatucci. 1993. "A Linkage Between DNA Markers on the X Chromosome and Male Sexual Orientation." *Science 261*: 321–327.

Hamill, John. 1995. "Dexterity and Sexuality: Is There a Relationship?" *Journal of Homosexuality* 28 (3/4):375–396.

Harman, Gilbert. 1986. *Change in View: Principles of Reasoning.* Cambridge, MA: MIT Press.

Hausman, Bernice. 1995. *Changing Sex: Transsexualism, Technology, and the Idea of Gender.* Durham, NC: Duke University Press.

Heger, Heinz. 1980. *The Men with the Pink Triangle.* Translated by David Fernbach. Boston: Alyson.

Hendricks, S. E., B. Graber, and J. F. Rodriquez-Sierra. 1989. "Neuroendocrine Responses to Exogenous Estrogen. No Differences Between Heterosexual and Homosexual Men." *Psychoneurobiology* 14:177–185.

Hendriks, Aart, Rob Tielman, and Evert van der Veen, eds. 1993. *The Third Pink Book: A Global View of Lesbian and Gay Liberation and Oppression.* Buffalo: Prometheus Books.

Henry, George. 1941. *Sex Variants: A Study of Homosexual Patterns.* 2 vols. New York: Hoeber.

Herdt, Gil. 1984a. "Semen Transaction in Sambia Culture." In *Ritualized Homosexuality in Melanesia,* Berkeley: University of California Press.

——, ed. 1984b. *Ritualized Homosexuality in Melanesia.* Berkeley: University of California Press.

Herrn, Rainer. 1995. "On the History of Biological Theories of Homosexuality." *Journal of Homosexuality* 28 (1/2):31–56.

Herrnstein, Richard. 1971. *I.Q. in the Meritocracy.* Boston: Little, Brown, and Co.

Herrnstein, Richard, and Charles Murray. 1994. *The Bell Curve: Intelligence and Class Structure in American Life.* New York: Free Press.

Herzer, Manfred. 1985. "Kertbenny and the Nameless Love." *Journal of Homosexuality* 12:1–26.

*High Tech Gays v. Defense Industrial Security Clearance Office,* 895 F.2d 563 (9th Cir. 1990).

Hirschfeld, Magnus. 1903. "Heredität und Homosexualität [Heredity and Homosexuality]." *Jahrbuch für sexuelle Zwischenstufen [Yearbook for sexual intermediates]* 5 (1):138–159.

——. 1914. *Die Homosexualität des Mannes und des Weibes [Homosexuality in Men and Women].* Berlin: Louis Marcus.

Hodges, Andrew. 1983. *Alan Turing: The Enigma.* New York: Simon and Schuster.

Hollandsworth, Marla. 1995. "Gay Men Creating Families Through Surro-Gay Arrangements: A Paradigm for Reproductive Freedom." *American University Journal of Gender and Law* 3:183–246.

Holmes, Helen. 1984. "Sex Preselection: Eugenics for Everyone?" In *Biomedical*

*Ethics Review*, edited by James Humber and Robert Alemeder. Clifton, NJ: Humana Press.

Holtzen, D. W. 1994. "Handedness and Sexual Orientation." *Journal of Clinical and Experimental Neuropsychology* 16:702–712.

Horgan, John. 1993. "Eugenics Revisited." *Scientific American* 268:122–131.

Hu, Stella, Angela Pattatucci, C. Patterson, L. Li, D. W. Fulker, S. S. Cherny, L. Kruglyak, and Dean Hamer. 1995. "Linkage Between Sexual Orientation and Chromosome Xq28 in Males But Not in Females." *Nature Genetics* 11:248–256.

Hull, David. 1976. "Are Species Really Individuals?" *Systematic Zoology* 25:174–191.

Hull, David, and Michael Ruse, eds. 1998. *The Philosophy of Biology*. Oxford: Oxford University Press.

Hume, David. [1748] 1977. *Enquiry Concerning Human Understanding*. Indianapolis: Hackett.

Hunt, George, and Mary Warner Hunt. 1977. "Female-Female Pairing in Western Gulls (*Larus occidentalis*) in Southern California." *Science* 196:1466–1467.

Hutchinson, G. E. 1959. "A Speculative Consideration of Certain Possible Forms of Sexual Selection in Man." *American Naturalist* 94:81–91.

Hyde, J. S., B. G. Rosenberg, and J. Behrman. 1977. "Tomboyism." *Psychology of Women Quarterly* 2:73–75.

Inglehart, Ronald. 1990. *Cultural Shift in Advanced Industrial Society*. Princeton: Princeton University Press.

Irvine, Janice. 1990. *Disorders of Desire: Sex and Gender in Modern Sexology*. Philadelphia: Temple University Press.

Isaacs, Tracy. 1997. "Cultural Context and Moral Responsibility." *Ethics* 107: 670–684.

*J.E.B. v. Alabama ex rel T.B.*, 511 U.S. 127 (1994) (Justice Scalia, dissenting).

Jefferson, D. J. 1993. "Science Beseiged: Studying the Biology of Sexual Orientation Has Political Fallout." *Wall Street Journal*, August 12, A1, A4.

Jencks, Christopher, Marshall Smith, Henry Acland, Mary Jo Bane, David Cohen, Herbert Gintis, Barbara Heyns, and Stephan Michelson. 1972. *Inequality: A Reassessment of the Effect of Family and Schooling in America*. New York: Basic Books.

Johnson, W. A., and L. Tiefer. 1972. "Sexual Preference in Neonatally Castrated Male Golden Hamsters." *Physiology and Behavior* 9:213–218.

Kallman, Franz. 1952a. "Comparative Twin Study on the Genetic Aspects of Male Homosexuality." *Journal of Mental and Nervous Disease* 115:283–298.

———. 1952b. "Twin and Sibship Study of Overt Male Homosexuality." *American Journal of Human Genetics* 4:135–146.

Kamm, Frances. 1992. *Abortion and Creation: A Study in Moral and Legal Philosophy*. New York: Oxford University Press.

Kaplan, Lawrence, and Rosemarie Tong. 1994. *Controlling Our Reproductive Destiny: A Technological and Philosophical Perspective*. Cambridge, MA: MIT Press.

Kaplan, Morris. 1997. *Sexual Justice: Democratic Citizenship and the Politics of Desire*. New York: Routledge.

Kaplan, Morris, and Edward Stein. 1996. "Review of *Virtually Normal*, by Andrew Sullivan." *Constellations: An International Journal of Critical and Democratic Theory* 3:261–265.

Katz, Jonathan Ned. 1976. *Gay American History.* New York: Thomas Crowell.

———. 1995. *The Invention of Heterosexuality.* New York: Dutton.

Keen, Lisa, and Suzanne Goldberg. 1998. *Strangers to the Law: Gay People on Trial.* Ann Arbor: University of Michigan Press.

Keil, Frank. 1989. *Concepts, Kinds, and Cognitive Development.* Cambridge, MA: MIT Press.

Kelley, Ken. 1978. "Playboy Interview: Anita Bryant." *Playboy,* May, 73–96, 232–250.

Kendler, K. S., M. C. Neale, R. C. Kessler, A. C. Heath, and L. J. Eaves. 1993. "A Test of the Equal-Environment Assumption in Twin Studies of Psychiatric Illness." *Behavior Genetics* 23:21–28.

Kennedy, Hubert. 1988. *Ulrichs: The Life and Works of Karl Heinrich Ulrichs, Pioneer of the Modern Gay Movement.* Boston: Allyson.

Kessler, Suzanne. 1990. "The Medical Construction of Gender: Case Management of Intersexed Infants." *Signs: A Journal of Women in Culture and Society* 16:3–26.

———. 1998. *Lessons from the Intersexed.* New Brunswick, NJ: Rutgers University Press.

Kessler, Suzanne, and Wendy McKenna. 1978. *Gender: An Ethnomethodological Approach.* New York: Wiley.

Kiernan, James. 1892. "Responsibility in Sexual Perversion." *Chicago Medical Recorder* 3:185–210.

Kinsey, Alfred, Wardell Pomeroy, and Clyde Martin. 1948. *Sexual Behavior in the Human Male.* Philadelphia: W. B. Saunders.

Kinsey, Alfred, Wardell Pomeroy, Clyde Martin, and Paul Gebhard. 1953. *Sexual Behavior in the Human Female.* Philadelphia: W.B. Saunders.

Kirby, David. 1998. "The Second Generation." *New York Times,* June 7, section 14, The City, 1, 12–13.

Kirsch, John, and James Rodman. 1982. "Selection and Sexuality: The Darwinian View of Homosexuality." In *Homosexuality: Social, Psychological, and Biological Issues,* edited by William Paul, James Weinrich, John Gonsiorek, and Mary Hotvedt. Beverly Hills: Sage Publications.

Kitcher, Philip. 1985. *Vaulting Ambition: Sociobiology and the Quest for Human Nature.* Cambridge, MA: MIT Press.

Kitzinger, C., and S. Wilkinson. 1995. "Transitions from Heterosexuality to Lesbianism: The Discursive Production of Lesbian Identities." *Developmental Psychology* 31:95–104.

Klassen, Albert, Colin Williams, and Eugene Levitt. 1989. *Sex and Morality in the United States: An Empirical Enquiry under the Auspices of the Kinsey Institute.* Middletown, CT: Wesleyan University Press.

Klein, Fritz, Barry Sepekoff, and Timothy Wolf. 1985. "Sexual Orientation: A Multi-Variable Dynamic Process." *Journal of Homosexuality* 11(1-2):35–49.

Klein, Fritz, and Timothy Wolf, eds. 1985. *Two Lives to Lead: Bisexuality in Men and Women.* New York: Harrington Park Press.

Knox, R. A. 1993. "Existence of Gay Gene Raises Ethical Concern." *Boston Globe,* July 18.

Kolata, Gina. 1998. "Researchers Report Success in Method to Pick Baby's Sex." *New York Times,* September 9, A1, A22.

Kolker, Aliza, and B. Meredith Burke. 1994. *Prenatal Testing: A Sociological Perspective.* Westport, CT: Bergin and Garvey.

Koppelman, Andrew. 1988. "The Miscegenation Analogy: Sodomy Law as Sex Discrimination." *Yale Law Journal* 98:145–164.

———. 1994. "Why Sexual Orientation Discrimination is Sex Discrimination." *New York University Law Review* 69:197–287.

Krafft-Ebing, Richard von. [1886] 1965. *Psychopathia Sexualis: A Medico-Forensic Study.* Translated by Harry Wedeck. New York: G. P. Putnam.

Kuhn, Thomas. 1957. *The Copernican Revolution: Planetary Astronomy in the Development of Western Thought.* Cambridge, MA: Harvard University Press.

———. 1970. *The Structure of Scientific Revolutions.* Rev. ed. Chicago: University of Chicago Press.

Kurjack, Asim, and Frank Chervenak, eds. 1994. *The Fetus as Patient.* New York: Pantheon.

Kushner, Tony. 1992. *Angels in America: Part One, Millennium Approaches.* New York: Theater Communications Group.

Kussum. 1993. "The Use of Pre-natal Diagnostic Techniques for Sex Selection: The Indian Scene." *Bioethics* 7:149–165.

Laumann, Edward, John Gagnon, Robert Michael, and Stuart Michaels. 1994. *The Social Organization of Sexuality.* Chicago: University of Chicago Press.

Law, Sylvia. 1988. "Homosexuality and the Social Meaning of Gender." *Wisconsin Law Review* 1988:187–235.

Leplin, Jarrett, ed. 1984. *Scientific Realism.* Berkeley: University of California Press.

LeVay, Simon. 1991. "A Difference in Hypothalamic Structure Between Heterosexual and Homosexual Men." *Science* 253:1034–1037.

———. 1993. *The Sexual Brain.* Cambridge, MA: MIT Press.

———. 1996. *Queer Science: The Use and Abuse of Research into Homosexuality.* Cambridge, MA: MIT Press.

LeVay, Simon, and Dean Hamer. 1994. "Evidence for a Biological Influence in Male Homosexuality." *Scientific American* 270 (May):44–49.

Levin, Michael. 1984. "Why Homosexuality Is Abnormal." *Monist* 67:251–283.

Lev-Ran, A. 1974. "Sexuality and Educational Levels of Women with the Late-Treated Adrenogentical Syndrome." *Archives of Sexual Behavior* 3:27–32.

Lewes, Kenneth. 1988. *The Psychoanalytic Theory of Male Homosexuality.* New York: Simon and Schuster.

Lewis, David. 1973. *Counterfactuals.* Cambridge, MA: Harvard University Press.

Lewontin, Richard, Steven Rose, and Leon Kamin. 1984. *Not In Our Genes.* New York: Pantheon.

Lim, L. C. C. 1995. "Present Controversies in the Genetics of Male Homosexuality." *Annals of the Academy of Medicine of Singapore* 24:759–763.

*Loving v. Virginia,* 388 U.S. 1 (1967).

Lyons, William. 1986. *The Disappearance of Introspection.* Cambridge, MA: MIT Press.

Macedo, Stephen. 1995. "Homosexuality and the Conservative Mind." *Georgetown Law Journal* 84:261–300.

Mackie, John L. 1964. "Self-Refutation: A Formal Analysis." *Philosophical Quarterly* 14:193–203.

Marshall, Eliot. 1995. "NIH'S 'Gay Gene' Study Questioned." *Science* 268:1841.

Mason, Jackie. 1991. *Brand New.* New York: Sony Music Entertainment.

*Massachusetts Board of Retirement v. Murgia,* 427 U.S. 307 (1976).

Matuszczyk, J. Vega, A. Fernandez-Guasti, and K. Larssen. 1988. "Sexual Orientation, Proceptivity, and Receptivity in the Male Rat as Function of Neonatal Hormonal Manipulation." *Hormones and Behavior* 22:362–378.

McCaughey, Martha. 1996. "Perverting Evolutionary Narratives of Heterosexual Masculinity." *GLQ: A Journal of Lesbian and Gay Studies* 3:261–287.

McCormick, C. M., S. F. Witelson, and E. Kingstone. 1990. "Left-Handedness in Homosexual Men and Women." *Psychoneuroendocrinology* 15:69–76.

McFadden, Dennis, J. C. Loehlin, and Edward Pasanen. 1996. "Additional Findings on Heritability and Prenatal Masculinization of Cochlear Mechanisms: Click-Evoked Otoacoustic Emissions." *Hearing Research* 97:102–119.

McFadden, Dennis, and Edward Pasanen. 1998. "Comparison of the Auditory Systems of Heterosexuals and Homosexuals: Click-Evoked Otoacoustic Emissions." *Proceedings of the National Academy of Science* 95:2709–2713.

McGue, M., and D. T. Lykken. 1992. "Genetic Influence on Risk of Divorce." *Psychological Science* 3:368–373.

McGuffin, Peter, M. Sargeant, H. Heft, S. Tidmarsh, S. Whatley, and R. M. Marchbanks. 1990. "Exclusion of a Schizophrenia Susceptibility Gene from the Chromosome 5Q11-Q13 Region: New Data and a Reanalysis of Previous Reports." *American Journal of Human Genetics* 43:524–535.

McGuire, R. J., J. M. Carlisle, and B. G. Young. 1965. "Sexual Deviations as Conditioned Behavior: A Hypothesis." *Behavior Research and Therapy* 2:185–190.

McGuire, Terry. 1995. "Is Homosexuality Genetic?: A Critical Review and Some Suggestions." *Journal of Homosexuality* 28 (1/2):115–145.

McIntosh, Mary. 1968. "The Homosexual Role." *Social Problems* 16:182–192.

McKnight, Jim. 1997. *Straight Science: Homosexuality, Evolution, and Adaptation.* New York: Routledge.

Meyer-Bahlburg, Heino. 1984. "Psychoendocrine Research on Sexual Orientation: Current Status and Future Options." In *Progress in Brain Research,* edited by G. J. Devries, J. P. C. DeBruin, H. M B. Uylings, and M. A. Corner. Amsterdam: Elsevier.

Micklem, Neil. 1996. *The Nature of Hysteria.* New York: Routledge.

Miller, Barbara. 1981. *The Endangered Sex: Neglect of Children in Rural North India.* Ithaca, NY: Cornell University Press.

Mitchell, Alison. 1998. "Lott Says Homosexuality Is a Sin and Compares It to Alcoholism." *New York Times,* June 16, A24.

Mohr, Richard. 1990. *Gays/Justice: A Study in Society, Ethics and Law.* New York: Columbia University Press.

———. 1992a. "The Outing Controversy: Privacy and Dignity in Gay Ethics." In *Gay Ideas: Outing and Other Controversies.* Boston: Beacon.

———. 1992b. "The Thing of It Is: Some Problems with Models for the Social

Construction of Homosexuality." In *Gay Ideas: Outing and Other Controversies.*
Boston: Beacon.

Money, John. 1955. "Linguistic Resources and Psychodynamic Theory." *British Journal of Medical Psychology* 20:264–266.

———. 1988. *Gay, Straight, and In-Between: The Sexology of Erotic Orientation.* New York: Oxford University Press.

Money, John, M. Schwartz, and V. G. Lewis. 1984. "Adult Erotosexual Status and Fetal Hormonal Masculinization and Demasculinization: 46, XX Congenital Virilizing Adrenal Hyperplasia and 46, XY Androgen-Insensitivity Syndrome Compared." *Psychoneuroendocrinology* 9:405–414.

Moore, G. E. 1903. *Principia Ethica.* Cambridge: Cambridge University Press.

Morin, Stephen, and Stephen Schultz. 1978. "The Gay Rights Movement and the Rights of Children." *Journal of Social Issues* 32:137–148.

Mulaikal, R. M., C. J. Migeon, and J. A. Rock. 1987. "Fertility Rates in Female Patients with Congenital Adrenal Hyperplasia Due to 21-hydroxylase Deficiency." *New England Journal of Medicine* 316:178–182.

Murphy, Timothy. 1987. "Homosexuality and Nature: Happiness and the Law at Stake." *Journal of Applied Philosophy* 4:195–204.

———. 1990. "Reproductive Controls and Sexual Destiny." *Bioethics* 4:121–142.

———. 1992. "Redirecting Sexual Orientation: Techniques and Justifications." *Journal of Sex Research* 29:501–523.

———. 1997. *Gay Science: The Ethics of Sexual Orientation Research.* New York: Columbia University Press.

Nadler, Ronald. 1990. "Homosexual Behavior in Nonhuman Primates." In *Homosexuality/Heterosexuality: Concepts of Sexual Orientation,* edited by D. P. McWhirter, S. A. Sanders, and J. M . Reinisch. New York: Oxford University Press.

Nagel, Thomas. 1979. "Sexual Perversion." In *Mortal Questions.* Cambridge: Cambridge University Press. First published in *Journal of Philosophy* 66 (1969): 5–17.

Nanda, Serena. 1993. "Hijras as Neither Man Nor Woman." In *The Lesbian and Gay Studies Reader,* edited by H. Abelove, M. A. Barale, and D. Halperin. New York: Routledge.

Needham, Joseph. 1959. *A History of Embryology.* New York: Abelard-Schuman.

Newton, Esther. 1972. *Mother Camp: Female Impersonators in America.* Englewood Cliffs, NJ: Prentice-Hall.

Newton, Huey. 1997. "A Letter from Huey to the Revolutionary Brothers and Sisters about the Women's Liberation and Gay Liberation Movements." In *We Are Everywhere: A Historical Sourcebook of Gay and Lesbian Politics.* edited by M. Blasius and S. Phelan. First published in *The Black Panther,* August 21 (1970).

Nicols, R. C., and W. C. Bilbro. 1966. "The Diagnosis of Twin Zygosity." *Acta Genetica Statistica Medica* 16:265–275.

Nussbaum, Martha, and Cass Sunstein, eds. 1998. *Clones and Clones: Facts and Fantasies about Human Cloning.* New York: Norton.

*Olmstead v. United States,* 277 U.S. 438 (1928) (Justice Brandeis, dissenting).

Ortner, Sherry, and Harriet Whitehead, eds. 1981. *Sexual Meanings: The Cultural Construction of Gender and Sexuality.* Cambridge: Cambridge University Press.

Overall, Christine. 1987. *Ethics and Human Reproduction: A Feminist Analysis*. Boston: Allen and Unwin.

Padgug, Robert. 1992. "Sexual Matters: On Conceptualizing Sexuality in History." In *Forms of Desire: Sexual Orientation and the Social Constructionist Controversy*, edited by Edward Stein. New York: Routledge. First published in *Radical History Review* 20 (1979):3–23.

Paley, William. [1802] 1963. *Natural Theology*. Indianapolis: Bobbs-Merrill.

Pare, C. M. B. 1956. "Homosexuality and Chromosomal Sex." *Journal of Psychosomatic Research* 1:247–251.

Patel, Vibuti. 1989. "Sex Determination and Preselection Tests in India: Recent Techniques in Femicide." *Reproductive and Genetics Engineering* 2:111–120.

Pattatucci, Angela, and Dean Hamer. 1995. "Development and Familiality of Sexual Orientation in Females." *Behavior Genetics* 24:407–420.

Pennsylvania. 1989. *Pennsylvania Consolidated Statutes Annotated*. 18 § 3204 (c).

Peplau, L. Anne, L. D. Garnets, L. R. Spalding, T. D. Conley, and R. C. Veniegas. 1998. "A Critique of Bem's 'Exotic Becomes Erotic' Theory of Sexual Orientation." *Psychological Review* 105 (2):387–394.

Perlman, David. 1991. "Brain Cells Study Finds Link to Homosexuality: Tissue Differs Between Gay and Straight Men." *San Francisco Chronicle*, August 30, A1, A12.

Perry, Michael. 1995. "The Morality of Homosexual Conduct: A Response to John Finnis." *Notre Dame Journal of Law, Ethics, and Public Policy* 1:41–73.

Phelan, Shane. 1995. *Getting Specific: Post-modern Lesbian Politics*. Minneapolis: University of Minnesota Press.

Pillard, Richard. 1990. "The Kinsey Scale: Is It Familial?" In *Homosexuality/Heterosexuality: Concepts of Sexual Orientation*, edited by D. P . McWhirter, S. A. Saunders, and J. M. Reinisch. New York: Oxford University Press.

———. 1997. "The Search for a Genetic Influence on Sexual Orientation." In *Science and Homosexualities*, edited by Vernon Rosario. New York: Routledge.

Pillard, Richard, and James Weinrich. 1986. "Evidence of Familial Nature of Male Homosexuality." *Archives of General Psychiatry* 43:808–812.

Pinker, Steven. 1994. *The Language Instinct: How the Mind Creates Language*. New York: Morrow.

———. 1997. *How the Mind Works*. New York: Norton.

Pinker, Steven, and Paul Bloom. 1990. "Natural Language and Natural Selection." *Behavioral and Brain Sciences* 13:707–784.

Piskur, J., and D. Delegman. 1992. "Effect of Reading a Summary of Research about Biological Bases of Homosexual Orientation on Attitudes Towards Homosexuals." *Psychological Reports* 71:1219–1225.

*Planned Parenthood v. Casey*, 505 U.S. 833 (1992).

Plant, Richard. 1986. *The Pink Triangle: The Nazi War Against Homosexuals*. New York: Henry Holt.

Plato. 1934. *The Laws*. Translated by A. E. Taylor. New York: E. P. Dutton.

———. 1935a. *Theaetetus*. Translated by F. M. Cornford. London: Routledge and Kegan Paul.

———. 1935b. *The Symposium*. Translated by Michael Joyce. New York: E. P. Dutton.

————. 1952. *The Statesman*. Translated by J. B. Skemp. New Haven: Yale University Press.

Plomin, Robert, J. C. DeFries, and G. E. McClearn. 1990. *Behavioral Genetics: A Primer.* New York: W. H. Freeman.

Plummer, Kenneth. 1975. *Sexual Stigma*. London: Routledge and Kegan Paul.

*Plyler v. Doe*, 457 U.S. 202 (1982).

*Policy Concerning Homosexuality in the Armed Forces*. 1994. U.S. Code Vol. 10 § 654.

Popper, Karl. 1959. *The Logic of Scientific Discovery.* New York: Basic Books.

————. 1962. *Conjectures and Refutations*. New York: Basic Books.

Posner, Richard. 1992. *Sex and Reason*. Cambridge, MA: Harvard University Press.

Posner, Richard, and Katharine Silbaugh. 1996. *A Guide to America's Sex Laws*. Chicago: University of Chicago Press.

Purdy, Laura. 1996. *Reproducing Persons: Issues in Feminist Bioethics*. Ithaca, NY: Cornell University Press.

Putnam, Hilary. 1987. *The Many Faces of Realism*. LaSalle, IL: Open Court.

"Queers Read This; I Hate Straights." 1997. In *We Are Everywhere: A Historical Sourcebook of Gay and Lesbian Politics*, edited by Mark Blasius and Shane Phelan. Routledge. First published and distributed in 1990, n.p.

Quine, Willard V. O. 1961. "Two Dogmas of Empiricism." In *From a Logical Point of View*. Cambridge, MA: Harvard University Press.

Radicalesbians. 1973. "The Woman-Identified Woman." In *Radical Feminism*, edited by Anne Koedt, Ellen Levine, and Anita Rapone. New York: Quadrangle Books.

Raymond, Janice. 1993. *Women as Wombs: Reproductive Technologies and the Battle over Women's Freedom*. New York: Harper Collins.

Rekers, George. 1982. *Growing Up Straight: What Families Should Know about Homosexuality*. Chicago: Moody Press.

Rice, George, Carol Anderson, Neil Risch, and George Ebers. 1999. "Male Homosexuality: Absence of Linkage to Microsatellite Markers at xq28." *Science* 284:665–667

Rich, Adrienne. 1980. "Compulsory Heterosexuality and Lesbian Existence." *Signs* 5:631–660.

Richards, David. 1982. *Sex, Drugs, Death, and the Law*. Totowa, NJ: Rowman and Littlefield.

————. 1994. "Sexual Preference as a Suspect (Religious) Classification: An Alternative Perspective on the Unconstitutionality of Anti-Lesbian/Gay Initiatives." *Ohio State Law Journal* 55:491–553.

————. 1998. *Women, Gays and the Constitution: The Grounds for Feminism and Gay Rights in Culture and Law*. Chicago: University of Chicago Press.

Risch, Neil, and K. R. Merikangas. 1993. "Linkage Studies of Psychiatric Disorders." *European Archives of Psychiatry and Clinical Neuroscience* 243:143–149.

Risch, Neil, E. Squires-Wheeler, and B. J. B. Keats. 1993. "Male Sexual Orientation and Genetic Evidence." *Science* 262:2063–2065.

Robertson, John. 1995. *Children of Choice: Freedom and the New Reproductive Techniques*. Princeton: Princeton University Press.

Robeson, Ruthann. 1992. *Lesbian (Out)Law: Survival Under the Rule of Law*. Ithaca, NY: Firebrand.

Robinson, Paul. 1989. *The Modernization of Sex: Havelock Ellis, Alfred Kinsey, William Masters, and Virginia Johnson.* Paperback ed. New York: Cornell University Press. Original edition, New York: Harper and Row, 1976.

*Roe v. Wade,* 410 U.S. 113 (1973).

*Romer v. Evans,* 517 U.S. 620 (1996).

Rorty, Richard. 1979. *Philosophy and the Mirror of Nature.* Princeton: Princeton University Press.

Rosen, Alexander, George Rekers, and Peter Bentler. 1978. "Ethical Issues in the Treatment of Children." *Journal of Social Issues* 32:122–136.

Rosenberg, Alexander. 1988. *Philosophy of Social Science.* Boulder, CO: Westview.

Ross, Lee, and Craig Anderson. 1982. "Shortcomings in the Attributional Process: On the Origins and Maintenance of Erroneous Social Assessments." In *Judgment under Uncertainty: Heuristics and Biases,* edited by Daniel Kahneman, Paul Slovic, and Amos Tversky. Cambridge: Cambridge University Press.

Ross, Lee, M. R. Lepper, and M. Hubbard. 1975. "Perseverance in Self Perception and Social Perception: Biased Attributional Processes in the Debriefing Paradigm." *Journal of Personality and Social Psychology* 32:880–892.

Ross, Michael W. 1980. "Retrospective Distortion in Homosexual Research." *Archives of Sexual Behavior* 9:523–531.

———. 1983. *The Married Homosexual Man: A Psychological Study.* New York: Routledge and Kegan Paul.

Rothman, Barbara. 1986. *The Tentative Pregnancy.* New York: Viking.

Rowse, Alfred. 1977. *Homosexuals in History: Ambisexuals in Society, Literature, and Art.* New York: Macmillan.

Rubin, Gayle. 1984. "Thinking Sex: Notes for a Radical Theory of the Politics of Sexuality." In *Pleasure and Danger: Exploring Female Sexuality,* edited by Carol Vance. Boston: Routledge and Kegan Paul.

Rubinstein, William, ed. 1997. *Sexual Orientation and the Law.* 2d ed. St. Paul, MN: West.

Ruse, Michael. 1988. *Homosexuality: A Philosophical Inquiry.* New York: Blackwell.

Russell, Bertrand. 1956. "The Value of Philosophy." In *Problems of Philosophy.* New York: Oxford University Press.

Rust, Paula. 1992. "The Politics of Sexual Identity: Sexual Attraction and Behavior among Lesbian and Bisexual Women." *Social Problems* 39:366–386.

Schmalz, Jeffrey. 1993. "Poll Finds Even Split on Homosexuality's Cause." *New York Times,* March 5, A14.

Schmidt, Gunter. 1984. "Allies and Persecutors: Science and Medicine in the Homosexuality Issue." *Journal of Homosexuality* 10 (3–4):127–140.

Schüklenk, Udo. 1993. Editorial. *Bioethics News* 12:1–5.

Schüklenk, Udo, and Michael Ristow. 1996. "The Ethics of Research into the Causes of Homosexuality." *Journal of Homosexuality* 31:5–30.

Seaborg, D. 1984. "Sexual Orientation, Behavioral Plasticity, and Evolution." *Journal of Homosexuality* 10(3-4):153–158.

Sedgwick, Eve Kosofsky. 1990. *Epistemology of the Closet.* Berkeley: University of California Press.

Sherrington, Robin, Jon Brynjolfsson, Hannes Petursson, Mark Potter, and Keith

Dueston. 1988. "Localization of a Susceptability Locus for Schizophrenia on Chromosome 5." *Nature* 336:164–167.

Silverstein, Charles. 1991. "Psychological and Medical Treatments of Homosexuality." In *Homosexuality: Research Implications for Public Policy*, edited by J. C. Gonsiorek and James Weinrich. Newbury Park, CA: Sage Publications.

Sinfield, Alan. 1994. *The Wilde Century*. New York: Columbia University Press.

Singer, Peter. 1990. *Animal Liberation*. New York: Random House.

Skinner, B. F. 1965. *Science and Human Behavior*. New York: Free Press.

Sleek, Scott. 1997. "Concerns about Conversion Therapy." *APA Monitor* 20 (10).

Sober, Elliott. 1984. *The Nature of Selection*. Cambridge, MA: MIT Press.

Somerville, Siobhan. 1994. "Scientific Racism and the Emergence of the Homosexual Body." *Journal of the History of Sexuality* 5:243–266.

Spence, Janet, R. L. Helmreich, and J. Stapp. 1974. "The Personal Attributes Questionnaire: A Measure of Sex-role Stereotypes and Masculinity and Femininity." *JSAS Catalog of Selected Documents in Psychology* 4:43.

———. 1975. "Ratings of Self and Peers on Sex Role Stereotypes and Masculinity-Femininity." *Journal of Personality and Social Psychology* 32:29–39.

Spira, Alfred, Nathalie Bajos, and Le Groupe ACSF. 1993. *Les comportements sexuals en France: rapport au Ministre de la recherche et de l'espace* [*Sexual Behaviors in France: Report to the Minister of Research and Aerospace*]. Paris: La Documentation Français.

Stein, Edward. 1990. "Essentials of Constructionism and the Construction of Essentialism." In *Forms of Desire: Sexual Orientation and the Social Constructionist Controversy*, edited by Edward Stein. New York: Routledge.

———. 1993. "Evidence for Queer Genes: An Interview with Richard Pillard." *GLQ: A Journal of Lesbian and Gay Studies* 1:93–110.

———. 1994. "The Relevance of Scientific Research Concerning Sexual Orientation to Lesbian and Gay Rights." *Journal of Homosexuality* 27(3/4):269–308.

———. 1996. *Without Good Reason: The Rationality Debate in Philosophy and Cognitive Science*. Oxford: Oxford University Press.

———. 1998. "Review of *Queer Science: The Use and Abuse of Research on Homosexuality* by Simon LeVay." *Journal of Homosexuality* 35 (2):107–119.

———, ed. 1990. *Forms of Desire: Sexual Orientation and the Social Constructionist Controversy*. New York: Routledge.

Stein, Edward, Jacinta Kerin, and Udo Schüklenk. 1998. "Sexual Orientation." In *Encyclopedia of Applied Ethics*, edited by Ruth Chadwick. San Diego: Academic Press.

Steinbock, Bonnie. 1992. *Life Before Birth: The Moral and Legal Status of Embryos and Fetuses*. New York: Oxford University Press.

"Stereotaxic Surgery Results in 'Cures' of German Sex Offenders." 1974. *Journal of the American Medical Association* 229:718.

Stich, Stephen. 1990. *The Fragmentation of Reason*. Cambridge, MA: MIT Press.

Storms, Michael. 1979. "Sex-Role Identity and Its Relationship to Sex-Role Attributes and Sex-Role Stereotypes." *Journal of Personality and Social Psychology* 37:1779–1789.

———. 1980. "Theories of Sexual Orientation." *Journal of Personality and Social Psychology* 38:783–792.

———. 1981. "A Theory of Erotic Orientation Development." *Psychological Review* 88:340–353.

Sullivan, Andrew. 1995. *Virtually Normal: An Argument about Homosexuality.* New York: Knopf.

Suppe, Frederick. 1984. "Curing Homosexuality." In *Philosophy and Sex.* Rev. ed., edited by Robert Baker and Frederick Elliston. Buffalo: Prometheus.

———. 1994. "Explaining Homosexuality: Philosophical Issues, and Who Cares Anyhow?" *Journal of Homosexuality* 27 (3/4):223–268.

Swaab, Dick, and E. Fliers. 1985. "A Sexually Dimorphic Nucleus in the Human Brain." *Science* 228:1112–1114.

Swaab, Dick, and M. Hoffman. 1990. "An Enlarged Suprachiasmatic Nucleus in Homosexual Men." *Brain Research* 537:141–148.

Symonds, Donald. 1979. *The Evolution of Human Sexuality.* New York: Oxford University Press.

Terry, Jennifer. 1990. "Lesbians under the Medical Gaze: Scientists Search for Remarkable Differences." *Journal of Sex Research* 27 (3):317–340.

———. 1997. "The Seductive Power of Science in the Making of Deviant Subjectivity." In *Science and Homosexualities,* edited by Vernon Rosario. New York: Routledge.

"Thinking about Social Values." 1998. *The Public Perspective* 9 (2):15.

Timmons, Stuart. 1990. *The Trouble with Harry Hay: Founder of the Modern Gay Movement.* Boston: Alyson.

Tooby, John. 1988. "The Emergence of Evolutionary Psychology." In *Emerging Syntheses in Science: Proceedings of the Founding Workshops of the Santa Fe Institute,* edited by David Pines. Redwood City, CA: Addison-Wesley.

Tooby, John, and Leda Cosmides. 1987. "Evolutionary Psychology and the Generation of Culture: Part I: Theoretical Considerations." *Ethology and Sociobiology* 10:29–49.

———. 1990. "On the Universality of Human Nature and the Uniqueness of the Individual: The Role of Genetics and Adaptation." *Journal of Personality* 58:17–67.

Tooley, Michael. 1983. *Abortion and Infanticide.* Oxford: Oxford University Press.

Trebilcot, Joyce. 1984. "Taking Responsibility for Sexuality." In *Philosophy and Sex.* Rev. ed., edited by Robert Baker and Frederick Elliston. Buffalo: Prometheus Books.

Trivers, Robert. 1974. "Parent-Offspring Conflict." *American Zoologist* 14:249–264.

Ulrichs, Karl Heinrich. [1898] 1994. *The Riddle of "Manly Love": The Pioneering Work on Male Homosexuality.* Translated by M. A. Lombardi-Nash. 2 vols. Buffalo: Prometheus Books.

van Inwagen, Peter. 1993. *Metaphysics.* Boulder, CO: Westview.

Vasey, Paul. 1995. "Homosexual Behavior in Primates: A Review of Evidence and Theory." *International Journal of Primatology* 16:173–204.

Voeller, Bruce. 1990. "Some Uses and Abuses of the Kinsey Scale." In *Homosexuality/Heterosexuality: Concepts of Sexual Orientation,* edited by D.P. McWhirter, S.A. Sanders, and J.M. Reinisch. New York: Oxford University Press.

Waal, Frans de. 1989. *Peacemaking among Primates.* Cambridge, MA: Harvard University Press.

Warner, Michael. 1993. *Fear of a Queer Planet: Queer Politics and Social Theory.* Minneapolis: University of Minnesota Press.

Warren, Mary Anne. 1985. *Gendercide: The Implications of Sex Research.* Totowa, NJ: Rowman and Allenheld.

*Watkins v. United States Army,* 847 F.2d 1329 (9th Cir. 1988).

Watson, Gary, ed. 1982. *Free Will.* New York: Oxford University Press.

Watson, John B. 1913. "Psychology as the Behaviorist Views It." *Psychological Review* 20:158–177.

Weeks, Jeffrey. 1977. *Coming Out: Homosexual Politics in Britain from the Nineteenth Century to the Present.* London: Quartet Books.

Weil, Arthur. 1921. "Die Körnermasse der Homosexuuellen als Ausdrucksform ihrer besonderen Veranlanlagung [The bodily measurements of homosexuals as an expression of their particular sexual disposition]." *Jahrbuch für sexuelle Zwischenstufen [Yearbook for sexual intermediates]* 21 (3/4):113–120.

Weinberg, Martin, Colin Williams, and Douglas Pryor. 1994. *Dual Attraction: Understanding Bisexuality.* New York: Oxford University Press.

Weinrich, James. 1982. "Is Homosexuality Biologically Normal?" In *Homosexuality: Social, Psychological, and Biological Issues,* edited by William Paul. Beverly Hills: Sage.

———. 1987a. "A New Sociobiological Theory of Homosexuality Applicable to Societies with Universal Marriage." *Ethology and Sociobiology* 8:37–48.

———. 1987b. *Sexual Landscapes: Why We Are What We Are, Why We Love Who We Love.* New York: Scribners.

Weinrich, James, Peter Snyder, Richard C. Pillard, Igor Grant, Denise Jacobson, S. Renée Robinson, and J. Allen McCutchan. 1993. "A Factor Analysis of the Klein Sexual Orientation Grid in Two Discrete Samples." *Archives of Sexual Behavior* 22:157–168.

Weiss, Gail. 1995. "Sex-Selective Abortion: A Relational Approach." *Hypatia* 10:202–217.

Wertz, Dorothy, and John Fletcher. 1992. "Sex Selection Through Prenatal Diagnosis: A Feminist Critique." In *Feminist Perspective in Medical Ethics,* edited by Helen Holmes and Laura Purdy. Bloomington: Indiana University Press.

West, Donald, and Richard Green, eds. 1997. *Sociolegal Control of Homosexuality: A Multi-nation Comparison.* New York: Plenum Press.

Whisman, Vera. 1996. *Queer By Choice: Lesbians, Gay Men and the Politics of Identity.* New York: Routledge.

Whitam, Frederick. 1983. "Culturally Invariable Properties of Male Homosexuality: Tentative Conclusions from Cross-Cultural Research." *Archives of Sexual Behavior* 12:207–226.

Whitam, Frederick, and Mary Jo Dizon. 1980. "Occupational Choice and Sexual Orientation in Cross-Cultural Perspective." In *Homosexuality in International Perspective,* edited by Joseph Harry and Man Singh Das. New Dehli: Vikas.

Whitehead, Harriet. 1993. "The Bow and the Burden Strap: A New Look at Institutionalized Homosexuality in Native North America." In *The Lesbian and Gay Studies Reader,* edited by H. Abelove, M. A. Barale, and D. Halperin.

Whitley, B. E. 1990. "The Relationship of Heterosexuals' Attributions for the Causes of Homosexuality to Attitudes Towards Lesbians and Gay Men." *Personality and Social Psychology Bulletin* 16:369–377.

Williams, George C. 1966. *Adaptation and Natural Selection*. Princeton: Princeton University Press.

Williams, Walter. 1986. *The Spirit and the Flesh: Sexual Diversity in American Indian Culture*. Boston: Beacon Press.

Wilson, Edward O. 1975. *Sociobiology: The New Synthesis*. Cambridge, MA: Harvard University Press.

———. 1978. *On Human Nature*. Cambridge, MA: Harvard University Press.

Wilson, Robert. 1999. "Realism, Essence, and Kind: Resuscitating Species Essentialism?" In *Species: New Interdisciplinary Essays*, edited by Robert Wilson. Cambridge, MA: MIT Press.

Wintemute, Robert. 1995. *Sexual Orientation and Human Rights: The United States Constitution, The European Convention, and the Canadian Charter*. Oxford: Oxford University Press.

Witelson, S. F. 1991. "Neural Sexual Mosaicism: Sexual Differentiation of the Human Tempero-Parietal Region for Functional Asymmetry." *Psychoneuroendocrinology* 16:131–153.

Wittig, Monique. 1993. "One Is Not Born a Woman." In *The Lesbian and Gay Studies Reader*, edited by H. Abelove, M. A. Barale, and D. Halperin. First published in *Feminist Issue* 1 (1981):47–54.

Wittman, Carl. 1997. "Gay Manifesto" (speech given in 1969). In *We Are Everywhere: A Historical Sourcebook of Gay and Lesbian Politics*, edited by M. Blasius and S. Phelan. New York: Routledge.

Wyden, Peter, and Barbara Wyden. 1968. *Growing Up Straight: What Every Thoughtful Parent Should Know about Homosexuality*. New York: Stein and Day.

Yoshino, Kenji. 1996. "Suspect Symbols: The Literary Argument for Heightened Scrutiny for Gays." *Columbia Law Review* 96:1753–1834.

———. 1998. "Assimilationist Bias in Equal Protection: The Visibility Presumption and the Case of 'Don't Ask, Don't Tell.'" *Yale Law Journal* 108:485–571.

Zucker, Kenneth. 1990. "Gender Identity Disorders in Children: Clinical Descriptions and Natural History." In *Clinical Management of Gender Identity Disorders in Children and Adults*, edited by Roy Blanchard and B. W. Steiner. Washington, DC: American Psychiatric Press.

Zucker, Kenneth, and S. J. Bradley. 1995. *Gender Identity Disorder and Psychosexual Problems in Children and Adolescents*. New York: Guilford Press.

# INDEX